Thomas Adams and the Modern Planning Movement

FIGURE 1. THOMAS ADAMS, c. 1921.

Thomas Adams and the Modern Planning Movement

Britain, Canada and the United States, 1900–1940

MICHAEL SIMPSON

An Alexandrine Press Book

MANSELL, London and New York

This book is part of the series
Studies in History, Planning and the Environment
Series editors: Professor Gordon E. Cherry and Professor Anthony Sutcliffe

First published 1985 by Mansell Publishing Limited
(A subsidiary of the H. W. Wilson Company)
6 All Saints Street, London N1 9RL
950 University Avenue, Bronx, New York 10452

This book was commissioned, edited and designed by
Alexandrine Press, Oxford

British Library Cataloguing in Publication Data

Simpson, Michael
    Thomas Adams and the modern planning movement:
    Britain, Canada and the United States, 1900–1940
    (Studies in history, planning and the environment)
    1. Adams, Thomas   2. City Planning
    I. Title   II. Series
    711′.4′0924   HT166

    ISBN 0-7201-1714-3

Library of Congress Cataloguing in Publication Data

Simpson, Michael
    Thomas Adams and the modern planning movement,
    Britain, Canada, and the United States, 1900–1940

    (Studies in history, planning, and the environment)
    'An Alexandrine Press book'
    Includes bibliographical references and index
    1. Adams, Thomas, 1871–1940. 2. City planners—Great Britain—Biography. 3. City
planning—Great Britain—History. 4. City planning—Canada—History. 5. City
planning—United States—History. I. Title. II. Series
HT169.G78545   1985   711′.4′0924   [B]   84-21785 ISBN 0-7201-1714-3

Text set in 11/12pt Ehrhardt and printed in Great Britain by Henry Ling
Limited, Dorchester, bound by Green Street Bindery, Oxford.

Contents

Acknowledgments

A research project as extensive as this one necessarily calls upon the help of many individuals and institutions, not all of whom can be mentioned here. Throughout my studies, I have enjoyed the warm support, ready co-operation and kind hospitality of the Adams family: the late James Adams, Mrs. Constance Adams, and their sons and granddaughters; the late Professor Frederick Adams, and Mrs. Keith Adams; Mrs. Margaret Adkins; and Mr. and Mrs. John Adams.

Professor Tony Sutcliffe of the University of Sheffield has read the manuscript with his usual acute perception and despatch and has saved me from several blunders; I have profited richly from his learning and wisdom on many other occasions. Ann Drybrough-Smith has brought to the editorial work not only patience, cheerfulness and literary skill but also a shrewd understanding of planning. I am grateful for the wise counsel and friendship of colleagues at the University College of Swansea, particularly Professors Glanmor Williams and Ralph Griffiths. I have benefited enormously from long conversations on planning with Dr. Arwel Edwards and have drawn upon the learning of Mr. Neville Masterman and Dr. David Howell. Numerous other people in Britain have given generously of their time and knowledge, notably Adams's former associates Mr. Maxwell Fry, Sir Geoffrey and Lady Jellicoe, Sir Colin Buchanan, the late Sir Frederic Osborn, and Mr. Bernard Collins; Professors Gordon Cherry, George Shepperson and Michael Thompson; Drs. Tony Badger, Martin Gaskell, Martin Hawtree, J. D. Marshall, David Massey, Mervyn Miller and Stephen Ward; Mr. Kenneth Hanning and Mr. Michael Harrison; Dr. E. A. Cormack, the late Mr. D. Wilson and Dr. J. Simpson, all of Corstorphine, Edinburgh, Mr. W. John Smith of Alkrington, and the residents of Glyn Cory near Cardiff. I am grateful to the Marquis of Salisbury for permission to consult his family's Liverpool archives and to the Hon. David Lytton Cobbold for granting access to the Knebworth records. Mr. B. D. Beckett, Chief Planning Officer, Barrow-in-Furness, generously supplied me with material otherwise unobtainable, Mrs. Doreen Cadwalleder, curator of the Garden City Museum at Letchworth, and Mr. John Barrick, Librarian of the Royal Town

Planning Institute, have been stalwart friends and helpers for many years. Other libraries and institutions which have generously opened their materials and facilities to me include the public libraries at Bristol, Cardiff, Dundee, Edinburgh, Letchworth, Liverpool, Manchester, Middleton, Stalybridge and Wolverhampton; the Public Record Office; the General Register Office, the Registers of Scotland, and the National Library of Scotland in Edinburgh; the Department of Civic Design Library, University of Liverpool; the Library of the Royal Institute of British Architects; the Town and Country Planning Association; the National Housing and Town Planning Council; and the Landscape Institute; in Canada, the National Library of Canada, the Public Archives of Canada, Archives of Ontario, Canadian Institute of Planners, and the libraries of the University of Toronto and Carleton University; in the United States, the School of Design Library at Harvard, the Olin and other libraries at Cornell and the library of the Massachusetts Institute of Technology. To a novice in Canadian history, Professors Alan Artibise, David Hulchanski, Gilbert Stelter and John Taylor and Mr. Lloyd Evans gave much-needed and greatly-appreciated advice. In the United States, Professors Stephan Thernstrom (Harvard) and John Reps (Cornell) kindly assisted with accommodation and other facilities, while Professors Blaine Brownell (Alabama) and David Goldfield (North Carolina) read the American chapters, making several sage comments. Without David Hulchanski's painstaking and comprehensive bibliography of Thomas Adams's writings, this study would have been impossible, and he has furnished me with much other material.

I wish to acknowledge with gratitude the financial assistance of the Research and Fieldwork Fund of the University College of Swansea; the Wolfson Foundation; the Royal Institute of British Architects; the Leverhulme Trust; and the Council for Comparative British and American Studies (Wales and the West of England). I am grateful to the Editors of the *Town Planning Review*, the *Journal of American Studies*, the *Urban History Review*, and to the Architectural Press, for permission to reproduce certain material from their publications. Mrs. Glennis Jones and Mrs. June Morgan have typed part of the manuscript with promptness and good humour. I am grateful to Mr. Guy Lewis and to Mr. R. P. Davies, F.R.P.S., for assistance with the illustrations.

John and Ann Charrington, John and Maureen Clachan, Bob and Giesele Mennel, David and Angela Pratt and Bob and Alice-Jo Taylor have provided a wandering scholar with warm hospitality. Fellow-authors will appreciate the value of a happy home and family life and also how difficult it is to thank those who provide these blessings; a dedicatory note seems poor recompense for their love and support. This book is for Sue, Alison and Richard, and in memory of my parents.

Michael Simpson

Chapter One

Home and Family
1871–1900

Late Victorian Edinburgh was 'a sort of three distinct cities' – the medieval Old Town, the Heart of Midlothian, tumbling down the narrow ridge of the Royal Mile from the Castle to Holyrood; the classical Georgian New Town, on the lowlands to the north, arranged in what Robert Louis Stevenson called 'draughty parallelograms'; and the transport-led Victorian suburbs, rolling outwards along the main lines of communication, flowing over (but not always subduing) the adjacent village communities[1]. One of the villages threatened by spreading suburbia was Corstorphine, situated just above the flood plain, about three miles to the west of Edinburgh. In the eighteenth century a health resort, it was in Victorian times a parish of dairy farms and market gardens. In the last quarter of the nineteenth century it was still separated from Auld Reekie by the meadows and orchards bordering the Water of Leith. Corstorphine's view of the great city was of 'the pile of building on the hill-top, and the long plume of smoke over the plain'. While Edinburgh was confined to the hill-top, Corstorphine's rustic virginity was safe but by Stevenson's day Edinburgh had descended to the plain and the comprehensive suburbanization of the village was only a generation away; indeed, the first substantial villas had appeared on the slopes of Corstorphine Hill around 1830. The real invasion of suburbanites, however, followed the opening of the North British Railway's Corstorphine branch in 1902[2].

Lying below the hill, on the south side of the Edinburgh road, was Meadow House Farm, almost certainly of less than a hundred acres. The farmhouse, its outbuildings and the cottages for the byreman and ploughman stood practically on the roadside. Running south from there was a sizeable orchard and several fields, stretching to the Stank, a major drain. The tenant of Meadow House Farm in 1870 was James Adams, aged twenty-eight, the son of Thomas Adams, a horse-dealer. On St. Andrew's Day, 1870, James

1

brought to Meadow House his bride, Margaret Johnstone, a housekeeper in Canongate, Edinburgh, and the daughter of a gardener. There on 10 September 1871, Thomas, their first child, was born. He was followed by another son, William, and two daughters, Margaret and Sarah[3].

In 1884 Thomas entered Daniel Stewart's College, one of the city's leading day schools, where he received a good if rather conventional general education. It is not known what kind of a scholar he was but it is probable that he left school by the age of sixteen. In later life, Adams referred to an early acquaintance with the law and it is possible that he was articled to a solicitor upon leaving school. The most significant event of his youth, however, was the sudden death in May 1888 of his father from a stroke at the age of forty-six[4]. The eldest of the four children, Thomas had to devote himself to the running of the family business. At the time of his father's death, the enterprise was carried on from a shop in the Haymarket and a dairy farm close by at Wester Coates. It is not known when the move was made from Meadow House but Wester Coates was a small property of $23\frac{3}{4}$ acres, extending from the Glasgow road northwards to the Water of Leith, eastwards to Donaldson's Hospital and westwards to the railway line from Murrayfield to Granton. Wester Coates was much closer to Edinburgh than Meadow House and by the last decade of the nineteenth century it was being covered rapidly by suburban terraces and tenements. At some point in the 1890s, the Adams family returned to Meadow House Farm. This movement back and forth suggests short, perhaps annual, leases[5].

FARMING, MARRIAGE AND FAMILY LIFE, 1893–1900

Thomas did not stay long with his family after his father's death for early in 1893 he took up the tenancy of Fairslacks Farm at Carlops in the Pentland Hills, about seven miles south-west of Edinburgh and almost a thousand feet above sea level. A lonely spot, Fairslacks was a 48-acre holding consisting of three large fields surrounded by copses and situated on the south side of the Lyneton road, facing the steep scarp slopes of Windy Gowl, a rough sheep run. It is likely that Adams worked it with the assistance of a ploughman, for whom there was a cottage, and it must have been a tough experience among 'the wild heathery peaks' which gave extensive if desolate views and were described by Stevenson as still and lonely. In 1894, at the age of twenty-three, Adams became one of the first batch of parish councillors, serving on the council for West Linton. He claimed later that his career in planning derived from his successful campaign to remove squatters' shacks from the village green[6]. However, his existence as an independent farmer did not last long for he had formed an attachment to a Corstorphine girl and tramped regularly over the Pentlands to court her. She was Caroline Bertha Weierter, daughter of an immigrant German music teacher, Frederick Weierter, and his wife

Sarah (née Kay). Weierter had been in Edinburgh since at least 1887, when he was teaching music at his home in London Street. Moving later to Corstorphine, the family lived in Manse Road. Weierter continued to give music lessons and also helped his wife in their village grocery store on the main road. On 22 December 1897 their daughter Caroline, aged twenty-two, married Thomas Adams and the couple settled at 25 Downie Terrace, a new house adjacent to Meadow House Farm[7].

For Caroline Weierter, marriage to Thomas Adams was to mean a bewildering succession of homes in Britain, Canada and the United States. Adams did not acquire a house of his own until 1930, when he bought a property in Sussex. In the meantime, his wife bore five children – James (born in Downie Terrace in 1898), Frederick (born at Dulwich in 1901), Neville (born at Hitchin in 1904), Margaret (born at Wolverhampton in 1908) and John (born in Ottawa in 1916) – and coped with great patience and good humour with the frequent removals. From a family gifted in the arts, she was herself an accomplished musician. She supported her husband's career decisions, so disruptive to her own and her children's lives, with unstinting loyalty. A woman of firmness, not to say strictness, she was nevertheless compassionate. Surviving her husband by a quarter of a century, she died in 1965, aged ninety, having lived to see her two eldest sons, James and Frederick, become distinguished planners in their own right. James became County Planning Officer for Kent and followed his father in the Presidency both of the Town Planning Institute (1948–49) and the Institute of Landscape Architects (1949–53). Frederick was for many years Chairman of the Department of City Planning at the Massachusetts Institute of Technology and President of the American Institute of Planners in 1948–49, the same year in which his elder brother headed the British professional body. The two younger sons, Neville and John, both read engineering at the University of London, while their sister Margaret had a musical education and later married a farmer. Home life, wherever the family happened to be, was happy. Adams himself, though inclined to shyness on first acquaintance, was a generous, humorous man who loved family gatherings. His grandchildren remember him as a first-rate Santa Claus and fond of little conjuring tricks. Dedicated to his work, he was rarely clear of it, even on Atlantic crossings and on holidays. He thus had little time for leisure pursuits but he was always a voracious reader of catholic tastes and a regular churchgoer, having been brought up as a Presbyterian. A keen golfer and tennis player in his youth, in later years gardening became his principal recreation[8].

ENTRY INTO PUBLIC LIFE, 1897–1900

Adams's return to Corstorphine in 1897 was due only in part to his marriage to a village girl. At about the time of his marriage, he 'became enthusiastic about writing rather than farming', though he continued to assist in the family business. He had given a hint of his literary proclivities when in 1898 he had founded *The Progressive Youth of Great Britain: An Amateur Monthly Journal for Young Authors;* later he edited another little magazine and had about a score of his poems – generally on religious or romantic themes – published in a variety of papers. At the age of twenty, he had attended in London the first annual convention of the British Amateur Press Association and was elected its inaugural President – the earliest in a long line of 'firsts' in his career. In Corstorphine, he became an active member of the village Literary and Debating Society, succeeding to the Presidency in 1900[9].

From 1897 to 1900, however, the two principal thrusts of his career were in journalism and politics. The two were related for most of Adams's early writing turned upon the 'Land Question', a major issue in contemporary politics and 'nowhere was the land reform movement stronger than in Scotland'. His earliest articles, advocating tenants' rights, a free market in land and an equitable land tax, appeared in local papers from 1894. Publicizing the plight of small farmers like himself was, however, only half the battle. Action could come only from a sympathetic Parliament, which meant one with a strong Liberal majority. In consequence, Adams followed up his journalism by becoming the secretary of the Midlothian Liberal Association. His brief party-political career reached its apogee in the autumn of 1900, when at the General Election of that year he acted as the agent to the constituency's Liberal candidate, the Master of Elibank. In a bad year for Liberals, Elibank retained the seat (held by Gladstone between 1880 and 1895). Following the election, Adams joined with a number of other young Scottish Liberals, dissatisfied with their seniors' lamentable performance in the late election, to form the Young Scots Society, of which he became the first chairman. A ginger group of radical activists, its objects were 'To stimulate interest in progressive Politics, to encourage the study of History, Social and Industrial Science, and Economics, and generally to promote Liberal Principles; to further the interests of Scotland, and to secure for Scotland the right of Self-Government'. An intellectual, Edinburgh-based group, it held discussions led by notable public figures and remained in being well into the inter-war period, Adams later identifying it as the precursor of the Scottish Nationalist movement[10].

Adams did not long remain a part of the Edinburgh literary and political scene, for in December 1900 he sought his fortune as a man of letters in London, the heart of empire offering far greater opportunities for an aspiring writer. Moreover, he felt little obligation to remain in Edinburgh. He had lost interest in both farming and politics as possible careers. His mother had died in July 1899, aged fifty-one, after a long illness, and the family business was in the highly capable hands of his sister Margaret, who had married a Murrayfield cab proprietor, Thomas Hall. Nevertheless, it took much courage to move to London with little but his own self-confidence to sustain him in his literary ambitions[11].

The Influence of Edinburgh upon Adams's Career

Adams's early life in and around Edinburgh had a crucial influence upon him in two respects. In the first place, family background, personal experience in farming, participation in local public life and his extensive reading helped to mould a personal philosophy which thereafter underwent only marginal changes. To his demands for a new order in agriculture, Adams, being a literary man, added the sentiments of the Ayrshire ploughman, Robert Burns, 'the poet of the Scottish peasantry'. Adams, also an advocate of peasant proprietorship, did not anticipate an enlarged role for the state but rather the application of free trade and classical economics to the agricultural sector, still the prisoner of feudalism. Adams wanted a revived yeomanry, allotments and decent housing for labourers, the better integration of farming and manufacturing, and a fairer balance of population between town and country – the accepted agenda of agrarian radicalism. However, Adams was as much a townsman as a countryman and his political philosophy was grounded also in the Whiggism which was the dominant strain of Liberalism in Edinburgh. He was therefore profoundly distrustful of the power of the state and a champion of individual liberty[12].

Adams's reading was concentrated upon poetry, philosophy and political economy and included most of the nineteenth-century British and foreign luminaries in those fields – for example, Tennyson, Longfellow, Carlyle, Emerson, John Stuart Mill and Kropotkin. He had 'a belief in a conception of society in which self-reliance of the individual is regarded as of vital consequence'. Though he recognized that some major problems, such as housing, were not soluble entirely by *laissez-faire* means, in general he sanctioned state intervention only to prevent abuses of freedom, fearing the loss of liberty seemingly inherent in collectivism. A *via media* between absolute liberty and the public welfare had to be found which would reverse the nation's rapid drift into hostile camps of labour and capital, restore society's natural harmony, and vanquish domestic ills without increasing the authority, cost and scale of government. Adams's version of this refurbished voluntarism was 'associated individualism', the co-operation of individuals to achieve by free association those ends beyond their capacity to attain alone[13]. Adams's cautious and fundamentally negative Liberalism thus excluded any sympathy with socialism. Unlike Raymond Unwin, Adams had no acquaintance with socialist thinkers or with the working class, to which he manifested a somewhat patronizing if sympathetic attitude. His insistence on the natural harmony of society ruled out the notion of an inevitable conflict of classes and he refused always to countenance redistributive measures (such as council housing) which benefitted one group at the expense of others. Adams was also a confirmed Utilitarian and, having a scientific cast of mind, he was convinced that the greatest good of the greatest number could be ascertained by scientific enquiries conducted by experts. Later, in his 'scientific town planning', he held that 'The general objective to be kept in mind should be to do that which is best for the general welfare'. He was, finally, a pragmatist and a meliorist, remarking characteristically that 'It is a waste of time to set up idealistic utopias of what we would like to do but cannot'. The ideas of balance and interdependence between city and country, of the state as the moderator of private initiative, of voluntarism as the organizing principle of society, of society itself as a seamless robe and of the professional planner as the disinterested rationalist dominated Adams's conception of planning throughout his career[14].

Adams was influenced also by his Edinburgh environment, a unique one in that it embraced both town and country. This unusual perspective helps to explain his consistent attempt to restore a viable balance between rural and urban life and to compel acknowledgement of their interdependence. It was clearly of benefit to him in both site planning and comprehensive planning. As he himself noted late in his career:

> It is to his early life on the farm that he is indebted for his appreciation of natural beauty and his understanding of the city from the outside. This explains his frequently expressed conviction that the city cannot be seen and understood in broad perspective from within; that it must be visualised in the first instance from the vantage point of open situations in the environs[15].

His good fortune in spending his formative years on the outskirts of a great city led to an early appreciation of the need to take into account the whole of a city's cultural hinterland in planning its development and helped to make him a pioneer of regional planning, while his close association with the land gave him a fine natural eye for the possibilities inherent in a landscape.

Edinburgh constituted an admirable case study for a putative town planner, 'one of the classic examples where good city planning and good architecture combine to create a high standard of design'. Acknowledging its pervasive influence on him, Adams wrote in 1924 that

> The experience of growing up in a city like Edinburgh is necessary to the preparation of a state of mind that accepts the beautiful in architecture at its true value as a force in moulding character and in developing a sane outlook on life[16].

The rehabilitation of the dilapidated and overcrowded Old Town was only just beginning in his youth but it was nonetheless testimony to his belief that 'Some of the best features of cities are the result of accident'. The New Town of 1768–1837 – in his view the first one worthy of the name – was well suited to its topography and architecture and it was 'difficult to conceive that any more appropriate plan could have been prepared'. It was timeless in its relevance and blended successfully with the Old Town, thus giving the city an enviable combination of 'medieval picturesqueness with the orderly dignity of classical forms'. He praised the Georgian civic leaders for their vision and willingness to acquire strategic sites and employ notable architects[17].

In his awareness of the effects of unplanned development, Adams shared the views of Stevenson, Ruskin and most subsequent writers on the drab and tasteless suburban tenements of the Victorian era and the more recent 'monotonous bungalow neighbourhoods with no architectural quality'. This regrettably haphazard growth had come about since 1830. 'After the coming of the railways,' he complained, 'civic art in Edinburgh was neglected'. Although the Victorian city had 'a heritage of incalculable wealth', its ruthless inner-city redevelopment and unregulated suburban accretions threatened to dissipate the priceless legacy of the more sensitive and aesthetically aware past[18]. Despite these rude assaults upon its matchless artistic integrity, he concluded that 'Edinburgh is still one of the finest cities and one of the best examples of the value of employing the art of the planner'. His own contribution to Edinburgh's planning history was made in his recommendations for a general development plan in 1929–31[19].

Adams's Midlothian environment and upbringing had a deep and persistent influence upon his career and philosophy. As he and his family departed from Auld Reekie towards the end of 1900, he may have recalled Stevenson's perceptive conclusion to his often waspish but essentially affectionate vignette of late Victorian Edinburgh:

There is no Edinburgh emigrant, far or near, from China to Peru but he or she carries some lively pictures of the mind, some sunset behind the Castle cliffs, some snow scene, some maze of city lamps, indelible in the memory and delightful to study in the intervals of toil[20].

Chapter Two

Launching
the First Garden City,
1901–1906

Organizing the Garden City Association, 1901–1902

In London, Adams sought his destiny as a writer and found it as a planner. He rented a house in Dulwich and subsisted on freelance journalism. He retained a vestigial interest in politics and the first meeting he attended after his arrival in December 1900 was of the Fabian Society, where he 'listened to the cynical Bernard Shaw, the serious Ramsay MacDonald and the dapper Hubert Bland enunciating the claims of Socialism'. However, this presaged no political conversion, for Adams was intent upon making his own way in life without being 'coddled' by the state[1].

Adam's literary career was over almost before it had started, for by the beginning of April 1901 he had become the first full-time secretary of the Garden City Association. His acceptance of a salaried position may have been prompted by a desire for security but the infant G.C.A. could scarcely offer that and it is more likely that he was attracted by the prospect it offered of realizing his ideals. The advertisement called for a sympathetic acquaintance with Ebenezer Howard's book, *Tomorrow: a Peaceful Path to Real Reform* (1898). Adams reputedly bought a copy at a station bookstall and read it *en route* from Edinburgh to London, being excited initially more by its 'underlying philosophy' of 'associated individualism' than by its proposals for garden cities. After a preliminary screening by the treasurer, he was offered the appointment by a committee late in March and entered upon his duties at once[2].

Howard's book, a last hurrah for Liberalism, appeared at a time of psychic crisis. At the turn of the century, Britain experienced a wave of self-doubt and introspection. International tensions were rising and there was an accelerating arms race. There was acute concern over German and American business competition. The countryside was still largely in a state of depression and rural depopulation was still common. In the towns there was gross overcrowding and considerable unemployment; the working class – and the Irish – were becoming restive, while social inquiries revealed that perhaps a third of the people were living on or below the 'poverty line'. There were fears of class warfare and a growing dissatisfaction with the ugliness resulting from industrialization. Howard's project appeared to offer solutions to many of these problems. He envisaged a network of economically self-contained medium-sized towns built on large rural estates, of which about one-sixth would be devoted to urban purposes, the remainder forming a permanent greenbelt of parkland and farms. Each city was to have a civic centre, a separate factory district, ample open space, tree-lined avenues, neighbourhood units and single-family homes with gardens. Anticipating what was to become the conventional wisdom of professional planning, Howard called for designs made by teams drawn from all the environmental professions. Intended as a combination of all of the advantages of both town and country without the disadvantages of either, the Garden City was to be a co-operative commonwealth, the increment in land values consequent upon the conversion of the estate from rural to urban uses being reserved to the community[3].

When he launched the Garden City Association in London in June 1899, Howard mustered no more than a dozen adherents but the tide of social and environmental concern was flowing in his favour. By October 1899, he claimed that:

> The Association numbers among its members manufacturers, co-operators, architects, artists, medical men, financial experts, lawyers, merchants, ministers of religion, members of the London County Council (Moderate and Progressive), socialists and individualists, Radicals and Conservatives[4].

Howard had a clear strategy: after hard promotional work, chiefly by his own lectures, a company should be formed to secure an option on a suitable property, followed by the establishment of First Garden City, Limited. Attractive though his utopia may have seemed, the pioneer company floated in May 1900 was stillborn. Reformers' enthusiasm faded swiftly when financial commitments were called for and Howard concluded that insufficient groundwork had been done; another winter propaganda campaign was necessary. Further exertions raised the membership to over 350 by early 1901, including the Liberal statesman James Bryce and other M.P.s. The Association's income exceeded £200, its organization had been streamlined and it enjoyed a better press[5].

Nevertheless, what Howard really needed was a breakthrough into definite action. In March 1901 he read an article by Ralph Neville, Q.C., Chairman of the Land Nationalization Society, and a former Liberal M.P., entitled 'The Extension of Co-operation: Garden Cities' in which the writer argued that co-operation could do 'practically everything' and recommended Howard's scheme as 'based upon a sound economic principle'. His vigorous endorsement of the Garden City concept led Howard to invite him to become chairman of the council. Neville's accession was a decisive event. It brought to the movement an authoritative leadership, an objective and thoroughly practical approach, a high public reputation and a wide circle of influential friends. 'People who were hesitating as to the project came in because they had confidence in Neville and believed he knew what he was about', wrote Howard's biographer. Neville's first act was to obtain a resolution 'that a paid Secretary be appointed, and that offices be obtained for the Association'. Thus Adams began work in a top floor room at 77 Chancery Lane[6].

The events of March and April 1901 created the team which was chiefly responsible for the realization of the Garden City idea. In complete agreement on social, economic and political philosophy, Neville, Howard and Adams brought to these 'very intimate days . . . days of ideals' complementary qualities. Neville contributed sagacious strategic direction, Howard evangelistic fervour and Adams, a prodigious worker and a highly effective organizer, had abundant energy, imagination and a sense of initiative. All were convinced of the need for an immediate and successful practical demonstration, yet in the spring of 1901 there seemed no clear way forward[7].

Adam's duties were ill-defined and the organization was still somewhat casual. Thirty years later, he recalled that:

> In a one-room office at 77 Chancery Lane, approached through a lawyer's office occupied by a white-whiskered, frock-coated gentlemanly clerk of seventy years of age, I sat at a desk and wrote out receipts for half-crown subscriptions and a few guineas. Howard came in daily to confer and occasionally discuss matters with Neville[8].

Apart from keeping the books, Adams was the association's press officer and one of its principal lecturers. He established immediately a monthly Garden City spot in the *Municipal Reformer* and seized every opportunity to follow up news items and correspondence on environmental issues. Having experienced a conversion to Howard's ideas as total as Saul's on the road to Damascus, he told the readers of the *Morning Leader,* with all the conviction of the practised public relations officer, 'Garden City is going to be built in the near future by practical men and then everyone will say: "Why was this not done before?" Characteristically, his lectures also stressed the practicality of Howard's proposals[9].

Shortly after taking up his post, Adams seems to have visited the new model industrial villages at Port Sunlight and Bournville. It was his recognition that they were close approximations to much of what was intended in Garden City that led to the next breakthrough for the G.C.A. In his column in the June issue of the *Municipal Reformer*, he floated the idea of a major public meeting of the association at one of these villages. He suggested that:

> If such a conference were held at Bournville, for instance, members would be able to study the satisfactory conditions under which the workpeople of Messrs. Cadbury are employed, and the best existing illustration of the advantages, which accrue to the manufacturer and his employees, from a combination of town and country life[10].

This tentative proposal was well received, for George Cadbury immediately offered the G.C.A. full facilities for a conference in September[11].

The Bournville conference gave itself a wide remit:

> To consider the experiment of Mr. George Cadbury in removing his works from Birmingham to Bournville; the difficulties which attend the removal of works from large cities to new districts; how local authorities and other organisations can co-operate with such movements; and the desirability and practicability of a movement of manufacturers and co-operators to new areas, so that new towns may be established on land purchased for the community[12].

The known attractiveness of Bournville and Adams's publicity secured an attendance of over 300, including Earl Grey, a number of M.P.s, G.B. Shaw, and representatives of municipalities, the professions, churches, trade unions, reform groups and co-operative societies. The addresses, by professional men, politicians and others were for the most part patronizing, moralistic and nationalistic, Neville's being typical of the genre. Calling for 'more air and less alcohol', he warned that inattention to the health of the masses would lead to the 'ultimate destruction and decadence of the race'. Reflecting current concern with national efficiency, he argued that 'if they fell below the physical standard of the rivals their bolt was shot and they must fall before them'. The most significant paper, however, was Raymond Unwin's Ruskinian, collectivist, neotechnic exposition on 'Housing in Garden City'. Laying down hitherto unimaginable standards for working-class housing, he called for light, airy houses with a cheerful outlook, facing the sun and with open space on two sides – a conception utterly removed from 'the dismal monotony of the narrow (by-law) street'[13].

The Bournville gathering was a great triumph for the association and especially for its new secretary. It picked up over one hundred new members – 'many of them,' noted Howard, 'men of light and leading.' The association of the Garden City with such an agreeable and patently successful experiment resulted in extensive and generally respectful press coverage. The wide geographical and institutional spread of the delegates led to intensified discussion of not only the Garden City but of the housing question in general, Neville asserting that 'It would be impossible to over-rate the value of the conference at Bournville,' adding that 'If the reason for its success was largely due to the fact that the conference was held on the site of a practical experiment, then the moral was that the Association could not too soon follow Mr. Cadbury's example and create an object lesson of its own'. An exhilarated Ebenezer Howard declared that 'A Garden Village has been built; a Garden City is but a step beyond'. This euphoria caused the G.C.A.'s council to resolve in December 1901 that 'nothing should hinder the immediate acquirement of a site and the carrying out of the first experiment'. In the most succinct summing-up of what was his first significant contribution to the British planning movement, Adams remarked that 'After the Bournville Conference it began to be recognised that we had a definite aim, that there was a solid foundation for Mr. Howard's proposals, and that the central idea of the project was feasible'[14].

The triumph was not unalloyed for there were hidden features later to prove troublesome. The many local authority representatives could have little part to play in the establishment of garden cities but they were presented with the vision of the more easily realizable garden suburb which they were later to embrace. One group vital to the success of a garden city was virtually unrepresented – the businessmen who would have to find not only the bulk of the capital it required but also furnish it with its economic basis. Finally, the mountain-top re-affirmation of faith and the urge to 'create an object lesson of our own' soon evaporated and the chance to launch Garden City immediately after the conference was lost. As so often in early Garden City history, caution ruled when boldness might have paid a better dividend. The failure of the first pioneer company was fresh, the money market was still slow, and the G.C.A. lacked the organizational resources to capitalize on its publicity triumph. Adams in particular felt frustrated; he had exclaimed in July: 'Let us act, and leave off talking until we have tried an actual experiment'. Once again, the Association settled down to a winter of propaganda. Membership rose from 530 to 1500 and now included, besides many M.P.s, leading literary figures like H. G. Wells, Marie Corelli, Madame Sarah Grand and Anthony Hope (Hawkins), appropriately a writer of Ruritanian fantasies. Other eminent recruits included J. S. Nettlefold, chairman of Birmingham's housing committee, and Alfred Marshall, the most distinguished economist of the day. Adams and Howard were tireless in building links with other reform bodies – the National Housing Reform Council, the Co-operative Union and the Ruskin Society, for example – and in the spring of 1902, they formed G.C.A. branches at Liverpool and Manchester[15].

Meanwhile, it was coming to be recognized that 'There is no question at present of greater social importance than the Housing of the Working Classes' and that there was 'an urgent need to relieve overcrowding and rural depopulation'. Over three and a half millions were living in unhealthy conditions, some 690,000 houses needed to be demolished and the estimated rehousing cost was £69 m. Moreover, in the previous generation, over a million people had left the land. The conversion to the cause of Alfred Harmsworth, proprietor of the *Daily Mail* and George Cadbury's purchase of the *Daily News* helped enormously to create an awareness of these conditions and to spread Garden City propaganda. In 1902, Howard brought out the definitive edition of his gospel, retitled *Garden Cities of Tomorrow*[16].

LETCHWORTH GARDEN CITY:
CONCEPTION, GESTATION AND BIRTH, 1902–1905

By July 1902, the Association was ready at last to launch the Pioneer Company and did so in connection with a second conference, at Port Sunlight. William Lever presided and about 900 delegates, representing nearly 100 organizations, attended, while press coverage was even more extensive than at Bournville. Taken together, 'These two conferences were decisive steps in the propaganda which led to the creation of Letchworth, for they showed to a large public concrete examples of the application of those methods of industrial development which were involved in the Garden City idea'. Like the Bournville meeting, however, the Port Sunlight gathering was a mixed blessing. Once again, there were few businessmen and the range of bodies represented led to serious divisions of opinion on environmental reform[17].

The Garden City Pioneer Company was the Association's council in business garb, Neville becoming the chairman, Howard the managing director and Adams the secretary. With the exception of Howard Pearsall, a civil engineer, the five other directors were leading Liberals and businessmen. Given a board of proven business acumen, the company could have expected a smooth passage but it was no ordinary business venture. Of itself, it offered no return, for its task was simply to reconnoitre sites and acquire one, whereupon its shares would be exchanged for those of its successor, the First Garden City Company, which was to build and operate the model community. To have launched the First Garden City Company at once would have required several hundred thousand pounds. The directors were doubtful of doing so without an actual site to display, and may well have had grave misgivings as to the practicality of the whole project and therefore limited the initial call to the £20,000 required for the pioneering operation. They may have judged, too, that it was about the amount they could expect to raise from philanthropists. As Adams remarked shrewdly, 'If the whole of the £20,000 is raised on the conditions named in the prospectus it will undoubtedly be a triumph for social reform'[18].

The first appeal brought in only a quarter of the required amount but it was decided to open for business on 18 August 1902. A second appeal had to be made but by the end of the year the issue was over-subscribed by £2000, due chiefly to a handful of large shareholders, notably Lever, George Cadbury, Harmsworth and the Lancashire cotton spinner J. P. Thomasson. Among smaller investors were many M.P.s, members of the Cadbury and Rowntree families, Barry Parker, Raymond Unwin and Thomas Adams[19].

The division of the Garden City movement into a propaganda body and a prospecting firm compelled organizational adjustments, though the two were run as parts of one household. The 'poor and dilapidated' Chancery Lane office was vacated for more commodious accommodation in Holborn and additional staff were recruited. They included a general clerk, C. B. Purdom, a young Londoner and a disciple of Howard whose lifelong devotion to the Garden City idea was second only to the founder's, and an 'impeccable' young accountant, Harold Craske, who 'treated the affair as rather amusing'. Initially, the directors seem to have had little idea how to proceed and 'the office floor was covered with maps and offers of sites'. They decided eventually on a number of essential requirements. A suitable site should be freehold and of four to six thousand acres, with good railway and, if possible, waterway connections, a satisfactory water supply and good drainage. It had to be close to a major source of labour, preferably London. That there was 'no scarcity of estates suitable for our purposes' had been established by a G.C.A. committee in July 1901[20].

Prospecting work began in the damp, cold autumn of 1902. By November, Adams had a list of over thirty properties, including 'Letchford Manor, Near Hitchin'. He ran a parallel campaign to interest businessmen in locating their factories in the first garden city, involving a questionnaire on their requirements. By December, the sites under serious consideration had been reduced to Grendon (Warwickshire), Kelham (Nottinghamshire), an estate on the River Crouch (Essex) and – everyone's favourite – Chartley Castle, eight miles east of Stafford. Howard, Adams and the directors in twos and threes visited every one of them. Doctors, engineers and surveyors were asked for advice on healthiness, water supply and drainage, and general physical characteristics. By May 1903, all eyes were on Chartley. The property of Earl Ferrers, it was compact, breezy and attractive. It lay close to the Potteries and the Black Country and possessed good transport facilities and drainage. The only problem, which was resolvable, was the water supply. Howard gave it a decisive vote – 'it is the only site on which what I have set out to do can be accomplished' and urged no timidity. Adams, who was sent there in January 1903, did most of the detective work, enquiring about local industrial development and labour supplies and arranging for a valuation. Howard invited Unwin to join Adams in a trek round the property and the two confirmed Howard's favourable opinion of it. The asking price (£285,000) was high but not enough to prevent the directors taking a three months' option on Chartley in April 1903[21].

One major doubt, largely unspoken, prevented the directors from closing the deal. Chartley was 140 miles from London and it seemed vital that the first garden city should be close to the capital, the likely source of most of its funds, support, labour and industries. Important potential backers should be able to visit it easily, within an hour of town. At the eleventh hour, the company's solicitor, Herbert Warren, produced dramatically what was 'very nearly an ideal site'. This was the Letchworth Hall estate, just to the east of Hitchin in Hertfordshire and 35 miles from London. The main property amounted only to 1800 acres but Warren's Baldock office was confident of putting together about 4000 acres. A year of secret and delicate negotiations with no less than fifteen owners then ensued. Adams, who was still busy with Chartley and other possibilities, was detailed to work closely with local solicitors and surveyors. He had no part in the initial selection of Letchworth but on seeing it endorsed Neville's view of it. The chairman, who had probably the decisive voice, was 'very favourably inclined' to Letchworth. By early autumn, the long and complex negotiations, which were carried through with great skill and complete success, were over. The package totalled 3818 acres but the shortfall was slight and quite outweighed by Letchworth's enormous advantages. It lay astride a main railway and was only a couple of miles off the main East Coast road and rail routes to Scotland. The site was level, well-drained and had ample water supplies. The County Medical Officer pronounced it healthy. Its three parishes had a total population of just over 400. At £40 15s per acre, its price was remarkably close to Howard's 1898 estimate and its cost (£155,587) reflected the poor quality of the land and the fact that in 1903 20 per cent of Hertfordshire's farms were unoccupied[22].

Once the Letchworth contracts were exchanged, Adams liquidated the Pioneer Company, receiving a bonus of £50 'for services rendered in the flotation of the company'. For Howard and his fellow explorers, the discovery and acquisition of Letchworth marked the end of the beginning[23].

The promoters of planned decentralization now came face to face with the tasks of organizing the First Garden City Company, raising adequate capital, devising a management structure, adopting a ground plan, settling on a development procedure and setting out the terms upon which land was to be leased. Since entry to the estate was not possible until 1 January 1904, they had a short breathing space in which to resolve these issues. First Garden City, Ltd., was registered on 1 September 1903 with an authorized capital of £300,000, of which only £80,000 in £1 and £5 ordinary shares was to be raised at once. The maximum dividend was the philanthropic five per cent. The movement's chief supporters – Ralph Neville, William Lever, the Cadburys, J. P. Thomasson and others – gave the company a good launch with promises amounting to £40,000. On this foundation the directors (who were the same as for the Pioneer Company with the addition of Lever and H. B. Harris, a solicitor) were able to go to allotment after three days. Thomas and Caroline Adams each contributed one £5 share[24].

The directors' timid decision to raise initially only £80,000 precluded the rapid provision of Letchworth's infrastructure and its early financial viability. Moreover, it dashed Howard's hopes that an immediate triumph of planned decentralization would touch off a spontaneous nationwide Garden City movement. The depressed agricultural properties generated little rent and much of the £80,000 would have to service the mortgage on two-thirds of the purchase price. The weak state of the capital market was the likely explanation of directoral caution – new issues had fared badly in the past two years – and even the remainder of the £80,000 took a great deal of getting. With money hard to come by, it made sense to keep as much of it as possible as working capital. The board counted also upon a rapid build-up of commercial rents and outside provision of housing. It was hoped that as the practicality and success of the scheme became known it would take off into self-sustained growth[25].

Strategy was the concern of the directors; the success of the tactical battle among the hedges and ditches of a bleak stretch of north Hertfordshire would be in the hands of the local management team. First Garden City was an extraordinary project calling for an extra-ordinarily able, experienced and adequate staff yet no attempt was made to assess the management requirements of the scheme or to recruit a manager familiar either with the development of a great estate or the promotion of a large-scale enterprise. It is scarcely credible that a board of successful businessmen should proceed in so casual a fashion. Adams was appointed secretary while continuing to run the Garden City Association, though when development got underway in March 1904 and he added the managership of the company he retained only a watching brief over the affairs of the G.C.A. While he was given a subordinate staff with clearly defined duties – a civil engineer, a highway engineer, a surveyor, a forester, a general clerk and a financial assistant – his own functions, apart from the superintendence of others, were ill-defined. He became director of operations and factotum, covering the areas not dealt with by his underlings, notably publicity, agricultural supervision, the attraction of industry and trouble-shooting. While he had abundant personal qualities of energy, imagination, shrewdness, charm and tact as well as unfailing good humour and recognized organizing ability, he lacked experience in management. The board seems to have given him few firm directions on how to proceed, in part because it lacked a clear policy of its own[26].

The essence of the Garden City was that it should be planned in advance of development. Even in this matter, obvious though it was, the board appears to have adopted no uniform procedure. Several architects, probably known to members of the board, were invited to submit plans. They included Richard Norman Shaw, W. R. Lethaby and Halsey Ricardo, Barry Parker and Raymond Unwin and possibly Sir Aston Webb. Ultimately three plans were submitted – one by the local architects Geoffrey Lucas and Sydney Cranfield, similar to the Parker and Unwin plan, one by Lethaby and Ricardo, a formal and relatively compact design, and the successful one by Parker and Unwin. It is likely that Howard had already determined upon Unwin as his planner having been drawn to him by Unwin's architectural vision of Garden City revealed at the Bournville conference[27].

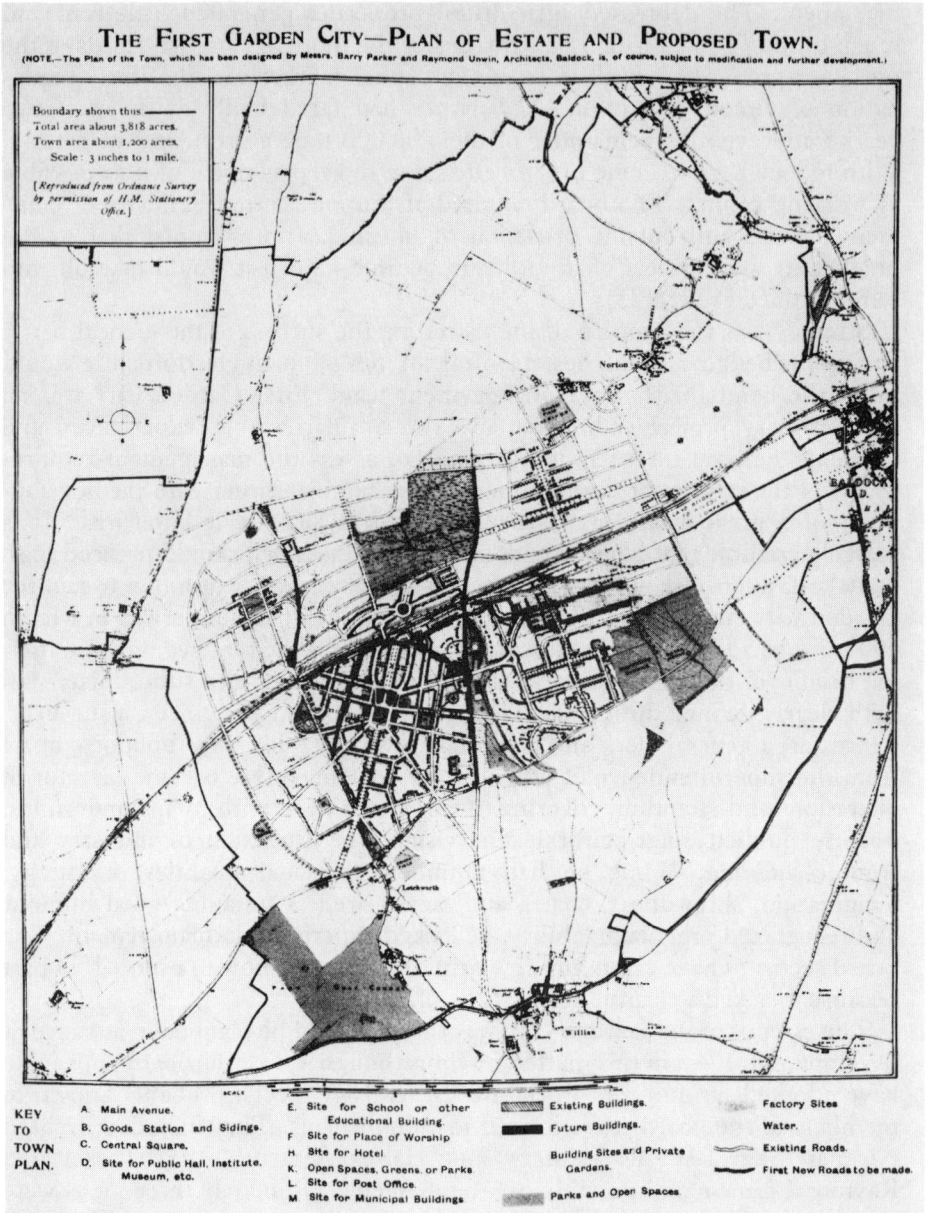

FIGURE 2. Letchworth Garden City: Plan by Raymond Unwin and Barry Parker, 1904.

A blend of the formal and the informal. The severence of the estate by the railway was a major handicap. (Thomas Adams, *Garden City and Agriculture*, 1905)

With the plan – a curious mixture of formal avenues, contoured housing layouts and village greens – Adams had nothing to do though the appointment of Parker and Unwin as architectural consultants in 1904 created some difficulties for him, for they were answerable not to him but to the board and he had some differences with the architects. Adams wanted less artistic cottages than Unwin and Parker were intent on designing, arguing for cheap, plain dwellings affordable by unskilled labourers[28]. Unwin counselled against such utilitarian policies. He told Adams that:

> People are expecting that Garden City will be a more interesting and beautiful place than an ordinary new building suburb, and its practical success will depend largely on this expectation being realised. The general effect of the town may yet be made or marred by the way in which the plan is carried out in detail[29].

Unwin argued constantly that even temporary buildings should be 'creditable and attractive' and was disappointed that Adams should have permitted the town's first cottages to be built speculatively without architectural control[30]. Through Adams and Unwin were to evince profound respect for one another and to co-operate fruitfully throughout their careers, this early clash reflected their respective approaches to environmental design. Unwin's was aesthetic, radical and abstract while Adams, though by no means dismissive of the aesthetic, was characteristically more conservative, pragmatic and businesslike.

In implementing the Parker and Unwin plan, the redoubtable Neville insisted upon adherence to Howard's essential principles. The work was in the hands of Adams, who moved from Dulwich to Hitchin in the spring of 1904 and who understood clearly what his priorities should be. The first requirement was roads and services and Adams applied his formidable energies to the task with such success that, despite the company's meagre resources, by the summer of 1905 Letchworth had about five miles of made-up roads and many more miles of mains water, gas, drains and sewers, serving over one thousand people in more than five hundred houses, twenty-five shops, seven factories and numerous public buildings. 'There is no doubt', reported the *Daily Express* in May 1905, 'that First Garden City is rapidly materialising' and Purdom, a hard man to please, acknowledged that 'the credit must go to Adams' for Letchworth's swift urbanization[31].

As an exercise in planned decentralization, Letchworth was moving with the industrial tide though it had many established competitors, such as Hitchin, which were receptive to footloose factories. The principal responsibility for luring firms to Garden City devolved upon Adams. His strategy was to circularize companies, mostly in London and covering a wide range of non-offensive trades, at regular intervals, outlining Letchworth's advantages. Once the town had something to show in the way of urban form, he followed this with an illustrated guide, supplemented by frequent press releases and articles of his own. Members of the board exploited their business connections, too; one of them, T. H. W. Idris, moving his noted table water concern to Garden City. Of the thirteen companies which had chosen to locate in Letchworth by the time Adams left in the autumn of 1906, the first, Garden City Press, was a new undertaking, two moved from other small towns and several more came from London. Adams was responsible for most, if not all, of these acquisitions but his greatest triumph was the translation from central London in the summer of 1906 of the printing and binding division of Dents, the well-known publishers. J. M. Dent had become interested in Letchworth at a lecture given by Adams and 'With the settling of this firm on the Estate it may confidently be said that a new era has begun'. Letchworth had attained industrial viability. The capture of Dents was justifiably celebrated on a Mafeking Night scale. One local paper declared that 'It is entirely due to Mr. Adams's exertions that this firm have decided to move to Letchworth'. This and other successes speak volumes for his persuasiveness, business sense and diligence. Adams's Garden City experience led him to one of his fundamental planning principles – that a city's *raison d'etre* is economic and that the first duty of a planner is to secure adequate provision for its industry, commerce and communications[32].

Much of Adams's time was spent on public relations, congenial work for which he had a recognized talent. His handling of the company's publicity reveals a careful strategy. One facet was the attraction of commercial enterprises. A second was regular and favourable press coverage. Thirdly, he sought to nail promptly the many slurs on Garden City. Fourthly, he endeavoured to extend the movement's basis of support and finally, he appreciated the need to dispel local suspicions and cultivate the goodwill of the neighbourhood.

Before Adams joined the G.C.A., it had received only minor and intermittent press coverage, most of it derisive. Now that a practical experiment was under way, it was vital to establish consistent and sympathetic exposure and the company went for a grand opening to its publicity campaign. Adams arranged two open days at Letchworth in October 1903, one on the 6th for the press and one on the 9th for the movement's supporters and the general public. He led the train-load of pressmen over a part of the estate to a field near Letchworth Corner where over lunch Neville and Howard addressed them on the principles and proposals of Garden City. Unfortunately, even Adams could not arrange the weather, which was nothing short of Noah's Ark conditions. The great press day went off like the proverbial damp squib, and, the dreadful weather and glutinous mud apart, it would have required more than even a journalist's fertile imagination to picture utopia on the dreary Letchworth plateau. Moreover, it was apparent from Neville's and Howard's addresses that there was 'no very clear scheme agreed upon'[33]. Part of the damage done to the Garden City's press image was repaired by a subsequent press day in June 1906, by which time the growing town was assessed as a 'sound and realisable' venture. Once again the reporters had 'an able conductor in Mr. Thomas Adams, the popular Secretary of the Company, whose courtesy and urbanity are only equalled by the ability he possesses to impart, in a lucid and comprehensive manner, interesting information about the Estate'. Adams and his successors secured by means of interviews, tours, press releases, articles and letters an increasingly substantial and favourable treatment for the infant city[34].

There were many misconceptions to be dispelled. The prevailing scepticism was summed up by *The Builder:* 'Much as we wish success to the enterprise . . . we still have grave doubts about the scheme'. Most reservations concerned Garden City's practicality, critics arguing that it could succeed only if stripped of Howard's 'poetic conceptions'. Adams defended its viability but stressed that 'we shall not depart from customary business principles'. A further common charge was that Letchworth was the creation of 'faddists' and the home of 'cranks'. Adams replied that Garden City was not 'a haven of refuge for the elect who wished to escape from the sins and temptations of the world' nor were its inhabitants 'a set of cranky idealists'[35]. Furthermore, there was 'not the slightest basis for the suggestion that the scheme is an attempt to create a socialistic paradise'. Indeed, the project earned the distrust and distaste of the labour movement which viewed it as 'a happy hunting ground for capitalists on the lookout for cheaper labour' and as a diversion of the housing reform movement from its true path towards subsidized municipal housing[36].

It was to be expected that Garden City's supporters would demand an early sight of the promised land and Earl Grey, assisted by other prominent figures, opened the estate formally on 9 October 1903 in the presence of about a thousand people. As always, Adams's organization was faultless, his shepherding unobtrusive and his manner genial, the local paper reporting that the visitors were 'unanimous in praise of the kindly efforts of the Secretary (Mr. Thomas Adams) and his staff of helpers, who were here, there and everywhere, ready to attend to all inquiries and hear complaints'[37]. Adams realized the need to broaden the base of the movement's support and cultivated assiduously any band of enthusiasts or reformers likely to share its ideals. Most visits amounted to no more than a conducted tour of the estate, lunch or tea and a speech or two by Garden City leaders, but some centred round conferences at which major economic and social issues of the day were debated. Among the groups attracted to Letchworth were Esperantists, vegetarians, cyclists, adult education bodies, ramblers, women Liberals, Shoreditch councillors, Y.M.C.S.s, and the Economic Section of the British Association. One of the last important groups to which Adams played host was a large, all-party Parliamentary delegation of July 1906. In the summer of 1904, he had instigated a series of open air meetings, beginning with the American social gospeller Josiah Strong on 'The Industrial Revolution: its influence on Urban Development' and Seebohm Rowntree on 'Constructive Temperance Reform'. The G.C.A. held joint meetings with the Christian Social Union and the Co-operative Union and in 1906 regular Saturday excursions from London were organized. By these means, Adams spread the word of Garden City and helped to integrate it into the mainstream of social reform[38].

FIGURE 3. Letchworth Garden City: Open Air Meeting, 1904.
Rev. Josiah Strong addressing Garden City pioneers. Adams is seated behind the speaker, furthest from camera. (Mrs. Constance Adams)

The announcement that a garden city was to be built in north Hertfordshire was 'the one great absorbing topic locally' and both Howard and Adams devoted a good deal of time to outlining their plans, emphasizing the non-offensive nature of the town's industries, its essential practicality and its wish to be on good terms with its neighbours. After initial rural suspicion, rustic humour and countryside curiosity, both press and public reaction in the neighbourhood was benign and the company had far less trouble with the natives than with the settlers. Adams thus carried off the burdensome task of publicity and public relations with characteristic flair and aplomb[39].

HOMES AND FARMS IN FIRST GARDEN CITY

One of the conferences which Adams organized was on 'Garden City in Relation to Agriculture', held on 10 September 1904, at which he was himself the principal speaker. Though Howard and another director, Aneurin Williams, attended, it was very much Adams's own occasion. At this time, the issue closest to his heart was the revival of rural life and agriculture and as manager of the Garden City scheme he felt he had a perfect opportunity to implement both Howard's recommendations and his own[40].

Despite a brief youthful encounter with farming in the United States, Howard was never an agriculturalist nor even a countryman. Though he

FIGURE 4. Letchworth Garden City: Garden City and Agriculture Conference, 1904.

Adams is seated, hands on knees, to the right of Ebenezer Howard, with a child on his knee; H. Rider Haggard is next to Howard and Raymond Unwin is standing, far left, in Norfolk jacket. (Thomas Adams, *Garden City and Agriculture*, 1905)

sought genuinely to solve rural as well as urban problems and believed that his garden city would do both, he had little specific to say on the rural side of his scheme. Of the 3800 acres in the Letchworth package, 2500 were scheduled for farming. At the outset, there were eleven sizeable tenancies and one smallholding and initially they presented Adams, who was in effect the company's factor, with more problems than opportunities. About a quarter of the land was down to pasture and the soil was reckoned by Adams to be of a 'good average' quality but yields were low, capitalization minimal and the state of the properties downright shabby. Most of the tenancies were annual

ones and the tenants themselves, with one exception, were sullenly obstruc-
tive. Adams assured them that the company proposed to leave them as undis-
turbed as was consistent with the prompt establishment of a major road
system and public utilities and the more gradual requisitioning of land for
houses, shops and factories. Indeed, the company was in no position to do
otherwise and was able to invest only a meagre £5000 in the rundown farmland. Nor was a more dynamic policy ever likely for all the directors were
townsmen, at best *ersatz* country gentlemen, neither inclined nor fitted to lead
a crusade to reinvigorate the British countryside. In any case, the building of
the city was necessarily their immediate priority[41].

By the summer of 1904, it had become clear to Adams that he alone possessed the interest, experience and imagination necessary to make good the
second half of Howard's promise. As the company's prospectus said, 'The
root idea of Mr. Howard's book is to deal at once with the two vital questions
of the *overcrowding* in our towns and the *depopulation* of our rural districts'.
Thus Adams organized his conference to draw attention to the unwonted
neglect of the rural possibilities of Garden City. He persuaded the well-
known novelist, Norfolk squire and veteran of the land campaign, Henry
Rider Haggard, to chair the meeting and also present were other leaders of
the countryside lobby – Constance Cochrane of the Rural Housing and Sanitation Association, J. Nugent Harris, secretary of the Agricultural Organization Society, and the chairman of the highly-successful South Lincolnshire
Small Holdings Association, Alderman Richard Winfrey. Rider Haggard, in a
pungent and witty introduction to Adams's paper, adduced three reasons for
the deplorable rural situation – the want of cottages, the dullness of country
life and the pathetically low pay of the farm labourer. To overcome these
problems, he proposed a national policy of smallholdings to give labourers a
personal stake in the land, co-operative purchasing and marketing organizations, people's banks for loans to smallholders and an agricultural 'parcel
post' to get products to market quickly and above all more cheaply than by
rail. These proposals were in fact the common currency of most agrarian
reformers[42].

Adams's own paper developed the arguments advanced in his Edinburgh
articles of 1897[43]. Dismissing low prices as the major factor in the
depression, he pointed out that many prices had held firm while feeding costs
had fallen sharply and identified legal and social rather than economic causes.
He demonstrated the iniquity of annual tenancies and the difficulty of
transferring land ownership. The game laws, which entailed great crop losses,
were obsolete feudal remnants. The transportation of produce was difficult
and expensive. Agricultural education and research had been neglected and
farmers, historically staunch individualists, had been reluctant to co-operate.
The drift to the towns was due less to poverty than to the greater freedom and
opportunities of urban life. The collapse of rural industries left the labourer's
family without additional income while the lack of cottage gardens deprived

the man of a leisure interest and the opportunity to supplement the family budget. By 1900 there was a serious shortage of cottages for by-laws were rigid, materials dear and practicable rents too low to justify either building new, or repairing old, cottages.

Garden cities could never be plentiful enough to effect a complete remedy and so Adams called for general agricultural reforms. Arguing that a rise in wages would result in higher productivity, he recommended that British farming should concentrate on lines unaffected by foreign competition – market gardening, dairying and sheep. The restoration of cottage industries and gardens would give labouring families a stake in the land and enhanced incomes. Ingenuity should be exercised to reduce housing costs. Longer tenancies, offering a measure of security and incentives to tenants to effect improvements, should be granted while land should be easy of transfer, thus encouraging greater investment in agriculture. Farmers should form co-operatives and land banks to raise capital, purchase in bulk, market collectively and negotiate cheaper freight rates. National and local government should support the acquisition of smallholdings, backed up by expert assistance and training. Given this comprehensive attack on rural problems, Adams believed that farming would revive, depopulation would be stemmed and

> when the labourer gets proper opportunity, when he is encouraged to give of his best, when the land is made to produce its full complement of food, and when nature is thus induced to restore capital to our chief industry, cottages will come as a natural sequence, and a new race of sturdy English yeomen will grow up to form the bulwarks of our Empire[44].

Fleshing out Howard's vague and uninformed proposals for Garden City agriculture, Adams declared that 'The really great advantage of the Garden City scheme is the opportunity it provides to establish a just and equitable system of tenure, and for giving the labourer a personal interest in the land'. The company should create 200 smallholdings averaging five acres each, and allotments for labourers and factory hands. Local farm credit banks and co-operatives would assist with capital and marketing. Much of the farm belt would remain in units of 150 acres, on long and equitable leases, serviced by adequate communications and utilities. Suitable village industries would employ farm wives and, like the produce, find a ready market in Garden City. The company should establish a demonstration farm, a technical institute, a fruit tree nursery and a research and advisory centre. The investment would be modest, probably under £10,000. Moreover, the company should expect a return on its outlay, for 'No scheme of social reform that does not pay can be permanently successful'. Externally-financed contributions would be a rural university settlement, bringing students into contact with country life, and a farm colony for the London unemployed[45]. Convinced that the directors' interest 'is entirely in the social as distinct from the purely commercial side of the scheme,' he believed that

> they may be fully relied upon to use their best efforts to make the agricultural part of the project of real value as an object lesson to the nation. No doubt the industrial point of view is of more pressing importance but no-one who has followed me thus far can believe it to be independent of the development of the agricultural estate[46].

Altruism and equal priority, however, lost out to a frankly commercial, primarily industrial and essentially urban policy. All that Adams secured was a 152-acre smallholding centre at Norton Hall farm, where the Co-operative Small Holdings Society used the farm buildings as a demonstration and training centre and let units of up to 25 acres on long leases, building cottages and undertaking co-operative buying and selling. A small industrial bank was set up to lend to smallholders and in March 1905 a Smallholdings and Allotments Society was formed. Even these little ventures failed. Smallholders, who worked desperately hard and always on the margin of existence, found the local soils either too heavy or too chalky. Furthermore, the local market grew only slowly (perhaps a function of encouraging workers to grow their own food), most smallholders lacked capital and experience and, after Adams left, received no encouragement from the company[47].

While Adams remained, he lost no opportunity to expound his comprehensive vision of 'a democratic city of self-reliant citizens – surrounded by an agricultural belt occupied by a sturdy and independent yeomanry'. Shortly after his departure, however, he admitted the failure of his lone crusade and criticized the company for its lack of a constructive rural policy. 'To some of us,' he wrote, 'that aspect of the problem was as important as that of moving industries out of the large towns' and he lamented that 'The importance of the agricultural side of the scheme does not seem to be realised by some of those who are the warmest supporters of the industrial side of the movement'. The rural belt was destined to be the Cinderella of Garden City, a mere backdrop to the urban scene and the lungs of the lusty young town. Given the nature of the directorate, the company's lack of capital and the prevailing depression in farming, no other outcome was likely. Moreover, Adams's prescription, which was that of agricultural reformers in general, was already obsolete. The decline of the rural population was arrested after 1900 and agricultural returns were beginning to improve. The national smallholdings campaign was an almost total failure and the trend in farming was from tenancy to ownership. Adams's proposals were characteristic of both Liberals and Unionists and kept the state firmly in the background. Insofar as the farm problem was to be solved, however, it was to involve positive intervention by the state and a massive commitment of public money[48].

Adams ran up against similar problems in the housing field. A major inspiration of the Garden City movement was the desire to find an effective answer to the slum. It was essential, therefore, to assure decent standards of accommodation to all inhabitants, regardless of income. Raymond Unwin expressed the point succinctly: 'If Garden City stands for anything, surely it stands for this: a decent home and garden for every family that comes there. That is the irreducible minimum. Let that go and we fail utterly'[49]. From its inception, therefore, Letchworth was committed to a housing policy which became ultimately the national norm. The standard Letchworth house had three bedrooms, a kitchen and a reception room; all houses had baths, though not necessarily bathrooms. Mains services were laid on and all that was necessary for health and convenience, especially adequate light and air, was provided. Houses were to be within walking distance of the town centre, employment, shops and services, recreation spaces and the surrounding countryside. There were to be no differences between urban and rural standards and roads were lined with verges and trees. Great care was taken to avoid monotony in design and layout.

The Garden City fathers knew what kind of housing they wanted but had few clear ideas on how it was to be provided. They knew only that they would not build themselves – indeed, they lacked the capital to do so. Letchworth was no less open to the speculator than anywhere else. Almost from the day the company took possession in January 1904, houses began to go up in widely scattered locations and Letchworth's first inhabitants were solidly middle class – tradesmen, professional workers, retired folk and people of leisure. Many (of whom Howard was one) commuted to London, only forty minutes away, and the character of the new town seemed to bear out Howard's opinion that 'Garden City will be a splendid place to live in for those who want a pretty home near London'. There was no shortage of £250–400 villas in large gardens and the company encouraged a substantial middle-class presence. Adams stated that 'the Company will provide social facilities to induce a good class of residents', while Howard appealed for 'people of leisure and culture' to assist in the development of the town's social, artistic, educational and religious life – an elite to civilize the rude labourers who would soon form the bulk of the town's population[50].

The middle class was well able to fend for itself and so also was the aristocracy of labour, thanks largely to a new device which appealed greatly to the Garden City movement's liberalism. Co-partnership housing, which appeared at the end of the Victorian age, was an attractive blend of working-class self-help and thrift, philanthropy and good business. A limited dividend society was formed by philanthropists and prospective tenants, drawn largely from the great army of clerks and artisans. Tenants paid rent and received their shares of the profits in the form of reduced rents or of improved services and amenities. Estates were well equipped with community halls, recreation grounds, allotments and gardens. They were self-governing and developed lively cultural, sporting and horticultural activities[51]. At Letchworth,

Garden City Tenants was formed in 1904 and by 1906 had constructed about one hundred houses on four sites. Howard and Henry Vivian, M.P., the chairman of the parent body, Co-Partnership Tenants, Ltd., often shared the same platform. Adams, who saw 'a great future for co-partnership housing', remained committed to this form of 'associated individualism' throughout his life and recommended it in Canada and the United States in the inter-war years. However, the houses, though attractive and well-appointed, commanded rents 'beyond the means of any save the higher paid kinds of skilled workers and artisans'[52].

Adams, as the director of construction and recruiter-in-chief of population and industry, was more aware than most that a large body of people remained ill-housed. Some three hundred construction workers had to live in Hitchin and Baldock, often in overcrowded lodgings, rising at 5 a.m. to trudge three or four miles to be at work for 6.30 a.m., returning late in the evening. For a city designed to obviate the excessive separation of home and work and to dispense with overcrowding, the situation was naturally embarrassing. Declaring that it was 'time for someone to speak out strongly,' Adams insisted that 'Cottages must be provided for labourers at rents they can afford to pay, and the sooner the problem is faced the better for the Garden City scheme'. He took a number of initiatives to deal with it. In the spring of 1904, he persuaded a local builder to erect half-a-dozen small cottages for sale and pressed others to speculate in the local housing market, but demand always outran supply and the better-off forced up rents beyond the means of those earning less than twenty-five shillings a week. He then publicized the willingness of the Co-operative Permanent Building Society to lend 85 per cent of the purchase price at 5 per cent and the Hitchin Rural District Council's power to lend the balance on a £180–250 cottage provided the prospective purchaser could raise £40 or £50. This, too, was out of the reach of the labouring man and Adams believed that major reasons for the high costs of Garden City housing were that it was too ornate and had a higher than necessary standard of amenity, though Unwin rebutted the charges[53].

Though it was widely accepted that 'the very germ and principle of the Garden City idea largely depends on a satisfactory solution of this problem of the housing of the working classes being found', several remedies were not feasible. It was unlikely that there could be a significant increase in real wages and job security for the unskilled. Experiments with new and cheaper forms of construction had proved disappointing. Most reformers abhorred the prospect of state-subsidized housing, insisting that decent housing could and should be built 'without loss to the community' and, like Adams, they would have echoed the *Birmingham Gazette's* warning against getting into 'the dangerous position that every citizen has a right to ask the municipality to provide him with a house'. By the time Adams left, the directors were sufficiently exercised to ask Howard to give four months to propaganda work with a view to getting cheap houses for the town and eventually arrangements were made with a local builder to construct over one hundred houses letting at 4s and 4s 6d a week and returning 5 per cent. Ultimately the company sponsored the Howard Cottage Society to provide good basic accommodation[54]. The problem of low-income housing, however, was not solved until subsidized local authority housing became general after the First World War. At the time of Letchworth's establishment, the prevailing social philosophy and costs precluded a satisfactory solution; the means to overcome the difficulty could not be sanctioned by the liberal minds of the Edwardian age.

Adams's most remarkable contribution to the solution of Letchworth's housing difficulty was the Cheap Cottages Exhibition of 1905. It capitalized on a growing concern among the landed classes at the virtual cessation of rural cottage building. This perturbation reached a climax with the publication in the *County Gentleman* of a series of articles on the question, the most influential of which was by the paper's proprietor, J. St. Loe Strachey, entitled 'In Search of the £150 Cottage'. Though his assertion that 'If the agricultural problem and the problem of rural depopulation are ever to be solved they will be by the £150 cottage' was highly debatable, he was on firmer ground in complaining that it was 'yearly becoming more difficult for the labourer to obtain house room'. Even a regularly-employed labourer could afford no more than £8 a year for rent and this was insufficient to meet 'the interest on capital, rates, insurance and repairs'. A new cottage cost at least £250 and consequently there were 'fewer new houses built than old ones allowed to go to ruin'[55].

Seeing a range of possibilities in the article, Adams suggested to Strachey an exhibition of model rural cottages at Letchworth and believed that the directors would be pleased to make available the land and other facilities. Having aroused Strachey's interest, he then proposed to the board an exhibition lasting several months. The company would have the option to purchase the cottages but would in any case guarantee to let all of them. It would approve the plans and rents were to show a return of 5 per cent. Strachey offered £100 towards a prize fund of £1000. In proposing the exhibition, Adams had in mind several motives, as he told the directors:

> I am quite sure that if this exhibition is properly organized, and is held on the Estate it will be of tremendous advantage to the Company not only because it would advertise the scheme, but because of the attraction it would be to bring visitors to the Estate. The Exhibition should be made of a national character[56].

In this instance, Adams's longstanding interest in rural welfare seems to have run second to Letchworth's immediate needs of publicity and a hundred or so cheap homes for town labourers. The directors endorsed his initiative and he organized a list of distinguished patrons, an influential committee with a paid secretary and a panel of eminent judges. Adams and his colleagues were keen to amend 'old-fashioned by-laws, inelastic in their character and stupidly administered'. Fortunately, the local building code was lax, thus permitting a great variety of experiments. They sought to foster the use of both cheap local materials and of new techniques. Prizes were offered for four classes of cottages and for the best ones in wood and concrete, and for the best model of a smallholding. A sideshow displayed building materials, equipment and housing and planning exhibits. One hundred and twenty-one cottages were built, about evenly divided between detached, semi-detached and terraced homes[57].

Though welcome, the exhibition created headaches for Adams and Unwin. No satisfactory site was available and it had to be laid out in two parts, one to the south of the town centre and one north of the railway. A full range of services had to be supplied to areas as yet undeveloped, straining still further the company's slender capital resources. Arrangements had to be made for the reception of thousands of visitors who would want to see not only country

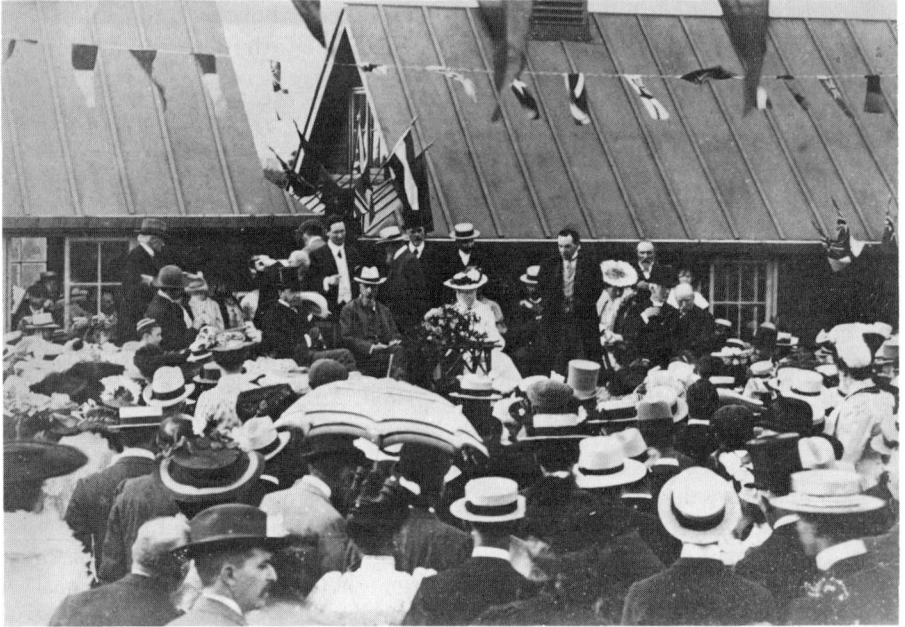

FIGURE 5. Letchworth Garden City: Opening of Cheap Cottages Exhibition, 1905.

The ceremony was performed by the Duke and Duchess of Devonshire (seated, centre). Adams is standing behind the Duke. The speaker is J. St. Loe Strachey. Ralph Neville is seated to the Duke's left and Ebenezer Howard is seated extreme right. Other Garden City directors and prominent supporters are on the platform. (Mrs. Constance Adams)

cottages but also a garden city in the making. The Great Northern Railway built a temporary station in the spring of 1905 but of Garden City itself there was still precious little to be seen. Construction was still at the roads and services stage, with a few dozen scattered middle-class houses, a handful of shops and no proper town centre. Dispersed over an often bleak landscape, Letchworth was the target of chill east winds and often as deep in mud as a Wild West town[58].

With his customary enthusiasm and dynamism, Adams had everything ready for the opening by the Duke of Devonshire on 25 July 1905. The judges reported that the exhibition had given 'valuable assistance towards the general objective' of lowering housing costs, but called for more ingenuity to overcome the defects and limitations encountered in the exhibits and they had reservations about the comfort and healthiness of one or two cottages in which tiny rooms denied adequate light and air. Visitors came from all over Britain, most by special trains, and from the four corners of the globe, a grand total of 60,000 by the time the exhibition closed in October. The Garden City board welcomed the publicity and the visitors and, even more, the substantial addition to the housing stock. On the face of it, Adams had inspired a triumph[59].

The Cheap Cottages Exhibition met a great deal of adverse comment, however, the press reaction being largely unfavourable. While it was acknowledged that 'The buildings demonstrate clearly that great savings could be effected in the erection of workmen's houses', experienced builders declared the £150 cottage to be a myth and put the true cost of the examples at £250–275 (and thus well beyond the scope of those for whom they were designed) since their costs did not include the price of the land, architects' fees, builders' profits, roadmaking, fencing, drainage and the transport of materials. Moreover, the by-laws in most districts would not permit the erection of many of the examples. Plainly, architects had much to learn in designing working-class accommodation. 'The general impression', the *Times* concluded, 'is less of genuine labourers' homes than of tasteful little week-end or summer holiday cottages for town dwellers'. As Constance Cochrane commented, 'That was to pass upon them the severest condemnation'. Many were disappointed that model cottages should be more concerned with aesthetics than serviceability and criticized their impracticality, poor materials, shoddy workmanship and low standards of light, air and space. 'The labourer's wife', it was said, 'cares a great deal more for 6d a week less rent than for all the art in all Ruskin's works'[60]. Arty cottages 'gave the place a name for cranky buildings' and 'the idea got fixed in the public mind, especially the journalistic mind, that Letchworth was a town of cheap country cottages'. Considering the distinguished work being done in the town by Baillie Scott, H. Clapham Lander and Parker and Unwin, the tag was undeserved. Many visitors were dismayed also by the apparent lack of progress with Garden City. The exhibition 'brought crowds of people to see a Garden City which had not yet been built, and gained the place a bad reputation before it deserved one'[61]. Like many of the movement's leaders, the general public seem to have expected an instant utopia. Letchworth paid a heavy price for its publicity, visitors and new cottages.

The exhibition nevertheless had some more substantial and general benefits. Adams could argue that even a bad press was better than no publicity at all and Garden City was certainly now known throughout the country and indeed the world. The show 'gave a powerful impetus to the better planning and reduction of cost of the small cottage' and led to a series of similar displays – urban cottages and smallholdings at Letchworth again (1907) and others at Wolverhampton, Sheffield, Newcastle, Glasgow and Swansea. While Adams's initiative had not suggested a convincing answer to the longstanding question 'Is it possible to provide a decent and wholesome dwelling for a married man earning low wages at a rent which he can afford to pay?' it had given rise to extensive discussion of the housing issue which, said the *Birmingham Gazette*, 'is exercising the public mind more acutely at the present moment than any other subject'[62]. The majority of visitors were drawn from local councils, medical officers of health, architects, builders, building trades and other unions, women's organizations, churches, co-operatives and reform bodies, and one of the most profound results of Adams's great exhibition was to stimulate a debate which was to have immense implications for the Englishman's future home.

UTOPIA IN HERTFORDSHIRE

In Adams's time, Letchworth was a remarkable community. Though mostly middle class in composition, the few who were not – largely independent-minded, self-organizing and ambitious artisans and market gardeners – displayed many of the same characteristics and interests. Garden City represented their Utopia though the term meant something different to each of them and the town became an open debating forum as the most advanced ideas of the day were canvassed and more specific social experiments took place under the umbrella of the larger one. Notable among these was the colony of artists who raised more than local eyebrows by going around in skirts of knee-length, smocks and sandals. At the Cloisters, an open-air school, 'the leisured classes' exchanged comfort for Spartan rigour. Aneurin Williams and a former East End settlement worker, the Rev. J. Bruce Wallace, founded the Alpha Union, a quasi-Christian fellowship 'for the deepening of spiritual life'. S. W. Palmer recalled that 'Socialism, vegetarianism, the simple life, bare legs and so on were our peculiarities at first . . . We were out to convert the world and each other'. Not unnaturally, the press seized on these 'peculiarities' and the reputation of being a community of freaks 'hung over Garden City for years'[63].

Though disputation was incessant and often fierce, there was at the same time a sense of 'good fellowship – the genuine brotherliness of those early days'. The unity of the inhabitants was scarcely surprising – differences were generally kept in the abstract and the fragility of the enterprise and the suspicion of the natives ensured a high degree of social cohesion. Nevertheless, the plethora of alternative visions of the social order led to intense activity and 'before Letchworth was four years old it had one committee for each inhabitant, and all of them uplift ones'. In this maelstrom of earnest endeavour, Howard, Parker, Unwin, Adams, Purdom and F. J. Cole, the forester, and the wives, all joined[64].

Adams moved to Punchardon Hall in Letchworth itself in 1905. He was not enamoured of many of the departures from the social norm but he shared the belief that Garden City was a *tabula rasa* on which a happier, more just and more efficient society could be erected. What Purdom said of Raymond Unwin applied equally to Adams: 'He threw himself into the town's incipient life, and everything that was to be done there was dear to him'. Despite his work as the company's secretary, manager and factotum, Adams found time to indulge in every one of his interests – religion, education, politics, debating, public speaking, gardening, golf and tennis. His principal identification was with the Free Church, of which he was president. A Presbyterian of tolerant views, he aimed to make the congregation the centre of local Nonconformity and 'the most alive body on the estate'. Establishing a wide variety of activities, by the time he left he had led it to the point of erecting a permanent building and appointing a minister. A frequent speaker to religious groups, he addressed the Y.M.C.A. on 'The Religious Teaching of John Ruskin' and 'Wilberforce', and the Anglican Men's Adult School on 'Cranks'. Caroline was a faithful supporter of his church work, inevitably playing the piano at services and musical evenings[65].

Though Adams did not match Unwin's involvement in education, he endorsed the latter's initiative in setting up evening classes and a county school with resident governors and supplemented by a voluntary local rate. With Howard Pearsall, a Garden City director resident in Letchworth, and Herbert Warren, the company's solicitor, he became a vice-president of the Liberal and Radical Association, while his wife was president of the Women's Liberal Association. He was president of the Debating Society, with Purdom as secretary-treasurer, and was treasurer of the Horticultural Society, of which Neville was the President, and he was active in the local branch of the Garden City Association. A keen tennis player, he was also the instigator of the Letchworth Hall Golf Club. Caroline became the unofficial social worker for the little community and the Adams's knew also how to enjoy themselves, initiating regular Christmas and New Year parties at Letchworth Hall[66].

The frenetic social life was, however, special to the years 1904–1906 and by the time the Adams's left, the sense of community was breaking down, some of the excitement was evaporating and pressures were being exerted on

Letchworth which turned it ultimately into a rather ordinary if pleasant
moderate-sized industrial town. In the first place, the company adopted a
sternly commercial policy, discouraging the unorthodox, and secondly there
was a massive shift in the social balance following the rapid growth of the
factory district in 1906. 'So sudden an influx of people,' noted Purdom,
'swamped the first comers and their idealistic notions'. By 1907, there were
4300 people in Garden City. The new inhabitants were the very people for
whom Letchworth had been founded yet they met there an atmosphere to
which they were either hostile or indifferent[67].

Adams recognized early the need to discover common ground between
'old' and 'new' residents and encourage communication between them. Like
most of his fellow-pioneers, he was a patron of labour, intent upon educating
the working-class into middle-class beliefs and patterns of behaviour. He
encouraged working-class self-help so long as it did not take the form of trade
unions or political parties. It was in this spirit of moral elevation that Adams
suggested an organization to provide 'instruction and recreation' for the
London unemployed then engaged on construction work at Letchworth.
Towards the end of his stay, since the middle-class churches were 'not getting
hold of the working man', he founded a Pleasant Sunday Afternoon, inform-
ing the working class that 'In this society is none of the asceticism, the dull
cold religion of the churches, rightly or wrongly attributed to them'. Calling
it 'an outspreading of the hand of fellowship to the working man', he
deprecated rigid class distinctions between labourers and professional and
managerial people, observing that it was 'peculiarly appropriate to build up
Garden City citizenship . . . Labour is noble and man should cultivate his
mind so that it would be a complement to his physical energy put forth
day-by-day. Cultivate independence of character, true nobility and thrift, and
good will will result to all'. Along with these ventures, Letchworth's leaders
established a workmen's social club, a 'beerless pub' (the famous Skittles Inn)
and the Howard Memorial Hall (for which Adams proposed an 'advisory
committee' of six workers)[68].

The vision of a community of interests between the classes was already a
part of the past. Few of Letchworth's new mass army of machine minders
heeded the call. They were being offered only a minimal share in the
power structure and Letchworth's social order and assumptions were as
anachronistic as the idea of a private Garden City itself, a last-gasp extension
of Victorian utilitarian liberalism. The newcomers were already identifying
with trade unions and by 1906 socialism was the strongest political creed in
the town[69]. Yet despite the inevitable submerging and disintegration of the
first Garden City community, it has to be acknowledged that in those early
years there was an extraordinary flowering of community organization and
citizen participation. In that tale of the strenuous life, Thomas and Caroline
Adams played an honoured and, characteristically, a leading role.

ADAMS AS SCAPEGOAT

Adams was transcendentally happy at Letchworth but the days of wine and roses were not long for in August 1905 he was relieved of managerial responsibilities. At the root of this decision lay First Garden City's chronic lack of capital and organization. The struggle to raise capital was constant and largely unavailing. When Adams departed in the autumn of 1906, the sum raised (£148,000) amounted to less than the purchase price (£155,000). At the same time, over £200,000 had been invested in the town's infrastructure. A combination of loans and mortgages kept the company going. 'Money was so tight,' recalled Purdom, 'that the Company was only barely able to carry on'. The directors, a constantly changing group, were nervous men, anxious for instant profitability and fearful of imminent collapse. Adams, an inexperienced manager, was given little more than a year to prove himself. He displayed great energy, high organizing skill and a clear-sighted realization of immediate needs but only an impossible overnight success could have satisfied the fidgety board. He was replaced by W. H. Gaunt, manager of the Trafford Park industrial estate at Manchester and the kind of man who ought to have been appointed at the outset. Though compelled to hand over to Gaunt all responsibility for the building of the town, Adams bore him no ill will and referred to him often with approval[70].

Adams continued to act as company secretary, which necessitated regular commuting to London. Gaunt meanwhile adopted a strictly commercial policy which seemed to Adams and other pioneers destructive of many of the essentials of Garden City. In a famous passage Purdom accused Gaunt of trying to establish 'the characteristics of a Manchester suburb and the features of a Lancashire industrial town' but Gaunt lacked both the desire and the opportunity to do so. He liked Letchworth enough to remain there for the rest of his life, long after he had ceased to work for the company, and became a town councillor. He adhered to the essentials of a limited dividend and the retention for the community of the increment in land value, though he was fully aware of the difficulties that this philanthropic policy created. However, he pressed ahead with rapid industrialization, the cheapest possible housing, high ground rents and the cutting of aesthetic corners. The so-called 'New Policy' was extremely unpopular in the town. The hard-headed approach met resistance also on the board, particularly from Neville, and there were frequent squabbles, culminating in Gaunt's dismissal in 1917. Gaunt had been no more able than Adams to generate instant success for the first net profit was not made until 1911 and the first dividend was declared only in 1915. Indeed, such industrial advances as Letchworth made before 1907 were all due to Adams[71].

THE REVIVAL OF THE GARDEN CITY ASSOCIATION, 1904–1906

Despite his disappointment at being relieved of the key post in the building of the town and his misgivings over Gaunt's 'New Policy', Adams remained loyal to the idea of Garden City and to his closest associates, Neville and Howard, and seems to have had no thought of resigning in 1905. Indeed, his demotion was a blessing for the Garden City Association and now that he had time on his hands, he was asked to serve as the honorary secretary *pro tempore*. The Association was then in a state of lethargy and disorganization and suffering a crisis of identity. Its troubles had begun with the formation of First Garden City for supporters switched funds from the association to the company. Adams served on a 'Special Sub-Committee to enquire into the Financial Position of the Association' and the company twice had to bail out its parent body. Even more disruptive was the virtual loss of Adams's energetic and imaginative guiding hand as he, along with Neville and Howard, became absorbed in the Letchworth experiment. The daily routine fell to a new organizing secretary, George J. H. Northcroft, a journalist returned recently from ten years abroad. However, Adams remained 'the nominal chief official in the Association, with authority over the actual working Secretary of the Association, whenever he may claim to exercise it'. It was an unsatisfactory situation but the association was reluctant to part entirely with Adams, both on account of his knowledge of its work and of his position at Letchworth. Northcroft was unhappy with Adams looking over his shoulder and after two years he resigned in August 1905. He lacked Adams's organizing ability, energy and commitment and when Adams regained the reins he found the office in total disarray, new subscriptions had almost dried up and old ones had not been renewed, the branches were complaining of neglect and 'very little has been done to organise lectures'. The whole organization of the association 'seems to require attention'. The situation was tailor-made for Adams's zeal and drive[72].

The association's essential problem was stated by Herbert Warren, chairman of the executive and the company's solicitor: 'the objects of the Association were to some extent attained by the floating of the Company and unless fresh objects can be given to the Association it seems likely to languish'. Between 1903 and 1905 it spent much time discussing what future, if any, it had. A disposition to superintend the company was quashed by Adams who asserted that it had 'no claim to dictate the policy to be adopted'[73]. Most importantly, he recognized that a broader role had to be found for it and proposed that

> The function of the Garden City Association is surely the higher one of teaching sound principles in regard to a particular aspect of social reform, ... there is a room for a strong, active, educational institution to take up a *definite line of action* and press its objects forward not only on the public generally but on all public bodies throughout the country[74].

By the autumn of 1905 Adams knew better than anyone the strength of the movement throughout the country, the prospects for Letchworth and the proposals of other environmental reformers. The trend was towards garden suburbs, a bastard form of Howard's vision and indeed contrary to it in that they would exacerbate the urban sprawl he sought to eliminate. Nevertheless, their widespread realization promised better environmental conditions for many and the movement could hardly condemn that. Ever a realist, Adams recognized that Letchworth's financial difficulties would render it an only child and believed that the association, while still committed to 'taking initial steps to establish Garden Cities', should promote the 'scientific' development of existing towns and the planned decentralization of industry and population. When Hampstead Garden Suburb was founded, he counselled, 'Let the Garden City Association as the parent body, look with equal favour on all its offsprings, and welcome the suburb and the village as well as the city, so long as its principles are maintained'. In thus broadening the scope and therefore the appeal of the association, Adams launched it on the path which was to make it the principal voice of town planning in general and laid the basis for its eventual transformation into the modern Town and Country Planning Association[75].

Adams took over at the G.C.A. in September 1905 and quickly revitalized the organization. He circulated fresh appeals for subscriptions, arranged winter lectures and toured provincial cities reviving or founding branches. The one gain of Northcroft's stewardship, the quarterly, *Garden City*, was reshaped as a monthly. Edited for a time by Adams himself (he was always a major contributor), it remained primarily 'a record of progress' at Letchworth but introduced also news of environmental reform elsewhere and discussed the intellectual origins of the movement. Virtually self-supporting, it was described as 'one of the chief factors' in the association's revival. The association's propaganda service recovered its vigour and advised government and industry on new residential projects. Local branches became strong and active and finances were 'thoroughly sound'[76].

By the spring of 1906, the G.C.A. was enjoying a remarkable turn round in fortune and Adams was able to withdraw from his temporary role on the appointment of a new organizing secretary, the journalist Ewart G. Culpin, a man his equal in energy, ability and devotion to Howard's principles[77]. Adams received a well-justified encomium from the council:

> When, nine months ago, Mr. Adams resumed the work of organization which he had been so conspicuously successful in bringing into prominence, the Association was in a moribund condition, and the state of its finances were very unsatisfactory. With his characteristic energy, however, the honorary secretary at once infused his own enthusiasm into the members, and it is safe to say that the credit of the Association never stood higher in the general estimation than it does today[78].

Not only had Adams revolutionized the association's structure and prospects, he had pointed it also in the direction it was henceforth to take, at some cost to its purity but grasping firmly the realistic possibilities of the time.

LEAVETAKING, 1906

Adams's relinquishment of his honorary duties presaged his resignation from the company's service. It was scarcely to be expected that he was happy to hand over the responsibility for building Garden City and that he would endorse the 'New Policy', but what probably determined him to quit was Neville's departure from the chairmanship and the board in April 1906, on his elevation to the King's Bench. Neville, Howard and Adams had formed a triumvirate crucial to the early realization of the Garden City vision. Of Neville's contribution, Adams wrote justly that 'None gave greater or more valuable service at the cost of his health'[79]. Neville was unable to prevent Adams from being made the scapegoat for Letchworth's failure to attain immediate profitability but while he remained Adams felt that he had some influence and an obligation to stay. His departure left Adams dependent on the ineffectual Howard, whose influence faded rapidly once Garden City began to be realized. As Adams explained later:

> A mind like his – broad-visioned and idealistic – was not the kind that throve when preoccupied by detail, and from the time that Letchworth was begun, very naturally, he became more absorbed in problems of development than was good for his expansive and sensitive nature. Little irritations that do not much disturb the equanimity of the ordinary man were real afflictions to him. In time they reduced his resistance to those who had a narrower, more erroneous but more immediately practical way of doing things[80].

Frankly, Howard was out of his depth. He had neither the wealth, the experience, the prestige or the expertise to hold his own with the captains of industry who soon came to dominate the board. Letchworth, his child, was fostered by others, often on lines he must deeply have regretted. By the summer of 1906, Adams concluded that his influence on policy was negligible and submitted his resignation, effective at the end of October. Though he refrained from publishing his reasons, the local press speculated freely that the cause was his opposition to the 'New Policy'[81].

The Adams's going was the occasion of much lamentation and praise. A string of farewell events culminated in a presentation evening in the Howard Memorial Hall. The place was overflowing with townsfolk and the luminaries of the movement, Ralph Neville speaking for all present in asserting that Adams

> had shown ability of no mean order, and untiring and persistent energy in his work. He had compressed as great an amount of useful work into the time

of his connection with the movement as it was possible for any man to do. To Mr. Adams's devotion to the scheme they owed its success[82].

In the press, further tribute was paid to his 'unsparing energy and enthusiasm' and it was argued that 'in a very large measure – how large, perhaps not even Mr. Adams's warmest admirers quite realise – the success of the Garden City movement and the Garden City Company is due to his ability, tactfulness and capacity for hard work' and it was noted also that a number of local societies 'owe their very existence to him'. Rarely can so short a residence have generated such universal feelings of approbation[83].

That appreciation was not misplaced for with Howard himself, Neville and Unwin, Adams was a vital factor in the realization of Howard's dream. 'He has Atlas-like carried Garden City on his shoulders', wrote one eulogist, but Adams was no overpowering bureaucrat. He and Caroline were crucial figures in the evolution of Letchworth's political, religious, educational, cultural, sporting and social life. Only Howard himself and the equally-dedicated Raymond Unwin matched Adams's social commitment. It is from Letchworth that one has the richest insights into Adams's personality. Remembered as 'a tall, lithe, ruddy son of the Scottish countryside', he was described as 'Genial to his fingertips yet with a twinkle of his eyes and a smile as potent in disarming too great a familiarity and inquisitiveness as in inspiring confidence in the man behind' and as 'friendly and unassuming, kindly and hearty'. With 'his usual anxiety to please', he achieved excellent relations between the company and the initial settlers. The local embodiment of the Garden City idea, he was imbued with 'the spirit of the place'[84]. A rock of fortitude and encouragement, his critical importance to the young Letchworth was summed up much later by a retired nurseryman:

> ... if it had not been for Mr. Adams, with his untiring energy, I doubt very much if Letchworth ... would have survived ... No other man, in my estimation, could have given the inspiration and help that were so needed to the very early settlers. We could all go to him with our anxieties and, believe me, there were some in those days. He had the gift of infusing hope and courage when it was most needed. I always felt better after a talk with him and ready for battle again. What he was to us struggling men, Mrs. Adams was to our womenfolk ... He realised the vital importance for Letchworth, in those early days, that if possible there should be no failures, however small the venture[85].

This comprehensive tribute goes far to explain the widespread appreciation of the Adams's contribution expressed at the farewell gatherings. The churlish treatment meted out to him by a board which used him as a scapegoat for its own shortcomings masked his highly successful initiation of an experiment the sages had prejudged as impracticable. Letchworth's later vindication of its founders' hopes and principles might well have been impossible without Adams's skilful pilotage of the fragile vessel through the troubled waters of 1903–1906.

Chapter Three

The Establishment
of British Planning,
1906–1914

The First Town Planning Practice, 1906–1909

When Adams resigned from First Garden City in July 1906, he had no other position in prospect. However, during his five years of hectic activity on behalf of the Garden City movement, he had made many influential contacts, he was experienced, talented and ambitious, and the field of what came to be known shortly as 'town planning' was clearly a burgeoning one. For the next three years he became in effect the first man to earn his living solely from town planning work.

He began his planning career at an auspicious moment for 1906 was a critical year in British planning, a year in which it took off into self-sustained growth. Letchworth at last developed the industrial base on which its success depended while the earlier model villages were coming to maturity. The garden suburb movement, led by Hampstead, blossomed as from nothing and the co-partnership movement flourished. The day of the environmental idealists appeared to have dawned yet their triumph was shortlived for 1906 marked also a watershed after which a more pragmatic meliorism came to dominate the British planning scene. It borrowed from the idealist school only its techniques and standards, grafting on to them foreign ideas of development control. This fusion, the work principally of the Birmingham councillor J. S. Nettlefold, became the basis of statutory town planning and led to the routinization of the planning process[1].

However, statutory planning did not come into operation until 1910 and in the meantime, the garden suburb movement reached its peak, a growth in which Adams played a significant part[2]. His entrée was almost accidental. The Pagets, Staffordshire landowners who were also supporters of the Garden City movement, asked Adams to recommend an agent for their

estates who would develop them on garden city lines. Seeing a life-raft,
Adams offered to take the post himself and moved to Wolverhampton in
November 1906[3].

He described his new milieu in Stevensonian terms:

> ... a black and smoky wilderness, permeated with reeking canals, covered with
> pit banks, and slummy rows of jerry-built houses, with here and there a stunted
> tree raising its skeletal form against the horizon, as if in protest against the
> destruction of nature[4].

The bearer of the Garden City gospel fell upon Wolverhampton with all of
the hand-rubbing glee of the evangelist cornering the rake. The 'Capital of
the Black Country', a county borough of over 100,000 people, suffered doubly
in 1906 – from a dreary, dirty and devastated environment and from
depression. The work force, though generally well-paid, was ill-housed and
unwilling to pay for decent accommodation. There was severe overcrowding
and large numbers of two-roomed back-to-back houses, while of over 1000
vacant houses, some two-thirds were unsanitary[5].

The Pagets had several properties in Staffordshire and Adams was agent
for all of them. His principal responsibility, however, was for the Fallings
Park estate. A compact, picturesque, elevated, well-wooded and well-drained
piece of 400 acres, it was conveniently situated a mile or so to the east of the
town, off the Cannock road. The Pagets intended to build a garden suburb
there and engaged the well-known Arts-and-Crafts architect Detmar Blow to
plan it. From a central hub, Blow proposed radials leading to four subsidiary
foci. The roads were generally straight, punctuated by frequent set-backs of
houses fronted by greens. Ample open space was reserved in advance and the
housing was a mixture of detached and semi-detached villas and short
terraces. At ten houses per acre, the ultimate population was to be 20,000.
Road widths varied according to function and streets were tree-lined and
verged. Urban services were available and sites were reserved for public
buildings. Adams had a hand, albeit an unspecified one, in the making of
the plan. It was an effective if somewhat pedestrian and stilted design.
The principal attraction of the scheme for Adams was the opportunity it
offered for 'associated individualism'. There was cordial co-operation
between the landowner and local authorities, much of the housing was to be
by co-partnership societies and Adams hoped that the residents would
ultimately manage the estate themselves[6].

He realized that the success of Fallings Park depended upon a rejuvenation
of the local economy and quickly got himself appointed convenor of the
advertising committee of the local Industrial Development Committee,
writing a boosterish history, guide and promotional handbook aimed
primarily at London businessmen but also at American and German firms.
The one major success of his campaign was the location, on ten acres of

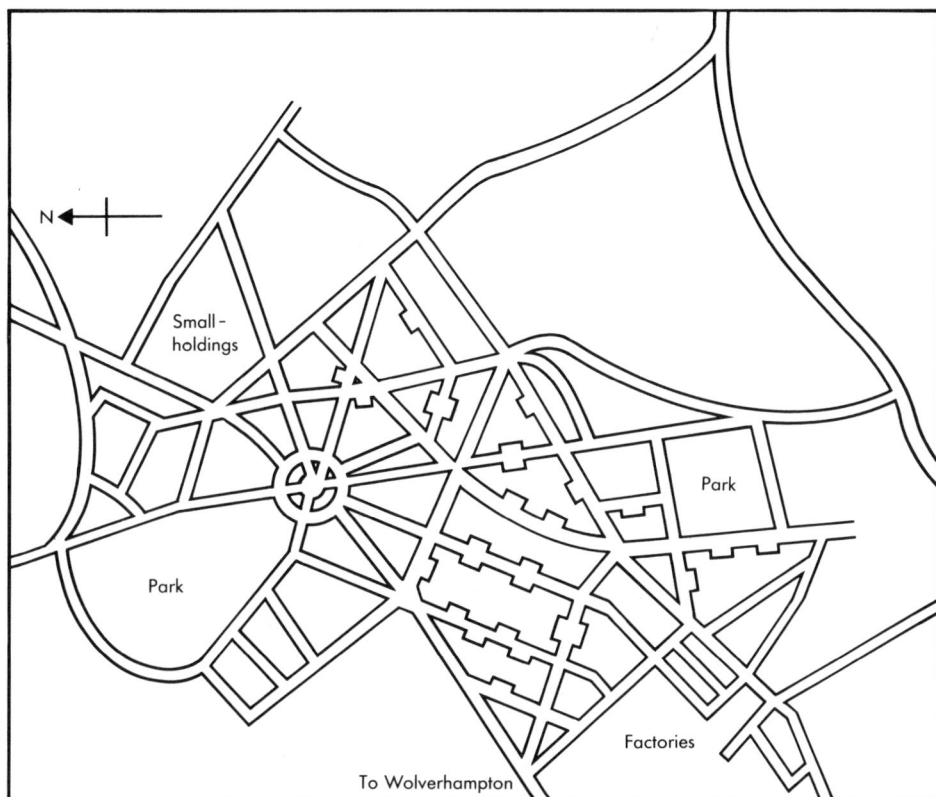

FIGURE 6. Wolverhampton: Fallings Park Garden Suburb, 1907–8.
Designed by Detmar Blow assisted by Thomas Adams. Note the numerous residential set-backs and the designers' attachment to hubs and radials. (*Book of the Model Housing Exhibition, Wolverhampton*, 1908, p. 12)

Fallings Park land, of a new Chubb lock and safe factory. Adams pressed other improvements on local leaders – better communications by road and rail, a decent hotel for visiting businessmen, a local insurance society to invest in the area, and boundary extensions. He drummed up support for the garden suburb from municipal leaders, local business magnates like the Manders, clerks and artisans; secured the patronage of the Lord Mayor of Birmingham, the Bishop of Lichfield, Sir Oliver Lodge, the eccentric Principal of Birmingham University, and Nettlefold; and brought in outside speakers like Henry Vivian. He obtained for the scheme extensive press coverage, the *Primitive Methodist Leader* remarking, with a combination of gruffness and millenialism, 'Nowhere is it needed more. Wolverhampton is not exactly a garden city. All hail to the new departure. Flowers and fresh air for the workers will help to bring the Kingdom of Heaven nearer'[7].

The suburb was inaugurated in the summer of 1907, following which there was a conference at which the principal speaker was a leading housing reformer, Sir John Dickson Poynder, M.P. The first houses, built by a co-partnership society and letting at four to six shillings weekly, were occupied in February 1908 and by the opening of the Chubb works in July over forty had been completed. A housing exhibition scheduled for 1907 was postponed until September 1908, as a consequence of the building depression, but even when it opened, with a typically rumbustious address by Lodge, the number of entries was disappointing. Moreover, many were repeats of successful designs from other competitions, though the entrants were divided fairly evenly between local architects and familiar names from elsewhere — Pepler and Allen, Crickmer, and Bennett and Bidwell. By the end of the year, seventy-five houses had been built on seven acres. Development then ceased, killed off by the local slackness of trade and the persistence of the national building depression. Fallings Park thus achieved little, either as an exercise in housing improvement for the masses or in pointing the way to a new guild-like urban community[8].

Despite this disappointment, Adams's two years in the Black Country brought three distinct gains. Acquaintance with the desolate landscape, the legacy of two hundred years of extractive and industrial exploitation, led to his involvement with Lodge's Midland Re-afforestation Association, which planted over 100,000 trees in three years and aimed to restore to public use the 30,000 acres of wasteland, replacing the mounds of grey shale with young saplings, a profitable as well as an aesthetic investment.

Adams had high hopes of the programme, for he believed it would result in

> . . . the conversion of . . . the most desolate industrial region of the country into a commonwealth of garden cities. Nothing will help to bring about that result more speedily than the success of the Afforestation Movement. . . The work is immediately practical on lines that are far from the pauperising elements of many schemes of social reform . . .[9].

Secondly, Adams was introduced to what later became regional planning. The Mayor of Dudley in 1907, Alderman Frank W. Cook, conceived the idea of a federation of Black Country municipalities with the aims of improving the communications between them, co-ordinating their public services, reclaiming wasteland and enlarging county boroughs to improve health and economy. In 1908, twenty-six councils, including Birmingham and Wolverhampton, with a combined population of 1.3 millions, set up an Association of Midland Local Authorities. Discussions took place on sewage disposal and the improvement of highways and waterways. Nettlefold, a prominent supporter, recommended the co-ordination of planning schemes, should the town planning measure then before Parliament become law. The boldest proposal, however, was that of Adams and a local business leader, G. H. Sankey, for a new trunk road from Wolverhampton to Birmingham. Described as 'Perhaps the most important scheme of new roadmaking contemplated in this country for a good many years', its preliminary planning was undertaken by Adams. Regarding existing communications as 'quite inadequate', he proposed the improvement of five miles of old road and the construction of six miles of new road. The total cost was estimated at £76,136 and it was to be thirty-five feet wide, verged and tree-lined. Adams intended that seventy per cent of the work should be undertaken by the unemployed. He acted as spokesman for the association, endeavouring to interest the Government in afforestation and the new road. He urged John Burns, President of the Local Government Board, to inspect the area and attend a conference. Unfortunately, nothing seems to have come of the organization but in its attempted rationalization of local government and its services and in its co-ordinated attack on environmental problems, it represented what was probably the earliest attempt at regional planning in these islands. From his experience, Adams derived a belief in metropolitan regions and spent much of the rest of his career in urging regional planning[10].

Finally, the Wolverhampton episode enabled Adams to get a start in planning practice. Once construction was under way at Fallings Park, he set up in practice as a 'consulting surveyor and land agent' with chambers in Wolverhampton and, from January 1909, in Pall Mall, London. His connections with progressive landowners, the current high demand for garden suburbs and the lack of experienced planners brought him commissions for five garden suburb schemes by the summer of 1907[11].

His first engagement appears to have been at Glyn Cory in South Wales. Reginald Cory, of the great Cardiff shipping, coalowning and philanthropic family, joined the board of First Garden City in June 1906 and was thereby inspired to set up a garden suburb on his estate at Duffryn, seven miles west of Cardiff. It was to be a commuter village for businessmen and clerks and the landscape architect Thomas Mawson was commissioned to design it. Mawson emphasized the florid, grandiose and picturesque and at Glyn Cory he had a fine site for his proclivities. A natural amphitheatre on the wooded slopes above the River Ely, the place was easily accessible by rail from Cardiff. Mawson aimed to provide 'a quiet retreat where, in forgetfulness of the stress and strain of business, lovers of country pleasures may find suitable homes' and he sought 'to conserve almost all the existing features and supplement them with effective combinations of trees and gardens grouped and arranged to achieve consummate effects, with which the houses will accord in happy combination and repose in their fitting and restful settings'. He made good use of his opportunity. A new road led from the station to a fine river bridge, beyond which was a hundred-foot Main Avenue culminating at a church. Subsidiary avenues radiated from the bridge, along with a riverside

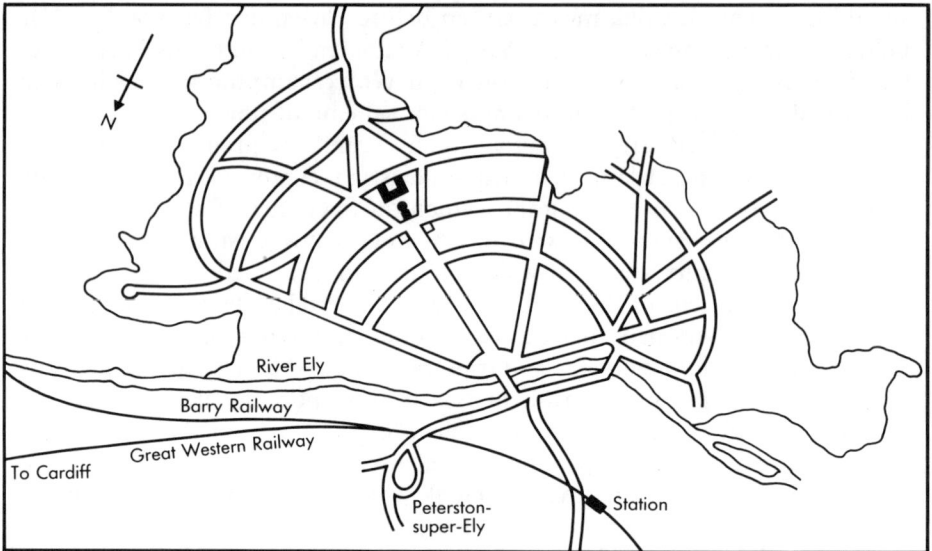

FIGURE 7. Cardiff Glyn Cory Garden Suburb, 1907–9.
Designed by Thomas Mawson and revised by Thomas Adams, who simplified the
design substantially. The lower crescents were intended for artisans' terraces and the
highest ground was reserved for villas. (*Town Planning Review*, Vol. 1, no. 2, July
1910).

promenade, and crescents intersected the radials, with cheaper terraced
houses on the lower slopes and villas on the commanding heights, all in local
materials and vernacular style. The public facilities were lavish, there were to
be no advertisements and the village was to be teetotal. Cory leased plots on
generous terms, placing 'the welfare of its inhabitants before pecuniary gain'.
Attractive mortgages were offered and it was hoped to form a co-partnership
society, Adams entertaining a party of Cardiff philanthropists at Fallings Park
to explain the idea. When complete, Glyn Cory would house five to six
thousand people in 1400 houses[12].

Adams was called in to supervise construction while Mawson was lecturing
in America in 1907. He made several modifications to the plan, moving the
housing well above the flood level, foreshortening the promenade and re-
aligning and extending other roads. By the spring of 1909, rapid development
was under way, a co-partnership society had leased a considerable area, and
the bridge, the main avenue, two crescents and four houses had been completed. Though it was claimed that Glyn Cory 'bids fair to be one of the most
successful and interesting projects of its kind', only twenty-four houses had
been built by the outbreak of war in 1914. The plan was in the grand manner,
quite unnecessary for a homely commuter suburb, and it failed also because it

was too far from Cardiff, which had attractive competing suburbs closer at hand, and because of the all-pervading building depression[13].

The first plan for which Adams was wholly responsible was Alkrington garden suburb, near Middleton in Lancashire. It was familiar ground, for in 1905 the trustees of the late James Lees had offered it to the Garden City Association as the core of a possible northern garden city. Adams, Herbert Warren and the Manchester branch of the G.C.A. investigated the possibility and took an option to purchase the 700-acre estate. However, it seemed unwise to compete for scarce funds with First Garden City, the land was only a tenth of what was desirable and there was little prospect of the remainder becoming available, while the asking price of £219 per acre was considered excessive. Howard thought the property – which was rugged and dissected by ravines on the west though more gently graded on the east – was better left wild and both the Manchester and the London leaders of the G.C.A. were lukewarm about the project[14].

FIGURE 8. Alkrington Garden Suburb, Middleton, near Manchester, 1908–9.

Highly formal on level ground to the right; bending with contours on rugged, fissured ground to the left. Interiors of blocks to be used for recreation. The grand avenue was intended to lead to a square with shops and public buildings. As at Wolverhampton, there are numerous residential set-backs and half-a-dozen radial hubs. (*Town Planning Review*, July 1910)

The Lees Trustees thereupon formed their own garden suburb company and engaged Adams. His plan was completed in 1908 and made public in January 1909, with the intention of beginning work in the summer. As with other garden suburbs, there were to be villas and co-partnership housing, at a density of fifteen to the acre, laid out on tree-lined, grass-margined roads of varying widths with allotments, playgrounds and recreation areas in the interiors of blocks and a park on the bluff round the old hall. On the west, the ravines and a lake compelled roads to wind along contours but east of the Middleton–Manchester road, the ground, though undulating, was easier and a more formal street plan was laid out — a rectangular framework divided by diagonals with a wide grand avenue on the south side, with a central reservation, leading to a square for public buildings. Substantial areas on the north and west were left for future development. The plan was clearly derived from Adams's knowledge of the Letchworth, Fallings Park and Glyn Cory designs and, following Hampstead, made extensive use of footpaths and culs-de-sac. However, it demonstrated Adams's fine natural eye for landscape and the plan was sympathetic to the site, at once attractive, economical and compact[15].

Little progress was made before Adams entered government service in March 1910 and it was his successors, George Pepler and Ernest Allen, who oversaw the first phase. T. C. Horsfall, the Manchester businessman, philanthropist and advocate of German planning, opened a fifty-acre section on the west side in August 1911 but by 1914 only 40 houses on ten acres had been completed. Though there was heavy local demand for decent accommodation, the building depression continued to blight new projects[16].

One of the great landowners with whom Adams had become acquainted at Letchworth was the second Earl of Lytton, whose seat was at nearby Knebworth. A supporter of the Garden City movement, he attempted in 1905 to create a model village there. Knebworth was only twenty-five miles from King's Cross and 'It is, perhaps, to the City man that the offer will most appeal'. Though steady growth took place, there was no clear plan and Lytton became aware that it was 'on old-fashioned lines'. In the summer of 1908, he determined on a fresh start, becoming president of Garden Villages, Ltd, and appointing Adams to draw up a plan in association with the renowned architect Edwin Lutyens, Lytton's brother-in-law[17].

The 800-acre site was divided almost equally by the main line of the Great Northern Railway, running at the foot of a chalk ridge; the land was level to the east but rose steeply on the west. Great care was taken to retain the natural beauty and character of the neighbourhood and, apart from the straggling development around the station, Adams had a greenfield site. The Earl laid out a golf course on the north-west, seemingly for the House of Lords and the two front benches. Ample open spaces and sites for shops and public buildings were reserved, while the inhabitants were to control the public utilities. The average housing density was eight per acre and the classes were

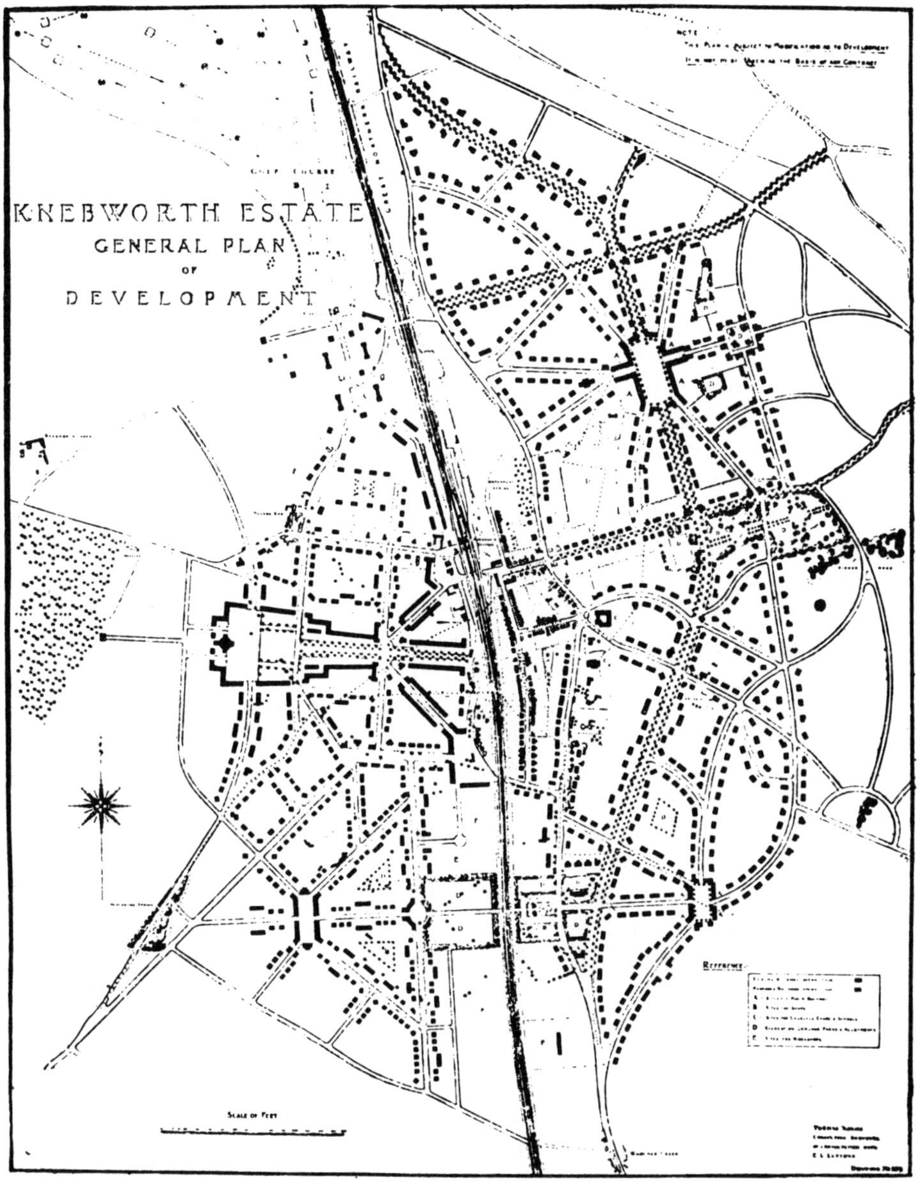

FIGURE 9. Knebworth Garden Suburb, Hertfordshire, 1909.

The distinguished architect Edwin Lutyens was associated with Adams in this design. Artisans' co-partnership housing and factories to the south; villas and golf course to the north; commercial and public buildings largely east of the railway.

segregated rigidly, with villas ranging from £360 to £1000 on the higher ground and co-partnership terraces around greens on the flat, adjacent to a small industrial estate. There were to be eventually 6400 houses and 30,000 people. Launching the venture in September 1909, the Earl suggested a residents' council to assist in managing the enterprise[18].

The bulk of the planning was done by Adams, Lutyens acting as a consultant. The layout was more formal than his other designs, essentially a series of rectangles divided by diagonals with on the west a hundred-foot grand avenue with a tree-lined central reservation leading to a great square set in a bowl in the folds of the chalk ridge. On hilly ground the roads paid court to the contours in gentle curves. The railway, as at Letchworth, was a nuisance but, inexplicably, Adams failed to improve the awkward east–west communications and modern inhabitants must curse him for having left untouched the four narrow, angled lanes which dip under the line. Knebworth, only 38 minutes from London, was marginally more successful than other schemes; by 1914, it had 250 houses and 1250 people[19].

'The way Bristol houses its poor is a scandal', said Henrietta Barnett, the creator of Hampstead Garden Suburb, with characteristic pungency at a public meeting in the city in 1909. Bristol had a high proportion of people of conscience, many of them Quakers, and it had been felt for some time that 'Housing reform is one of the most pressing questions in Bristol'. Proposals for a garden suburb had been made in 1903 and in 1906, Philip Napier Miles, owner of the 3000-acre King's Weston estate, outlined a project for a 'garden city'. Both schemes proved abortive and it was only in 1907 that real progress was made. Elizabeth Sturge, a leading Quaker, organized a public meeting addressed by Alfred Lyttelton, chairman of Hampstead Garden Suburb, and in July 1909 a Bristol Garden Suburb Company was formed at last. It intended to demonstrate that decent housing for the working class was a paying proposition and would strike a blow at major social problems while avoiding the 'ghastly uniformity' of by-law housing. Among the sponsors were members of the Wills and Fry families and Miles offered the site — $26\frac{1}{2}$ acres on a south-facing hillside at Shirehampton, overlooking the River Avon. Frank Bromhead was engaged as architect and Thomas Adams as planner. It was intended to develop $7\frac{1}{2}$ acres immediately though ultimately there were to be 280 houses at fourteen to the acre, with ample gardens, trees and open spaces. A site for non-offensive industries was reserved adjacent to the Avonmouth branch railway and there was easy access to the station. Prospective residents were assured that 'every care will be taken to avoid interference with existing trees and to afford picturesque views'[20].

Adams was faced with a more or less virgin, oval, upland site. He enclosed it by east to west roads to both the north and the south. The heart of the estate was a diamond containing a site for a church and tennis courts. Adams positioned the houses, almost all semi-detached or in short terraces, so as to give each one sunlight in its living room for the greater part of the day.

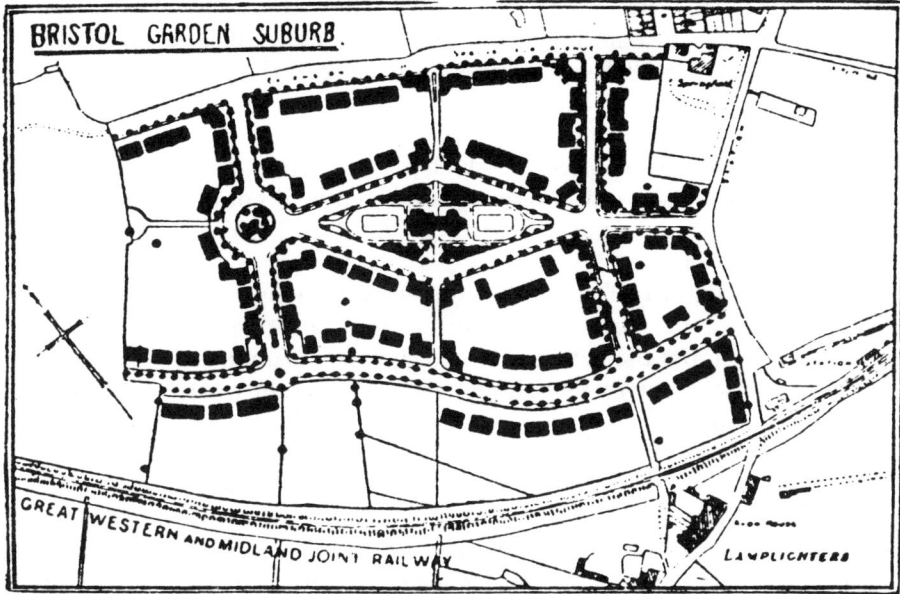

FIGURE 10. Bristol: Shirehampton Garden Suburb, 1909.

An attenuated design, to be extended if demand warranted it, this was a fairly formal layout on a south-facing slope, dominated by a central island featuring a church. (From the promotional booklet, courtesy of Avon County Libraries)

Though simple and compact, the design was but a fragment of the larger projected scheme. In the event, Shirehampton grew no more for the company was unable to raise further funds and only forty-four houses were built[21].

Two of Adams's largest designs never got beyond the drawing board. The great cotton spinning family of Ashtons of Hyde, south-east of Manchester, invited him to lay out a garden suburb on their 200-acre Newton Moor estate, lying just to the north of one of their mills. A bleak plateau, it had been subject to some haphazard building and Adams commented that 'the working in of a garden suburb plan round an "island" of existing houses has afforded an interesting opportunity of blending the new with the old'. His design retained the two east-to-west roads already there and these were intersected by residential streets forming a series of rectangles, with a couple of crescents at the east end. The houses were to be semi-detached pairs and short terraces, some of them set back behind small greens. No start was made, however, and subsequent development has been on very different lines[22].

The other abortive exercise was an ambitious design for Lord Salisbury's Liverpool estates at Childwall and Wavertree, east of the city. The third Marquess was president of the Garden City Association and with his lands, some 1500 acres, about to fall to the march of suburbia, he wished to have them planned properly on garden suburb lines. Little is known about Adams's plan save that it seems to have been a series of hubs and radials. It was superseded in 1909 by the new local project, the Wavertree Garden Suburb, in which Henry Vivian was prominent. The plan for this was the result of a competition promoted by the *Town Planning Review* and judged by Raymond Unwin. Adams's design, which may have been simply a main road and basic land-use plan, was described as 'influential if not binding' upon the competitors. By 1914, of the 185 acres involved, $25\frac{1}{2}$ had been built upon, with a total of 260 houses[23].

Even less is known of Adams's other commissions. In the summer of 1909, he advised the second Viscount Ridley, owner of 10,000 acres in Northumberland, but the nature of the engagement is unknown. At about the same time, he laid out two small co-partnership estates – at Brackenlands, near Wigton, and at Portinscale, near Keswick – for the lawyer J. S. Birkett, a director of Garden Villages, Ltd.[24].

Within three years of deciding to leave Letchworth, seemingly with no future in the infant planning movement, Adams had established himself as one of its leaders, despite sparse experience and a lack of formal qualifications. He had shown a remarkable capacity to learn quickly from other pioneers and to grow with the subject. Even so, his high reputation rested on a slender base for all of his projects had been marred by attenuated growth or had failed to get under way. Moreover, the only sizeable plan for which he was wholly responsible and which was in part realized was Alkrington.

Though the terrain on which he worked varied greatly, his plans display common features. On hillsides, his roads wound about the contours but on anything approaching a level, he favoured either hubs and radials or squares and diagonals. His larger designs feature broad grand avenues leading to the central focal point. Trees and verges universally lined his roads, which varied in width according to function, residential streets being kept to about twenty feet where possible to reduce construction costs, while use was made, somewhat sparingly, of footpaths, culs-de-sac and of set-back greens. A high proportion of ground (often one acre in ten) was reserved for allotments, playgrounds, tennis courts and the like (frequently in the interiors of blocks) while public buildings were placed in formal squares. Housing was normally set back from roads and corners, to break up the vista, and it was generally placed to catch the maximum amount of sunlight throughout the year, in response to the gathering attack on tuberculosis and similar illnesses, which could best be combatted by maximizing domestic light and air. It was a *sine qua non* of the Garden City movement, even before Unwin's famous dictum, that housing densities should be low and that every house must have a garden. Adams and his clients sought to avoid the extreme degree of class segregation characteristic of contemporary suburban growth and catered for most social groups though generally separating villas from co-partnership rows in deference to market forces.

Quite as important to Adams as the physical aspect was the hope that the suburbs would demonstrate a new form of social organization. He advocated turning each one over to its residents, making them responsible for its management. A classless society would be constructed, imbued with the virtues of individual freedom and voluntary co-operation. Social justice and harmony would be achieved without recourse to a collectivist bureaucracy, class warfare or the subsidizing of one class at the expense of others. Adams was convinced, as were many liberals of his ilk, that 'associated individualism' was the trend of the times but none of his projects matured to the point of testing his proposals.

Adams's garden suburbs were derivative, for he was never an innovator in Unwin's class, rather a superb synthesizer. Since Parker and Unwin had made their three great designs before he began, it was difficult for anyone else to be other than imitative. Though lacking the fluency and sheer inventiveness of Unwin at Hampstead, Adams's plans were neat, compact, attractive and made efficient use of their space. Well-serviced, generous in amenity and open space, appropriate to traffic requirements, they were generally fit for their purpose. They displayed, too, one of Adams's principal qualities – that perceptive eye for fine landscape and elemental rapport with nature born of his Edinburgh and farming origins and evidenced by his willingness to bend to the lie of the land and work with the grain of nature.

Adams remained in the mainstream of the planning movement. He was a frequent visitor to Letchworth and served on the executive committee of the Garden City Association until his departure for Canada in 1914. A familiar speaker at planning meetings up and down the country, he contributed to the *Garden City* and other magazines. He was one of the eighty members of the National Housing Reform Council who inspected 'the example of Germany' in 1909. In about 1907, he served as a Smallholdings Commissioner in three southern English counties. By the end of 1909, he had forced himself to the front of a still-limited but burgeoning field. Dynamism, adaptability and shrewdness more than overcame a lack of professional training and experience. His career was now about to take a more professional tack[25].

STATUTORY TOWN PLANNING, 1909–1914

When the Housing, Town Planning, etc., Act became law in December 1909, Thomas Adams was appointed to the new post of Town Planning Assistant at the Local Government Board, taking up his duties in the spring of 1910. His move from the private to the public sector mirrored the shifting emphasis of town planning itself. The act was the result of several years of sustained pressure by the environmentalist lobby. The conjunction, early in the new century, of the Garden City movement, the example of Germany, the revival of the 'condition of the nation' question, the evolution of thought on

environmental issues and the incisive, determined and galvanic leadership
of J. S. Nettlefold brought about a statutory planning structure which has
continued in its essentials down to the present day[26].

The National Housing Reform Council had taken steps to secure legislation enabling local authorities 'to prepare building plans definitely planning
the lines of development of new areas' as early as 1905. However, it was not
until 1907, following further pressure from the N.H.R.C. and the Association
of Municipal Corporations, both advised by Nettlefold, that the President of
the Local Government Board, John Burns, drew up a bill. It proposed to
give to local authorities optional powers to plan new development, control
street patterns, limit building densities, reserve sites for public purposes,
acquire land to enable schemes to be carried out and halt building while a
scheme was in preparation. It provided cautiously for betterment levies, the
apportionment of expenses, compensation and arbitration. It encouraged
co-operation with landowners and adjacent local authorities and permitted the
inclusion in schemes of land in adjoining municipalities. Land already
developed was excluded because of 'the many difficulties' of vested interests,
lengthy negotiations and heavy compensation[27].

Presented to Parliament in April 1908 as an omnibus measure embracing
housing and public health, the bill received a qualified approval from
planning leaders. Adams was lukewarm, doubting whether the bill took 'full
advantage of all the experience that has been gained', probably a reference to
the increasing conviction among planners that towns should be comprehen-
sively planned. He complained that 'there is far too much red tape and
Local Government Board control about the measure' and criticized the bill's
lack of compulsion; backward councils needed a scourge for 'They will go on
neglecting protection until they are compelled to cure'. Characteristically,
however, he accepted pragmatically Burns's half-measure: 'While it is desirable that all of us should make suggestions for its improvement, let us
withhold any criticisms that may imperil the passage of the Bill into law
during the present session of Parliament'. The most urgent need was to secure
the acceptance of the principle of statutory planning; experience in working
it would bring about improvements. Burns took the same view; he 'put just
sufficient into the Bill to allow it to get through Parliament this year'[28].

However, the bill took over eighteen months to become law, despite all-
party support for its principle. It was caught up in the constitutional crisis of
1909 and met Conservative opposition to interference with landowners' rights
and to the growth of administrative law. Described as 'cumbersome' and
'absolutely unintelligible', it was subjected to extensive redrafting and
numerous concessions were made; that it survived at all was due to the skill of
Burns's Parliamentary Secretary, Charles Masterman. Parliament lengthened
still more the already tedious procedure. Sponsors of planning schemes had to
notify all interested parties; the Local Government Board then held an
enquiry to determine whether there was a *prima facie* case for planning. If

approval was given for the preparation of a plan, a second round of notification and a further enquiry were necessary before the Board granted final approval to a scheme. In an untried line of public policy, it was not unreasonable to hasten slowly and most planning leaders endorsed Burns's caution. Nevertheless, the procedure had a deterrent effect and the act was obsolete for by 1909 many supporters of planning were calling for compulsory powers, central area redevelopment and comprehensive metropolitan regional planning[29].

In setting up machinery to work the act, Burns took good care to keep firm control of the new powers. A Housing and Town Planning Department was formed under the Comptrollership of J. A. E. Dickenson, a long-serving official, who was given three housing inspectors and a town planning assistant. Adams's appointment to the latter post earned wide approval, Adams himself attributing it to lack of competition. Though Burns assured the Tory spokesman Alfred Lyttelton that he would do his 'best to secure the services of the most highly qualified man or men for this particular work', he pointed out that experienced planners could be numbered 'on the fingers of one hand'. Adams had as much experience as anyone, he was well-known and highly respected and had influential friends on both sides of Parliament, for whom he had provided briefs on the bill. He had been acquainted with Burns since 1906 and his Liberal background may have been significant. His personal qualities of patience, good humour, energy, commitment to environmental reform and capacity for seizing up situations shrewdly and swiftly fitted him well for the task. He may have taken the post simply for security but it is more likely that he saw it as an opportunity to preach the cause to a wider audience, to establish planning as an accepted, everyday function of government and to set high professional standards[30].

The Board's *Procedure Regulations*, issued in 1910, maintained a grudging attitude to local authority powers and displayed a continuing tenderness for private property. Adams himself explained the Board's thinking:

> In drafting his Bill, the astute President of the Local Government Board, aware that the resulting Act would invest all local authorities with novel and drastic powers over property, realized that some effective restraint was required to prevent the abuse of these powers. So he wrote *festina lente* over the fourth and fifth schedules and took care that the regulations observed the precept[31].

The official emphasis was on co-operation between public and private interests for 'if town planning were to make headway commensurate with its merits, the goodwill of owners was imperative'. Adams regarded the new legislation less as a vehicle for rapid action than as a learning instrument by which 'the pioneering local authorities must educate the public and owners in the general benefits of town planning'. However, the Board was far from rigid or negative in its interpretation of the act and the regulations. 'It is our desire', said Dickenson, 'to take as broad a view as possible in regard to land which may be included in a scheme'. The Board was ready to advise municipalities and landowners and sought 'to impress upon local authorities the importance of making their schemes as simple as possible'. In the main, this cautious but flexible approach was endorsed by local authority organizations and by prominent planners[32].

Adams was also sent abroad to study planning in Europe and the United States. In June 1910, he attended an international planning conference in Berlin and then travelled through Germany, Denmark and Sweden. He returned to Berlin in 1912, this time giving a paper on British planning. He gained little from Continental practice, being more impressed with its shortcomings than its achievements. He remarked unfavourably upon the squalid, sordid, sardine-packed tenements that lurked behind the elegant Beaux Arts frontages and wide boulevards of European cities. Civic pomp and circumstance should follow the satisfaction of basic human needs for decent and healthful accommodation and he entertained a lifelong dislike for the 'City Beautiful' school, whether European or American. He was one of five Board representatives at the Royal Institute of British Architects' great international conference in London in 1910 and in 1911 he made his first visit to the United States, 'bent on making a study of housing and city planning conditions and ideas in that country'[33].

The American scene exercised over him an immediate and lasting influence and the visit set in train the events and connections that were to lead to his most mature achievements. The main purpose of the journey was to attend, with Unwin and Mawson, the Philadelphia meeting of the National Conference on City Planning and he later visited other major cities, notably New York. He made several long-lasting friendships, based on a common outlook in which practicality, efficiency and utility were the guiding principles. Among them were Nelson P. Lewis, chief engineer of the City of New York, the landscape architect John Nolen and the architect George B. Ford. The high technical proficiency of the Americans, their willingness to take a comprehensive view of city planning in scope and scale and their businesslike methods had an immediate impact on Adams and, while he felt they had much to learn about housing the poor, he attempted to apply their approach in Britain. He thus became a vehicle for the transatlantic traffic in ideas then approaching its peak[34].

Adams's principal function at the Local Government Board, however, was to conduct public inquiries at both stages of the planning process. The Board endeavoured to hold them within two months of receipt of applications and Adams's report on the initial inquiry was normally circulated to officials at the Board within two weeks of the hearing. Adams's procedure was invariable. Prior to an inquiry, he went over the ground with local officials and others interested. At the inquiry, he outlined the procedure, heard the council's submission, studied maps, sought clarifications, heard supporting statements and objections and made copious notes (his reports ran to 250 pages of foolscap on occasion). Scrupulously fair, he injected humour into the proceedings and dealt tactfully with pompous aldermen, loquacious town clerks and indignant opponents[35]. That he gave statutory planning as good a start in life as was possible was acknowledged by Patrick Abercrombie:

> How many inquiries can one call to mind at which the influence of Mr. Adams, exercised during the lunch hour, has led to the removal of opposition or bickering between rival local authorities? The spirit of co-operation, the first essential of town planning in its initial stages, could not have had a better encourager than Mr. Adams[36].

Town planning schemes worked infinite sets of variations upon the basic theme of development control but though there were bold and interesting projects, most plans were unexciting. A typical early statutory plan covered an average area of over 2000 acres and called for the widening, straightening and linking of existing roads; short stretches of new road to improve exits from towns or cross-town communications; the limitation of housing densities to 20 per acre or less; the setting back of building lines; the restrictive zoning of factories and noxious industries; and the reservation in advance of need of sites for public purposes. These plans, generally the work of municipal engineers or surveyors, represented in many cases incremental extensions of their normal work[37].

There was remarkable accord between councils and landowners on the uses to which suburban land should be put but only in two cases – at Alkrington, where Middleton Council wished to adopt Adams's plan, and at Ruislip-Northwood, where joint plans were submitted by the council, the principal landowner and the main developer – did the initiative for a scheme arise from private interests. There were rare objections to the expense of schemes, the iniquity of compensation and betterment conditions (condemned as 'a flagrant denial of democratic and legal rights') and the limitation of housing densities (attacked as 'impracticable and will prevent the erection of weekly houses at rents which the working man can afford to pay'). More frequently, local Liberals, trades councils, churches, co-operative societies, amenity and reform groups supported planning with enthusiasm and occasionally galvanized councils into action[38].

Some authorities used planning powers to achieve ends other than those intended and some waved the bogey of the act at landlords to obtain their agreement to a policy without going to the trouble of a scheme. Other councils used the density limitation powers to maintain their exclusive suburban status, as Adams and working-class spokesmen were well aware[39]. Two of the most comprehensive schemes were put forward by rural district councils – the Wirral and Wrexham – which, anticipating early development, were anxious to plan their whole areas. Two of the boldest and most extensive schemes were by smaller authorities. At Sutton Coldfield, an exclusive suburb of Birmingham, the Clerk to the Council was R. W. Reay-Nadin, later President of the Town Planning Institute (1921–22). Sutton Coldfield's scheme froze its character into an upper middle-class mould but it was notable for its emphasis on the preservation of natural amenities and historic sites. Luton, developing as an automotive and light engineering centre, was experiencing rapid growth and the threat of extensive redevelopment of its built-up area. This central area and much of the rural surroundings were allowed to be included in the scheme to prevent speculators nullifying the plan by jerry-building over the boundary and to allow an integrated radial and circumferential road network, which would relieve central business district congestion. The borough wished to limit housing densities, secure open spaces and control the location of factories. In most respects, Luton's plan was ahead of its time[40].

In general, the most comprehensive proposals arose from the great cities, used already to working on the grand scale. Birmingham, Leeds, Liverpool, Manchester and Sheffield all proposed to control the development of their entire suburban areas and induced neighbouring authorities to prepare compatible schemes; none of these metropolitan ambitions seem to have been realized. They intended to restrict factory location, reserve land for highways, parks and public services, promote low-density housing, create new radial and ring roads, control the redevelopment of country house estates, preserve picturesque and historic sites and segregate social classes[41].

Adams recommended the granting of permission to prepare schemes in all the cases he examined. Most authorities had little difficulty in demonstrating the imminence of development and their plans, if unexciting, were sensible and well within the act's scope. Such reservations as Adams made were minor ones – the addition or subtraction of small pieces of land, the realignment of roads, co-operation with neighbouring councils or suggestions to adjoining municipalities that they should prepare complementary schemes. In all cases, too, his recommendations were endorsed by the Board[42].

Local authority response to the act was disappointing. Of some 1500 local authorities in England and Wales, only about one-tenth had shown an interest by the outbreak of war in 1914; very few Scottish councils had responded. Some thirty authorities had sought advice, twenty had applied for permission to prepare plans, and seventy-four had been granted authority to prepare schemes. Four schemes had received final approval and three were awaiting it. Three of these seven schemes were Birmingham's – hardly surprising in view of the city's tradition of bold corporate action and dynamic leadership. The poor response was due to indifference to environmental conditions, ignorance of planning as an instrument of improvement, the absence of local reformist pressure, the fear of heavy expense and the lack of sufficient or of competent staff. Few councils had councillors or officials committed to planning. The architect and councillor Frank Elgood and the town clerk Edmund Abbott at Ruislip, Reay-Nadin at Sutton Coldfield, the engineers John Brodie of Liverpool and J. W. Cockrill of Great Yarmouth and the politicians J. S. Nettlefold and Neville Chamberlain in Birmingham were exceptions to the rule. Some authorities, anxious to stimulate development, feared rightly than planning would retard it and others were prisoners of vested property interests[43].

What prevented most councils from taking up planning was their dislike of the Local Government Board, the complexities of the act and the obstacle race imposed by the tedious regulations. The act was described by Alderman William Thompson as 'a clumsy measure', its clauses 'by no means clear in their wording' and it was alleged that 'it hardly provides enough machinery for rectifying existing wrongs'. German observers were amazed at the discussion of whether town planning was necessary in a given place. More sustained criticism was directed at the procedure regulations which 'do not encourage local bodies to do town planning; their effect is rather deterrent'. The procedure was attacked for unnecessary mapping and notification, for its length (which discriminated against builders by halting their operations), its cost and the failure to require a preliminary survey. One of the most acute yet balanced critics of the statutory planning process, Stanley Adshead, warned that 'handled entirely by a powerful bureaucracy, town planning cannot help but be subject to the dangers of petrification'[44].

The critics were met by a defence as resolute as it was justified. The faults of the act, said Abercrombie, arose from having to create a planning tradition out of nothing but at least it was elastic and the Board had wide discretionary powers. Culpin, though agreeing that 'one could have welcomed less ambiguity and simpler procedure in several directions', argued that a lengthy process was a safeguard against 'hastily and ill-conceived planning'[45]. Adams was also a staunch upholder of the act and its procedure. It gave 'an opportunity to proceed, with caution and comparative rapidity, along lines of real progress in social reconstruction'. He argued pragmatically that 'It is better to begin with a sound basis, and proceed step by step, assimilating experience as you go along, changing with the altered habits and tendencies of the time than to attempt to include in one Act a counsel of perfection'[46]. He was less concerned to cover the country overnight with a patchwork quilt of plans than to stimulate a greater general awareness of environmental problems:

I look to town planning and the co-operation which it sets in motion to widen the outlook of members of the local authorities, and to increase their interest in the future of their districts. I look to it to improve public taste and awaken the public spirit. I look to it to bring many hitherto conflicting elements into co-operation in connection with land development and local government. It will awaken a consciousness of social responsibility and a desire for social improvement . . .[47].

Acknowledging that the present procedure was irksome and sometimes superfluous and that an amending act and simplified regulations were necessary, he counselled patience, arguing that 'Once town planning has firmly established itself on its merits, it will be stripped of its swaddling clothes of notices and formalities by an amendment of the present laborious procedure regulations. In the meantime it may well pray to be saved from some of its friends'[48].

Like Adams, Burns was as content to watch the gospel spread and hear the public discussion as to encourage schemes. He claimed that the act had inspired 'good results in securing a better development of land by owners' even where schemes were not proposed and he asked that it should be judged not on completed schemes but on its success in building up a sound planning tradition based on co-operation. Moreover, the Board operated the act and the regulations with more flexibility and a greater sense of initiative than has been generally supposed. Adams and Dickenson were always ready to advise and were willing to listen to suggestions for improving and simplifying the regulations. They waived notification requirements in many cases. The Board goaded authorities to process schemes without undue delay and reprimanded them sharply if they were dilatory following authorization. It discouraged schemes launched for purposes other than planning and proposals for very small areas, favouring large-scale schemes which formed part of an over-all strategy for the whole of a town's fringe. Aware that completed and successful plans were the best exemplars, it encouraged the early realization of the first two schemes at Ruislip and Birmingham (Quinton-Harborne). Nevertheless, the Board doubted 'whether public opinion on the subject of town planning is ripe for any material lessening of the safeguards to the parties interested'[49].

However, following a deputation to Burns led by Neville Chamberlain, who had succeeded Nettlefold as chairman of Birmingham's town planning committee, revised regulations were announced in February 1914, reducing notification and mapping requirements. At the same time, Burns was succeeded by Herbert Samuel, a far abler and more progressive figure who proposed to amend the act and introduce compulsory planning. The pace of statutory planning was accelerating by 1914, necessitating the appointment of a second inspector, George Pepler. The very real improvement in procedure and leadership and increased municipal interest suggest that statutory planning might have been at take-off point when the First World War broke out and terminated progress[50].

One area in which the Board's thought matured and led to an initiative from the centre was regional planning. In the Doncaster area, it responded to news of a new coalfield by recommending to local authorities in the district a combined plan. Adams attended several conferences in the locality between 1912 and 1914 and urged regional representatives to take prompt action ahead of mining development. Unfortunately the response was sluggish and the

Board was disappointed. More was achieved in London, despite the indifference of the L.C.C. Here, Adams was in his element and his metropolitan inquiry reports were more lively and more suggestive than others. It is clear from his first report on Ruislip that he had a firm grasp of Greater London's problems and possibilities[51].

London's difficulties were well-known by 1900. It suffered from acute traffic congestion, overcrowding at the centre and haphazard sprawl on the margins. Environmental responsibility was divided between the L.C.C. (the planning authority), the metropolitan boroughs and a host of small councils on the fringes and the confusion was added to in 1907 when a London Traffic Branch was set up at the Board of Trade following the *Report of the Royal Commission on London Traffic* (1905) and again in 1909 when a Road Board was established to provide the nation with a network of trunk roads for the motor age[52].

Adams's reports on planning inquiries in Greater London reveal three major concerns. He refused to treat individual authorities and their plans in isolation and urged co-operation with their neighbours. Secondly, he evinced a strong interest in the preservation of the amenity of the lower Thames valley in the vicinity of Richmond. Finally, his principal anxiety was to integrate major road projects into a definite system of arterial and ring roads.

The need to co-ordinate the development of a suburb with that of those adjoining it was obvious, though many of the little outer zone councils remained deaf to Adams's pleas. The preservation on a regional scale of the great amenity of the Thames above Kew Bridge was necessary because of its scenic qualities, historic associations and recreational possibilities. The river was fringed by trees and meadows, by great houses and their parks, and the whole was rounded off by the justly celebrated view from Richmond Hill. By 1910, this fine regional asset was threatened by headlong speculative development, including the demolition of large houses and the intensive use of their grounds. Adams advocated the co-operation of authorities on both sides of the river for 'whatever is done on one bank will have as direct an effect on the other as if the two banks formed two frontages of one street'. Recommending a long-term view (twenty-five to fifty years), he advised that 'The Board should stretch its powers to the utmost to allow the inclusion of all the land' necessary in Richmond, Ham, Twickenham and Teddington[53].

Though Adams attempted to steer small districts in the direction of constructing their sections of an outer circular road, he recognized that this was a stop-gap measure and that it was unfair to expect those councils to shoulder the responsibility for a task that should be the joint concern of the Local Government Board, the Treasury's Road Board, the London Traffic Branch and the L.C.C. The normal difficulty of obtaining the concerted action of several bodies was rendered much worse by the L.C.C.'s unco-operative attitude to planning. The replacement of Liberal–Labour control of the L.C.C. by the Tories in 1907 resulted in a totally negative response to planning, made more irritating by the L.C.C.'s refusal to permit the metropolitan boroughs to use the act. As Culpin commented, 'It is tragic that while outside the Council area local authorities are progressing in one stage or another, London County is still without a policy'[54].

The L.C.C.'s obduracy delayed proper planning for London before the war but, with Adams's encouragement, the outer authorities sent a deputation to the Prime Minister in July 1913, calling for a major road plan for Greater London. Burns thereupon summoned 115 councils, twelve voluntary bodies, the Road Board and the London Traffic Branch to a conference in November and this was followed by six sectional conferences, which continued to meet after the war began. The agenda was chiefly the discussion of new arterial and ring roads but open space planning was also considered. In part, this latter topic arose from Lord Meath's proposal for a 'green girdle round London' made in 1901. Meath, who had chaired the L.C.C.'s parks committee, had visited Chicago and had been impressed with Olmsted's park system. He suggested a string of outer London parks linked by parkways, 35 miles in length and up to one mile wide. Not only would this ring reserve essential open space for the metropolitan millions, it would act also as a great green wall halting the wen's outward sprawl at a point five to nine miles from the centre. Though making little impression at the time, Meath's idea was revived by the *Garden City* in the wake of the report on London traffic and elaborated later by Abercrombie, Pepler, the surveyor W. R. Davidge and others. By 1913, professional planners were agreed that there should be a Greater London planning authority, a communications and development plan for the metropolis, the acquisition of land for roads and open spaces while it was still cheap and available, the integration of the various forms of transport, better inter-suburban connections, the relief of central area traffic and population congestion and the co-ordination of public services[55].

Even with the restricted remit of the Arterial Roads Conferences, 'very substantial progress' had been made by the outbreak of war with the collection of information and the exchange of views on roads and planning schemes. Adams, who was responsible for organizing the conferences, spent the greater part of his time on them from the beginning of 1914, a congenial task. Given his intimate association with the conferences and his hope that they would be the precursors of a true metropolitan regional plan, it was not surprising that his valedictory speech in Britain before leaving for Canada should be on 'Town Planning in Greater London', the most refined and comprehensive treatment of the case thus far. Arguing for a skeleton communications and land-use plan, he intended that all land should be included. He called for the identification of suitable secondary centres, for use zoning, the control of building heights, character and elevation, the integration of transportation, the acquisition ahead of need of land for public purposes, power to regulate frontages, preserve gardens and widen roads, a hierarchy of highways related systematically and a central planning authority. As usual, he urged the co-operation of public and private interests and detailed local plans compatible with the regional strategy. On his departure, he handed the conferences over to George Pepler but the capital's problems continued to intrigue him and he must have envied Raymond Unwin his opportunity to devise an outline plan for the metropolitan area in 1929[56].

In assessing Adams's impact on the Local Government Board and on statutory planning and the influence of his four-and-a-half years in the civil service upon himself, it must be remembered that he, too, was a Liberal of a stamp not dissimilar from Asquith, Burns and the bulk of the party and that he was a junior appointee and not a career civil servant. He had the capacity only to advise his seniors on their decisions and his powers over local authorities were only such as his personality, tact and diplomacy could command. Though he gave advice before plans were made and suggested amendments in the course of his examinations, he had but minor influence over most of the plans made. Most were fairly and squarely within the terms of reference and in most cases as much as could have been expected from the municipal engineers and surveyors of the day. His scope for taking bold initiatives was severely circumscribed and is seen at its greatest extent in the London context. However, the planning world felt happy with him in Whitehall; he was one of them, and a trusted one at that. His position gave him prestige, authority, a vantage point from which he could comprehend the drift of planning thought and practice at home and abroad and an opportunity to assess what was needed next in terms both of legislation and of professionalization.

Adams conceded readily that his term of office had considerable effect on his own thought and practice. Always conciliatory, the job made him 'more balanced and impartial towards opposite points of view'. He came to believe that planning should be made compulsory and comprehensive and felt by 1914 that 'the time had arrived when it would have been reasonable and desirable for the Board to insist on completed schemes being submitted by many more authorities'. The Board, however, had no sanctions it could impose upon recalcitrant authorities and even when ministers had compulsory powers from 1919, they made no use of them. One major influence his inspectoral experience had on him 'was to prove the need of regional planning'. Perhaps the greatest effect of his appointment was to convince him of the necessity for trained town planners bound together in a professional institute and capable of tackling bolder and more comprehensive planning projects[57].

THE FOUNDATION OF THE TOWN PLANNING INSTITUTE, 1909–1914

During the passage of the act, Adams foresaw that its operation would fall largely to existing municipal technical and legal staffs, few of whom had any experience in or indentification with planning. Cautious men in general, they were unlikely to make grave errors but equally unlikely to handle schemes with imagination or comprehensiveness. He began to conceive a professional body to train those who would work the new machinery, to act as a forum for all of the environmental professions and as a sponsor of research into planning problems. He came early to the firm conclusion that each profession had something to contribute to planning and that the new field was beyond the capacity of any one of them totally to subsume. For a decade, he had worked with lawyers, engineers, surveyors and architects and now, without a professional home of his own (and therefore unprejudiced), he recognized the strengths and weaknesses of each profession. Initially, he did not articulate the case for a new independent profession or discipline; he saw town planning as a complex amalgam of individual professional techniques and believed always that planners must come to it from a basic training in one of the participating professions; thus a course in planning should form a kind of postgraduate education. Nor did Adams consider planning a mere technical exercise; he had come to it as a social reformer and wished to infuse into statutory planning a commitment to 'social reconstruction' lest it became merely a bureaucratic routine[58].

Aware that the nature and parameters of British planning had been framed by amateurs – Cadbury, Lever, Rowntree, Howard, Henrietta Barnett, Geddes, Horsfall and Nettlefold – he determined to find a place for them in his proposed 'central Consultative Body' along with medical officers, lawyers, economists and sociologists. Thus, though an institute would re-integrate the sharply-divided environmental professions, and oversee technical training, Adams saw no fundamental distinction between professionals and amateurs and believed both needed education in the appreciation of environmental problems and possibilities[59].

Adams was not unique in his thinking and it is likely that a professional body would have been organized by leaders of the movement soon after planning had attained the respectability of becoming a public function. Stanley Adshead remarked in 1910 that 'It would seem to be an opportune moment for the formation of a Society of Town Planners' and shared Adams's view that planning co-ordinated other specialisms. Abercrombie expressed similar sentiments and put down gently Thomas Mawson's plea for an English Association of Landscape Architects. Mawson, the sole British representative of the genre, lamented the low status of the art in Britain compared with America, where it was a recognized profession and academic subject. The boldest declaration of independence was made by C. H. Reilly, Professor of Architecture at Liverpool University and the instigator of the School of Civic Design there: 'Town Planning, although intimately connected with Architecture and Engineering, is a distinct and separate study in itself and the primary object of the school is to equip Architects, Engineers and others with a knowledge of the supplementary subjects that Town Planning connotes'. The leaders of the planning movement were thus developing an increasing self-confidence, independence and a sense of unity. However, it was Adams who took the initiative and he was admirably fitted by position, experience, temperament and personal qualities to do so[60].

On the return leg of an N.H.R.C. visit to Germany at Easter 1909, he expounded his ideas to several companions. A year later informal discussions began between Adams, Unwin, Adshead, Pepler, J. S. Birkett and the architect H. V. Lanchester. In attaining their object of welding together professions engaged in planning, they faced a difficult task because each profession claimed primacy in the planning process and there was already much rivalry, not to say hostility, between them[61].

Most plans in the private sector had been made by architects and by virtue of this, their assured social position, cultivation, idealism, long-standing professional organization and their general articulateness they had reason to regard themselves as leaders of the new field. Raymond Unwin exemplified their attitude:

> Town planning is finally an architectural problem. In some respects the work of others is of more importance. . . But when we come to the final stage of putting something down on paper in the way of a definite plan, that is an architectural problem . . . if there are to spring up in our cities . . . dwelling places of a degree of beauty such as I think we have a right to expect[62].

Adams, who did not wish any one profession to be pre-eminent and was more inclined to stress utility than art, was concerned to put the architects in their place. 'It is not the architect *qua* architect who is best fitted to become a town planner', he declared, 'but architectural training and insight are necessary qualifications of anyone who presumes to advise in any department of civic design'[63].

The Royal Institute of British Architects was quick to appreciate that Burns's bill might well divert the control of planning to engineers and surveyors and therefore set up a Development of Towns and Suburbs Committee in 1907. It was active in lobbying and in 1910 sponsored a huge international congress to celebrate the act's passage. Adams was well aware that this was a display of enlightened self-interest and criticized it as a 'town planning conference promoted by Architects for Architects'. The R.I.B.A. had made 'little or no attempt to give guidance' to municipal councillors and officials 'on how to use the powers conferred upon them by the Town Planning Act'. Moreover, a conference dedicated largely to civic splendour represented unwise publicity for it implied that planning was a necessarily costly exercise. While affirming that 'town planning schemes will only be truly successful if the architect is allowed to take his proper place in their preparation', he warned that 'under the new Act the scope for architects is limited' and acknowledged that 'the work to be performed will fall for the most part into the hands of local engineers or surveyors'[64].

The Surveyors' Institution, a body of far less prestige than the R.I.B.A., showed little concern for planning until Burns introduced his bill, most members being engaged in private practice. Sir Alexander Stenning, President of the Institution in 1909, supported by Pepler and Adams, persuaded it to set up a Town Planning Committee, though it was less active than that of the architects[65].

Engineers tended to be self-effacing and lacking in propaganda skills. Most of those who had to do with planning were members of the relatively humble Institution of Municipal and County Engineers, which moved towards planning in fits and starts. Horsfall addressed its conference in 1906 and it formed a joint committee with the N.H.R.C., though this was largely a paper exercise. The President in 1907 was the great City Engineer of Liverpool, J. A. Brodie, who preached the gospel with little effect until the passage of the act brought home to his colleagues the fact that they would have to do the bulk of the work. A Town Planning Committee was established in 1909 and thereafter the I.M.C.E. took planning seriously at its conferences and instituted an examination in it in 1914[66].

Adams's small group, joined occasionally by others, continued to meet informally for three years, constituting itself a Provisional Committee in the summer of 1913, with Pepler as Secretary-Treasurer. It drew up a list of people to be invited into membership of a Town Planning Institute, its objects being 'to advance the study of Town Planning and Civic Design, to promote the artistic and scientific development of Towns and Cities, and to secure the association of those engaged or interested in the practice of Town Planning'. Full Membership was to be confined to 'members of the professions who have attained to a special degree of eminence in connection with the planning of cities and towns'. Associates were to be qualified members of the R.I.B.A., I.M.C.E. or Surveyors' Institution or lawyers 'who have acquired an approved standard of efficiency in town planning'. The Associate Member category was for those 'who have taken an interest in one or more of the many aspects of Town Planning'. Honorary Membership would be conferred on 'Distinguished persons who have taken a special interest in Town Planning'. A Council representative of all classes of membership was to be formed and on 21 November 1913 the proposed constitution was to be discussed at an invitation dinner. This meeting agreed to establish a Town Planning Institute and approved the draft constitution and the list of those invited to become members. A month later, the Council unanimously elected Adams to the Presidency, with Unwin and Cockrill as Vice-Presidents, Patrick Geddes as Honorary Librarian and Pepler as Honorary Secretary-Treasurer[67].

By February 1914, the Institute was functioning vigorously, negotiating for the acquisition of Geddes's Cities and Town Planning Exhibition, lobbying Parliament against a railway bill threatening Hampstead Garden Suburb and pressing the Local Government Board and the Board of Agriculture for public money for housing. Amendments were made to the membership requirements and it was resolved that after 1916 admission should be by examination, which implied a drift towards professional exclusivity and away from catholicity. On Adams's nomination, three of his American friends – George B. Ford, John Nolen and Frederick Law Olmsted, Jr. – were admitted to membership. One of the Institute's first functions was a dinner in honour of John Burns on the occasion of his retirement from the Local Government Board in January 1914[68].

Adams departed for Canada in the autumn of 1914 and at an informal farewell dinner in September, Raymond Unwin paid tribute to his wisdom, level-headedness, impartiality, wide outlook on the planning movement, all-round knowledge and experience and sound judgment – a verdict readily seconded. Adams, who was persuaded to remain as President despite his emigration, deserved the encomium. The basic conception of the Town Planning Institute was his and he was responsible for its constitution. His well-known diplomatic skills had subjugated the incipient rivalries of the constituent professions and knitted them together in a body which did not challenge the existing institutions but rather acted as a complement to them. That the Town Planning Institute came about was due principally to his wise statesmanship and, as Abercrombie said, 'It was a foregone conclusion when the Town Planning Institute was founded that Mr. Adams should be its first President'[69]. Adams was aware that it had far to go before it obtained recognition on a par with the older bodies and before it redeemed its promise as an instrument of scientific research, systematic training and professional discussion. He was too shrewd to challenge the older professions with a declaration of total independence before planning had matured as a normal public function with a legislative framework which enjoyed public confidence as a desirable social exercise and before it crystallized as a recognizable subject in its own right with an established body of doctrine. Nevertheless, under his auspices it got off to a very busy and productive beginning and, summing up his stewardship, he commented that:

> The meetings held by the Institute during the year have given a striking justi-
> fication both for its existence and for the varied professional character of its mem-
> bership. They have also helped to show the complex character of Town Planning,
> and therefore of the need for an educational body to study and investigate the
> numerous problems to which town planning gives rise[70].

Adams was almost in the position of being unable to join his own foundation for he qualified as a surveyor only in 1913. He may have taken up pro-
fessional studies simply to meet the T.P.I.'s membership requirements or to reinforce his authority as the Local Government Board's Town Planning Advisor. It is more likely, however, that he resolved to acquire a professional diploma on entering private practice, both to provide him with a 'fall-back' career if planning failed to develop and to give him recognized credentials to

help his quest for commissions. The choice of surveying was a congenial and logical one, given his background and experience. He studied part-time, often on the bus from his home at Dulwich to his London offices[71].

ADAMS AND BRITISH PLANNING, 1900–1914

The state of British planning on the outbreak of war in 1914 was an odd mixture of frustration and hope. Government remained largely indifferent to planning and in respect of comprehensive and monumental planning it was acknowledged that Britain was behind Germany and the United States. The great British contribution to modern planning, the garden city, no longer represented the mainstream of British thought and practice. It had been debased and replaced as the characteristic form of British planning by the ubiquitous garden suburb, attacked by the architect A. Trystan Edwards as elitest, essentially anti-urban, unrealistically romantic and devoid of the culture and amenity associated with the true city. In place of this 'fiction of rusticity', he wanted 'a compact town'. However, Letchworth itself was both successful and profitable by 1914, public environmental standards were rising, Britain was exporting her approach to planning on a large scale and the country had well-established voluntary bodies and the first professional institute, university courses and journals in the field[72].

Thomas Adams had grown up with British planning and in 1914 stood abreast of the latest thought. His was a more utilitarian, pragmatic and scientific planning philosophy than that of most of his fellows and it is possible that already he felt more in tune with his American friends than with his compatriots. He had limited experience as a designer and in this sphere, while highly competent, he lacked Unwin's originality and artistry, though he was the finest landscapist of his generation. His principal contribution to early British planning, however, was a managerial, administrative, educational and institutional one. He was crucial to the early realization of the Garden City idea and was vital to its survival in infancy. One of the most active and respected spokesmen for planning, he gave statutory planning as sound a start as it could have hoped for in the circumstances. Since his own fortunes were bound up with the future of planning, he took a more advanced view of the functions and identity of the planner than did most of his colleagues. Though much of his success was attributable to his exceptional organizational and elucidatory talents, much was due also to his genial and universally popular personality.

By the summer of 1914, though sharing the general hopes for a more productive future for planning, he experienced also some of the frustrations. He was becoming bored with 'the routine of planning control' and chafed at 'the lack of opportunity to do constructive work in planning'. Most of all, he was unhappy with the straitjacket of Local Government Board bureaucracy. It made him

> ... resentful of the subordination of the technical branch to the super-educated administrative branch of the English civil service. The latter is an outcome of the 'sense of leadership' which is supposed to be a privileged creation of Oxford and Cambridge. I came to realize that 'sense' was not always 'actual' in capacity for leadership; and that the subordination of the technical men in the service is mistaken in the public interest[73].

It is possible that Adams was prevented by his superiors from making his office a more dynamic and constructive one, though in the everyday routine of planning inquiries and reports they deferred to his recommendations and suggestions despite occasional reservations. His characteristic impatience with the slow progress of statutory planning and his immediate rapport with the North American milieu combined to leave him open to a lucrative offer from Canada in July 1914 and he resigned with effect from 30 September, leaving almost immediately for Ottawa.

Between 1901 and 1914, Adams had been one of the half-dozen critical influences on the shape, pace and substance of British planning. The Carnot of the Edwardian transformation in environmental attitudes and policies, he was described aptly by Abercrombie as 'justly looked up to as the head of the profession in this country'[74].

Chapter Four

Canada: the Years of Hope, 1914 – 1919

Before the accession of the Laurier administration in 1896, Canada had struggled to fulfil its apparently boundless promise, but from 1898 the Dominion enjoyed a fifteen year boom during which 'Optimism was Canada's most striking characteristic'. The Prime Minister himself termed the new century 'Canada's century'. The great economic bonanza led to the settlement of the vast virgin Prairies and to the explosive expansion of the cities[1].

The presiding genius of the Prairie land rush was the able but enigmatic Minister of the Interior, Clifford Sifton, 'a no-nonsense Manitoba business-man'. The Prairie population rose by over a million in the first decade of the new century, most of them immigrants; in the peak year of 1913, over 400,000 people entered Canada. The West that the boom and Sifton built was free-booting, individualistic, extravagant, opportunistic and optimistic[2].

Remarkable as was the settlement of the Prairies, Canada's rural population rose by only 17 per cent between 1901 and 1911, whereas the urban figure climbed by 62 per cent, resulting in the near-balance of the city and country populations by 1914. Apart from the Maritimes, scarcely warmed by the boom, most towns recorded steep rates of growth. Vancouver, 14,000 in 1891, reached 115,000 in 1914; Winnipeg, 25,000 in 1891, stood at 136,000 in 1911. In the new Western townships, planted annually by the hundred, the ubiqui-tous grid, heedless of topography, was the norm and the countryside was quartered also in the standard North American fashion. Market forces largely determined land use and single-family housing encouraged speculative sub-division and municipal annexation on the grand scale, for 'Western cities felt they had all God's room to grow in'. Local elites were universally boosterish and in their cities, Adams noted, 'the wildest ideas prevailed as to their future progress'[3].

Environmental Problems

Private aggrandisement, however, begat public misery and the unacceptable face of unbridled capitalism was portrayed by W. F. Burditt of Saint John, New Brunswick, a businessman with a social conscience:

> For a quarter of a century or so preceding the outbreak of war, so rapid was the development of Canada, so great were the opportunities for gain, that as individuals we became almost wholly absorbed in the acquisition of wealth, and, as communities, in the increase of population and the expansion of our commerce and industry, while the amenities of life, health and happiness of the masses received scant consideration[4].

Reformers linked social evils with land speculation which had 'spread like measles in a country school until west and east were down with it'. Speculators bought up and subdivided farm land round each city; by 1913 Calgary and Edmonton were both sub-divided for populations of over a million before they had 50,000 people. The boom's collapse in 1913 stung many a family, municipality and speculator[5].

Adams later identified two disastrous consequences of this speculative orgy. Municipalities 'seeing enormous prices paid for land adjacent to their limits, and being little lacking in optimism themselves . . . desired to see this territory within the limits . . . the result was that large areas of land were taken into cities', much of which had no prospect of being developed and thus became sterile. Secondly, 'the assessment of all this land . . . was based upon the fictitious values then prevailing'. This led to 'an accumulation of taxes which . . . now exceeds or approximates the present value of the land . . . Taxation has reached a stage that approaches confiscation'. Towns also serviced new lots at their own expense, an uneconomic undertaking since subdivisions were laid out at unrealistically low densities. Private and municipal extravagance set in motion a spiral of tax delinquency, abandoned lots, sequestration and ultimately the threat of municipal bankruptcy[6].

Suburban residents faced high land and transport costs and many homes were slums. 'The person who has paid heavily for his site and has little capital', it was stated, 'contents himself with the erection of a "shack" and does without local improvements'. Reformers argued that 'shack life is so bad for family life that it ought to be prohibited'. Slumdom was even more pervasive in the inner city, where high costs led to overbuilding on lots and to poor standards. Congestion of population approached London and New York levels. Slums, it was alleged, were sources of vice, crime, disease, pollution and fires and caused sharp falls in moral standards and racial vitality – issues of great concern to old-stock Canadians for many of the slum dwellers were rude peasants from eastern and central Europe. A significant element in city populations – over a half in Winnipeg in 1911 – recent immigrants were blamed for society's problems. It was a commonplace of the time that environment as well as race determined behaviour. 'The environments in which the children of the poor and degenerate classes are reared,' it was said, 'are such as must necessarily breed immorality, crime and vice'. Foreign observers like Raymond Unwin warned that Canada's cities were repeating Victorian Britain's errors. 'Every city' reported one housing committee, 'has in one form or another its "Housing Problem"'. Utility and transportation monopolies were often accused of providing deplorable services at exorbitant prices and the urban public felt little confidence in city hall. Moreover, cities wore a grim, workaday visage, for there was little public investment in the arts, parks or playgrounds; civic dignity was notably absent in towns dedicated to headlong growth[7].

Canada's century thus had a sombre side with which government at all levels seemed unable to cope. The Dominion authorities, anxious for settlement and development, exercised little control over land use and natural resource exploitation. The provinces, largely rural-dominated, evinced little interest in their towns. Hundreds of communities had to construct local governments from scratch. Boomers feared that regulation would reduce 'opportunities for gambling' and 'it was therefore not encouraged'. Even older centres lacked a substantial municipal tradition but it is likely that any municipal system would have been overwhelmed by the boom's tidal wave. 'It was', said the evangelical reformer, the Rev. J. O. Miller, 'the old bad time of individualism. Civic consciousness had not yet been born'[8].

Country areas suffered also from unregulated growth. Speculators held the best land, close to railways, off the market; other land was sterilized through premature subdivision. Settlements were scattered, inconveniently located, lacking in services and amenities, laid out without regard to the terrain, in homestead units too small for successful Prairie farming. Settlers, often poor and ignorant, endured appalling conditions and lacked decent education, health care and alternative occupations. Disenchantment with grim country life and the bright lures of the town led to extensive rural depopulation, even in the west by 1914[9].

THE 'CITY BEAUTIFUL', 1896–1910

An awareness of urban problems gave rise to reformism in the 1880s but the take-off came in the 1890s, piloted especially by a Social Gospel movement and fuelled by British and American influences. By 1914, 'the Social Gospel was entering a crest of influence' and progressivism peaked about 1918. A confluence of twenty years' campaigning and the sense of community born of total war, it was summed up in *The New Era* (1917), edited by Miller, which might have been subtitled 'The Promise of Canadian Life'[10].

From about 1905, city planning became a feature of Canadian progressivism. Initially, architects and businessmen promoted the American 'City

Beautiful', stressing civic pride and dignity, Renaissance order and harmony, monumental architecture and the regimented insertion of nature into the urban scene. It was believed that a well-laid out, aesthetically-pleasing city would reduce social tensions, secure property values, promote contentment, stability and efficiency and outbid rivals for new investment and population. A 'City Beautiful' plan was also a mark of urban maturity. 'We do not want to remain a wooden backwoods place with narrow provincial ideas', remarked a Torontonian in 1906, 'We aim to be cosmopolitan, to have a larger outlook'. However, the 'City Beautiful' was a rush of blood to the civic head which faded after 1910, taxpayers fearing crippling assessments and chauvinists denouncing its old world fripperies. 'Town planning broke upon the Canadian people as an expensive decorative luxury', the grandiloquent flourishes obscuring the many sensible proposals which took metropolitan perspectives, stressed that planning was 'a business proposition', paid attention to housing, public health, playgrounds and utilities and stated firmly that 'The primary requirement of city planning is convenient, economical and easy transportation'[11]. Adams believed that the 'City Beautiful' simply had the wrong priorities:

> When the City planning movement takes the form of creating Civic Centres, wide boulevards, extensive parks and parkways, it is apt to overlook the problem of the individual home. The former are desirable luxuries which should be supplements to decent healthy home life and not alternatives which should be adopted in preference to the work of making actual living conditions, the environment and the sanitation of humanity itself above reproach[12].

THE 'CITY SCIENTIFIC', 1910–1914

From about 1910, planning priorities were re-ordered to 'health, economics and beautification in that order' as British ideas on health and housing swept across Canada. This 'City Scientific' approach differed from the 'City Beautiful' largely in emphasis and was promoted by successive Governors-General with strong backgrounds in the British environmental movement, who sponsored lecture tours by major British planners such as Henry Vivian, Thomas Mawson, Raymond Unwin and Thomas Adams[13].

Their Canadian converts – mostly doctors, clergymen, academics, social workers, journalists and engineers – preached that 'We must use as our ideal Garden Cities', described as being 'perhaps the greatest contribution of modern times to the well-being of urban populations'. Many visited Letchworth, Hampstead and other model communities. It was engineers who best represented the new consensus on planning which was emerging in the Western world by 1914. 'The design of a city', one proclaimed bluntly, 'is in the main, an engineering one'. Calgary's City Planning Commission, affirming the cost-effectiveness of utilitarian, long-term trend amelioration and development control planning, adopted the motto: 'Town planning is not another way of spending money; it is a method of saving it'. By 1914, sobriety had supplanted flamboyance as the directing influence and it was the Imperial umbilical cord which truly brought Canadian planning to birth[14].

Planning made no more than a modest beginning before 1914. The all-conquering British influence led to three provincial planning acts – in New Brunswick and Nova Scotia (1912) and Alberta (1913). Slavish copies of the British act of 1909, adopted hastily and without adequate means of implementation, they were failures and 'subsequent experience has shown that these Acts were passed without full consideration of the character of the British statute and the general object that they had in view, or of the entire difference in conditions in Canada as compared to Great Britain'[15]. The two major planning schemes that got under way were the result of indefatigable local pressure. The Halifax plan was the culmination of a civic improvement league campaign begun in 1907 and Saint John owed its plan to W.F. Burditt, who had been inspired by hearing Henry Vivian and reading Nettlefold. Co-partnership housing, which it was felt 'Makes for better citizenship by the cultivation of the two most vital factors – Self-Reliance and Individualism', made its appearance in the shape of the Toronto Housing Company. 'Organized to help solve the housing problem in Toronto upon sound economic principles', its hopes of a substantial garden suburb never materialized; its legacy was two small pseudo-English housing estates. An ambitious garden suburb for Saint John remained unbuilt and the boldest plan of the time was Edward H. Bennett's Ottawa-Hull federal district project, emphasizing a civic centre, communications and a park system[16].

THE COMMISSION OF CONSERVATION, 1909–1914

The British connection was reinforced by the work of the Commission of Conservation, an autonomous Federal-provincial body established in 1909 following widespread concern in North America at the rapid destruction of natural resources. Its function was 'to investigate, enquire, advise and inform' the nation on the scientific farming of its natural resources, including human life. Headed by Clifford Sifton, it conducted detailed inquiries into the use and state of Canada's resources and made proposals for their conservation and economic development, refining the 'doctrine of usefulness' by marrying it to modern scientific management[17].

It was the Commission's Medical Officer, Dr. Charles Hodgetts, who was largely responsible for the reshaping of the Canadian planning movement between 1910 and 1914. A trenchant critic of 'the army of land speculators and jerry builders' who had blighted Canada's cities, Hodgetts was 'an expert-with-a-mission', a Canadian Edwin Chadwick. Well-acquainted with foreign practice, Hodgetts formulated a programme for Canadian planning embracing the planning of Ottawa as an object lesson, adequate housing for all, long-term master plans, land-use zoning, factories downwind, dignified civic centres and a dispersed suburban population served by rapid transit. Aware that 'public opinion must be aroused before the necessary legislation can be hoped for', he started a broadsheet, *Conservation of Life*, in 1914 and inspired the Commission's draft town planning act. Outlining the aims of planning as 'efficiency, economy and vision', it called for provincial departments of municipal affairs to give professional advice to towns and approve local plans. Schemes were to cover traffic control, transportation, sanitation, amenity and convenience. Unfortunately the draft was criticized as impracticable, undemocratic, authoritarian and likely to incite intra-municipal friction[18].

Hodgetts believed that Canadian planning's most urgent need was for a professional director, who would have to be imported for 'The country is young and we lack qualified men', and from 1912 he set about recruiting one. It was evident that he had Thomas Adams in mind, having been impressed by him at the National Conference on City Planning at Philadelphia in 1911; 'he was the one man there who apparently had very sound and business-like ideas on the subject of housing and town planning'. Initially, Hodgetts wanted Adams to address a conference in Ottawa and then take a swing around the country, dispensing lectures and advice, 'probably taking two or three months'. Backed by 'a very large number of the most prominent citizens of Canada' and major organizations, the Prime Minister, Sir Robert Borden, requested the loan of Adams. Much was anticipated from the visit, Hodgetts declaring with some exaggeration that 'Mr. Adams is the one man in England who has had to meet with and grapple with the difficulties that we have today . . . I am satisfied . . . that he . . . will make suggestions and recommendations to the municipalities of Canada, that will be far more practical than those of any other man'[19].

Unfortunately, the 'Local Government Board was unable to spare Mr. Adams'. However, Hodgetts was determined to get his man and persuaded the Commission to host the 1914 National Conference on City Planning at Toronto 'with the object of strengthening and advancing the movement in favour of more scientific town planning and more vigorous attention to the housing requirements of Canadians'. Adams accepted an invitation to attend and told the delegates 'Do not let us underrate how extensive and how broad town planning is', adding that 'town planning is no mere dream of a few sentimentalists, but is a practical proposition for saving money'. He refrained from commenting on specific Canadian problems, especially the draft act, but signified a willingness to discuss matters with Hodgetts[20].

ADAMS APPOINTED TOWN PLANNING ADVISOR

Adams's authoritative performance at Toronto led to an invitation to become

Town Planning Advisor to the Commission of Conservation, and on 23 July James White, the Commission's secretary, cabled Sifton from London:

> Can get Thomas Adams man we requested come Canada last year best man in England come three years fee $7500 and $1000 travelling expenses to Canada[21].

It is clear from the Canadian response to this news that Adams was virtually deified well in advance of his arrival. Stating that he was 'peculiarly fitted' for the post, Hodgetts claimed that 'The Commission of Conservation has secured the services of one who is considered as the highest authority upon the subject, perhaps in the world'[22], while White told a member of the Commission that

> Mr. Adams has been employed by us because we desired to have available a man whose professional ability and experience would give weight to any advice that he may give the cities and towns of Canada, respecting town planning, housing, and, on cognate subjects . . . It is not too much to say that Mr. Adams stands at the head of his profession[23].

Eulogies flowed also from unofficial sources, the general view of the new man being that he was 'the greatest expert in the world today' and the pragmatic Canadian public was assured that he was 'Essentially practical and direct in his methods'. Much was looked for in his tour of duty and it was said that 'If the Commission of Conservation had done nothing but engage Thomas Adams for the conservation of the best in our civic life, it would have paid for its existence'[24]. Deification might have endowed Adams with a divine authority in planning matters but he must have been aware that it placed a great burden upon him, too.

Given that the trend of Canadian planning, assisted energetically by Hodgetts, was moving firmly in the British direction, a British appointee was likely. In any case, Hodgetts would have none of 'the noon-day effulgence of the City Beautiful' still thought (wrongly) to dominate American planning[25]. Adams was in any case the most suitable candidate, not least because he had for four years held successfully a national post broadly similar to that he was asked to fill in Canada. His temperament, personality, breadth of experience and gifts as an energetic organizer and lucid communicator commended him, too. More significantly, he was at home in the North American milieu and at one with the Commission's dedication to the conservation of life and the efficient and scientific management of resources. In tune with the Canadian psyche, crossing the Atlantic compelled no philosophical adjustment. The utilitarian and pragmatic Adams had found a congenial home.

Adams's prestige no doubt permitted him virtually to define the terms of his appointment though he was constrained by the fact that both he and the

Commission possessed only advisory powers. It was a situation to test his well-known and extensive gifts for persuasion, diplomacy, communication and organization. Furthermore, October 1914 was hardly the most propitious moment to begin an evangelical mission. The immigrant and land boom had collapsed in 1913 and the environmental reform movement thereby lost some of its sense of urgency, reduced further by the cessation of development by 1915. Though Canada had been engaged in hostilities since August 1914, the full effects of the war were slow to emerge. However, the early departure of Hodgetts for war service robbed Adams of invaluable guidance; it may also have been a blessing in disguise for both were strong personalities with definite views; a prolonged acquaintance might have promoted friction[26].

ADAMS TAKES CHARGE

Adams's first task was to familiarize himself with Canadian conditions, communities and leaders. Making the first of many tours of inspection and lecturing, he visited all of the provinces by early in 1915 and was then in a position to devise a strategy. His aim was to establish planning as a central function of government at all levels, buttressed by an integrated structure of legislation, administration, public support and professional organization, education and expertise. Though developing hesitantly along British lines, the fragile and rudimentary state of Canadian planning, the exigencies of war and the short-term nature of his appointment left him with only one feasible strategy – the more or less simultaneous promotion of legislation, propaganda, advice, demonstrations, research and professionalization[27].

Before Adams, like some great Ionan saint from over the water, could convert Canada to planning, he had to exorcise two irksome ghosts – the indigenous fondness for the traditional but wasteful 'doctrine of usefulness' and the wide-spread belief that planning meant the ruinous excesses of the 'City Beautiful'. Bitterly critical of the heedless speculative growth of cities, he enquired, 'Is it not time to pay more regard to human life and less to the sanctity of that kind of property that injures it?' The grid he denounced as 'a crime against both nature and society, and an economic blunder of the worst kind', inefficient, costly and unattractive. The slum, he noted hopefully, was not yet firmly entrenched: 'In Canada we have an opportunity to prevent the slum from coming into being, except in a few cases where it has already gained a foothold'. Nevertheless, 200,000 lives had been lost in five years, largely through preventable diseases in unsatisfactory homes. Decent housing was the inalienable right of all but 'land gambling, overcrowding of buildings, and the inefficiency of our schemes of land settlement in the past' denied it to many[28]. Exposing the problems of congestion and Canada's backwardness in dealing with it, he asked:

Should it not be a crime in Canada, as in England, to erect crowded wooden tenements for habitation, to permit old decayed timbers to be used in construction, to build what are admitted to be fire traps, to crowd up rear lots intended for gardens and have hundreds of vacant lots unbuilt on?[29].

Acknowledging that it was 'difficult to convince the average man that the planning of towns and the adequate control of building development and public health are not fads of well-meaning but impracticable enthusiasts', the functionalist Adams sought to erase the 'erroneous impression of what town planning is', dismissing the 'City Beautiful' as 'of comparatively little value', rating 'aesthetic features' as 'in the nature of luxuries'[30].

The philosophical basis of the gospel which Adams expounded was the advanced utilitarianism of J. S. Mill which had formed a major strand of Liberal reformism in Britain. In terms redolent of Mill, Adams asserted that a landowner had no 'right to use his property to injure his fellows. Life is higher and more valuable under the law than real property . . . we have either to control the right to property so that it shall not endanger the right to live in wholesome surroundings or face inevitable decay'. However, the negative restraint of private activity did not imply a positive collectivism for 'we do not want to inaugurate socialistic extremes but to forestall them'. His liberalism was further displayed in his assumption of an essential social unity and his utilitarianism in his belief in 'scientific town planning' by which experts could discover and cater for the general good. He was a functionalist, holding that 'Orderly development and health will produce beauty without seeking beauty as an end in itself'. Above all, he was a strict pragmatist, urging 'the necessity of preparing schemes that are practical . . . one must be practical in method to get a thing done at all, and it is a waste of time to set up idealistic utopias of what we would like to do but cannot'. It was a philosophy well calculated to appeal to Canadian reformers though there is no evidence that his Canadian experience had any significant effect on either his philosophy or his technique. He considered his already-established Anglo-American 'City Practical' approach to have a universal validity and kept up to date with advances abroad. Sympathetic to specific conditions in Canada, nevertheless he made little but institutional concessions to the general Canadian situation[31].

'The keynote of town planning' he defined as 'the conservation of life and economy in the system of developing land' so as 'to secure efficiency, convenience, health and amenity'. Within this general objectival framework, he laid down two specific priorities. Aware of the need to canvass business support, he described the city as primarily an economic organism for which 'the first concern of a town plan should be to provide for the proper and efficient carrying on of business'. However, mindful of his reformist background, he added that 'Complementary to the business side of a city is the provision of satisfactory and healthy living conditions for the people'. Cognisant of the acute financial embarrassment of many municipalities, he stressed the cost-effectiveness of planning. 'By preparation of a town planning scheme at comparatively small cost', he advised, 'we would save much money and wasted effort, and we could avoid mistakes which are caused by the want of planning'[32].

Cost, together with the exigencies of war and the existence of vested interests, ruled out both garden cities and urban renewal. However, Adams endorsed 'the soundness of the principles' of garden cities and felt that Canada needed 'an object lesson' which would enjoy 'the combined advantages of town and country'. He advocated the foundation of small new towns, well-sited, fully-serviced and provided with light industries, in rural areas and welcomed the trend to industrial and residential decentralization. Observing of great cities that 'it is desirable that they should be spread out over wide areas, and that the penetration of rural districts by industrial plants should continue', he argued that 'the more widespread the population is the more healthy it will be'. Urging the integration of rural and urban planning, he emphasized that 'You cannot separate the problem of the town from the problem of the country'. Nevertheless, he was no rural sentimentalist, acknowledging that Canada was becoming an essentially urban nation. He asserted flatly that 'We must make up our minds that the increase in the city population will continue and that no extensive back-to-the-land movement will counteract it' for 'the movement of population cityward is determined by economic and social causes which it is impossible to resist'. Should urban redevelopment become feasible, he counselled that compensation should not be over-generous and that landowners should undertake public improvements. Comprehensive zoning ordinances governing height, bulk and use should be introduced, roads varied in width according to function and one-tenth of the land reserved for public open space[33].

Explaining that planning 'seeks to prevent rather than cure', he affirmed that 'The most urgent need is to safeguard future growth'. Thus what he offered Canada was conventional trend-ameliorating, development control planning, in which public authority laid down a broad framework within which private enterprise took most initiatives. Even this fundamentally negative vision was most comprehensive for 'There is nothing in the development of a city which does not come under the purview of town planning properly understood'. He hoped to avoid 'uniform geometrical patterns' and undue speculation, to match roads to the topography, regulate building construction, co-ordinate manufacturing areas with transport and power systems, zone residential areas and ensure adequate light, air and space in and about homes. His vision was also a metropolitan one for he suggested that 'the most important, if not the most urgent of our problems is the preparation of comprehensive schemes for large regions, embracing the large city, its adjacent satellite towns, and the whole of the intervening lands that make up the metropolitan area'[34].

Though he observed that 'Owing to the war there has been a considerable difficulty in attracting widespread public interest in the matter of planning, which seems to most people who look on the surface to be a question which can be left in abeyance until the return of peace', Adams attempted to turn the conflict to good account. He wished to take advantage of the cessation of development which meant that Canada was 'free from the injurious effects of gambling in fictitious land values which characterize periods of boom'. Wartime was a good time to plan, untrammelled by normal pressures but 'Immediate action is necessary therefore before there is a resumption of building activity and land sub-division'. He attempted also to tap the patriotic well, arguing that 'The very sacrifices which are being made in the war demand that we who are at home should devote our attention to laying foundations which will insure healthy living conditions and increased efficiency in the future'. As peace drew near, he urged planning for post-war reconstruction, pointing out that 'Peace is certain – then why be unprepared?[35].

CIVIC IMPROVEMENT LEAGUE

Adams made use of many vehicles for his propaganda. He spoke about twice weekly to universities, Canadian Clubs and other civic groups. His presence, plans and pronouncements were always newsworthy and he was a frequent contributor to both the general and the professional press. Taking over Hodgett's broadsheet, he renamed it *Town Planning and the Conservation of Life*, reflecting its new emphasis. Adams wrote most of the copy himself – the news items on housing and planning progress at home and abroad and homilies on the necessity for and the practicality of planning[36].

His chief instrument for winning public support was the Civic Improvement League. Within a few months of his arrival, he discerned that 'An organization is required to stimulate public interest in municipal affairs, with special regard to public health, town planning and housing and to encourage the study and advancement of the best principles of town planning and urban growth'[37]. Under the auspices of the Commission of Conservation, Adams organized a preliminary national meeting at Ottawa in November 1915, attended by members of the Commission, headed by Sifton, national and provincial politicians, municipal councillors, government officials, clergymen like J. S. Woodsworth, newspapermen like Sir John Willison, the Toronto editor, members of the professions, women's leaders, civic improvers and academics. The meeting, stage-managed by Adams, resolved

That a Civic Improvement League for Canada be formed, with the general object of promoting the study and advancement of the best principles and methods of civic improvement and to secure a general and effective interest in all municipal affairs and to encourage and organise in every community all those social forces that make for an efficient Canadian citizenship[38].

It pledged itself to pay 'special attention' to the form and character of local government, municipal economy, adequate housing, health and utilities, city planning, civic education and the agricultural cultivation of idle suburban lands. Adams gave it a wide ambit for, though planning was to be 'a central plank' in its platform, it was as yet a novel and minute interest and needed the enveloping support of related causes which would maximize its audience. The League took its cue from existing local civic groups in North America and also from British environmental lobbies. It was markedly elitist in character, generally melioristic and quintessentially progressive. Adams, who became Acting Secretary, was left to draft a constitution, form a provisional council and arrange further meetings. He believed the League had 'enormous potential for the future welfare of Canada' and mused euphorically that 'it seems difficult to anticipate anything but great success'[39].

Its inaugural meeting in January 1916 was also well attended. Adams again ran the show, while Willison became chairman of the provisional council, which included Sifton, Woodsworth and the planner Noulan Cauchon. Opinion ranged from muscular Christianity to socialism and the ever-practical Adams urged delegates to 'keep our discussions along practical lines and conclude our deliberations with definite recommendations on what action can be taken'. He steered through resolutions calling for planning legislation in all provinces, the better settlement of land and the proper reception of returned veterans. By the end of 1916, he could record some thirty local leagues but then the war began to divert the nation's attentions and energies and a second national meeting in May 1917 was less well attended. Still the puppeteer, Adams then switched tactics to regional meetings, the formation of local branches and the provision of a national information service. Though ultimately the war made it 'impossible to arouse much interest and enthusiasm on the subject of civic improvement', Adams was confident that in peacetime 'We may now expect the restoration of interest in civic improvement matters' and declared that 'a serious effort must be made to create a permanent organization'. His own drive and enthusiasm had sustained the League throughout the war, for he regarded it as a vital adjunct to his legislative proposals. 'Legislation', he said, 'cannot be effective unless the people are educated to appreciate it'[40].

PROVINCIAL PLANNING LEGISLATION

Legislation, clearly, had to be the core of Adams's strategy and his object was to draw up a model act and get it adopted by all of the provinces, thus ensuring uniformity of law and practice throughout the Dominion. Much of his time between 1914 and 1919 was occupied in pursuing this aim. His own draft act was not unveiled until January 1916 for he had to proceed with caution and tact. Apart from the need to acquaint himself with Canadian conditions, needs and governmental structures, he had to overcome diplomatically the obstacles posed by the three existing provincial measures and the Commission's own draft act.

The object of Adams's act was 'primarily, to secure that new growth will be properly regulated, that the evils which have resulted from haphazard growth in the past will be avoided in the future, that such public monies as are expended on local improvements will be spent to the best advantage, and the conditions of the environment in urban communities will not continue to cause unnecessary loss of life and impairment of health'. The crucial role in the planning process was to be played by an expert provincial bureaucracy and, believing that there was 'a pressing need for a central department in each Province to deal with all questions of local government, including highways, town planning and local improvements', Adams urged parallel legislation to establish departments of municipal affairs. These would play the overlord role of the Local Government Board – advising, stimulating, vetting, arbitrating and compelling activity at the municipal level. Equally vital was a comptroller of housing and town planning, for 'until we get such a director for each Province, we shall not get much effective work done'. Adams envisaged the appointment of architects or engineers, men of action who could play in provincial life the galvanizing role he performed for the Dominion[41].

On the municipal level, there was to be indirect democratic control of the planning process, as local boards were in most respects autonomous and only partly composed of councillors. A familiar device in North America, it has been suggested that the planning board was a reflection of current distrust of politicians and that Adams inserted it with some reluctance. Executive responsibility was to be placed in the hands of a professional town planning surveyor. Planning was to be made mandatory, it being assumed that towns would adopt long-term schemes and rural areas the simpler method of by-laws. Permission to prepare a scheme, approval of the draft scheme and of the final plan would have to be obtained from the provincial authorities, accompanied by a lengthy procedure involving extensive mapping, notification and hearings. Only land in the course of development or likely to be developed in the near future could be included. All subdivisions had to be approved by the local board and street widths were to vary, according to function, from 40 to 100 feet. Provision was made for arbitration, betterment, compensation, the limitation of building densities, the reservation of open space and future street lines, the protection of beautiful and historic sites, and co-operation with landowners and adjacent municipalities. Zoning for use, height and bulk was permitted and the act was reinforced by four schedules covering by-laws, planning schemes, procedure and the expropriation of land[42].

Adams's act was much as might have been expected, given its author's and Canada's essential conservatism. It posited no threat to the established political and economic order, suggesting only modest adjustments to the private development process to avoid past evils and safeguard the future general welfare. It steered clear of controversial areas like public housing, urban renewal and publicly-sponsored new towns. It assumed a knowable common good and proceeded more by co-operation than by compulsion. Planning was envisaged as an essentially negative promoter of efficiency and economy and as a guardian of the public health.

The British pedigree was unmistakeable. Departments of municipal affairs were to exercise the same stranglehold over local powers as the Local Government Board and the fussy, cumbersome British procedure was retained. In scope and operation, it followed closely its Imperial progenitor. The most significant new features were its mandatory nature, unsurprising in view of Adams's consistent advocacy of compulsion in Britain, and the pre-eminence of the professional planner. This was equally to be expected for Adams was the archetype of the professional planner and it reflected his frustration at being subjected to lay civil service control at the Local Government Board. It represented, too, an innocent assumption, easily made in those days, that a professional planner could be relied upon to discover and implement impartially a universally agreed public good, a utilitarian notion subscribed to as widely in Canada as in Britain. The by-law procedure for small communities presaged outline zoning plans while, reflecting recent developments in planning thought, zoning provisions were more explicit than in the British act.

In view of Adams's expressed wish to adjust his planning to Canadian requirements, there was little truly Canadian about the measure save for the necessary institutional arrangements. Even more surprising was the absence of any significant contribution from American planning experience, in spite of Adams's extensive acquaintance with and general endorsement of recent planning in the United States, though there was then precious little American legislation on which to draw[43].

It was a disappointing act, Adams failing to take the opportunity to set precedents in the object, scope and procedure of planning. The act was as tortuous and almost as timid as its British exemplar. It offered no invitation to public authorities to take positive environmental initiatives and it naively presented experts with dangerously extensive powers. Little concession was made to the fragility and novelty of the Canadian municipal tradition. Though it represented probably a shrewd estimate of what provincial legislatures could be persuaded to accept, the act lacked imagination and was far too complex. Simpler, general enabling legislation along the lines shortly to become familiar across the border would have been more suitable for a young nation demanding immediate action and early results. Adams conceded, however, that 'frequent modifications will be necessary, as experience is gained, until a satisfactory measure can be evolved', more effective and wider in scope[44].

Adams was active on the legislative front even before his model act was published but his principal campaigns date from its appearance. He was optimistic of early and complete success. 'It will be disappointing', he remarked, 'if all the provinces do not have town Planning Acts in force by this time next year, and the satisfactory feature is that they are likely to be really practical and effective measures, and comparatively uniform throughout the Dominion'[45].

His first opportunity came early, in Nova Scotia, which found its act of 1912 unwieldy and irrelevant. He largely drafted the new act of April 1915. Virtually identical with the model act, it was amended in 1919 on his advice, to strengthen the compulsory powers and ensure its application to rural areas. He was pleased with his original measure, claiming that 'we have found a method by which the maximum amount of compulsion can be introduced into a Town Planning Act in a democratic country'. He continued to press the provincial authorities for a department of municipal affairs and an overhaul of the highway administration[46]. In New Brunswick, though working for a broader measure 'to enable the whole province to be planned under comprehensive schemes', he managed only to revise the procedure regulations[47]. Especially friendly with the Prime Minister of Prince Edward Island, by 1918 he had prepared and seen passed a package of measures including a planning and development act, a commission of planning and development with a director, had suggested transport improvements and a concentration on tourism and was advising on a new ferry port[48].

In the Prairie provinces, he enjoyed varying fortunes. In Alberta, where he felt planning had a low priority, he was able only to simplify the procedure regulations[49]. Saskatchewan towns were petitioning the province for a planning act from 1915 and, reinforced by Adams, secured a quite advanced measure, based on his advice, in 1918. He drew up the procedure regulations and persuaded the province to appoint a director of town planning and a town planning engineer[50]. Winnipeg, which had a prior interest in planning, took the lead in Manitoba, the Greater Winnipeg Town Planning Commission drafting a bill in 1915. Amended by Adams, it became law in 1916 and he produced also a set of model by-laws[51]. All three provinces had departments of municipal affairs.

Adams made frequent visits to British Columbia and was highly critical of conditions there. 'The rectangular system of subdividing lands is not good even in the prairies but it is the height of absurdity to apply it as a highway plan for such a province as British Columbia', he declared, deprecating the results of 'the get rich quick real estate speculator, with his corps of salesmen and prolific advertising'. He found the provincial authorities and public opinion receptive to his message but, despite sporadic local pressure for legislation and consideration from time to time of his draft act, nothing further was achieved[52].

Recognizing that Quebec had many other things on its mind, Adams handled it with great tact, establishing a close enough relationship with the government by 1916 to be invited to forward a draft statute. However, all he could extract from the cabinet were vague promises, never redeemed, to introduce a bill. A bureau of municipal affairs was introduced in 1917 and he gave advice on highway development and the resettlement of veterans. A housing act of 1915 permitted municipal loans to limited dividend housing companies and was used for a working-class housing experiment at Pointe-aux-Trembles, which Adams described as 'a valuable object lesson'. Even so, Quebec's response to his entreaties was disappointing[53].

Ontario was the most urbanized province and had perhaps the most serious problems of slums, speculation, poor communications, municipal financial instability and housing shortages. Industrial decentralization was in an advanced state and rural depopulation was more severe than elsewhere. There was widespread awareness of these problems and the towns of the south-western industrial belt had established a standing conference on housing and planning. The province had made a modest beginning with a railway and municipal board, a housing act permitting municipalities to guarantee the bonds of philanthropic housing companies and a City and Suburbs Plans Act allowing towns of over 50,000 people to control subdivisions within five miles of their borders. To Adams, these measures were inadequate for 'the Act is of comparatively small value in securing the proper development of even the few cities to which it applies', while 'the absence of any central departments to regulate and correlate such local activities limits the extent to which local councils are now entrusted to discharge the duties which only they can effectively perform'[54].

Adams was quick to see that Ontario was the most crucial province. The early success there of his proposals would impress the other provinces and thus he concentrated his efforts on the Ontario administration, beginning in March 1916. Pressing the Premier, Sir William Hearst, for a new planning bill, he referred to 'the great change which a town planning act would make in regard to giving local authorities an entirely new outlook on the question of their future development'. Liaising closely with the standing conference, he told Hearst, 'We are receiving increasing evidence of the strong demand on the part of public bodies and representative men in Ontario to have town planning powers granted to local authorities during this session of Parliament'. The struggle reached epic proportions, Adams stressing that 'the matter is one of the greatest urgency' and that 'opinion in support of the bill is practically unanimous'. He dropped the mandatory provisions to make it more palatable and professed himself 'anxious to come to Toronto immediately there is the slightest prospect of anything being discussed'. Hearst was not averse to the bill but clearly regarded it as postponable until peacetime and was inhibited by negative advice on municipal powers from his legal officers. A municipal deputation headed by Adams in 1917 was rewarded with a bureau of municipal affairs and a Planning and Development Act, though both statutes were drawn up without his advice. Adams welcomed the planning act as 'a good step in the right direction' but lamented that 'the bill does not meet the demand which has been made for legislation and covers what are perhaps the least important matters'. He complained to Hearst that 'Your advisors do not seem to have comprehended what is required . . . having regard to our wide experience in the application of similar legislation, we might have been of some service in assisting to frame it'. Enclosing a detailed criticism of the act, which was only a marginal improvement on the previous statute, he concluded, 'I do not think it will make much difference to the position in Ontario'. After four sessions of sustained pressure, the position remained as it was in 1916 and 'Ontario, the most important province of all, with the greatest population and the largest number of municipalities able to undertake this work, is still without legislation, and yet is most in need of it'[55].

ADVICE AND DEMONSTRATION

Adams realized shrewdly that 'The average man is not convinced by plans, by addresses, or by reports; he is convinced by what he sees', and a cardinal feature of the planning system he built up was his advisory and demonstration work. He sought to demonstrate the various aspects of planning – new industrial, resort or resource towns, metropolitan planning, long-term town development schemes and urban renewal. Arguing that 'The advantage of assistance in a few special cases, as object lessons, is obvious from an educational point of view', he aimed to have an advisory role or a demonstration project in each province. Nevertheless, he did not seek to monopolize planning work; he 'consistently followed the practice of assisting only in the initiatory stages of work' and 'In no case has the Town Planning Advisor assisted in preparing more than one scheme of the same kind'. A one-man band, he received many more requests than he could satisfy. He commented on proposals sent to him and drew up draft planning schemes, by-laws, maps and surveys. He recommended native planners for appointments, such as Cauchon for railway improvements at Hamilton and for a general development plan at London[56].

Adams never had the opportunity to assist in the planning of a metropolitan region but he had much to say on the subject. Conditions in Canada's largest urban centre, Montreal, were worse than elsewhere and Adams felt that it, 'more than any other city in Canada, needs town planning'. He urged the satellite towns to co-operate with Montreal in a plan to improve municipal economy and efficiency, raise health and housing standards, reduce population and traffic congestion, compel sounder and more compact suburban growth, considerably expand the region's amenity and develop industrial and transport facilities. Unfortunately, despite frequent efforts by the civic improvement league, Montreal remained indifferent to his call and blundered on, uncontrolled[57]. Toronto was actually engaged in several

planning enterprises – harbour, highway and transportation schemes – and
Adams pleaded, again in vain, for the co-ordination of this otherwise
creditable activity. In Ottawa, he called repeatedly but unavailingly for
the implementation of the Bennett proposals, which he described as both
attractive and functional[58].

He had most influence on medium and smaller-sized cities, notably Halifax
and Saint John. Following up local business support for planning legislation
and schemes, he hoped to create models for the nation and worked consistently in both places over several years, co-operating closely with the city
engineers. The plans were very close in character to British long-term
schemes and Adams ensured that the areas were extensive enough to cater for
all possible future growth, which entailed joint city-county commissions. The
time spans were up to a century. Built-up areas were excluded on grounds of
cost. Following civic surveys, emphasis was placed on highways, building
lines, subdivision control, economical utilities, adequate open space, height,
bulk and use zoning and low-density residential districts. Good progress was
made in both cities, the first stages being completed by 1917[59]. Many
smaller towns made use of Adams's services – places like Renfrew, Ontario,
for which he prepared an outline development plan, and Sudbury, Ontario,
for which he reported on park proposals, stressing the need to attract industry
by presenting a pleasant face. He lost no opportunity to preach the gospel
of comprehensive planning, as when he assessed the Vancouver civic centre
competition and urged a metropolitan plan. He co-operated with provincial
governments, as in the design of Port Borden, Prince Edward Island, and
with the Dominion Government, as in the revision of Mawson's plan for the
national park town of Banff[60]. He could be critical of earlier planning, too.
The Grand Trunk Pacific Railway had laid out and landscaped Prince
Rupert, British Columbia, at great expense, and took umbrage at his condemnation of its speculative excesses and poor housing. Adams, sticking to his
guns, argued that the grid design was unsuitable and that a development
scheme was necessary to prevent the plan miscarrying. His offer to report on
the necessary remedies was accepted and he advised a fifty-year view, a civic
survey, accurate maps, a planning commission, a development scheme and a
skeleton plan [61]. At times, he prescribed strong medicine, telling the leading
municipalities of Alberta to repair their battered finances by returning
unused subdivisions to farming, thus reducing assessments, banning further
subdivisions and providing services only at the landowner's expense[62].

THE RE-PLANNING OF HALIFAX, NOVA SCOTIA, 1918

Urban renewal was on scarcely any planning agenda at that time but Adams
took well his one opportunity. In December 1917, an explosion in Halifax
harbour wrecked the adjacent Richmond district, 325 acres of hillside

working-class and waterfront industrial land. At Sifton's suggestion, Adams offered his services to re-plan it. A Federal official, G. S. Campbell, commended him to the Relief Commission as 'a man of sound judgement and not a faddist. He has an attractive personality and would I think be *persona grata* to his colleagues . . . I don't think there is any man in Canada better qualified for the job'. Beginning in the spring of 1918, he was determined that 'a serious effort should be made to prepare a sound scheme of development worthy of the city'. Insisting on plenary powers to acquire land, impose zoning and plan for up to thirty years ahead, he wished to include an adjacent undeveloped area but was thwarted by the Commission's strict interpretation of its powers, though his outline street plan was largely implemented in subsequent years. In Richmond itself, he broke up the grid with diagonals, swung some roads along contours, eased grades, varied street widths according to function, avoided awkward junctions, improved access, provided a central square, park and playgrounds, reduced housing densities, expanded industrial space and established firm building lines. He was assisted by Horace L. Seymour, a surveyor and engineer loaned by the Surveyor-General, and the Montreal architect George Ross, who experimented with a variety of attractive working-class housing designs[63].

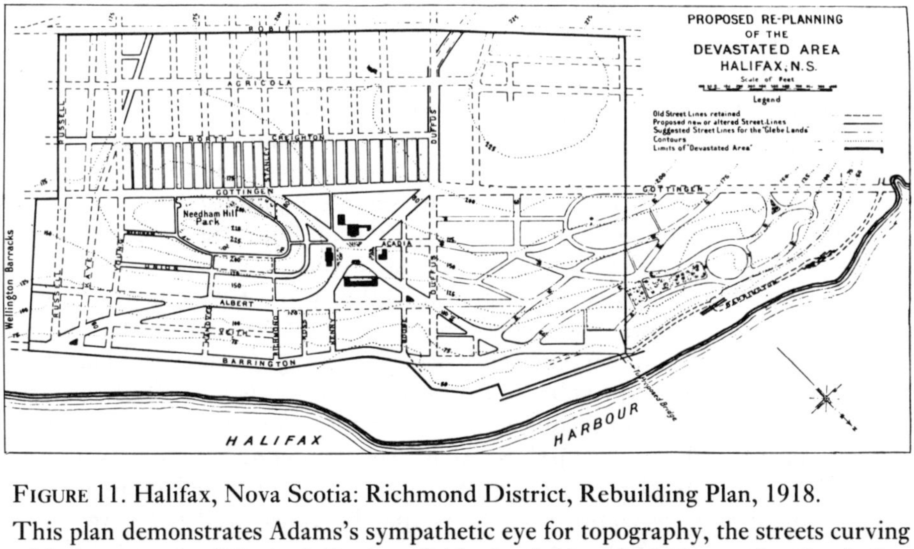

FIGURE 11. Halifax, Nova Scotia: Richmond District, Rebuilding Plan, 1918.

This plan demonstrates Adams's sympathetic eye for topography, the streets curving with the contours. Diagonals further divide the rigid grid which was the plan before the explosion and the remains of which can be seen to the South of the devastated area. The highest ground was reserved for a park and there was to be a central square. Adams hoped to include adjacent undeveloped land. (Commission of Conservation, *Tenth Annual Report*, 1919)

Adams demanded and very largely obtained a free hand. He was confident
of producing a scientific plan, at once impartial and in the best interests of
the community. The combination of a total war situation and a disaster
emergency freed him from the normal restraints on redevelopment – local
property owners and the municipality – and he was able to indulge in a technocratic exercise which was a fine example of the planner's art, functional yet
attractive, displaying an affinity with the topography and integrating the
various economic uses and social needs in a balanced whole. Nevertheless, he
incurred the displeasure of the residents for refusing to rebuild at once on
familiar lines and the wrath of the municipality for ignoring it, while he complained at the lack of support and appreciation from the Relief Commission.
In terms of physical planning, there is no doubt that he was right; the interference of other bodies would have produced probably an indifferent plan.
His utilitarian exercise gave the people of Richmond a distinctly improved
environment. Yet he failed in perhaps the most important respect; he hoped
that Richmond would constitute an example for the nation but it was treated,
not surprisingly, as a unique situation, not to be repeated in normal times and
circumstances[64].

NEW COMMUNITIES

Adams had been heralded in 1914 as a proponent of garden cities yet he
devoted little attention to the subject in Canada. He was above all a realist and
knew that a combination of the war, the lack of philanthropic capital and the
resistance of government to positive social expenditure ruled out a Canadian
Letchworth. His occasional remarks about a Federally-sponsored object
lesson lacked conviction but he did aim in all his planning at Garden City
standards of housing, amenity and general urban design. He vetted readily or
advised on plans for such new communities as were proposed, such as H. B.
Dunington-Grubb's garden village for the Riordon Pulp and Paper Company
at Hawkesbury, Ontario[65]. He was asked to vet the plans for the United
States Steel Corporation's new town at Ojibway, near Windsor, Ontario.
Projected during the war but begun only in 1919, it was designed by Owen
Brainard of the well-known New York planning firm of Carrere and Hastings.
Based on a modified grid split by diagonals, boulevards and 300-foot parkways, focusing on a central square, it was situated on virgin land adjacent to
transportation and power supplies. Adams recommended the reservation of
one-tenth of the 1000 acres for open space for the expected population of
20,000 but otherwise commented flatly that he considered the plan 'to be
satisfactory from the point of view of layout; the disposition and width of
streets'. It was probably more stereotyped and conventional than he would
have wished but he was more concerned at the likelihood that a shanty
town would spring up on the outskirts – a situation which, because of the
deficiencies of Ontario planning legislation, could not be prevented[66].

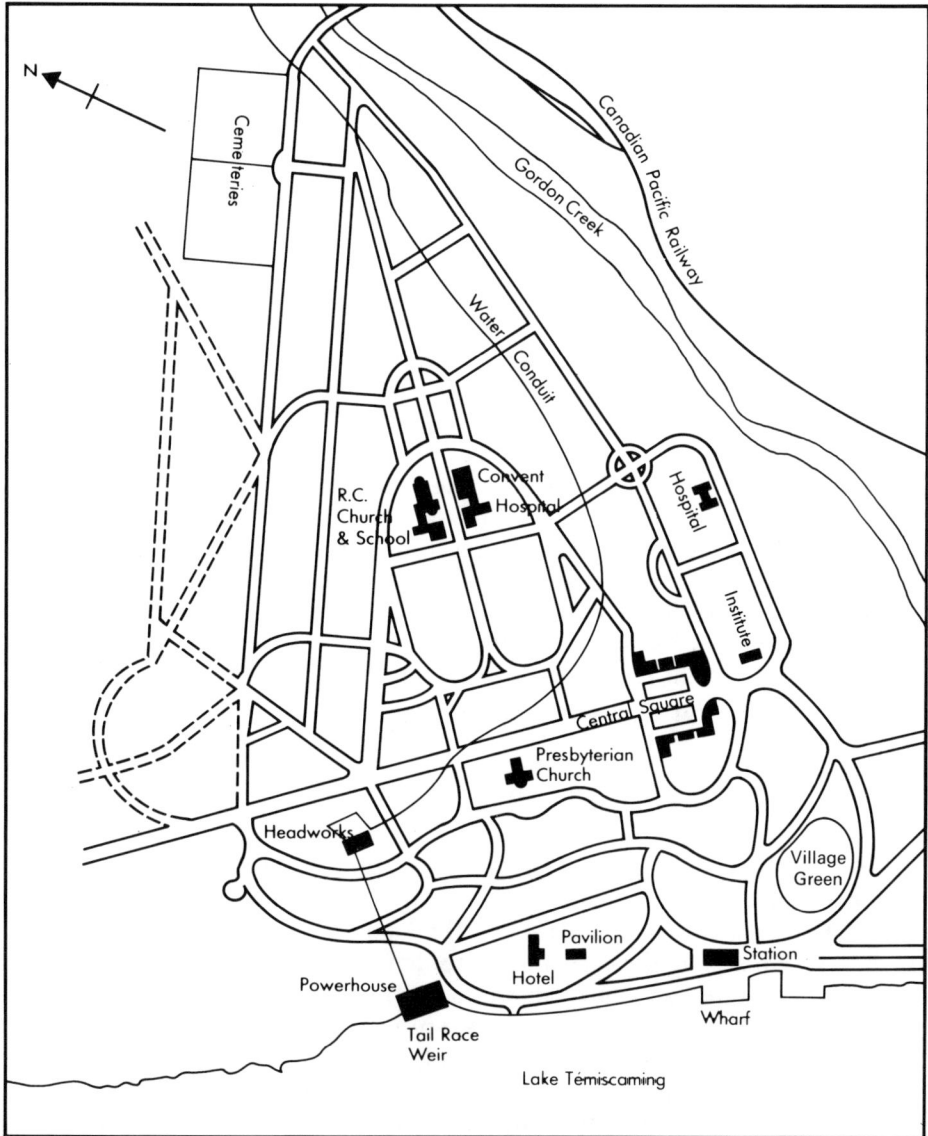

FIGURE 12. Quebec: Kipawa Resource Community, 1917.

Designed by Adams for a subsidiary of the Riordon Paper Company. Set in a remote location, it made skilful use of a hilly and wooded site. As was usual with Adams, shade trees were planted along verges and as many of the original trees as possible were retained, notably around the irregular roads near the lake. It was laid out to Garden City standards. (*Town Planning and Conservation of Life*, January 1919, pp. 12–13)

His one design for a new community was made in 1917 when the Riordon Company sought his advice on a proposed resource town at Kipawa (now Témiscaming) in northern Quebec. Generally rough-and-ready places, resource towns needed an exemplar. Devoting 'a considerable part' of 1917 to it, Adams advised on the site and co-ordinated the work of engineers and architects. His was the preliminary plan, fixing the street layout, the central square, open spaces and public buildings. Conditions were unfavourable – remote territory, the level lakeside ground pre-empted by the mill and its associated activities, leaving him with steep hillsides – but he resolved the site planning problems skilfully. Displaying his usual feeling for the topography, his contoured streets had a grade of only 5 per cent compared with 18 per cent for a grid pattern. The ten-square mile location was endowed liberally with a full range of community facilities, low-density housing, tree-lined and grass-verged roads. These were Garden City features but a stricter comparison would be with the contemporary company towns laid out in the United States by Adams's friends John Nolen and the younger Olmsted. Like them and parallel Canadian projects, Kipawa was an expression of welfare capitalism and the need to make remote resource towns more attractive at a time of labour scarcity. Moreover, Adams noted approvingly, 'It is recognised by the promoters that healthy and agreeable housing and social conditions are of vital importance in securing the efficiency of the workers'. A pleasant and successful example of its genre, the Kipawa plan was publicized widely as a model for other company towns[67].

RESEARCH

Adams was a product of the Chadwick tradition of scientific social investigation and in any case had an academic cast of mind. These influences, reinforced by the investigatory nature of the Commission of Conservation, his wish to give planning the cachet of an academic discipline and his perception that little concrete was known about many of Canada's environmental problems combined to inspire three research projects. One was to be a survey of the housing question, based on a case study of Ottawa. A second was to be an investigation into urban planning and development and a 112-question circular requesting information on municipal and economic matters was sent out to over two hundred towns. The pressure of other work cut short these enquiries at an early stage but the results of a third one were published in 1917 as *Rural Planning and Development*[68].

Based on his experience in rural Britain and his knowledge of rural policies in Europe and North America, *Rural Planning and Development* was his first major work and perhaps his most notable contribution to Canadian planning. Canada's countryside was facing problems quite as severe as those of the cities. Thin soils in some areas and maltreated ones elsewhere, an excess of small farms, under-capitalization, heavy indebtedness, the absence of non-farm occupations, public services, sanitation and facilities for social inter-course, inadequate education and transportation and high fire risks precipitated serious and accelerating depopulation. 'The main causes of these difficulties', stated Adams firmly, 'have been the scattered nature of settle-ment, the using up of capital in speculation which should have been devoted to production, the placing of men on unsuitable land, and inadequate means of communication'. Speculation, promoted by the grid survey and by 'going blindly for results', was the root of many evils – idle land, high land values, rising debts and absentee landlordism. Many of the best lands were held off the market for a greater future killing. Speculation 'has not only been injurious in its legitimate forms but . . . it has been accompanied by much dishonest dealing which has caused hardships to numerous purchasers and destroyed a great deal of confidence in real estate investment in Canada'. Sadly, these 'necessarily crude methods of the pioneer stage of development and civilisation still prevail'[69].

In their place, Adams proposed a radical and comprehensive policy involv-ing a dramatically expanded role for government at all levels. Envisaging a Federal department of development, he suggested that 'The primary and most important duty of governments which control the disposition of the public domain, is so to town-plan and dispose of it that the resultant social development will largely take care of itself'. Land should be surveyed accu-rately, classified and planned according to the topography and economic conditions for convenience, health, amenity and economy. Special attention should be paid to 'the location and grouping of farm buildings so as to secure the closest settlement practicable, the provision of radial highways and the reduction of the unnecessary length of roads'. Government should police private enterprise by strict control of railways, the licensing of real estate operations, the forcible disgorging of land held for profiteering and the payment of improvements by landowners. Substantial investment was recom-mended in university schools of civics and in scientific and vocational train-ing, especially in better farming techniques. Suitably-located new towns, financed by generous low-interest loans, combining the best features of town and country, would provide markets for farm produce, offer alternative employment and assist industrial decentralization. Dutch and Belgian experience demonstrated that 'by proper planning, together with the employ-ment of electricity for power, small village industries can be made as profit-able as those of large cities'. Country folk must be offered also a fuller life for 'We have placed too much on the magnet of ownership to attract the labour-ing farmer to the soil of Canada and too little on the more enduring magnets of social amenities and efficient organisation'[70].

A fundamental reversal of the freebooting doctrine of usefulness, *Rural Planning and Development* did not imply collectivism for 'If we would only apply sound social principles to the early stages of our individualistic system of developing land, we would be less in need of applying socialistic remedies of doubtful value in the later stages'. What Adams advocated was associated individualism, confident that

> Land can be planned and settled in a businesslike way, so as to facilitate co-operation and make social intercourse easy, without any great restraint on the individual, or anything more artificial in the way of organisation than we have at present. The merit of co-operation is that it recognises the individual as an independent unit and leaves unimpaired his self-reliance and initiative[71].

The distillation of over twenty years' study, this report represents Adams's vision of a co-operative yeoman commonwealth and the recognition of interdependence and equality between town and country. Matching the Commission's established high standards of scientific enquiry, it was a courageous challenge to tradition yet in the reform atmosphere of the time it was well received at home and abroad[72].

Post-War Housing and Reconstruction

Adams's contract ran out in 1917 and Sifton, observing that 'There is hardly a part of the country where his wisdom and experience has not made itself felt', promptly offered him a second three-year term. He accepted, there being much unfinished business and nowhere else to go[73]. At this time, there was much discussion of the resettlement of returning veterans. Adams recommended planned communities in rural areas and one such scheme, at Lens, Saskatchewan, was implemented. The Soldiers' Settlement Board, the Surveyor-General and the province's Director of Town Planning co-operated in laying out a 162-acre tract as a 'trading centre' for ex-servicemen farmers, with a civic centre, industrial and commercial districts adjoining the railway, parks and public buildings, zoning and advertising controls. Adams's assistant, Alfred Buckley, remarked sardonically, 'It may be that the better life that was to be the outcome of the war will not, after all, be an empty dream'. The Soldiers' Land Settlement Scheme ultimately placed 100,000 people on farms at a cost of $86,000.000. It enjoyed general support, though nothing was done for those who went to the cities and it was assumed still that Canada's future lay on the frontier[74].

The approach of peace brought also widespread agitation for government-sponsored low-cost housing of publicly-acceptable standard at prices affordable by veterans and workers for whom private enterprise currently was unable to provide. Opinion differed on whether or not the shortage was temporary and on the extent of government intervention required but private enterprise had never provided enough decent low-income housing. In the boom rents rose far faster than real wages and its collapse in 1913 terminated construction and intensified the shortage, soon exacerbated by the war, particularly from 1916 when the war economy got into its stride. Between 1916 and 1918, building costs went up by 48 per cent and rents by 50 per cent. Family formation far outran new construction, rural migrants added to urban overcrowding, half-a-million servicemen were about to return and mass immigration was expected to resume. Practically every town reported 'serious congestion'. Toronto needed 5000 new homes, Winnipeg 3000 and small towns like Welland 500, without considering veterans. Meanwhile, 'the dearness and scarcity of money and labour have prevented, and will continue to prevent, private builders from erecting small houses ... The situation may gradually right itself, but it will take many years and meanwhile much hardship and injury will be caused and serious discontent and dissensions may be created'. Adams blamed the situation on excessive site costs, unsuitable sites, speculation, poor public services, unsound construction, unregulated rooming houses and inadequate sanitation, and suspected that a ring was inflating the prices of building materials. Bad conditions and shortages were undesirable at any time but at the end of a total war, they posed other dangers, contributing to social instability, labour unrest, a debilitated workforce and reduced industrial efficiency[75].

By the summer of 1918, several proposals had been advanced by M.P.s, provincial authorities, the Great War Veterans' Association, manufacturers' associations, boards of trade and the Canadian Association of Building Industries. Most contemplated short-term, self-sustaining schemes of low-interest loans to home buyers. There was no question of subsidized public housing, the Winnipeg housing committee and the realtors of Vancouver advocating a property-owning democracy as a guarantee of social stability. 'Selling houses on the monthly plan', it was claimed, 'encourages the thrifty and the industrious'. Initially, there was a note of effusive patriotism and middle-class paternalism about the schemes, a determination to give 'the gallant sons of Canada ... a better land' and to outlaw the slum. Moreover, 'The home is the starting point for strengthening and elevating our national life, and good housing conditions are to the advantage of the state as well as to the advantage of the community', said one representative of the existing social and political order, upholding traditional values and controls[76].

The Federal Government felt obliged to make a gesture towards the solution of the housing crisis and Adams was requested to report on it to the Cabinet. In his report, made in November 1918, he seized the opportunity to recommend a national programme of reconstruction and development, warning that

> There is ... a danger of treating housing as an isolated problem of reconstruction ... no real success can be attained unless housing, local transportation and land development are dealt with together ... Any scheme to ameliorate the present housing conditions should be part of a scheme of general reconstruction[77].

The centralizing effects of the war upon the North Atlantic countries, his own extensive travels across Canada's vast interior and the influence of several years in a Dominion post encouraged Adams to think in national terms. Though he never believed in more than the most general form of national planning, he advocated Federal development and settlement policies leading to evenly-distributed and viable concentrations of population and economic activity without congestion, the fuller development of the nation's resources and a systematic search for new ones. He made an early attempt to analyse the Canadian urban system, identifying sixteen major industrial regions and a number of lesser ones of mixed industrial-agricultural character. He was concerned particularly that population should be built up in the west and maintained in the east while steps should be taken to halt rural depopulation and the heavy drain of migration to the United States [78].

Adams advised the Cabinet to establish an independent Development Board, composed of experts, to co-operate with both Federal departments and provincial development committees. It should outline a highways programme, sponsor railway extensions in the west, encourage closer settlement, place veterans on the land, establish new industrial centres, increase the agricultural labour force to expand farm output, invest in vocational education and rehabilitation, produce materials for European reconstruction and set up training farms for veterans in Britain. Many of the recommendations sprang from *Rural Planning and Development* and the whole report represented the apotheosis of the scientific manager in the public service, the dispassionate sage who would conserve, exploit and allocate resources on the basis of economy and efficiency, within a traditional framework of democracy and free enterprise[79].

'The supreme task of the next few years' he defined as 'How to stabilise industrial conditions, provide employment in reproductive undertakings and spend every dollar to the best advantage in building up the country'. In this effort, 'the stimulation of building is one of the best methods of promoting employment and stimulating industry'. It would aid adjustment to peace, encourage industrialists to house their workers, foster immigration and 'assist in avoiding industrial unrest'. Nevertheless, Adams had a genuine interest in the housing question apart from its 'multiplier effect' and its role as a social balm. Indeed, in these years, housing was often his chief preoccupation and his condemnation of slums was unequivocal. 'There should not be property rights in dwellings used for human habitation that are a menace to the health, morality and well-being of the race', he insisted, demanding that slumlords should either make good deficiencies or have their property demolished by municipalities without compensation[80]. Yet, however acute accommodation problems were, publicly-subsidized housing on British lines was anathema to him. He told Canadians that the British subsidy 'is, in effect, a gratuity to those who will live in the houses, and however justified to meet an emergency is, of course, economically unsound'. He championed the owner-occupier principle, which 'has become so engrained in Canada that it is best to encourage it in preference to renting'. Where this was not possible, he recommended co-partnership housing, remarking characteristically that 'co-operation is not like socialism – the antithesis of individualism – it is co-operative individualism'. He suggested an initial appropriation of $10 m for housing and $10 m for highways and land development, with matching contributions from the provinces; the bulk would be in loan capital. Experts would draw up housing specifications, designs and model by-laws, advise localities and approve their schemes, taking care to eliminate speculation. Housing estates were to be planned in advance, with adequate open space and services[81].

Not surprisingly, the politicians ignored his utilitarian but potentially expensive and bureaucratic national environmental and reconstruction policy but adopted the gist of his housing proposals. Adams was named as housing advisor to a Cabinet committee charged with disbursing $25 m in twenty-year loans at 5 per cent to individuals, housing societies and similar bodies. The general objectives were:

(a) To promote the creation of dwelling houses of modern character to relieve the congestion of population in cities and towns;
(b) to put within the reach of all working men, particularly returned soldiers, the opportunity of acquiring their own homes at the actual cost of building and land acquired at a fair value, thus eliminating the profits of the speculator;
(c) to contribute to the general health and well-being of the community by encouraging suitable town planning and housing schemes[82].

Municipal schemes had to be approved by provincial authorities, who had to conform to Federal standards laid down, in effect, by Adams. The maximum cost of a house including land and services was set at $4500 and the maximum income for beneficiaries at $3000. A dwelling was to occupy no more than half its lot, have four to seven rooms, house a single family and give adequate light, air and access. Improvements were to be constructed beforehand and one-tenth of the land was to be dedicated as open space. For Adams, who was generally delighted with the programme, 'the unique part of this legislation . . . is the introduction of town planning as an essential part of housing'. He began work eagerly in 1919[83].

He even managed a demonstration project of his own. The Ottawa Housing Commission, which had acquired a 22-acre plot east of the city, was persuaded to let him lay it out. Though it was subdivided already on a grid plat, Adams saw it as 'an exceptional opportunity to create an ideal suburb'. The site was accessible yet countrified but bosky and rocky and his design was 'a good example of Adams's skill in turning apparent difficulties into assets'. A tree-lined boulevard formed the axis and open spaces, one-eighth of the area, were linked into a Lilliputian park system. Residential streets were narrow to

reduce costs and rock outcrops were retained as scenic features, screened by
the site's many fine trees. Appropriately christened Lindenlea, it was a minia-
ture garden suburb paying 'full regard to the need for pleasant surroundings
to homes and for provision for social life and recreation'. Among facilities
were garages, a wading pool, playground, tennis, bowls and a community
hall. Intended to provide 'healthful accommodation purchasable at reasonable
prices', the high cost of the land put a premium on good planning. Every one
of the 168 houses was to have a garden and buildings were to be related to
each other and to the site. Adams intended it to be as much an example of

FIGURE 13. Ottawa: Lindenlea Garden Suburb, 1919–20.

Adams's design for the Ottawa Housing Commission on a rocky, wooded site east of
the city. Note the high level of community provision and the internal 'park system'.
(*The Contract Record*, August 1919, p. 776)

social possibilities as of housing and planning and hoped for co-operative management of Lindenlea by the residents on the lines of British co-partnership communities. Lindenlea was thus another symbol of his 'associated individualism'[84].

A splendid design, Lindenlea commanded the general satisfaction of the home-owners. Adams thought of everything – the optimum separation of pedestrians and traffic, the avoidance of awkward junctions and compact yet low-density housing. Not surprisingly, it was acclaimed by reformers. 'There is little doubt', wrote one, 'that the Lindenlea garden suburb . . . will form one of the most attractive housing developments in North America and that its educative effect upon residents and upon visitors from other cities will be very considerable'. It seemed to herald a new era, for it gave 'a freedom to domestic life which is spiritual as well as physical. Workers who have lived in such towns will not be content with less advantageous surroundings. Building operations must equal these developments or go out of business'. Lindenlea was probably the most complete planning triumph Adams ever enjoyed[85].

THE TOWN PLANNING INSTITUTE OF CANADA

Given his prominent role in the foundation of professional societies in Britain and the United States, it was always likely that Adams would seek to cap his Canadian planning structure with a similar body. However, the initiative which led to the Town Planning Institute of Canada came as much from surveyors and engineers, poorly remunerated and underemployed, seeking financial salvation in diversification and believing that peace would create 'an urgent demand for town planners'. Adams also anticipated a post-war development boom and hoped that the legislation and planning agencies which had been largely dormant during hostilities would then become active. Moreover, approaching the end of his second contract, he sought to organize indigenous professionals in order to maintain and extend his bridgehead. By 1918, he was acquainted with most of those in the environmental professions who were interested in planning and calculated that they constituted a sufficient core for an independent professional body. Furthermore, a planners' organization would assist in the professional, public and political acceptance of planning as a legitimate and beneficial community activity, though he anticipated no overnight success. 'We shall have to be content to grow slowly as a profession', he remarked[86].

The Dominion Land Surveyors began the process leading to a professional institute in 1917 and in the spring of 1918 Adams became the chairman of a sub-committee which included engineers like Cauchon. By May 1919, it was possible to launch the Town Planning Institute of Canada, accompanied, inevitably, by a paper from Adams on 'Prospects of a Town Planning Profession in Canada'. He took the initiative in practically every facet of the

Institute's early life, serving two terms as the inaugural President[87]. Other members deferred to his counsel and his hand can be seen in every statement. The Institute was described as

> a group of professional men interested in town planning and having some knowledge of one or more aspects of the subject for the purpose of advancing the study of town planning and civic design and of the arts and sciences as applied to those subjects, and, incidentally, to secure the association of those engaged in or interested in the practice of town planning as architects, engineers or surveyors[88].

Its structure followed closely that of its British model, with full, associate, legal and honorary membership categories. Full membership was obtainable by examination or by membership of the British institute or of the American Association of Landscape Architects (with which Adams had close connections). Though he was a founder and vice-president of the American City Planning Institute, Adams had too many reservations about its professional standing to offer automatic membership to his colleagues. Organization was completed by a Dominion charter in 1922 and the establishment of active branches in Toronto, Montreal, Ottawa and Vancouver, a journal and committees on legislation, education and publications. It enjoyed an early prosperity, quickly enrolling over a hundred members. About half of the 1920 total of 113 came from Ottawa (forty-eight), with nineteen from Toronto, seventeen from Montreal, nineteen from the west, eight from the east and two from the United States. In 1921, there were thirty surveyors, twenty-seven engineers, sixteen architects, five landscape architects, two town planners and twenty-four 'other' members[89].

Adams had great ambitions for his creation, though its concept of planning was still essentially one of rational land-use allocation, little advanced from 1914:

> Town planning may be defined as the scientific and orderly disposition of land and buildings in use and development with a view to obviating congestion and securing economic and social efficiency, health and well-being in urban and rural communities[90].

He intended to co-ordinate the environmental professions, promote 'the interchange of professional knowledge' and encourage research in planning and related subjects. In particular, he wished to create 'a trained class of professional men' and urged that the Institute should 'consider what steps should be taken to promote educational courses in the universities'. He aimed 'to make town planning a branch of applied science with the imprimatur of a university' and establish 'a course at one or more of the universities with a special diploma in town planning' following a first degree in architecture or engineering. For existing planners and interested laymen, there should be summer schools and extension classes. An association with the universities would enhance the prestige of planning, confirm its status as an independent discipline, endow it with 'the most authoritative qualification', facilitate research and furnish the new profession with a sound training. It was argued that 'the greater responsibility for the development of town planning in Canada rests with the universities' and they were wooed with the lure that they had 'a unique opportunity' to associate themselves with a coming subject of immense social and academic potential. Adams lectured at most universities in 1919–20, attempting to inspire the foundation of planning courses. Not everyone in the Institute shared his enthusiasm for university training, surveyors and engineers like James Ewing and Cauchon fearing that a stream of graduates would exacerbate their already-parlous employment and remuneration situation. Nevertheless, T.P.I.C. members lectured on extension courses at McGill and Toronto Universities and Horace Seymour was appointed a part-time lecturer at Toronto in 1923. In organizational terms, the Institute followed the British example but the university connection reflected developing American practice and more particularly demonstrated Adams's evolving conception of planning as a viable and independent academic discipline and profession[91].

HIGH-WATER MARK, 1919

By 1919, Adams had completed the outline of his intended planning structure, though some details were missing. Nevertheless, given the disruptive effects of the war, the infant state of Canadian planning in 1914 and the single-handed nature of his enterprise, his achievements were noteworthy. He had sustained a massive and pervasive propaganda campaign. Four provinces had accepted his legislative and organizational advice and he was on good enough terms with the remainder (and possessed the persistence) to entertain hopes that they would do so in peacetime. Like his fellow planning pioneers, he believed that time was on his side. The scope for impressive demonstrations of his art was circumscribed by war and the level of Canadian social progress but he had been active in every province and Richmond, Kipawa and Lindenlea exemplified brilliantly what he could achieve in the most difficult circumstances. *Rural Planning and Development* had won wide acclaim and had been adopted as a textbook in universities. The Federal housing programme had been organized with customary thoroughness and he had brought to birth a professional association representative of all sections of the Dominion and all the relevant professions. His charm, good humour, patience, tact, energy, commitment, lucidity and efficiency were legendary. In five years, he had made many friends and his enemies could be numbered on the fingers of one hand. He identified himself with his adopted country, for which he retained a genuine affection.

Above all, Adams had offered Canadians a comprehensive vision of an integrated planning system based upon inter-governmental and public and private co-operation, compulsion being confined to the elimination of abuses and to mandatory injunctions to plan rationally all future development. The embodiment of an assumed scientific professionalism, Adams placed great faith in the impartiality of experts, assigning them key roles at every stage of the planning process and providing for the establishment, training and recognition of a professional cadre. Though his perception of the possibilities and benefits of positive public intervention was hostile and conservative, he took into account economic and social as well as physical factors to a degree that few, if any, other contemporaries matched. His horizon embraced not only city and homestead but, at an earlier date than his fellows, metropolis, province and even nation.

In an extraordinary solo effort, he got through a prodigious amount of work during the war. The 'Grand Seigneur' of Canadian planning could boast that 'Probably in no country was there more activity than there was in Canada during the critical years 1914–19'. His opportune arrival at the outbreak of war may well have saved Canadian planning from nemesis. Now, he was convinced that he had attained his goal, that planning had become an established feature of national life. 'A widespread sentiment in favour of city planning has been created throughout the Dominion', he claimed, 'The town planning work of the Commission of Conservation is now beginning to produce substantial results'. He had built a platform from which Canadian planning could take off in peacetime. The auguries seemed favourable. Pre-war progressivism appeared to have been reinforced by the experience of total war. The passions of class and region (always excepting Quebec) had been submerged in a common cause. Traditional restraints upon government activity were loosened and Federal authority was enhanced, while emerging concerns with racial survival, economic efficiency, social justice and harmonious labour relations were encouraged. 'A nation of comrade workers' looked forward to 'nothing less than complete social reconstruction'[92].

Adams shared this euphoria, exclaiming that 'We are at the opening of a new era of social construction and national expansion'. He observed with pleasure 'a growing sentiment in favour of scientific methods' and counselled that 'The great need of the moment . . . is the prudent and intelligent direction of trends towards reform'. However, while acknowledging that 'There is a genuine striving after "the justice that is more than liberty" among a great many who see the need for sane reform', he warned that 'there is always a good deal of blind agitation for change and the levelling down of society which is nothing less than a form of public insanity'. Despite admitting that the war 'has brought new ideas', his own prescription remained unchanged – the *via media* of liberalism, seeking the maintenance of social unity and solving labour unrest by giving workers 'a common interest in their work by means of some form of co-partnership'. Given the persistence of a congenial social climate, the future of Canadian planning seemed bright with hope[93].

Chapter Five

Canada: the Years of Trial and Disappointment, 1919–1930

THE POST-WAR CLIMATE

Wartime idealism did not long survive the coming of peace. The 'New Era' was swept aside in 1919, a watershed year, by recession, disillusionment, strife, conservatism, business dominance and demands for 'Normalcy'. Class, sectional, ethnic and religious tensions replaced wartime unity and contentious issues appeared unresolvable. The bitterly fragmented politics of the 1920s were presided over by the frigidly-negative Arthur Meighen or the cunningly-vague Mackenzie King. The economy was sluggish and only in the late 1920s was Canada warmed slightly by America's heady prosperity. 'The desire for the improvement of social and economic conditions in Canada and the spirit in doing things for the public good during those (wartime) years', observed Adams ruefully, 'does not seem to have been maintained during the period of reconstruction since 1919'[1].

If peace seemed unpropitious for planning, the war had contrived to undermine Adams's structure even as he built it. Especially from 1916, when it became a total conflict, it diverted attention, resources and manpower from planning. Adams laboured under the disadvantage 'of undertaking the creation of a stronger public opinion in favour of town planning and housing in Canada, when the whole energies of the nation were occupied in the great and imperative duty of national defence'. Wartime shortages of funds denied him professional assistance until 1918 and effectively prevented him from training successors. Provinces postponed either legislation or enforcement until peacetime while municipal finances, already straitened by the deleterious effects of the boom, were driven to the point of collapse. Although transport and industrial bottlenecks were thrown into sharper focus and the cessation of housebuilding exacerbated existing shortages, the interruption of urban growth made planning seem irrelevant[2].

DEMISE OF THE COMMISSION OF CONSERVATION

An early casualty of wartime stringencies and post-war social bleakness was the Civic Improvement League, 'never properly constituted owing to the war'. Adams had 'expected that now that the war is over it will be thoroughly organized and become a powerful educational factor in the Dominion'. The downswing in the reform cycle and his own preoccupations elsewhere precluded that, and meekly it expired. Moreover, the progressive recommendations of *Rural Planning and Development* went unconsidered and played no part in post-war rural political controversy; freewheeling frontier individualism persisted. Furthermore, he had 'not much hope of some of the provinces doing anything' in housing and planning[3].

By the end of 1919, therefore, Adams 'seemed to sense the steam going out of the Federal leadership in the town planning field' and, feeling that he had accomplished all that he could hope to achieve, began to disengage himself from Canada and build a new career elsewhere. Sifton had retired from the Commission of Conservation in 1918, incensed, it was said, at the Dominion's refusal to increase staff salaries – Adams's salary had remained virtually unchanged from its initial figure despite massive wartime inflation. Since he had 'several other very lucrative offers open to him', he moved in February 1920 on to a part-time basis, at $625 a month for eight months of the year, enabling him to undertake private work as chief consultant on planning for a new firm, American City Consultants. It was pointed out that he 'could earn several times the amount Canada has been paying him' since he was 'so eminent in his profession that the undertakings for which his services are solicited must at times be of such character as to make irresistible appeal to his professional ambition'. Until his contract ran out in August 1923, he appeared to spend less time in Canada each year[4].

As Adams may have recognized, Sifton's departure and the new atmosphere of austerity and retreat from wartime powers in Ottawa numbered the days of the Commission of Conservation. It fell victim in January 1921 to a combination of intra-government jealousies, intrigues, policy conflicts and parsimony. Sifton's biographer, J. W. Dafoe, noted accurately that 'The wounded *amour propre* of Ministers was seconded by the jealousy of departmental officials who had long resented the activities by the Commission which they regarded as trenching upon their powers'. The Meighen government despatched it with relish despite Sifton's stricture that 'the whole course of the government's conduct . . . is entirely discreditable'. Other defenders in Parliament argued that the Commission was a 'pioneer in many lines' and achieved 'results of far-reaching importance'[5].

Adams regarded the Commission's demise as 'a great misfortune'. It was tragic that a body 'which endeavoured to give the country a lead in rural and city planning . . . should have been destroyed at the very time its activities were most needed'. He laid the blame on a lack of imagination and statesmanship on the part of the politicians. There is no doubt that Canada lost much for the Commission articulated a conception of national resource management founded upon scientific enquiry and the long view. It represented a timely reversal of historic attitudes to nature's bounty and the value of human life which bordered on the rapacious and callous. It was a unique co-operative enterprise between the Dominion and the provinces and between politicians, businessmen, academics, reformers and experts. It acquired a reputation for impartiality, outspokenness and authoritativeness. It introduced to the nation the incorruptible expert who would fashion a universally beneficial future on the basis of unimpeachable research. It was a legacy of British Utilitarianism and American Pragmatism, to both of which Adams subscribed[6].

Its going reduced Adams's influence still further. The Town Planning Branch was transferred to the National Parks Division at Interior. Though information and advice would be available on request, Adams told Burditt that 'we will not have the same freedom as before in advising municipalities'. For the most part, his work was on Federal sites at Ottawa and in National Parks administrative centres. The one plan of consequence that he made was for Jasper, in association with the Surveyor-General, E. G. Deville. As usual, he made good use of an attractive site, eliciting the approbation 'how admirably this little town fits its site on a plateau at the foot of the great mountain ranges'. Adams retained the wooded nature of the location, drawing roads in gentle curves alongside the railway which had a pleasant station approach surrounded by a business centre. Garden suburb housing for residents was complemented by abundant camping and recreational grounds. Designed in 1921, three years later it was 'a well built up and flourishing community'[7].

COLLAPSE OF THE FEDERAL HOUSING PROGRAMME

A second victim of post-war Federal retrenchment was the housing programme. Meighen wound it up from the spring of 1921, against a chorus of protests from housing associations, chambers of commerce, municipalities and veterans' organizations, replying brusquely to one petitioner, 'The matter of house construction is not one with which the Federal Government has really any responsibility'. Where the Dominion refused to tread, not unnaturally the provinces declined to go. The scheme had provided 6244 houses in 179 municipalities at a cost of $23.5 m. Adams celebrated it as 'completely successful' because 'It stimulated building at a time of great shortage and when money was difficult to obtain'. Moreover, 'the class of building is better because of the example afforded by the houses erected under Government auspices'. Timely and based on the right principles, it had ensured that 'With neither coddling nor interference with private enterprise, and in spite of combines, the erection of new houses is gradually overcoming the effects of the war shortage'[8].

In fact, the programme was a dismal failure. Housing was dealt with in isolation and its projects did not even fulfil the conditions Adams laid down. No systematic enquiry into needs was undertaken and municipal estimates of shortages were often far less than those of reformers. No provision was made for rural areas. The money available was no more than a token sum and, despite generous mortgage terms, the scheme failed to reach the lowest income groups. As the Winnipeg Board of Health explained, 'few working men are in a position to furnish the required $500 or $600 in cash'. It feared that 'the number of houses which will be erected under the present scheme will be but a drop in a bucket when considered as a means of rectifying the seriously bad housing conditions which have existed in our City for some years'[9].

The response from the provinces was anything but uniform. Quebec was indifferent and Adams angrily 'made it clear that this province has been very backward'. Alberta also did nothing while the rest numbered their construction in hundreds. Only Ontario tackled the problem with any vigour, investing of $2 m of its own funds and building, in co-operation with the Federal authorities, 3233 houses in seventy communities. A provincial committee headed by Sir John Willison had made recommendations similar to those advanced by Adams but though Ontario had the best record, it had also the greatest shortage, which remained substantial after the programme ceased[10]. Construction, which did recover after 1918, fell off again in 1923 and by 1926, Adams's former assistant, Alfred Buckley, was reporting that 'practically no homes are being built in Canada for the low-paid wage-earner other than shacks'[11]. The perceptive Burditt summed up the programme's shortcomings:

> The general feeling seems to be that at the present excessive cost of building, the proffered loan by Government will be of little or no advantage as it will not be possible even with capital at 5% to build houses that could be rented at any figure which it is possible for workmen to pay, and unless the Government can do something in the way of reducing cost I fear but little will be accomplished[12].

None of the parties involved – politicians, experts, reformers or the public – seem to have been clear on what the programme should do, whether it should attempt to house substantial numbers or whether it should give a temporary fillip to the construction industry and offer private enterprise a demonstration of low-cost housing. Many reformers and members of the public demanded that shortages should be met but most politicians and experts felt that a brief injection of public funds and a set of desirable standards were all that was necessary. The Federal Government's guiding principles were essentially negative – a short-term programme at negligible cost which would avert serious discontent, offer a modicum of stimulation to the private sector and the labour market and avoid the taint of collectivism. Within those limited terms, its programme was successful[13].

However, Adams and the government were dealing with a long-term problem of some magnitude having causes far deeper than a wartime upset of the free market. Had they really wished to solve it, a number of alternatives were possible. They could have relied on the private sector and imposed stringent regulations on the price of materials and ensured housebuilding priority in resource allocation. Such a degree of interference in the market economy in peacetime was unprecedented and never contemplated. The application of new, cost-reducing technology and materials was not generally possible for another generation. A third possibility was a very substantial increase in real wages but, given the reactionary nature of Canadian business and the chaotic post-war economic situation, this was not a feasible alternative. The final policy choice was outlined by Adams's administrative assistant, Alfred Buckley:

> The only way in which we can obtain the effective improvement of the housing conditions of the poorest wage-earners is in first carrying out a policy of building houses through municipalities by government aid, meeting the loss out of public funds, and simultaneously passing legislation to enforce higher standards in respect of existing houses and those erected by private enterprise[14].

Adams and his superiors, however, had rejected subsidies on ideological and financial grounds. It is hard to escape the feeling that they were more afraid of committing the sin of collectivism than of failing to satisfy the housing needs of the people. More than anything else, Adams's housing policy revealed his fundamental attachment to Victorian liberalism.

Even Lindenlea was not an unalloyed triumph for him. It failed to become a model project because the housing programme came to an early halt and in any case mostly ignored planning principles. High building costs delayed its completion and the design of the houses was put into other hands, several builders being engaged, without Adams being consulted. The housing, badly sited and often ugly, was out of sympathy with Adams's plan. The financial and housing difficulties brought criticism down on him. One architect maintained that the residents were unhappy with their homes while a city alderman described Adams as 'a faddist' and his design as 'a crazy quilt'. Adams responded vigorously, pointing to his excellent relationship with the residents. He had 'never heard criticism of the plan' and asserted correctly that 'as a town planning project Lindenlea was completely successful'. Despite high costs, it could have been made profitable had his advice been taken. Withdrawing from all connection with the project in April 1920, he pointed out that it was 'carefully laid out, with ample open space and the preservation of trees has been a distinct asset towards meeting any imperfections in the buildings and given them an added value without which there would have been much more room for criticism'. Others had degraded it into 'an ordinary real estate development'[15].

LEGISLATIVE CHANGES

The central feature of Adams's strategy, the campaign for provincial planning legislation and administration, came to a halt by the end of 1919 and subsequent efforts met with little success. Ontario, though adding new planning powers under a variety of acts, failed to co-ordinate them or to give municipalities sufficient authority[16]. The high point was a new act in Saskatchewan in 1920, 'probably the most advanced compulsory town planning act in existence', and 'aggressively administered' by a professional staff. Adams saw it as the cutting edge of his post-war policy, for 'When the whole of Canada has similar legislation and an equally efficient organisation we shall have an effective national town planning policy'. However, few of the provinces made much use of their acts. Even the Saskatchewan officials, though dealing with over two hundred applications in 1922, reported that 'It cannot be said that the rate of progress has been sensational'. Most of the work was elementary and they felt that 'The chief problem appears to be in persuading local authorities that orderly development is for the common good'. The growth-oriented west eschewed planning with its inherent delays and constraints and 'Owing to the existing building depression and the continued shortage of houses, councils are loath to discuss plans of future improvement or submit to building regulations'. The compulsory powers quickly proved inoperable and growing home rule sentiment resented provincial overlordship[17]. Manitoba also appointed a town planning comptroller, W. E. Hobbs, but he became frustrated with the insignificance of his work and resigned after a few years[18]. Horace Seymour, appointed Director of Town Planning in Alberta in 1929, updated its legislation, though retaining Adams's basic aims – the promotion of efficiency, health, natural beauty and convenience and the avoidance of residential and traffic congestion. It was thus still a development control measure on accepted 'scientific town planning' lines. Initially, Seymour was encouragingly busy with conferences, propaganda, education, advice and work with no less than fourteen planning commissions but he became an early victim of depression economies[19].

Adams's own legislation in fact proved a major handicap to planning activity and came under increasing fire. Noulan Cauchon, always one of his covert critics, indicting 'the rather wheezy band' of provincial acts, remarked that 'some of them are inoperative and well-nigh useless'. Critics in Saskatchewan and Nova Scotia complained that they were 'difficult to understand, cumbersome as to procedure for action thereunder with control too greatly centralized in the Minister' while 'exception was taken to the compulsory features'. Even Adams's loyal supporter W. F. Burditt concluded that the legislation was insufficiently adapted to Canadian needs and that the town planning scheme was not a suitable vehicle for Canadian planning[20]. More and more calls were heard for American-style acts and Seymour's Alberta statute and Hobbs's amendments to the Manitoba law began to move in that direction. The real pointer to the future, however, was the British Columbia act of 1925. The Vancouver branch of the Town Planning Institute of Canada organized the lobby which resulted in its enactment, though it was 'largely disembowelled in its passage' by real estate interests who wished to keep planning inexpensive and amenable to their influence. 'Based largely upon similar legislation now in force in a majority of States of the United States', it was a simple enabling act permitting municipalities to undertake comprehensive development control master planning and zoning[21]. For all that it favoured the realtor's rather than the planner's idea of planning, it was better adapted to a society much more closely related to American social and spatial patterns, especially in the west, than to those of the motherland, whose own legislation was a considerable disincentive to planning. Even the new and supposedly-celebrated Saskatchewan act of 1920 was replaced in 1928 by a simple, effective measure incorporating features of the British Columbia statute. The province's planning director, Stewart Young, in praising its simplicity, noted that more by-laws had been passed in one year under the new act than in the whole life of previous legislation. The planner A. G. Dalzell regarded the 1928 law as a hopeful stimulus to the other provinces to remove dead legislation by acts better suited to Canadian requirements, conditions and institutions[22].

THE DILEMMA OF THE PLANNING PROFESSION

Adams had hoped that a self-sustaining planning profession would consolidate his system but many planners came increasingly to dissociate themselves from it. Indigenous planners failed signally to measure up to the task he left them, lacking political 'clout', self-confidence, assured professional standing and general public approbation. Most members of the T.P.I.C. felt only a marginal commitment to planning; to them it was simply a source of additional income. Only Dalzell, Seymour, both former Adams assistants, and Cauchon devoted the greater part of their time to planning. Cauchon, the one Canadian with anything like a national reputation and highly respected by his fellow-professionals, was often ahead of his time, impractical or simply baffling[23]. Though all Canadian planners were meliorists, they lacked any other common perspective and missed the prestige, direction and cohesion that Adams and the Commission of Conservation had given them, as can be seen from their attempt to reconstruct the national advisory service in 1927. In a memorandum to the Mackenzie King government, they lamented that 'Since the close of the Great War the town planning movement has not advanced in our Dominion at a rate comparable with Canada's importance as a nation or with progress in other countries'. Calling for 'a Town Planning Advisor of high technical standing and practical experience', they described the existing provision via the National Parks office as 'entirely inadequate'. They lacked the political weight to compel King, despite his professed interest in planning, to take any action[24].

Most planners were lukewarm towards Adams's proposals for university planning schools and, after his departure, relations with universities were intermittent and desultory. Planners were unable to convince universities of either the intellectual worth of their subject or of a demand for trained planners. In 1931, the T.P.I.C. reported that 'In one or two Canadian universities, town planning has been recognised in Cinderella fashion but there is no recognition of it, so far as we know, as a vital subject in applied social science which cannot be neglected'. It was a disappointing outcome for Adams and ironic that at the time Canada's dons were turning a cold shoulder towards planning, the Massachusetts Institute of Technology called upon him to present a course there and that he went on to play a leading part in the establishment of American planning education. Canada lagged far behind her neighbour, and the mother country, in academic preparation for a planning career[25].

In the 1920s, Canadian planners remained committed to the ideology of the Commission of Conservation – rational resource allocation on a basis of survey data analysis and long-term, trend-ameliorating development control planning in a regional context. They sought core city containment, metropolitan regional decentralization, evenly-distributed compact settlement, the elimination and prevention of abuses, and the establishment of decent standards of accommodation, amenity, convenience and services. They offered Canada nothing revolutionary, believing that by 'scientific and practical' planning, eschewing the extremes of unbridled liberalism and socialist regimentation in favour of the liberal mean, they could achieve all desirable ends within the framework of democracy and private enterprise. Though Buckley and Dalzell could be described as social democrats, most went no further than Adams in holding that 'a great part of town planning consists in preventing owners of private property from erecting buildings and laying out land in a way that causes injury to their neighbours and the community'. Their middle-class sensibilities shaken rudely by syndicalist eruptions like the Winnipeg General Strike, they agreed with Alfred Buckley that 'decent living conditions for workers are not only possible but imperative if revolution and disaster are to be avoided'. Possibilists and marginal adjusters, science, a discoverable and even-handed truth, was their new god. Thus, 'Canadian planning did not go beyond dealing with symptoms to basic changes in the social structure'. It may have been true that 'Belief in philanthropy, social engineering and the salvation of science was its ultimate weakness' but, in the Canadian context, a truly collectivist alternative had no place[26].

Even this mild, technocratic reformism was unacceptable in the business-led society of the 1920s and planners found themselves in a dilemma. They had either to conform to current political and social orthodoxy or attack it. If they rejected it, they would be unable to exercise any influence but if they adopted it, their aims would be circumscribed. In the event, they were ambivalent, both critical and complaisant. Lamenting that 'Canada is not yet awake to the immense economic and sociological importance of town planning', they compared the Dominion unfavourably with its mentors:

> In the United States regional planning is growing and its importance is being realised. The same is true in Great Britain. It is hard to understand why Canada should be so timid in the matter of town planning. No country stands to gain more by proper preparation for a future population[27].

Warning that 'Canada is falling behind in the application of foresight and science to the development of its urban and rural growth', Adams still spent much of his time despatching myths and errors. He attacked the fallacy 'that complete liberty to the individual to use his land as he likes is good for business as well as a sound democratic principle' and the canard that 'land speculation is harmless'. He complained that 'Urban land is not planned and sub-divided to aid the worker to get a convenient and healthy home, nor to enable the city to obtain an economic system of development but principally to yield profit to the sub-divider'. Condemning municipal indifference to planning, he regretted that 'Many opportunities that exist for undertaking expert services are not made available by those in control of public affairs'. He abhorred the contemporary crazes for skyscrapers and municipal tax bonuses to industry – 'an immoral proceeding which should be stopped'. The albatross of the 'City Beautiful' still hung round planning's neck for 'The average man thinks of town planning in terms of increased expenditures on fanciful improvements instead of . . . the regulation of the growth of the city in the interests of economy'[28]. His confreres endorsed the view that 'Owners of property, particularly in the cities, do not appear to want the slightest restrictions to be placed on their holdings' and there was universal agreement that 'the last citadel of opposition to town planning in Canada is the real estate operator'. The country was 'in the grip of the land speculator who is little concerned about the civic drift to the slums so long as he can turn over his land'. Other sections of the community seemed equally indifferent, manufacturers failing to appreciate the beneficial effects on productivity and labour relations of good housing and efficient communities, while labour dismissed planning as 'a fad of the rich'[29].

Though they attacked bitterly the brash business ethos of the times and its leading environmental spokesmen, the realtors, ultimately planners sought to come to terms with them, some more willingly than others, and the reformist tinge plainly visible in the Adams era was bleached clean. In order to gain the ear of the elite, James Ewing declared that 'We shall have to show them that the expenditure of one dollar will bring in two or three more'. Apologists for accommodation with the prevailing philosophy proclaimed that 'Modern town planning is fundamentally and all the time a "business proposition"' and that 'All planning must be judged by marketable results'. By creating 'the City Useful and Usable', business-oriented planning catered for growth, since 'the essence of town planning is to provide for expansion'. Even more specific overtures were made to the property interests, the Regina Town Planning Association affirming blandly that 'the object of a town planning scheme or by-laws is primarily protective ... They are intended to ensure the permanence of investment in real property'. Far from reducing speculative investment, 'orderly development recommended by town planners *increases* values'. At times planning seemed to prostitute itself to real estate yet even this degree of abasement was insufficient to establish planning as a normal public function[30].

The Nature of Canadian Planning, 1919–1930

Given this equivocation and crisis of identity, it is hardly surprising that Canadian planning achieved little in the post-war decade. There were a handful of master plans, often sponsored by chambers of commerce, but for the most part planning was confined to sub-division layout, highways and zoning. As Seymour remarked disconsolately to Cauchon, 'Nearly every surveyor in town advertises himself as a town planner. Practically all of the work we have done connected with this has been in the layout of sub-divisions'. In a feverish bid to cope with the motoring explosion, road widenings, new circumferential and radial highways, by-passes and parkways were constructed with the object of smoother and safer traffic flows. Alternative strategies were not considered as 'Not one Canadian planner sought to reverse the increasing use of the automobile'. Adams articulated the universal view: 'The needs of motor traffic demand the construction of new and improved highways'. Thus planning came to serve vehicles before people and the profession was unable to foresee the anti-social effects of near-universal car ownership and truck-borne freight. Their anxiety to accommodate the motor vehicle underlined the planners' clear commitment to mere trend amelioration. Zoning spread from across the border like a prairie fire and, as in America, it was often carried out by laymen and served as a substitute for comprehensive planning, generally with the sole object of preserving residential class segregation and property values[31].

The struggle to complete and implement earlier plans continued. Burditt nursed the Saint John scheme to completion in April 1922 but then fell foul of county objections. Though he fought on, with occasional advice from Adams and Dalzell, he admitted that 'Saint John is growing so slowly that most people seem to be more interested in improving what we have than in planning for future development'. Finally approved in 1931, it seems to have been engulfed in the general depression, an unjust reward for Burditt's epic persistence over two decades. Halifax, like Saint John virtually stagnant, received provincial approval for its plan – described by Adams as 'the most advanced city plan in Canada' – in the early 1920s though it appears then to have been pigeon-holed[32].

In Ontario, the province laid out a small model town at Kapuskasing and Haileybury was replanned by Seymour after a fire. Hamilton flirted with planning, engaging Cauchon for separate railway and war memorial projects. Toronto continued with piecemeal improvements, much to Adams's chagrin. In Ottawa, Cauchon worked tirelessly for the implementation of the Bennett plan and had visions of a long-distance canal and parkway to the United States. He had some success with zoning and took up Adams's call for a Federal District Commission, eventually introduced by Mackenzie King in 1927 as part of a 'City Beautiful' exercise in national (and personal) prestige. The most advanced planning was done on the Essex Border. Nine small communities began co-ordinating utility projects in 1917 and later obtained other powers to include parks, highways, rapid transit, subdivision control and even airports. Conferring substantial public benefits, it had Adams's warm support and was 'the most significant example of regional planning in Eastern Canada before World War II'[33].

Montreal, castigated by Ewing as 'cumbersome and unwieldy' and 'a disjointed aggregation of inharmonious parts', was the subject of renewed attempts by the T.P.I.C., local architects and civic improvers to secure a metropolitan plan but their pressure achieved only a technical advisory commission and random zoning[34]. In the west, there were promising beginnings in many communities but work rarely got beyond the discussion stage, zoning and highway projects. The brightest spot in Canada was Vancouver. Energetic work by the local T.P.I.C. branch led to a long-term master plan for the urban region by the doyen of American planners, Harland Bartholomew. Its implementation with 'despatch and energy' between 1926 and 1931 was in distinct contrast to the long-drawn out British-style schemes elsewhere. There was 'slight disappointment that the work was not given to a Canadian planner' (though Seymour became resident engineer) but it was a commentary on the insignificance of the profession in Canada that this prize job went to an American. It was also a further landmark in the increasing identification of Canadians with American urbanism[35].

Adams's work as a consultant was concentrated in the industrial belt of Ontario, where he was well known. Between 1922 and 1930, he turned out development control plans for Kitchener, Welland, London and Windsor and was associated with his protégé Seymour at Kitchener's neighbour Waterloo. All were thirty-year flexible outline plans, based on thorough civic surveys, accurate and detailed maps and careful data analysis. Accepting the inevitability of growth, Adams told his clients, 'Your task is to make it a growth of quality' and anticipated two- or three-fold increases in population. In the hope of stimulating regional planning, he advised co-operation with neighbouring communities – Kitchener and Waterloo, Windsor with the Essex Border and Welland with the Niagara Frontier region. Advising that it was 'better and cheaper for the city to extend its boundaries before the land is sub-divided', he recommended that political boundaries should accord with economic and political realities. He set out to establish a regulatory frame-work for the private development process – firm building lines, subdivision control to ensure compact development, height, use and bulk zoning. The railways, whom he regarded as chiefly responsible for the urban mess, were told bluntly to pay for the cleaning-up operation – better station approaches ('the biggest defect' at Kitchener), and the elimination of cross-town lines and grade crossings. He proposed hierarchies of highway widths based on func-tions, the reservation in advance of need of land for streets, public buildings and open space, civic centres, park systems and self-financing parkways. Firmly attached to single family housing, he was also elitist in that he stressed the need to keep wealthy citizens in the community, not only for their tax contributions but also because he saw them as the natural civic and cultural leaders. Recommending patient municipal propaganda campaigns, he emphasized that it was 'necessary to "sell" the plan to the public'. He was, characteristically, a possibilist, telling the burghers of Welland that 'I have not attempted to put forward any idealistic scheme that is unattainable'[36].

The degree of success he achieved varied. At Welland, his plan was made following a park report in 1922 but its fate is unknown. His work at London was halted by municipal economies in 1923. The final report for Windsor, due in September 1930, seems to have been an early casualty of the depression. At Kitchener, he had to hand over to Seymour on his appointment as director of the Regional Plan of New York in 1923 and Seymour also took on the London contract when planning resumed, thanks to Chamber of Commerce sponsor-ship, in 1925. London watered down the planning and zoning recommenda-tions and blew hot and cold about planning for many years but Kitchener's was the first plan to become law in Ontario and the city further secured a provincial zoning amendment. Both the plan and the zoning scheme were well received locally and successfully implemented[37]. Adams's plans were made for local business and professional establishments and were unoriginal, flatly pragmatic and trend-adjusting exercises. Based on a settled, relatively simple technique, they differed little from contemporary master-plans in other parts of the English-speaking world.

Adams's most interesting commission was in fact in Newfoundland, then an independent dominion. In 1923, he and his partner Francis Longstreth Thompson designed a new resource community for the Newfoundland Power and Paper Company. Situated on the east coast, in 'a shallow, sunny valley', at the head of a fjord, rocky and bosky, it was attractive but a difficult design

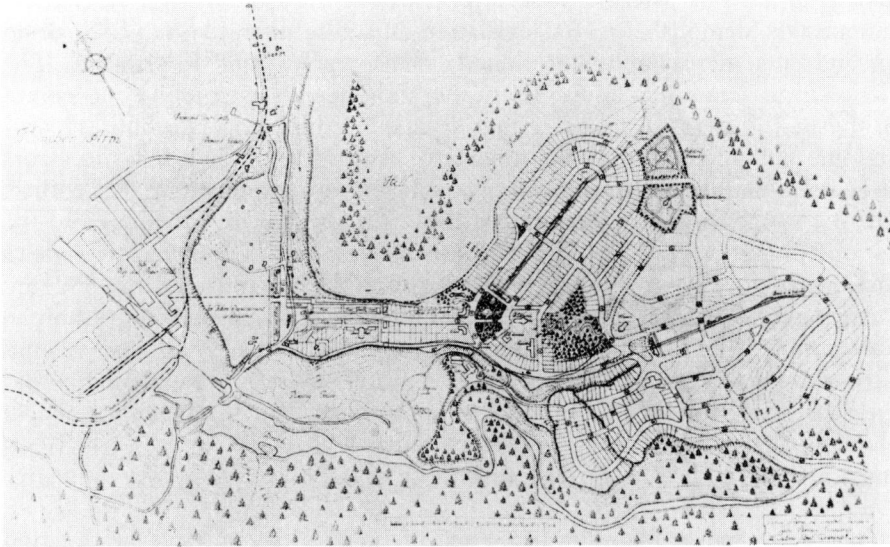

FIGURE 14. Corner Brook, Newfoundland: Resource Community, 1923.

By Adams and F. L. Thompson. They made optimum use of a narrow and difficult site, hemmed in by steep wooded hills. The pulp and paper mill is at the mouth of the creek and a jetty and railway station were proposed for the north shore. Playing fields lie alongside the creek and the civic centre is also set in park land. Two cemeteries lie at the back of the town which is protected by a firebreak on the north side. (Thomas Adams, *Recent Advances in Town Planning*, 1932)

problem. The town, named Corner Brook, was intended to house between five and six thousand people at Garden City standards. Adams, who seems to have been principally responsible for the plan, used the uneven terrain and valleys with his accustomed skill, fitting the street pattern to the contours. A full range of community services was provided on good sites and good use was made of streams as bases for parks. Unfortunately, the necessarily high cost of development in such a remote and inhospitable spot and the industry's depressed condition in later years prevented the full realization of the plan, one of Adams's most ingenious designs[38].

THE COLLAPSE OF THE ADAMS SYSTEM

The indifferent success of Adams's own planning was symptomatic of post-war Canadian planning. It was an ailing infant throughout the 1920s and Adams's system was collapsing before the Great Depression administered the *coup de grace*. His essential base of operations, the Commission of Conservation, was demolished. His legislative and administrative advance dried up and was increasingly questioned. Plans rarely came to fruition. The Civic Improvement League, his propaganda agency and lobby, never got established. His research was either stymied or ignored. The housing programme was denied the means to achieve the ends intended. His successors lacked the stature, commitment and cohesiveness to maintain his edifice. Finally, his gradual disengagement further diminished his influence and the aura of divinity which initially had surrounded him. Though earlier views that 'Canadian planning came to an abrupt and disastrous end in 1930' are exaggerated – planners in Toronto, Edmonton and Calgary, for example, were probably busier than in the 1920s, notably in zoning, highways and, later, slum clearance and public housing – it is nevertheless undeniable that the depression dealt Adams's hopes a mortal blow. Provincial and municipal planning agencies, the T.P.I.C. and its journal, all folded in the early 1930s and a national return to the level of activity of 1914–20 came about only after 1945[39].

The odds against planning being accepted as an everyday public function were substantial. Between 1900 and 1930, four major cataclysms affected its prospects adversely – the frenzied boom and its subsequent collapse, the trauma and totality of the Great War, the strife, uncertainty and disillusionment which haunted the peace, and the catastrophe of the Great Depression. Between them, they left Canada in turmoil and bereft of social resources, self-assurance and agreed goals. Progressive reform, seemingly firmly launched by 1914, lacked the pervasiveness, organization and persistence of its British and American counterparts and its rapid disintegration after 1918 left planners in an uncongenial social climate. Nor was progressivism an unmixed blessing for its earliest manifestation in planning was the 'City Beautiful' which had two deleterious effects on future planning. Firstly, it was devoid of accomplishments and, secondly, planning 'became associated in the common mind with fanciful and costly schemes of embellishment', a misconception difficult to dislodge[40]. However, Canada was not in any case fruitful ground for planning in those days. What principally defeated the first attempt to establish planning as part of the governmental and developmental process was simply the enmity and indifference of a frontier society, led by real estate speculators, to the very notion of resource management and environmental planning, as Adams recognized:

> The greatest difficulty in Canada was the strength of resistance to the ... proper use of land for healthful community use, even to the point of causing unhealthful conditions in town and country. This resistance is strong in other countries, but in Canada, still being exploited as a new country, it was exceptionally strong[41].

How far was Adams himself responsible for the debacle? He cannot be faulted on strategic grounds for he had little choice but to advance simultaneously on all fronts. His principal error was in persisting with a sophisticated British legislative and institutional framework which was far too complex for a relatively primitive society and did not work satisfactorily even at home. A greater willingness to follow American precepts and a more acute perception of social trends in Canada might have gained him a wider and more sustained influence. His energy, enthusiasm, charm and ability to communicate cannot be questioned.

The Significance of the Adams Era

What, then, was the significance of the Adams era in Canadian planning history? Philosophically, he offered Canada nothing new; indeed, he was invited precisely because he identified with the values and aspirations of the Canadian establishment, giving practical and institutional form to an already-entrenched utilitarianism. Though hurrying along Canada's apprenticeship in planning, he did not fashion a uniquely Canadian style of planning, nor did his native contemporaries. Rather, he and they saw Canadian problems as essentially those of all modern industrial societies, susceptible of the same general solutions. Canada was a 'borrowing' culture and thus Canadian planning ultimately 'represented the British mode moderated by American influence'. Modern Canadian planning owes little to Adams in a formal, institutional sense but, though his acts, plans and specific advice have been long superseded, his spiritual legacy is substantial and the utilitarian, pragmatic ideology still directs mainstream Canadian planning thought[42]. After a heroic and apparently successful crusade during the Great War, his Canadian experience turned sour. For all of its dazzling and purposeful activity, the Adams mission to Canada was tragically ill-timed and ultimately ill-starred.

Chapter Six

Towards a Regional Plan for New York, 1911–1929

THE EMERGENCE OF MODERN AMERICAN CITY PLANNING, 1890–1909

In May 1911, Thomas Adams, accompanied by Raymond Unwin and Thomas Mawson, paid his first visit to the United States. They were to attend the third National Conference on City Planning in Philadelphia but were also 'bent on making a study of housing and city planning conditions and ideas', an indirect testimony to the fact that the New World had now something to teach the Old[1].

Most American communities had been planned from the outset. The noblest plan was William Penn's for Philadelphia (1682). Intending it to be spacious and 'a green country town' which would 'always be wholesome', Penn emphasized the social features of town building. However, Philadelphia epitomized the fundamental dichotomy in American urbanism for it was not only an outpost of civilization in the wilderness but also a base for exploiting the natural resources of its hinterland. Under a merchant oligarchy in the eighteenth century, commercial considerations outweighed those of the community. 'By the eve of the Revolution', wrote Carl Bridenburgh, 'Philadelphia had assumed the appearance, and something of the ugliness, of any prosperous and rapidly growing city'[2].

The nineteenth century's model was the plan of Manhattan made in 1811. An unrelieved grid, heedless of topography, public health, amenity and the convenience of traffic, it was fashioned frankly for 'the buying, selling and improving of real estate'. The American city became a place in which to do business rather than a home for civilized life. Its development was in the hands of the vanguard of urban frontiersmen, the land speculators, the staunchest defenders of unbridled individualism. It was in the generation after 1865 that 'the American city faced its most desolate period'. The pace of

119

urban growth was such that by 1890 the United States was well on the way to becoming a predominantly urban nation and experienced the problems familiar to all industrial nations of the time – congestion of population, buildings and traffic, alarming levels of vice, crime and disease, economic inefficiency and inadequate government. Critics both domestic and foreign exposed its shortcomings and called for reform[3].

The urban reform movement which developed from about 1890 was a part of the Progressive crusade, an amorphous, largely urban and middle-class campaign for the amelioration of America's problems, imbued with an evangelical fervour. 'We have had a moral awakening, and are ready and anxious to do our duty', the banker Henry Morgenthau, Sr., told the first National Conference on City Planning in 1909. Progressives were alarmed for the nation's future and Adams warned that unless America reformed its cities, 'the physique of your race, its intellectual caliber, its moral strength will be lowered'. Some feared a revolution unless the sufferings of the masses were alleviated. 'Congestion', Morgenthau claimed, 'breeds physical disease, moral depravity, discontent and socialism – and all these must be cured and eradicated or else our great body politic will be weakened'. More positive Progressives like Frederick C. Howe viewed the city as 'the hope of democracy' and introduced Americans to the enlightened urban policies of Britain and Germany. This transatlantic traffic in ideas burgeoned with the introduction of cheap easy international travel. Numerous international organizations, journals and conferences were launched and American wandering scholars returned from European universities with the conviction that society was a malleable artefact susceptible of scientific management. Business began to be dominated by national corporations demanding a rational urban order as a basis for stability, investment and expansion. Urban boosters, anxious to attract new businesses to their towns, emphasized the competitive nature of the American city. 'Competition between cities', declared the St. Louis Civic League, 'is becoming keener. If one city makes itself more inviting than its neighbor it is bound to attract more people. A city, after all, is a great business in which hundreds of stockholders are interested'. By 1890, too, the environmental professions – notably that peculiarly American innovation, landscape architecture – were becoming self-confident and as American cities sought to fit themselves for admission to the league of world cities, planning appeared to be 'a badge of municipal maturity'[4].

Chamber of Commerce boosters were largely responsible for the first phase of modern American city planning – the 'City Beautiful'. It grew out of a municipal art campaign, a drive for park systems as a means of restoring the rural-urban continuum, and the impact upon American travellers of the baroque splendours of Paris, Rome and Vienna. It received its principal fillip from the Chicago world's fair of 1893 and the revitalization in 1901 of L'Enfant's plan for Washington, for both of which the great Chicago architect Daniel Hudson Burnham was the chief designer. The baroque halls and courts of the fair's 'Great White City' contrasted starkly with the drabness and squalor of the average American city while the strident nationalism of turn-of-the-century America demanded a Federal capital comparable in elegance and dignity to the capitals of older great powers. Thus inspired, cities of all ranks commissioned schemes for grandiose civic centres, ambitious park systems, monumental city gates and elegant station plazas. Burnham was connected with many of them but his 'unquestioned master-work' was the celebrated Chicago plan of 1909. Few other schemes got beyond the stage of lavish promotional folios, for taxpayers rebelled against costly fripperies while mundane necessities were neglected; a million dollars were to be spent on art, complained the *Chicago Post*, and nothing on smoke control or street cleaning. Chauvinists like the intellectual journalist Herbert Croly exclaimed, 'We do not want a Frenchified New York'. The 'City Beautiful' faded after 1909 but it had stimulated public interest in environmental design. 'Psychologically', observed the architect George B. Ford, 'it is quite justifiable that American city planning began with the "City Beautiful". The "City Scientific" would never have aroused such enthusiasm'[5].

The 'City Scientific' creed was disseminated by the National Conference on City Planning, established in 1909 by a group of New York social workers headed by the widely-read, idiosyncratic young radical Benjamin C. Marsh. Indeed, if Marsh and his colleagues had remained in the planning movement, the 'City Beautiful' might have been succeeded by a 'City Social' advocating drastic environmental controls and a positive low-income housing policy. However, apart from the fact that the 'City Social' would have been unacceptable to politicians and businessmen, it was a mirage which faded within two years as Marsh and his friends moved on to fresh woods and pastures new, leaving the more conservative politicians, lawyers and businessmen in command of the N.C.C.P. Their 'City Scientific' has become the dominant mode of American planning. It represented a re-ordering of priorities rather than a revolution. 'From a question of art', remarked the engineer Morris Knowles, 'town planning has become more and more one of engineering'. The new approach was a hard-headed, business-oriented, technical exercise in trend-adjusting, project-based development control planning. Economic efficiency, rational communications networks and zoning featured in its long-term master plans. These assumed the applicability of scientific method, a fundamental social harmony and the primacy of the economic function. 'All city planning', declared an authoritative survey in 1917, 'should start on a foundation of economic practicableness; . . . it should be something which will appeal to the businessman . . . as sane and reasonable'[6].

Two Traditions of American Planning

Both 'City Beautiful' and 'City Scientific' rested on a meliorist philosophy of which Burnham was the high priest. An architectural entrepreneur himself, he spoke the language of his clients, the great merchant princes. The dynamic Chicago of the late nineteenth century was his milieu and he was at one with its *zeitgeist*. He worked with the grain of America's business civilization and aimed to harness current economic and social trends to ameliorate rather than exacerbate urban ills. He welcomed urban growth and was confident of his ability to plan for it, regardless of a metropolis's ultimate size. Burnham represented the economically-oriented mainstream of American planning, evident in the Philadelphia of the Revolution and the Manhattan plan of 1811; his plans took frankly into consideration 'the fact that the American city . . . is a center of industry and traffic'[7].

Running alongside the mainstream was a thin brook whose line was defined by Burnham's contemporary, Frederick Law Olmsted, Sr., a self-confessed 'socialist-democrat' who struggled against the current of American society. Olmsted's urban vision descended from Penn's ideal for Philadelphia and placed social ends above economic ones. His richly varied cultural experience fostered an intellectual approach to city building and his New England small-town origins inspired him to restore to American cities the 'communicative-ness' of the relatively classless, rather genteel, cultivated, communitarian urban ethos of pre-Civil War America. He battled against the brash and brutal urbanism of the late nineteenth century and sought to maintain a rural–urban continuum, chiefly through his great city parks and parkways. His sylvan, contoured, intimate plans for the Chicago suburb of Riverside (1869) and Northern Manhattan (1878) reveal a bucolic vision sadly at variance with the ruling spirit of the age. The founder of modern landscape architecture, he regarded it not only as the art which unified all of the environmental professions but also as the potential instrument of a social-democratic urban regeneration. The trickling stream of insurgent opposition to the prevailing meliorism has rarely enjoyed success but it has contrived to breed disciples in almost every generation[8].

ADAMS'S ROLE IN AMERICAN PLANNING, 1911–1923

When the British delegates arrived in Philadelphia, therefore, they found the city attempting to revive Penn's vision and the national planning movement attempting to determine its ruling influences. Though they were confined to commenting on their hosts' papers, the Britons did something to offset the absence of native social reformers. 'Throughout the sessions', wrote the socially-concerned George B. Ford, 'the Social aspect would hardly have obtained full recognition if it had not been for our English friends'. Adams in particular emphasized the necessity of decent low-income housing, attacking the kind of individualism prevalent in the United States which interfered with the liberties of other citizens and the rights of the community. 'Whatever regard, then, you may have for the rights of the real estate owner', he told the delegates, 'it must be secondary to that first condition that every citizen should have the opportunity of obtaining a healthy home within the limits of his means'. He condemned also the general tendency to house the masses in tenements, commending to his hosts John Burns's dictum, 'Plan the town but spread the people'[9].

Following the conference, Adams made 'a very superficial inspection of most of the intensively developed regions', of the country, taking in New York, Washington, Baltimore, Pittsburgh, Chicago, Detroit, Cleveland and Boston and finding time also for Montreal and Toronto. It was New York which fascinated him most of all. In two subsequent articles, he discussed its planning problems. In a characteristically balanced assessment, he noted the splendid architecture of the Manhattan towers and the fine prospect of their massed ranks seen from an approaching liner but pointed out also the sunless, congested streets below them and the absence of light and air in many parts of the buildings themselves. He searched for a mean between the extremes of those who praised the skyscraper unstintingly as the highest expression of national art and those who sought its abolition on social grounds, concluding pragmatically that in lower Manhattan at least, 'the high-storeyed building must be the prevailing type of the future'. The planners' problem was 'how to limit and control it in accordance with a scheme of development for the whole city'. He laid down environmental conditions for skyscrapers which became the standards of the next generation. 'Conditions of health', he declared, 'can only be secured by preserving ample open space round high buildings so that there shall be ample light, air, and sun penetration of every part'. Adams was already a man of bold spatial vision and he was excited by the challenge of the great American metropolis. Recommending that the city should undertake a flexible, comprehensive, systematic and practical development plan for its region, he argued that

> the adoption of a city planning policy, which shall have for one of its main objects the wider distribution of its factories and population and the proper control of the consequent expansion of the city, is the most important and urgent duty of the city of New York as a means of solving its many problems.

Exemplifying his meliorism, these articles set out his approach to the problems of New York upon which he was to build a dozen years later when he became Director of the Regional Plan of New York[10].

Adams's first American tour had introduced him to an intriguing set of urban problems, a more commercially-inspired mode of melioristic planning and a group of pragmatic planners – the younger Olmsted, John Nolen, George B. Ford and Nelson P. Lewis – who were to become lifelong friends and professional associates. He found the general tenor of the country, the drift of its planning and the outlook of its practitioners largely to his liking.

For several years, Adams's contribution to American planning was that of an *amicus curiae* in the debate on planning which took place at N.C.C.P. meetings and in the press. The gist of his advice was that which he dispensed officially north of the border. He conformed to the 'City Scientific' norm, maintaining that 'Town or city planning is the application of scientific principles to all matters connected with towns or cities'. He stressed the economic basis of urban life and the cost-effectiveness of scientific planning 'to prevent future evils'. Liberty, he argued, must go with justice and civic virtue. He condemned both the 'City Beautiful' and land speculation and declared that there could be no property rights in slums: 'the poorest and meanest of our citizens', he said, 'have a claim for decent and sanitary shelter, which we have no right to withhold from them because of misfortune or inefficiency'. It was a radical sentiment in America. True to his Garden City antecedents, he suggested that 'America needs one thing almost more than any other, and that is an object lesson in city building'. He could have had little hope of its realization for he placed greater emphasis on planned decentralization from core cities into satellites separated from their parents by prosperous farm belts. His perspective on planning was more comprehensive than that of any of his American contemporaries:

> The first objective of town planning should be to conserve and provide for the extension of its business interests, and to apply healthy conditions to the dwellings of the people. Complementary to both these objects, it is desirable to secure efficiency in transportation and in the supply and distribution of food, etc., and lastly it is needful to give expression to those communal and social interests which are represented in universities, schools, parks, playgrounds, town halls, museums, churches, etc.[11].

He urged Americans to give force to their planning activities by passing enabling legislation on British lines and at the time most American planners were disposed to agree. For the most part, then, Adams endorsed the general professional support for the 'City Scientific' and preached the British gospel of statutory planning, housing reform and Garden City standards.

Adams made a breakthrough in planning thought which his native contemporaries seemed incapable of achieving. In addresses at Cleveland in 1916, he introduced the concept of regional planning and outlined a national planning framework. Given his Canadian experience, it was a natural progression to make. As in Canada, so in America he campaigned for a Federal Bureau of Civic Affairs working in harmony with State departments of municipal affairs which would co-operate with municipal planning boards. Though not yet ready to advocate national planning, he did propose state outline plans into which detailed local plans would dovetail, an elaboration of the structure he had outlined for London. He startled the American planning world at Cleveland by telling it that 'The first thing . . . is not to plan Cleveland, but to plan Ohio'. Adams was half a generation ahead of his audience; state planning came about only in the New Deal of the 1930s and then to an uneven extent. At least he gained the distinction of articulating the idea of genuine regional (as opposed to metropolitan) planning before anyone else[12].

The effect of the First World War upon America, especially after her intervention, intensified Adams's interest in the nation's urban policies and he was particularly loquacious in the era of war and reconstruction. Neutral America had been affected by the war as early as 1915 as Allied orders sparked an industrial boom, increasing pressure on an already-inadequate stock of low-income housing. 'Homes for workingmen! This has been the greatest problem of our American industrial cities during the past two years', wrote the designers of the model company town at Kohler, Wisconsin, in 1917. Numerous philanthropic expedients failed to overcome it. 'Low-cost houses of desirable types', reported Adams's friend the landscape architect John Nolen, 'cannot be built within the means of the workingman even at his present good wages'. As in Britain, however, belligerency broke the ideological log-jam and, thanks to the initiative of leading planners and housing reformers, the Federal Government was induced to appropriate almost $200m for over 150 model industrial communities. Laid out on the lines of the best company towns, few had progressed far before the simultaneous return of peace and *laissez-faire* compelled their cancellation and sale[13].

The model communities programme, in the minds of its initiators, was less a contribution to the war effort than a blueprint for a new form of urban development in peacetime, a campaign endorsed enthusiastically by Adams. Calling for 'real reconstruction', he advised Americans to 'Establish these new communities upon a permanent basis. Create garden cities now, because you have an opportunity you never had before'. As in Canada, he advocated a nationally-directed planning structure and co-partnership housing. Ample, decent low-cost housing would ensure an efficient, healthy, stable and contented labour force, while returned veterans could be settled on the land in planned villages. Co-operation was 'the force that is needed to give unity without the destruction of individual initiative and to create reform without dependence on governments'. John Nolen caught the exultant mood of his colleagues at the war's climax, proclaiming 'There is a new order. It is the order of the average man'. As in Canada, however, the reconstruction impulse died with the war itself; the hope of the 'City Social' perished with it. The average man demanded not a rejuvenated and more positive Progressivism but the routine conservatism and self-centred individualism of 'Normalcy'[14].

The determinants of post-war planning were the needs of business and especially those of real estate and the automobile industry. The planning of the 1920s was characterized by a narrow professionalism seeking technical solutions to specific problems and excluding social concerns from its purview. Planners concentrated upon the development of techniques, the incremental improvement of enabling legislation and the acceptance of their work as a normal and necessary component of public administration.

The characteristic feature of American planning in the post-war decade was zoning which, wrote the planning commentator Theodora Kimball, 'has taken the country by storm'. Often the only form of planning in a locality, it was instituted frequently without professional advice, subject to interminable amendment and served the interests of the suburban middle class and real estate boards. It earned the general support of established and substantial mercantile and property interests though small businessmen and individual speculators resented its curbs on their freedom of action, sensing that it protected the established interests from new competitors. The leading cities commissioned master plans – essentially highway and land-use maps and a shelf of engineering and recreation projects spread over thirty-year periods. Consultants were responsible for most plans since municipal planning offices were vestigial, capable only of token gestures, and John Nolen and Harland Bartholomew dominated the field. Metropolitan regional plans were adopted in a handful of the larger centres but achieved few concrete results. The governing features of plans were the stabilization of property values, residential segregation by class and race, the separation of urban functions, the accommodation of the automobile without consideration of alternative strategies, and the quest for urban efficiency and economy. American planning aimed to serve rather than transform the social and economic order and its values. Meliorism ruled virtually unopposed. In 1927, John Nolen reported that there were 390 city planning commissions, 525 zoning ordinances and 176 city plans. The Department of Commerce, under Herbert Hoover's aegis, circulated model zoning and planning acts and most states passed enabling legislation. Courses on planning were offered in the universities and there was a putative professional organization and an aspiring learned journal[15].

Thomas Adams had an intimate connection with most of these ancillary developments. In 1917, when leading members of the N.C.C.P. formed an American City Planning Institute, Adams became one of the first Vice-Presidents, though he felt that it was an unsatisfactory instrument of professional advancement. In both Britain and Canada, he initiated professional institutes which were exclusive, credential-granting bodies intended to define the nature of planning and the role of the professional practitioner and, above all, to confer upon the infant profession a distinct and corporate identity. At the time of the A.C.P.I.'s foundation, he had a somewhat limited influence in America and chafed constantly at its inadequacies. Its ambit was far more vague and its recruitment far broader than he would have liked. It remained tied to its parents' apron strings, lacked financial viability and meandered through the 1920s to no great purpose. Adams's friend George B. Ford argued that planning was too broad a subject to be a separate profession but Adams countered that 'the Institute should, as soon as possible, achieve the position of being a technical Institute, in which the members should be practising city planners'. The Adams view prevailed in 1927 when the A.C.P.I. organized itself on a more specifically professional basis. However, its other inherent handicaps continued and even after its metamorphosis into the American Institute of Planners in 1938, it was, if more active, little more purposeful[16].

The definition and validation of the professional planner was undertaken ultimately by the universities, planning having entered the curriculum at Harvard in 1909 as an adjunct to landscape architecture. Adams had lectured at practically all of the Canadian universities when in 1921 he was asked to give ten lectures to students of architecture at the Massachusetts Institute of Technology; he was quietly proud of this invitation and established planning as a major field of specialization at M.I.T., paving the way for the department headed ultimately by his second son, Frederick J. Adams. As was usual in those days, his lectures had a heavy historical base and dealt with planning chiefly in its legal, technical and physical aspects though treating also 'Economic and social problems related to planning of cities'[17].

For all of his activity around the fringes of American planning, however, it was many years before Adams was able to become a practising planner in the United States. Before 1920 his full-time post, first in Britain and then in Canada, prevented him from undertaking private work and even after his Canadian post became a part-time one, he took a self-denying ordinance, forswearing competition with native American planners. Following the running down of the Commission of Conservation, however, he had to build a new career, largely in private practice. His ambition was to head a trans-atlantic partnership. It was some time before he got the combination right. He turned down an offer of a partnership from Olmsted Brothers because it would have confined him to North America and between 1920 and 1922 he tried two other short-lived expedients. Early in 1920, he associated himself with a new firm, American City Consultants, which consisted of Adams (now described as a landscape architect) as chief planning consultant, an engineer, a lawyer and an economist. He undertook in 1920–21 'reconnaisance surveys' for a variety of small and medium-sized communities – among them Kansas City, Kansas, North Adams, Massachusetts, and Grand Island and the Tonawandas, on the New York side of the Niagara frontier. In 1922, he offered a similar service under the auspices of the American City Bureau. Since he confined himself to propaganda and preliminary work, advising the employment of native planners for detailed plans, there was little real satisfaction in this self-circumscribed activity[18].

The demise of the Commission of Conservation in January 1921 compelled him to make more substantial arrangements for his future and he formed a partnership with the young British engineer Francis Longstreth Thompson, with offices in both London and New York. In the main, Thompson was to look after the British work while Adams would use his presence in North America as a part-time advisor to the Canadian Government and as a visiting lecturer at M.I.T. to drum up contracts there. However, apart from the continuation of short-term consultancy work, a handful of Canadian contracts and a model industrial community in Newfoundland, the firm's early commitments were in Britain. Given his continuing rectitude with regard to actual planning in the United States, Adams might have been remembered in American planning history, if at all, as a marginal theorist, publicist, educator and organizer. His significance in the American planning movement was transformed by the most dramatic event yet witnessed in the nation's planning history – the launching in 1921 of the Regional Plan of New York and its Environs[19].

ORIGINS OF THE REGIONAL PLAN OF NEW YORK: METROPOLITAN PROBLEMS AND PLANS, 1811–1918

This great venture arose out of both the problems and the possibilities of New York. The city's rise to a metropolitan pre-eminence had been facilitated by its excellent location at the focal point of major sea and land routes and by its 500 miles of prime waterfront sites for port-related business. By 1920 it was America's leading commercial, financial and port city with a great industrial base and a regional population approaching nine millions. It was still developing and needed to do so if it was to maintain its primacy. There was widespread pride in the city's success and size and faith in its future. One of the plan's objects was to foster and direct future growth[20].

New York's previous growth had been largely unregulated and speculative, as had that of most American cities. 'In the American city', said Adams, 'the disposal of lots to individuals, with liberty to make the best use of them for their private purposes, was the governing factor in their development'. This untrammelled expansion led to congestion of one kind or another. There was congestion of population, especially in Manhattan where by 1920 there were two million residents crowded in at densities of over a quarter of a million per square mile and reinforced daily by nearly three million commuters. The city's buildings, both tenements and skyscrapers, were congested, more people being crammed into them than could be got safely onto the narrow streets below. Lots were overbuilt, especially in the skyscraper district where the great towers, a technological solution to the pressures of business centralization and soaring business district land values, greedily maximized the space potential of their lots and turned erstwhile residential streets into dingy, draughty canyons, each new cliff of steel and stone denying to its neighbours adequate light and air. Public open space was at a premium and the long waterfront had been usurped by wharfage and related industries. New York's magnificent backcloth of hills and water was almost invisible from Manhattan and other central parts. Even in the horse-and-buggy age, traffic congestion had been severe and the coming of the automobile had intensified it. Rail freight found it difficult to flow smoothly and efficiently while commuters suffered indignities of compression – each subway car was a microcosm of the manifold congestion above ground. Even the great port was congested. The rivers fragmented the shoreline and compelled both the transshipment of passengers and goods and the provision of costly tunnels and bridges to and from Manhattan. In 1927, it was estimated that traffic congestion cost the region one million dollars a day in delays and accidents[21].

Towards the end of the nineteenth century population and industry began to decentralize. Fingers of settlement spread out along trunk routes, leaving the interstices undeveloped. There grew up an interlocking combination of skyscrapers, commuter transportation and low-density dormitory suburbs, which lacked a sense of community and smothered old, organic settlements in a ceaseless sprawl of speculative construction. Uncontrolled suburbanization was 'one of the primary causes of the worst evils in city growth', outstripping demand, prodigal with land, destructive of the environment and under-endowed with public utilities and open space. The flight to the suburbs ever more remote from places of employment caused 'friction of space' – the excessive separation of home and work – which by 1920 had proceeded 'extravagantly far'. Decentralization relieved population pressure in central areas but decline there was more than offset by a rapid escalation of the commuting horde, an unprofitable burden to transportation services for expensive capital equipment lay idle between peak hours, when it was subjected to gross overcrowding. The arrival of the automobile assisted both centralization of employment and decentralization of residence. Inner-city streets were clogged on weekdays and country and seaside roads at weekends. There was also a developing awareness of new hazards – atmospheric and water-borne pollution and the prospect of a popular commercial and private aviation. By 1920, New York seemed to be a metropolis in chaos and crisis[22].

There was not an entire absence of planning in the New York region. The Manhattan gridiron plan of 1811, inefficient though it was, nevertheless gave the city a framework for incremental expansion. Olmsted's several attempts to moderate its unfortunate impact were defeated but throughout the region there were spasmodic public improvements after the Civil War. However, it was generally a case of 'piecemeal planning and of doing things when it was too late to do them right'. Before the Progressive era, authorities lacked the legal and financial powers and the organization, techniques and expertise to do more than catch up on some of the earlier neglect and arrest temporarily the onward march of urban chaos[23].

The Olmstedian vision informed the work of Progressive bodies such as the City Improvement Commission (1903–7) and the Advisory Committee on the City Plan (1913–15) which attempted to create the parks and parkways he had recommended. It was to little avail as the Progressives were 'mornin' glories' soon replaced by Tammany administrations unconcerned with the environment. Nevertheless, the Progressives' commissions gave them the group cohesiveness and range of expertise which served as the basis for the Regional Plan and they were able to introduce the celebrated zoning ordinance of 1916 which, while designed to protect the exclusive shopping district from penetration by the sweated trades and their sweaty hands, became a national panacea for urban ills. The City of New York, however, had no permanent planning commission until 1936 and the prime local examples of meliorist development plans were Chamber of Commerce-inspired reports for Newark (1913) and Brooklyn (1914) – practical if booster ish proposals to rationalize land utilization and improve civic and economic efficiency. The most august planning body, significantly, was one imposed on the region by the States of New Jersey and New York, the Port of New York Authority. Formed in 1921 to eliminate dockside congestion which had reached exasperating levels in World War One, it developed into an expert-dominated planning structure of considerable sophistication and purpose, taking a remarkably comprehensive view of economic and communications planning[24].

CHARLES DYER NORTON AND THE LAUNCHING OF THE REGIONAL PLAN OF NEW YORK, 1915–1923

Out of these tentative steps towards a rational metropolitan order and, more importantly, out of the experience of Chicago, there evolved a Regional Plan. The Second City had something to teach the First about planning and the communicator between the two was Charles Dyer Norton, a self-made financier and a leader of the Chicago business community. Norton had persuaded Burnham to undertake the great Chicago plan of 1906–9 and following that had served in the Taft administration before arriving in New York in 1911, rising in time to the presidency of the First National Bank. Described as 'not a mere dreamer' but as 'practical, able, endowed with common sense', Norton was the archetypal Progressive business advocate of meliorist planning, albeit with a bolder vision than most of his kind. Quickly integrating himself into the planning milieu in New York, he became Chairman of the abortive Advisory Committee on the City Plan and, helped by his Chicago experience, concluded that a mere city plan was inadequate and that it should be metropolitan in scope[25].

Norton's opportunity to realize his vision came with his appointment in November 1918 as a trustee of the Russell Sage Foundation, established in 1907 to promote 'the improvement of social and living conditions'. His fellow trustees were staid, patrician lawyers, bankers and merchants with impeccable old-stock pedigrees, Ivy League educations and distinguished public service records. Like most 'silk stockings', they distrusted both politicians and the urban masses and regarded themselves as disinterested public servants. The Foundation sponsored social and environmental studies, a garden suburb on Long Island (Forest Hills Gardens), the N.C.C.P., A.C.P.I. and National

Housing Association. However, its commitment to environmental betterment was circumscribed severely by its trustees' inherent caution, and Norton's initial suggestion of a regional plan was rejected in February 1919[26].

Securing the support of an influential trustee, Alfred T. While, and the technical assistance of the great City Engineer of New York, Nelson P. Lewis, who was about to retire, Norton at last obtained the trustees' consent in December 1920 to launch a feasibility study. In February 1921, his hand was strengthened by the addition to the trustees of Frederick A. Delano, a railroad president and his close friend from Chicago days. It was to Delano that Norton revealed his vision:

> From City Hall a circle must be swung which will include the Atlantic Highlands and Princeton; the lovely Jersey Hills back of Morriston and Tuxedo; the incomparable Hudson as far as Newburgh, the Westchester lakes and ridges, to Bridgeport and beyond, and all of Long Island. Let some Daniel Hudson Burnham do for this immense community what Burnham did for Chicago and its environs. . . Let him make a big daring imaginative plan such as George Washington and his French engineer L'Enfant had the courage to make for the City of Washington 115 years ago – and New York will not fail to recognize and adopt her City Plan[27].

The grandeur of the design was characteristic of Norton and it was equally typical of him and his colleagues that their conception was essentially one of a metropolitan region, with the harbour of New York as its hub. His project aimed at both solving the region's problems and realizing its potential to the full, and he espoused social as well as economic goals, calling for

> A Plan which shall offer particularly to the less fortunate hope and the prospect of better living conditions, and which shall realize to the maximum the economic, social and artistic values of this great port and world capital. When the plan is complete, it will be tendered as a free offering to the public of New York[28].

From the beginning of 1921 until early in 1923, the Regional Plan of New York and its Environs was under Norton's personal, strong-willed and sometimes idiosyncratic direction. He headed a Sage Foundation Regional Plan Committee, employed Sage staff and other experts on four major surveys – Physical, Legal, Economic, and Social and Living Conditions – and established an executive staff led by Frederick P. Keppel, an experienced administrator of comparable social standing to the Sage trustees. He added a Planning Advisory Group and architectural committees and presented the general project to the public on 10 May 1922. The invitations to this meeting read like the Social Register and included Secretary of Commerce Herbert Hoover and New York's senior Senator, Elihu Root, who both endorsed the scheme, which was well received also by the metropolitan establishment, professional leaders and the press[29].

While it did not clarify all of the plan's features, the Norton phase did define certain parameters. With its presumptive bias towards a command and support structure drawn from the metropolitan elite, the plan could not be other than a meliorist exercise in the satisfaction of the elite's demands and its paternalistic assumptions about community needs. Furthermore, Norton remained as much a mid-westerner as any character in *Gatsby*; Chicago's plan was the paragon and Norton's goals and methods replicated those of Burnham. His immediate constituency was a mirror image of the Merchants' Club and his public relations followed Walter D. Moody's successful pattern for the Chicago plan. Norton's vision, like Burnham's, was as much an aesthetic as a functional one, though he observed the lack of social welfare provision in the Burnham plan and intended to make the relief of urban deprivation a major feature of the New York plan. In this he was encouraged by the Sage chairman, Robert De Forest, an old housing reformer, who gruffly dismissed any 'City Beautiful' notions and called for 'the city whole-some, a city of homes'. The sage Lewis, too, advised in favour of urban efficiency rather than civic grandeur. The obverse of having the region's busi-ness, professional, cultural and social elite behind the plan was a marked lack of political figures (apart from ex-Governor Alfred E. Smith), representatives of labour and recent immigrants, and even notable Progressives. Norton and his associates were big city personalities and assumed that regional planning meant the continued and indeed extended domination of its hinterland by New York City; no alternative conception entered their minds. Any decentralization was to be local and not state-wide. Norton set the plan's boundaries at two hours' rail commuting from Manhattan, taking in substantial parts of New Jersey and New York and a small portion of Connecticut[30].

From the summer of 1922, Norton sought to integrate the separate groups and studies and to find a 'supreme commander' to play the Burnham role, though he was advised by his professional consultants that the task was beyond even a latter-day Burnham. They suggested a team of professionals drawn from architecture, engineering, landscape architecture, economics and law with a city planning specialist as co-ordinator. Accompanied by Keppel, Norton undertook a grand tour of Europe in the summer of 1922, visiting cities with something to show in planning. Like a Henry James character, Norton sent back to New York examples of European culture and wisdom, in this case, planners. From Paris he despatched the landscape architect Jacques Lambert to advise on parks and recreation, though this turned out to be an abortive mission. More significantly, from London he obtained Raymond Unwin, arguably the world's best-known planner[31].

Unwin visited New York in October 1922, gave several lectures at the Sage building and made three reports on the plan's progress, endorsing the need for a thorough survey. His emphasis was on the proper distribution of land uses and the planned decentralization of industry and population. Reiterating his famous theme 'Nothing gained by overcrowding', he advised the founding of self-contained satellite communities to help decongest the central area. On organization and procedure, he recommended an agreed broad outline, a well-focused survey and the appointment of one planner as a co-ordinator and another as director of research prior to the selection of a chief planner. Unwin's recommendations were little different from those of most contemporary planners save in two respects. He hinted that motor traffic might have to be restricted in central areas and he advocated stringent public controls over land development. In these suggestions he reflected his socialist background – and probably lost his opportunity to direct the plan, since they were unwelcome to its sponsors, who were more afraid of strong public authority than they were of unbridled *laissez-faire*[32].

ADAMS AND THE REGIONAL PLAN:
FROM OCCASIONAL ADVISOR TO GENERAL DIRECTOR, 1921–1923

Much the most important by-product of Norton's grand tour was the appointment as 'supreme commander' of Thomas Adams, who had been associated with the Regional Plan from its outset, endorsing the initial scope of the plan and its survey work. True to his oft-stated view that planning was a team game synthesizing the contributions of several professions, Adams recommended that the plan should be drawn up by a group including an engineer, an architect, a landscape architect, a lawyer and a regional planner, who would act as the co-ordinator. He became the front-runner for this appointment when, having agreed to serve on the Advisory Group of Planners, he was elected chairman by his fellow professionals – all Americans – in January 1923[33].

The Advisory Group contained all of the leading lights in American planning – the younger Olmsted, Edward H. Bennett, Ernest P. Goodrich, George B. Ford, Harlan Bartholomew, John Nolen and Henry V. Hubbard. Adams, a neutral on good terms with all of them and a well-known conciliator, was highly experienced in committee work. In collaboration with Olmsted he suggested individual sector studies and a final group report. He intended that the studies should be general reconnaissances, noting both problems and possibilities and suggesting points for consideration in the Legal, Economic and Social and Living Conditions surveys, with which they liaised. Their concerns were emphatically physical – land uses, development patterns, communications, open spaces and recreation. The plan's initial emphasis on a more even distribution of population and economic activity underlay the studies[34].

Adams's study of Westchester, Fairfield and the southern portion of

FIGURE 15. Regional Plan of New York: Advisory Group of Planners, 1923.

Thomas Adams, the Chairman, is second from left on the front row. The others are, left to right, Frank B. Williams, Edward M. Bassett, Frederick Law Olmsted, Jr., (unknown), John Nolen, Hale Walker (at back), Edward H. Bennett, (unknown), Harland Bartholomew (behind Adams), Henry V. Hubbard, Nelson P. Lewis, Ernest P. Goodrich (right of Adams). H. T. Frost, (unknown), Flavel Shurtleff (leaning), George B. Ford. (Courtesy of Olin Library, Cornell University. Identification by Professor D. A. Johnson)

Putnam counties was 'the best organized and most comprehensive' of the reports. Thoroughness in research and preparation were Adams's hallmarks and he was also the one best able to relate his sector to the region. Dealing with an area of some 1100 square miles with a varied and interesting topography, he accepted the current trend to smart dormitory suburbs, country clubs and parks and water recreation areas. Anticipating an increase in population from the 630,000 of his day to 850,000 in 1940, he stressed the urgent need of planning to preserve natural beauty, residential values and amenities and to promote industrial efficiency, chiefly by the sensible location of small factories. He wished Connecticut to bring its planning law up to New York's level. Referring to wasteful subdivision practices, expensive in public improvements, he called for more careful zoning, preferably in association with comprehensive local plans. Many of his proposals were for road improvements – arterials, radials, parkways and in particular east–west connections – which would facilitate the area's growth as an upper middle-class residential district and as one of the region's principal playgrounds. He was especially laudatory about Westchester's county park and parkway plan, which he referred to often as worthy of widespread imitation. Always eager to promote garden cities, he felt that the area had several suitable sites and he recommended also the reservation of areas for agriculture both as greenbelts and to ensure that farming was not wiped out by suburbanization or emparkment[35].

Given the length of experience and pioneering contributions of the distinguished panel, it is not surprising that there were substantial differences between them in both methods and emphases. In 'a masterful summary' of November 1923, Adams attempted to extract from the sector reports certain general themes. In doing so, he shaped the Regional Plan more precisely than anyone else. Frankly meliorist, he accepted the continued growth of the region. Acknowledging that Manhattan would remain its focus, he declared that some functions – for example, theatres and high finance – would continue to be centralized. Advocating more radial links between centre and periphery, more importantly he argued for a series of semi-circular road and rail by-passes round the region for through traffic. He pressed the advantages, social, economic and environmental, of satellite communities and scouted the formation of development corporations to encourage industrial decentralization and to build new towns. Though he ignored housing because it was already under investigation, he was scathing about the domination of residential development by real estate speculators; instead of their wasteful and substandard subdivisions, he wanted residential areas related to the landscape. He made an interesting proposal for more equitable property taxes, evening out the differences between industrial and non-industrial towns. A substantial increase in open spaces was proposed, particularly waterfront reservations and wedges of farmland dividing urban developments. With a great future for air travel predicted, Adams counselled the acquisition of an adequate number of landing sites ahead of need[36].

It was clear that the Regional Plan was to be no revolutionary prescription but rather the imposition of mild public controls on a free development pattern so as to improve metropolitan efficiency and curb the market's worst abuses while adding non-controversial public benefits like modern motor roads, parks and beaches. It represented what Adams had been saying about metropolitan regions since he had first studied London and New York a decade earlier. It was the sort of challenge for which he had hungered and thirsted during that time. When the Advisory Planning Group summary appeared, that challenge rested in his hands.

Norton had been in no hurry to appoint his 'supreme commander', preferring first to test the feasibility of the project, gauge public support and launch the necessary surveys and studies. However, by the beginning of 1923, he was aware that 'We shall soon reach the stage where we would welcome a chief planner'. He was more impressed with Adams than with any other contender. Adams had been a frequent correspondent since 1921 and in the summer of 1922 had escorted Norton and Keppel round the London region – and the British planning establishment. Norton felt he had the 'quality of practical sense' he desired in a supreme commander, finding him 'harder headed, more practical' than Unwin, whom he described as 'more the philosopher and idealist'. Adams was 'a man to do things and to do them well'. In short, Adams was a businessman's planner with a realistic notion of possibilities, a prior commitment to functionalism and economic efficiency, a dynamic organizer and a skilled and experienced administrator, able to moderate differences and harness awkward personalities in a common task. He had a more perceptive and rounded understanding of metropolitan planning than his contemporaries and his posts in Britain and Canada had been altogether more august than those attained by any American planner[37].

The need to appoint a chief planner was reinforced by the impending departure, in the autumn of 1923, of Frederick P. Keppel, the executive secretary. The situation was complicated further by Norton's unexpected death in March 1923. His former chief, ex-President Taft, summed him up succinctly: 'His interest was catholic, his mind constructive, and his vision broad and confident'. With his going, the Regional Plan lost much of its breadth of vision, imagination and galvanic spirit. Norton had devoted much if not most of his time to the plan; had he lived, he would have probably cramped the style of the chief planner and given the plan something of the aura of the 'City Beautiful' as well as a strong tinge of *noblesse oblige*. No one could truly replace him but there had to be a chairman of the Regional Plan Committee. The natural choice was Frederic A. Delano, a quieter, more deliberate man with experience of the Chicago plan, a genuine commitment to environmental reform, executive ability and a determination to honour Norton's memory. He was not, however, ordinarily resident in New York and had widely-scattered business interests which entailed lengthy absences. Moreover, he had doubts about the plan's viability and toyed with the idea of converting it to a planning advisory service[38].

Adams had been sounded out on his availability for more intensive work before Norton's death. There was a hiatus while the chairmanship was settled but in fact Delano's terms for taking it on involved Adams's appointment as chief planner. Delano accepted the leadership on condition 'that he would have approximately full-time help from some qualified planning expert of proved executive capacity. His candidate for the position would be Thomas Adams'. Following amicable discussions, Adams's appointment as General Director of Plans and Surveys (his own title) was confirmed on 3 July 1923.

He was to take charge from 1 October at an annual salary of $12,000 for four years with additional sums for travel, domestic expenses and termination of other contracts. He would give nine months of the year to the Regional Plan (including a month away from the city). He was given a free hand on personnel, ample funds and, as a result of Delano's frequent absences, responsibility for many of the organizational and planning decisions. Though the Sage staff were understandably apprehensive at having such a powerful head thrust upon them, the trustees were unanimously 'convinced of his exceptional ability and fitness for this job'. Adams was well aware of his delicate position in relation to the committee above him and the staff below him; no better diplomat could have been found. Furthermore, the Briton's restrained liberalism matched perfectly the Americans' cautious progressivism. The six months between Norton's death and Adams's arrival hid the subtle change in the plan's direction from gifted but slightly erratic amateurism to a methodical and possibilist professionalism[39].

ADAMS TAKES OVER

When Adams arrived at Sage headquarters in October 1923, he faced a number of problems. Finding a plan in which planners were peripheral beings, he had to establish the centrality of the planner's role, which he achieved by gaining approval for his suggested title of General Director of Plans and Surveys. Recognizing his sensitive position in relation to the committee on the one hand and the staff on the other, he paid a friendly deference to the former and built up an informal but intimate relationship with the latter based upon regular consultations and the occasional social gathering, at which Adams himself took a leading part in lampooning the Regional Plan. He had also to endow the plan with greater cohesion and efficiency and to speed its production. In this regard, he moderated the rather rigid proposals of Delano but gained effective personal control over staff organization, appointments and activity[40].

More difficult was the task of weaning the committee away from the younger Henry James's notion of replacing the projected regional plan by a planning advisory service, a proposal supported initially by Delano. As always, Adams compromised skilfully, enhancing the public relations and advisory functions of the staff but at the same time pressing ahead with proposals to complete the Regional Plan within four years, as Norton had intended. Within a few weeks of his arrival, he was able to inform Keppel that 'The Committee have now a clear objective and regard completion of the Plan as their first and most important task'. He brought the architectural committees under his control, thus avoiding too close and publicly-damaging an association with 'City Beautiful' ambitions. Always adept at public relations, he kept the Regional Plan in the news through a series of addresses and articles in a variety of journals[41].

A further group of problems was not so easily resolvable. There were in the Regional Plan's area three states and almost 500 other public bodies, including the young colossus the Port Authority of New York and the well-established but politically-troublesome City of New York. On the horizon was that remarkable proconsular figure, Robert Moses, baneful or benevolent influence, depending on one's standpoint, on New York, city and state, for forty years to come. The states played little direct part in the Regional Plan, though plan leaders supported moves to improve planning legislation. They liaised closely with counties and municipalities, intent on getting planning and the plan's specific proposals accepted at the local level. The City of New York was under Tammany domination during this time and there was little sympathy or indeed contact between the patrician leaders of the Regional Plan and the plebeian bosses of Gotham. The flamboyant Jimmy Walker, Mayor in 1926, invited the committee to take part in a bid to start planning in the city but an attempt to obtain the necessary enabling legislation at Albany failed in 1929 and it was not until 1936 that the city had a planning commission. In any case, once Nelson P. Lewis had retired in 1920, there was little awareness in the city administration of the need for comprehensive planning[42].

Much more receptive to the Regional Plan was the Port Authority, whose rationale was based on the planned development of the port and its communications and facilities. In general, the relationship between the Regional Plan people and the Port Authority was cordial, after some early disagreements on Hudson River crossings[43]. On the other hand, the regional planners' contacts with the ubiquitous Moses were often adversarial, due to Moses' aggressive posture and contempt for patricians and professional planners and his schemes for popularizing Long Island which were disagreeable to the plan's promoters[44].

Adams found, to his discomfort and embarrassment, that local institutions frequently cited the Regional Plan, sometimes inaccurately, in statements and that he and his colleagues were caught often in the cross-fire between bodies in dispute. He discovered, too, that no one agency had the purview or the power to represent the metropolitan region in a comprehensive fashion. The Regional Plan group possessed a conception of the urban region but lacked the muscle to implement its policies while groups which did have the executive strength lacked an overall view. The implementation of the plan would rest on its leaders' ability to persuade institutions with more specific remits to take its advice; alternatively, the planners could take on board others' projects and weave them into the plan's fabric. The experience of the New York region in the inter-war years demonstrated the inability of public authority to come to terms with social and economic trends which rendered nugatory old political boundaries, whether geographical or philosophical ones[45].

THE REGIONAL SURVEY OF NEW YORK AND ITS ENVIRONS

The Regional Plan team attempted to fill this gap in the political structure. It surveyed the region in detail before making its plan. Though conducted by experts, the surveys were established and broadly defined by Norton. Work began in 1921, individual reports were published at intervals and then gathered into eight volumes, which appeared between 1927 and 1931 and were under the general editorship of Thomas Adams[46]. He wrote much of the material and explained that:

> The survey has been made with the general object of examining the growth, characteristics, and needs of the communities in the whole urban region . . . and to summarize and present the results in a form that would offer guidance in the preparation of a plan so designed as to secure the best possible development of the whole Region[47].

Adams inherited several disparate surveys, vying with each other to form the basis of the Regional Plan. They seemed to him to be too broad, too leisurely, too distant from each other and ill-focused. He limited their scope and time-scales to what was strictly relevant to the formation of a plan, which he was anxious to draft by 1927. He suspended the legal survey, headed by Edward M. Bassett, a sage of environmental law, possibly because Bassett's strict constructionism was antagonizing other workers on the plan, and made him his personal legal advisor. The money thus saved was used to strengthen the staffs of the other surveys[48].

The eight volumes of the Regional Survey represented the most exhaustive and comprehensive study of an area ever undertaken, though it was not pretended that they were either conclusive or all-embracing – Adams admitting that more work needed to be done on the port and air travel, for example, while social and economic changes would require continuous data collection. There was a common format to the studies – each outlined problems and opportunities, identified trends and made specific recommendations – but the overwhelming impression (especially in the sections written by Adams) is of a massive educational exercise, disposing of popular misconceptions of urban growth and planning, often by well-chosen examples, and inculcating a broad perspective on regional planning[49].

The economic survey dealt with a dozen major industries and elucidated the principal trends in business. It was noted that 'The peak of manufacturing in the center of the city was reached about ten years ago, and a process of decentralization of factories appears to be already under way'. Manhattan continued to hold smaller, highly-skilled operations such as jewellery and printing. The retail trade was re-organizing in sub-centres which were challenging mid-town Manhattan's primacy. Transportation difficulties were inducing warehousing to relocate in the environs, though the authors warned

that cities in the South and West would soon challenge New York's grip on
the national distribution pattern. Manhattan was becoming a centre of economic management rather than one of production or distribution and this trend
seemed likely to spawn yet more skyscrapers – and still more congestion. The
whole tone of the report, however, was one of concurrence with developing
trends, which were assumed to be economically sound, and the region was
encouraged to 'go for growth' in the belief that stagnation or retrenchment
invited decay and that cities existed in a highly competitive league, one in
which New York was already falling behind its rivals[50].

From the physical survey came an encyclopaedic range of studies – on
geography and climate, water supply and sewage problems, the problems of
refuse disposal and oil pollution, power, light and other supply services, and
the distribution and site requirements of hospitals and prisons[51]. Four
enquiries were made into the likely regional population in 1965 (the end of the
plan's 'life expectancy') and while the estimates ranged from 14.5 m to 21 m,
all assumed substantial increases on the 1920 figure of just under 9 m; the
American economy, its urban bases and its managers and servants were
inherently growth-oriented[52]. The concentration of transportation facilities
and major economic institutions round New York gave it enormous potential
for continued expansion throughout the century. The motor age was just
coming into its stride and it was conceded that 'The automobile has helped to
spread residence and concentrate industry and business'. The effective commuting zone now reached up to 25 miles from Manhattan. The new residential development resulting from this spread was, however, repeating the evils
of the inner city, where new slums were arising. The researchers were unsure
of the automobile's long-term effects on the distribution of industry and
population[53]. Other transportation was generally in difficulties. The
renowned engineer William J. Wilgus pointed out that:

> The crisis is actually upon us, as evidenced by the universal outcry for quick
> relief from intolerable conditions in rapid transit, streetcar and bus service,
> suburban transportation, trunk line terminals, freight distribution, harbor
> facilities . . . street traffic and parks and playgrounds[54].

The social survey embraced public health, housing and recreation. In those
days of high incidence of rickets, tuberculosis and similar ailments, it was to
be expected that substantial attention would be paid to adequate standards of
sunlight and air and Adams observed that the chief problem in construction
was to provide enough space about buildings for these natural scourges of disease to wreak their beneficent influences. The whole region suffered from
defective development. Adams recited a long catalogue of evils – the unwise
conversion to multiple occupation of single family homes, the intrusion of
non-conforming uses in residential areas, poor construction and site planning,
overcrowding of dwellings and people in central districts but in the outskirts

settlements too scattered to be economic, lack of sanitation and amenities, and dilapidation of older property. Individual lots were overbuilt in that the building, whether cottage or skyscraper, took up far too much of the ground, creating problems of light, air and access for itself and its neighbours. Adams laid the blame for poor living conditions at the feet of public authorities. Deficient housing was due to 'a lack of public control in permitting bad building development, and not to anything inherent in the economic structure of society', though he somewhat contradicted this firm stance by admitting that three-quarters of the population did not earn enough to be able to purchase homes of their own, while a third of New York City's population (over two million people) lived in sub-standard accommodation, chiefly in 'old-law' tenements. The authorities, though culpable in failing to insist that property owners had duties as well as rights, were only as enlightened as their voters compelled them to be and Adams criticized 'the seeming acceptance by public opinion that the protection of property rights is more important than the health and general welfare of the individual and the family'. Many felt that overcrowding in central areas was inevitable as only then could property earn an economic return[55].

Adams was adamant that present urban conditions were the result not of overgrowth but of 'mis-planning'. In particular, he exploded some popular fallacies which led to this situation. One was that all urban land should be subdivided for building purposes, leaving nothing for public structures and open spaces. A second was that early subdivision of land would release an ample supply of cheap lots – though since sites were generally unimproved, the subdivider made a financial killing and the homeowner and municipality were left to pick up the bill for improvements, frequently more costly than they need have been owing to ill-considered planning. Finally, businessmen assumed that when they located their premises, it was economically essential to push the frontages up to the boundaries, despite the resulting inconvenience to the public. Good subdivision in the region was, unfortunately, the exception rather than the rule and then largely a matter of enlightened self-interest. Many sites remained vacant for years, often tax delinquent and reverting to county possession. Moreover, premature subdivision took good agricultural land out of commission unnecessarily and the public, wrongly, saw the retention of farmland in urban areas as an anachronism, yet the same public yearned for country week-end retreats[56].

Clarence Perry, a thoughtful architect of broad sympathies, contributed a notable personal statement on behalf of planned neighbourhood units, though he observed that these were being created willy-nilly by public reactions to private motoring which involved major thoroughfare widenings, leaving 'small islands separated from each other by raging streams of traffic'. The motor vehicle, Perry noted sardonically, took precedence over all other considerations. He concluded wryly that 'The cellular city is the inevitable product of an automobile age', while the planners' new magic toy, zoning, generally left for residential and community purposes what was not taken by alleged priorities such as industry, business and highways[57].

The recreation survey admitted also that 'The position of the motor car as the predominant user of the street surface is now impregnable, and every other use has to give way to it'. The region was gravely deficient in adequate park and playground provision, especially at the hub. The importance to the region of sufficient access to recreation space was shown by the deaths, injuries and queues on public holidays like the Fourth of July, when highways, railroads and ferries were all clogged with awayday pleasure seekers[58].

Though Adams readily acknowledged that the Regional Survey was not as comprehensive or as exhaustive as he and his colleagues desired, it was nevertheless the most substantial preparatory exercise ever conducted in planning. Handsomely produced, lavishly furnished with maps, graphs, diagrams, drawings and photographs, as well as an enormous range of statistics, it represented the consummation of a great combined operation, skilfully commanded by Adams, who welded the efforts of many contributors into a lucid and systematic dissection of most aspects of life in the New York metropolitan region. By 1927, with the bulk of the necessary data to hand, Adams felt that the decks were clear enough for his team to draw up the Regional Plan itself.

Chapter Seven

The Making of
the Regional Plan,
1929–1938

THE REGIONAL PLAN OF NEW YORK AND ITS ENVIRONS

The surveys were intended 'to get by an analysis of the whole of the elements, an understanding of what the city is, and where it is tending'. Following them, the Regional Plan was to be an attempt 'on the basis of this knowledge, to work out an imaginative conception of the best that can be made of it'. By November 1924, Adams, impatient to complete the great enterprise, was circulating a 'Brief Outline of the Scope of the Plan' and he followed this in December 1926 with the more substantial 'Basic General Assumptions Underlying the Regional Plan'[1]. The actual *Regional Plan of New York and its Environs* was published in two elegant and eloquent volumes, *The Graphic Regional Plan* (1929) and *The Building of the City* (1931). Written largely by Adams himself, the Regional Plan bore his stamp more than that of anyone else, with the debatable exception of Norton. Others, notably Nelson P. Lewis and Delano, had made significant contributions but the final presentation was a classic Adams statement. Its stylistic model was that of the great Edinburgh Whig, Lord Macaulay, its philosophy the pragmatic mean, and its planning a seasoned, measured professionalism[2].

The Regional Plan was fashioned within a framework composed of several constraints. The narrowness of the regular political spectrum permitted only incremental and essentially superficial reforms. Moreover, the 1920s were perceived widely as conservative times in which faith in individualism was renewed and collective prescriptions were unpopular. The mainstream of American planning dictated a meliorist approach, reinforced by the fact that planning was not yet accepted as a routine government function. Indeed, it was often regarded as visionary, impractical, expensive and unduly restrictive of the rights of private property.

The presumed conservatism of the region's public opinion was matched by
that of the plan's backers. Paternalistic *bourgeois gentilhommes,* their watch-
words were caution and consensus. Convinced of the basic soundness of the
American creed of free enterprise, they espoused a classical liberal conception
of the state in which a balance should be struck between the rights of the
individual and the needs of the community. Adams spoke for them in affirming that 'The Regional Plan goes far in proposing restrictions on the rights of
property but no further than it is reasonable to expect public opinion to go or
government to authorize in future'. Adopting a negative, regulatory view of
public planning authority, they agreed with Adams that 'The function of
government is to govern and not to compete with private enterprise in constructive undertakings'. They required of their professional advisors a blueprint for the maximization of regional economic efficiency and the winning
over of the public to their own values of stability, order and harmony. Looking towards an urban environment of classical dignity and a rural one of
tranquil beauty, they did not consider that a drastic shift in public
environmental policy was either desirable or possible, endorsing Adams's
disbelief 'that there would be any revolutionary change on the part of the
public in favour of a more ideal system of city development'. Their inherent
meliorism was cemented by their links, via Norton and Delano, with the
arch-priest of meliorist planning, Daniel Hudson Burnham[3].

By the time he took on the Regional Plan, Adams, who to some extent wore
Burnham's mantle, was in his fifties, his philosophical mould long set. A
possibilist, Adams's realism was well-honed by thirty years of battling his way
from a professional limbo to an international reputation as a master creator of
a new profession. Like his employers, he believed that the perimeters of
American planning were circumscribed strictly by current values, institutions
and conditions and also by trends of transcendent power which could be
moderated but not reversed. He sought 'an ideal based on realities' and held
that 'a plan of an urban region must present a picture of possibilities within
the limits of reasonable anticipation of what the collective intelligence of the
community will accept and promote'. Aware that the plan's implementation
depended upon an obvious moderation, an evident practicality and skilful
propaganda, Adams produced a plan in which an untutored and suspicious
public was led gently to endorse higher environmental standards within a
familiar philosophical and urban context. The Adams path was the middle
way between 'the visionless realist' and 'the unrealistic idealist'. The Regional
Plan attempted to ameliorate the problems identified by the surveys and to
direct known tendencies in regional growth to the community's benefit. It was
limited further by Adams's conception of regional planning, which was the
creation of a flexible outline structure plan within which detailed local plans
would fit with the precision of pieces in a jigsaw. Finally, it was restricted by
its reliance upon hundreds of other more specific or more localized agencies
to implement its recommendations. Thus it was often accommodationist,

incorporating almost verbatim existing proposals, such as Westchester County's park and parkway system and the Port Authority's suggestions on transportation and communications. The Regional Plan was, therefore, a conservative document, its temporizing opportunism conditioned by both internal and external constraints upon the planners' vision[4].

The Regional Plan's proposals were predicated on three principal assumptions – substantial further growth of the region's population and urbanized area, the primacy of the economic function in urban life and planning, and the continued domination of the region by New York City and in particular its great port. Acknowledging that 'we cannot overcome the economic forces that make cities as large as New York', the regional planners believed that they should 'make plans for what appears to be inevitable growth'. Arguing further that 'what matters is not quantity but quality of growth', they were confident of their ability as technocratic professionals 'to give that growth the right direction with more spaciousness'. Though the spread of hydro-electric power might enable other cities to reduce New York's dominance, the city had a great potential for sustained growth if artificial improvements could be grafted on to its natural assets. In order to give himself the maximum margin for error, Adams chose the highest of the projections for the 1965 population – 21 millions. Stating that 'The chief purpose of a city is to give satisfaction to human wants', he identified the first of these as 'the means of livelihood', placing 'an agreeable environment' second; in so doing, he remained faithful to the principle he had propounded for almost two decades, that planners must recognize that cities were primarily economic organisms. Finally, in all of the plan's recommendations it was evident that the whole of the 5000-square mile region was to be tributary to the port of New York, which 'will continue to be the most important focus of regional growth'. All other communities, whether existing or projected, were regarded at best as semi-independent satellites[5].

The basic conundrum facing the regional planners was how to accommodate, on a satisfactory land-use basis, twice the existing population and its accompanying urban functions while at the same time reducing the congestion in central areas. Thus, while introducing elements of regional economic and social planning to an extent greater than any previous plan, the Regional Plan of New York was still essentially an exercise in physical planning. 'What we have to pursue as our primary task', wrote Adams, 'is the making of a comprehensive ground diagram'. He was convinced that the expected population increase could be settled and environmental standards raised at the same time. By intelligent planning, New York City alone could house an additional three million people at a density of ten houses to the acre. Furthermore, a regional population double that anticipated in 1965 could be placed on a quarter of the region's land without overcrowding it. 'There is no want of land to enable twenty-one million people to live in spacious surroundings within a radius of twenty-five miles of Manhattan', asserted Adams. Forecasting that rapid

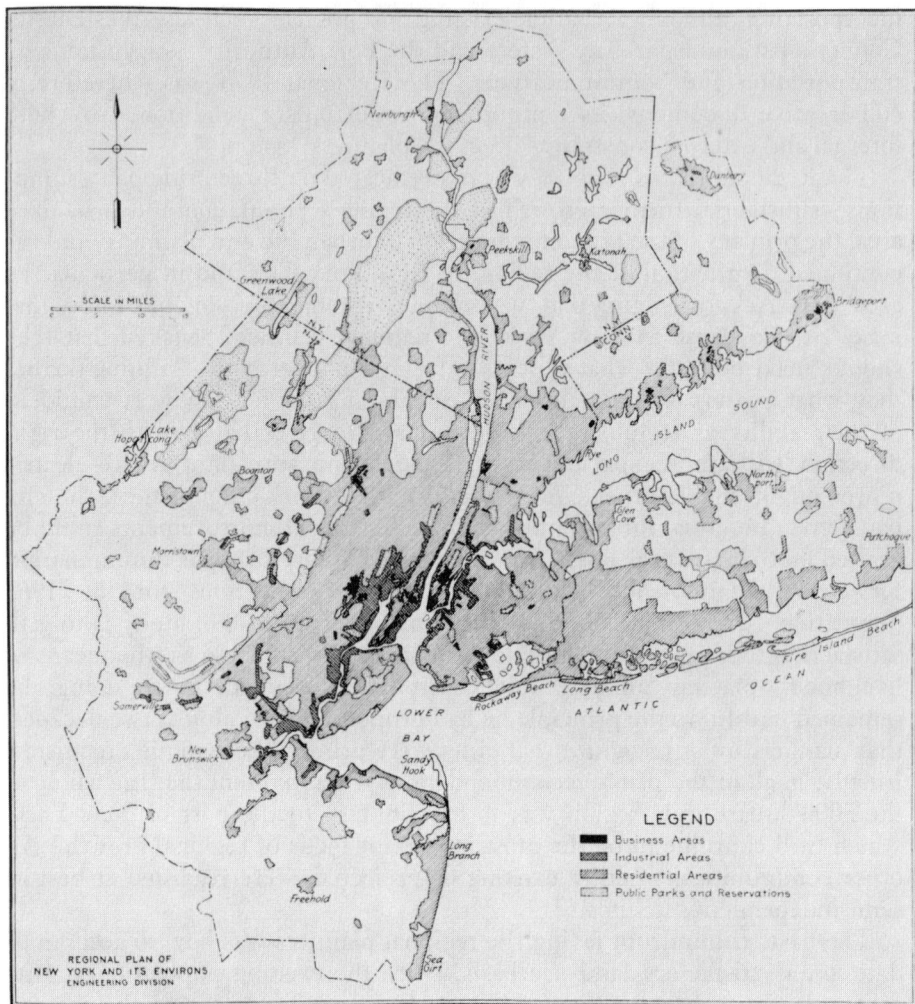

FIGURE 16. Regional Plan of New York: Proposed Land Uses, 1929.

Business and industrial areas occupy prime sites adjacent to the harbour. Residential settlement sprawls inland and along waterways and the coast. The regional planners could not seriously alter the existing pattern. (Thomas Adams *et al.*, *The Graphic Regional Plan*, 1929)

decentralization of industry and population would continue, he prophesied that if it was directed as suggested in the Regional Plan, 'we can visualize the spreading of urban growth outwards over great open spaces in the environs rather than adding in an unhealthy degree to its intensity in a few centres'. The means of distributing economic activity and residential accommodation over the region more evenly and rationally were land-use controls and an integrated transportation and communications network[6].

The regional planners' proposals for the use of land and the control of building were divided, in effect, into those for the built-up area and others for the still largely virgin outer districts. Adams explained the reason for this division:

> In an existing urban region where large areas are already built upon, and where building growth has taken place in a haphazard manner, so far as uses and the densities of buildings are concerned, nothing more can be done than to secure some amelioration of established evils. Fundamental planning which permits of adequate preventive measures is practicable only in areas that are not yet developed[7].

Thus the planners acknowledged defeat on central area planning before they had begun, eschewing compulsory purchase and redevelopment by civic authorities. 'Improvement in central areas', Adams felt, 'depends mainly on the voluntary action of owners of property and on their initiative in obtaining collaboration from the city in reducing densities'. Such proposals as they made for Manhattan were largely cosmetic or marginal improvements in transportation and street capacity. The skyscraper was accepted as an inevitable concomitant of a free market in land but Adams wanted to limit future giants to a lot occupancy not exceeding 20 per cent, thus allowing, for themselves and their neighbours, adequate light, air and access. Heavy port-related industries were to be encouraged to relocate in the Newark–Hackensack Meadows neighbourhood where seaborne and railroad freight facilities dovetailed and could be improved without undue difficulty[8].

Major recommendations were reserved, therefore, for the less developed and therefore more malleable hinterland. Local planning and zoning boards were urged to impose tough, permanent yet simple regulations on building heights and bulks, land uses and subdivisions on the basis that no property owner should have the freedom to injure his neighbours. Developers should be made to pay in advance for public utilities and amenities. A general reduction in suburban housing densities from 20 per acre to 10 per acre was advocated. In the main, Adams was intent merely upon supervising the trend to residential decentralization to ensure that it conformed to higher standards than in earlier suburbs. 'The suggested distribution of uses shown on the Graphic Plan', he admitted, 'does not indicate any radical change in the direction of growth'. Most industrial areas were already zoned as such and were in accord with the Regional Plan but he did recommend the setting up of a Regional Industrial Development Agency to relate new manufacturing plants to transport and port facilities and he advised local authorities to group industries on estates. Business centres should be located at major road intersections[9].

Adams's potentially most significant proposal was for the creation of satellite towns at the conjunction of the principal radial and circumferential arteries. He was careful not to describe them as garden cities for they would be still subservient to the great core city yet he hoped that they would share the same design characteristics. Among these were low-density housing of a uniformly decent standard, the combination of the best features of town and country, adequate provision for open space and public buildings and a skilfully-integrated hierarchy of highways. They were to be as self-contained economically as was consistent with their regional and ultimately dependent status and were intended to eliminate much of the 'friction of space' which was becoming the most notable feature of current regional development. Adams termed this planned reintegration of residence and employment 'recentralization', arguing that a reasonable degree of industrial concentration was necessary for business efficiency; properly handled, it need not degenerate into congestion. Factories, houses, commercial centres and other functions would enjoy local segregation but 'every area that is adaptable for industrial development should have, either contiguous or easily accessible to it, areas for the accommodation and recreation of its workers'. A satellite town would be, therefore, 'a well-balanced community' enjoying 'the highest efficiency, the most wholesome living conditions, and the greatest economy in work and travel'[10].

Adams averred that there were plenty of sites for satellite communities but refused to name them (other than general references to Jamaica Bay and Hackensack Meadows) for fear of starting off speculative rushes. Apart from suggesting the establishment of public development corporations to acquire their sites and commending the philanthropic model community at Radburn, New Jersey, as their exemplar, he made no specific recommendations for the implementation of his boldest initiative; in fact, a proposed survey volume on housing and new towns was shelved as potentially controversial. He concluded with the vague hope that regional development would be 'in the direction of a well-balanced distribution of buildings and avoid deflection toward the extremes of either excessive concentration or excessive diffusion'[11].

The ability to diffuse industry and population more widely throughout the region depended upon the provision of an integrated transportation system. There was a longstanding need for greater efficiency and economy of movement for both freight and passengers. The region's communications needed to be more closely related to land-use patterns. An adequate transportation system, particularly in the outer districts, would permit the establishment of new growth poles and open up the undeveloped webs between existing radial routes. It was intended further to make the whole system essentially self-supporting, including the major highways. Finally, there was a deliberate policy of separating through traffic from local movements and freight from cars. The principal means of rationalizing traffic flows, integrating the various modes of transport and promoting a more even distribution of business and

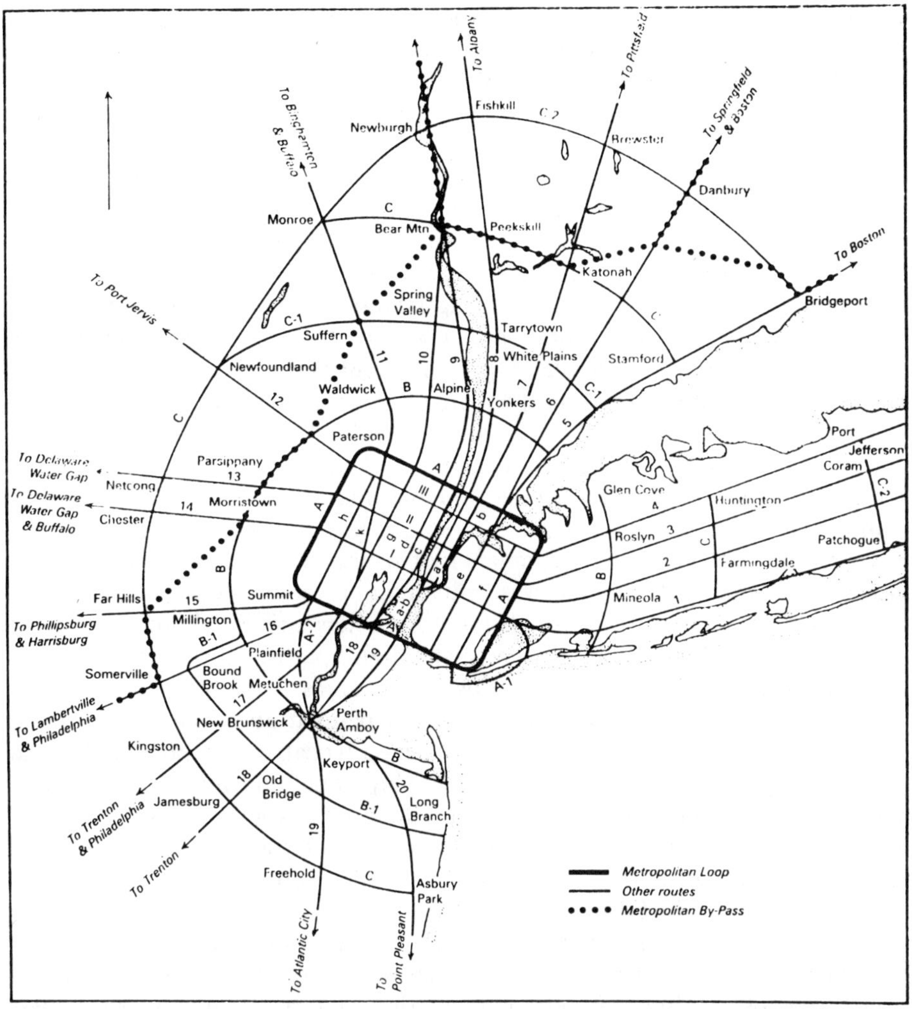

FIGURE 17. Regional Plan of New York: Diagrammatic Scheme for Regional Highway Routes, 1929.

The arcs were designed to route through traffic away from congested inner-city areas. It was hoped that satellite towns would be established at the intersections between arcs and radials. Rail and rapid transit proposals were along similar lines of circumferential and radial routes. (Thomas Adams *et al.*, *The Graphic Regional Plan*, 1929)

residence, including satellite centres, was to be by the construction of a series of loops, punctuated by radial spokes. The innermost loop served the metropolitan core around the harbour while others at intervals of several miles served the principal suburbs, a by-pass route from Philadelphia to

Boston, and the outermost towns on the regional frontier. Highways, rapid transit and railroads were intended to share some of these belts, with interchange points at regular intervals[12].

Of the various forms of transport, the regional planners laid most emphasis on the railroads, forecasting substantial increases in both freight and passenger traffic. They urged extensive electrification, unified management of the trunk lines, union passenger terminals, new crossings of the Hudson and numerous connecting lines. Rapid transit was to siphon off from the railroads many of the latter's commuters, engage in total electrification and develop connections between New Jersey, Long Island and Manhattan. A hierarchy of roads was proposed, embracing several limited-access expressways and regional highways, city boulevards and suburban and country parkways reserved for private automobiles, a score of new radial routes, the preparation of definitive street maps and the acquisition of land ahead of need. The trend towards mass car ownership was accepted and strenuous endeavours to keep pace with it in respect of driving and parking space were recommended. Guided wisely, the spread of private motoring could help to widen the corridors of growth. The new phenomenon of air travel was more difficult for the planners to cope with, since it was in its infancy yet developing rapidly, and they made only tentative proposals for sixteen new airports though they were imaginative enough to recommend safe flight paths, substantial terminal facilities and fast connections to downtown areas. Finally, reiterating the cardinal principle that New York's future depended upon the maximization of the potential of the harbour, the planners advocated new port facilities at Jamaica Bay and Newark, a New Jersey ship canal and improvements to a number of channels. Most of the proposals on transportation were derived from existing recommendations, notably those of the Port Authority and many highway authorities, the Regional Plan often suggesting merely co-ordination and the filling in of gaps[13].

There were three major problems relating to open space. One was that acreage per head was generally lower than was desirable. Secondly, built-up areas were often almost bereft of recreation facilities. Thirdly, wilderness areas were fast disappearing under various forms of urban development or were rising markedly in price. Adams advocated a regional standard of one acre of open space for every acre of building or, expressed another way, one acre to every three or four hundred people. The region possessed ample suitable land to meet these requirements. However, the planners acknowledged that in areas already developed the creation of new open spaces would be a slow and expensive task. Nevertheless, they advocated a steady policy of establishing neighbourhood parks and playgrounds. Given the grave shortage of inner-city open spaces, it was all the 'more necessary to preserve and extend' Central Park which was 'more in danger of injury and contraction than any city park in the region'. The regional planners were worthy heirs of Olmsted and Vaux in holding firm to the designers' intentions. Elsewhere in

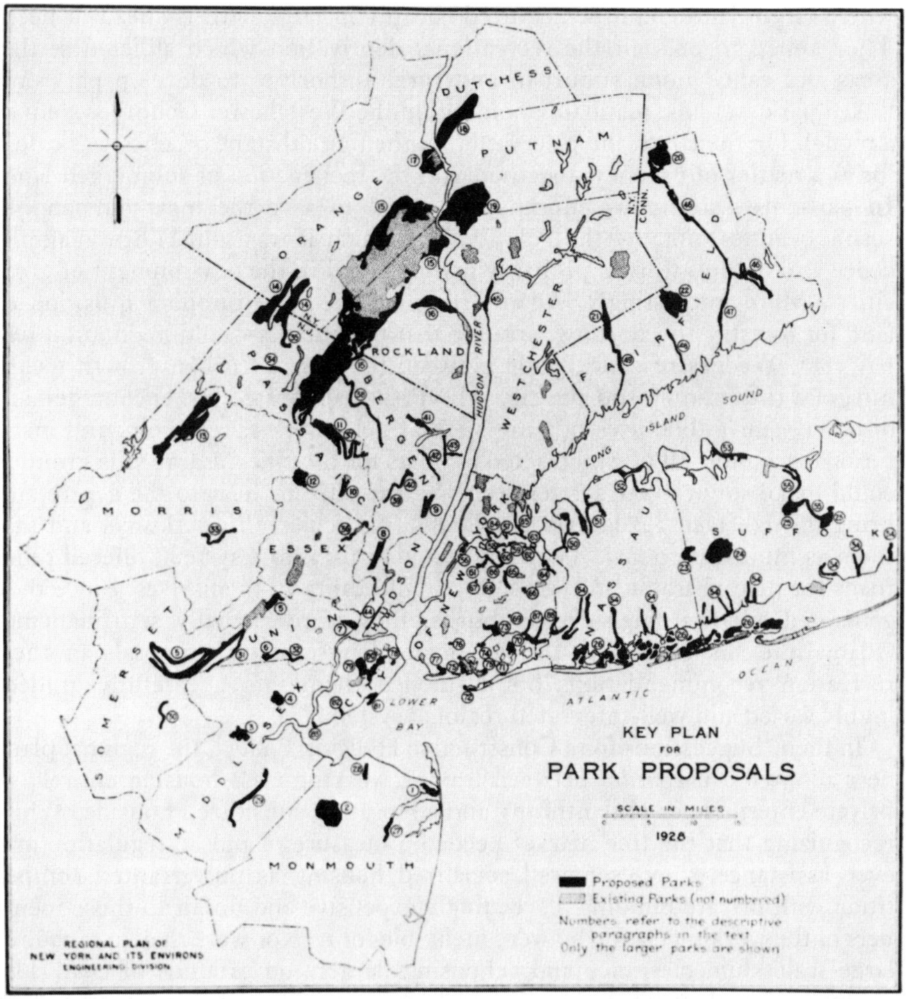

KEY PLAN
FOR
PARK PROPOSALS

SCALE IN MILES

1928

■ Proposed Parks
▒ Existing Parks (not numbered)

Numbers refer to the descriptive
paragraphs in the text
Only the larger parks are shown

REGIONAL PLAN OF
NEW YORK AND ITS ENVIRONS
ENGINEERING DIVISION

FIGURE 18. Regional Plan of New York: Key Plan for Park Proposals, 1928.
Major reservations were far out in the Adirondacks, beyond the suburban fringe. The long thin lines are parkways, intended to link the inner urban zone with the unalloyed countryside. Much of the Hudson valley shoreline had been pre-empted by other forms of development. (Thomas Adams, *et al.*, *The Graphic Regional Plan*, 1929).

New York City, they proposed an enlarged Battery Park, plazas, linear parks and parkways on the East and West Sides of Manhattan, parks on the East River islands and parkways for the Bronx. They had imaginative ideas for city centre waterfronts and playgrounds and even suggested roof-top recreation areas[14].

Their chief recommendations, however, related to more distant parts where virgin land could be acquired cheaply in large parcels ahead of need. They aimed to prevent the recreational deprivation which afflicted settled areas and called upon suburban and rural authorities to develop parkway-linked park systems, justifiably holding up the Westchester County system as a model. On the coast, the reservation of the more distant beaches was called for as a matter of urgency, together with the reclamation of submerged land. In particular, strenuous efforts were urged to save the most outstanding scenic beauties, notably the Palisades, of which it was said 'Their magnificence as a natural feature probably had no equal in the environment of great cities'. More interestingly, Adams recommended the public acquisition of land for forestry and farming, arguing that the tenants would maintain it *and* pay rent. Wedges of countryside between the arms of urban growth would integrate the country and the city. He further advocated the encouragement of other semi-public uses of land, such as golf courses, reservoirs and institutional grounds, all of which acted as lungs for the cities. Large villa grounds could make suburbs attractive, keep wealthy citizens near to the centre and bring in high taxes. Adams was addicted particularly to parkways and saw them as multi-functional. They connected parks into a system, offered relief roads for private traffic and were objects of beauty in themselves. Since they generated adjacent high-class suburbs, they were virtually self-financing. Adams and his colleagues utilized many longstanding proposals in their recreation recommendations but fashioned them into a carefully graded, highly varied and well-integrated regional system[15].

In their 'Suggestions for a Constructive Housing Policy', the regional planners adopted a *via media* between leaving working-class housing entirely to private enterprise or philanthropy and advocating subsidized housing. While recognizing that the free market needed a measure of public regulation and even assistance, they eschewed socialized housing as unwarranted competition with private building, exceedingly expensive and unfair to those members of the working class who were ineligible for it. Nor were they in favour of large-scale slum clearance and rehousing, largely on grounds of cost. The planners put their faith in new and cheaper materials and methods of construction, the example of Radburn and other model communities, co-operative savings and loan associations and low-interest mortgages. All housing should return a fair profit. These were familiar nostrums of most housing reformers but the regional planners sanctioned also the public acquisition, improvement and zoning of building land provided that it was then sold or leased, on strict conditions, to private builders; in this way, inner-city mistakes and the evils of speculation would be prevented and owner-occupiers would gain decent houses at reasonable prices in spacious surroundings and equipped with a full range of services and amenities. Thus the bulk of the working class was to be encouraged to relocate in undeveloped areas, hopefully in association with a similar shift in their places of employment[16].

It was acknowledged that improvements in central districts would be both slow and expensive to carry out. Public authorities were advised to widen streets, open lanes through congested blocks (thus reducing densities), and provide playgrounds and neighbourhood parks. Slum clearance was to be dependent, however, on tenants' demands for better conditions, the realization by landlords that slums were uneconomic and the gradual acquisition of land for public purposes by the authorities and the demolition of unfit houses. Housing had, however, a low priority in land allocation. 'Where land has a value based on a more profitable use than low-cost housing, such as business or expensive residences', wrote Adams, 'it should not be used for such housing'. Furthermore, in order to settle workers close to their places of employment, it might be necessary to compromise between healthy surroundings and the demands of economic efficiency[17].

THE PLAN'S RECEPTION: MELIORISTS VERSUS INSURGENTS

The two plan volumes were launched at sumptuous gatherings of the local establishment. It was their Regional Plan and they embraced it with enthusiasm. President Hoover, Governor Franklin D. Roosevelt of New York and the Governors of Connecticut and New Jersey all commended it. The extensive press comments were highly favourable, the *Engineering News–Record* describing it as 'a model for all similar studies made elsewhere'. Adams himself earned special encomiums. The *Survey Graphic* pronounced that 'Thomas Adams – America's best known Scotchman – his burr is even better than Ramsay MacDonald's – is the most distinguished city planner of our time'. John Nolen summed up the prevailing sentiment among meliorist planners and their supporters: 'The work accomplished in the New York region is not only large but significant, not only local in importance but national'[18].

The major discordant note amid the general paean of praise arose from the insurgent or radical strain of planning. This alternative tradition was now in the hands of the Regional Planning Association of America (R.P.A.A.), formed in 1923 by a small coterie as elitist in its own way as the Regional Plan group. Among its leaders were the architects Clarence Stein and Henry Wright, the housing reformer Catherine Bauer, the developer Alexander M. Bing, the economic journalist Stuart Chase, the forester Benton MacKaye and the precocious writer Lewis Mumford. Key members of the group came together in the wartime community planning programme and met informally in the R.P.A.A., making occasional sallies into print or the lecture hall. Grafting on to the elder Olmsted's communitarian principles the regionalism of the French human geographers and the related emphasis on the interdependence of town and country of Patrick Geddes, they drew also upon the Garden City philosophy and design standards of Ebenezer Howard and Raymond Unwin, adding finally a dash of the iconoclastic Thorstein Veblen. From this background there emerged a 'mildly socialist' conception of planning which aimed to subordinate 'speculation and profiteering to the welfare of the community'. It involved a rejection of the capitalist ethic in favour of a socialist one[19].

The insurgents' radical manifesto was the *Report* of the New York State Commission of Housing and Regional Planning (1926). Stein was the Commission's chairman but the report was written by its Planning Advisor, Henry Wright. Previous growth, largely uncontrolled, had resulted in 80 per cent of the state's population living on only 15 per cent of the land – mostly in the 400-mile long, 25-mile wide Hudson-Mohawk corridor. Congestion in the cities was matched by widespread rural depopulation. To reverse these unwholesome tendencies, Wright proposed a state planning agency which would co-ordinate the plans of the several regions, themselves overseeing local community plans. Articulating the insurgent philosophy, he declared that 'The aim of the state should be clearly to improve the conditions of life rather than promote opportunities for profit'. People and their work should be dispersed evenly throughout the state, the motor vehicle and 'giant power' having rendered industries and labour more mobile. Modern technology, applied effectively, would revitalize rural life and restore it to parity with urban life in terms of economic and cultural opportunities. Cities, limited in population and area, would benefit from easy access to the countryside and the rigid distinction between the two would disappear. Each would enjoy the advantages of the other without the disadvantages of either. 'By using nature and machinery intelligently', argued Wright, 'we can make them serve our human purposes'. On the fertile plains there should be truck farming, manufacturing and compact cities; dairying and crops would dominate the upland plateaux; and the highlands would be reserved for forests, reservoirs and hydro-electric plants. Wright believed that his sketch, an enticing blend of nature and technology, represented the true gospel, genuine regional planning as opposed to the metropolitan planning of the Regional Plan group. The sponsor of the state plan was Governor Alfred E. Smith but it was shelved when he fixed his sights on the White House and shifted his patronage to Robert Moses, who seemed to despise planners and was especially contemptuous of aesthetic social democrats like the R.P.A.A. group[20].

The relationship between the Regional Plan of New York group and the R.P.A.A. members was from the start an uneasy one, not unnaturally since they represented diametrically opposed views. From 1923 until 1932 there were intermittent attempts at co-operation and reconciliation, punctuated by polite though strong criticism. The youthful but formidable Lewis Mumford was the principal spokesman for the R.P.A.A. and threw down the gauntlet to the metropolitan regionalists as early as 1923, answering his own question 'Wilt thou play with Leviathan?' with a ringing 'Let Leviathan go hang'[21].

The fundamental antipathy between the two schools of regional planning was revealed most clearly in a special issue of *Survey Graphic* published to celebrate the New York meeting of the International Federation of Town Planning and Garden Cities in 1925. Declaring bluntly that 'This number has been written by a group of insurgents', the R.P.A.A. writers had two aims: to condemn what Stein called 'Dinosaur Cities' and those who sought to ameliorate and prolong their troubled and fragile existences; and to launch a preliminary version of their alternative strategy for town and country. At the conference itself one of their heroes, Ebenezer Howard, speaking of the Regional Plan proposals, lamented that 'Too little of your thinking is concerned with the vital factor – the decentralization of big cities – and too much with the sort of patching which will in the end aggravate the existing conditions'[22]. Reporting on the conference, Mumford noted that the two groups

> ... stand symbolically at opposite poles; one assumes that technical ability can improve living conditions while our existing economic and social habits continue; the other holds that technical ability can achieve little that is fundamentally worth the effort until we reshape our institutions in such a way as to subordinate financial and property values to those of human welfare[23].

Adams, who was also at the meeting, attempted to set up a dialogue with the R.P.A.A. but neither side was prepared to make any concessions and Mumford continued to snipe at Regional Plan statements and publications, dismissing the scheme as 'nothing bolder ... than an orderly dilution of New York over a fifty-mile circle'. His attack grew more savage over the years. Fearing the imminent consummation of a Boston–New York–Philadelphia megalopolis, he castigated the growth dynamic and its associated meliorism which informed the Regional Plan:

> Our technicians usually accept the fact of unregulated and unbounded growth as 'given'. So instead of attempting to remove the causes that create our mangled urban environments, they attempt only to relieve a few of the intolerable effects ... none of their remedies permanently remedies anything[24].

Mumford charged further that the regional planners were dominated by the privatism which had brought about 'intolerable' and 'botched' cities in the first place:

> Our municipal engineers and city planners, despite good intentions and technical skill, are all agents of a Higher Power, and the sort of city planning they continue to produce exists to protect and tenderly cherish the one function that all American cities have traditionally looked upon as the main end of human activity, namely, gambling in real estate[25].

Adams, clearly hurt by Mumford's repeated barbs, made a final attempt to

convert him in 1930, even offering him space for a statement in the second
plan volume. Mumford declined, pointing to 'fundamental differences of
principle and method' between them. Adams and his colleagues concluded
complacently that Mumford's 'premise is false and foolish'[26].

Given the frequent though amiable disagreements between Adams and
Mumford, it is perhaps surprising to find them and their respective colleagues
co-operating in the R.P.A.A. group's one practical venture, the model community at Radburn, New Jersey, designed by Stein and Wright for Bing's
City Housing Corporation and built between 1928 and 1932. A limited
dividend philanthropic enterprise on 1250 acres of virgin land within easy
commuting distance of Manhattan, Radburn was intended to cater for 'the
average family' and an ultimate population of 25,000, supported by some local
sources of employment. It aimed to make 'a scientific attack' on the problems
of community building. Advertised as 'The Town for the Motor Age', its
chief design innovation (adapted from Olmsted's Central Park) was the
separation of vehicles and pedestrians. Planned with a hierarchy of roads and
'super-blocks', it was given an interior park system, culs-de-sac and excellent
amenities and services. Its sponsors and consultants included leading New
York socialites, some of the Russell Sage people and two British advisors,
Raymond Unwin and Seebohm Rowntree. Bing asked the Regional Plan
Committee specifically for Adams's advice, which the latter gave with
enthusiasm though it is impossible to determine the nature of his contribution. He did, however, recognize in Radburn not only an American
descendent of the British Garden Cities but also a splendid example of his
'recentralizing' satellite cities. The two traditions of planning thus met fruitfully at Radburn though the coming of the Great Depression limited the venture to only a third of its intended size. Like so many model communities in
American history, before and since, Radburn remained a tantalizing vision of
what might have become the normal pattern of urban growth[27].

The climactic encounter between the meliorist and insurgent traditions of
American planning occurred in the *New Republic* in 1932. In a two-part
review of the Regional Plan volumes, Mumford was at his most magisterial: 'I
am frank to say at the outset that the Regional Plan of New York and its
Environs is a disappointment'. Not only was it bad for New York, it was 'a
warning rather than a good example' for other urban regions. Condemning its
vision as 'essentially parochial', Mumford complained that the definition of
the region was arbitrary, that the plan's conception lacked focus and consist-
ency and that its surveys were perfunctory. He challenged the assumption
that future metropolitan growth was inevitable, echoing Stein's belief that
urban expansion becomes ultimately uneconomic and ceases through the
operation of natural economic forces. No alternative strategies had been considered because the regional planners served slavishly the interests of the
urban establishment. Moreover, he indicated its timidity, which was due, he
believed, to Adams's 'genius for premature compromise'. This caution,

especially on the role of government, meant that the plan 'carefully refrains from proposing measures which would lead to effective public control of land, property values, buildings and human institutions, and leaves the metropolitan district without the hope of any substantial changes'[28].

Mumford was especially critical of the plan's acceptance of the skyscraper, 'a device for profiteering at the expense of the community'. He scolded Adams for resurrecting the discredited housing policies of the horse-and-buggy age and called for decent subsidized housing, particularly since two-thirds of New York City's population could not afford adequate accommodation. He chastized Adams further for being 'wilfully obtuse' on sites for satellite towns and for failing to lay down a concrete procedure for establishing them. The Regional Plan looked to the full realization of New York's potential, Mumford and the R.P.A.A. to its abandonment. If *he* could not destroy the metropolitan Leviathan, then the Regional Plan might actually do it for him, for 'One of the merits of the Regional Plan . . . is that it might, if thoroughly acted upon, hasten the inevitable collapse and deflation'[29].

In his rejoinder, Adams dismissed Mumford as 'an aesthete-sociologist, who has a religion that is based on high ideals, but is unworkable'. Refuting Mumford's criticisms of specific aspects of the plan, he emphasized that a reasonable degree of concentration was necessary in the modern economy. He acknowledged his willingness to compromise, for 'one must keep to the road, as nearly to the middle of it as possible, if any improvement is to be made'. Mumford had denounced the plan as a 'monumental failure' but Adams rejected his attack finally as 'based on a wrong diagnosis'[30].

Like many other conventional planners, Adams shared the ideals of the R.P.A.A. but, above all, he was a practical man and in practice dealt only with the real world and its more or less immediate and readily attainable possibilities. His utilitarian approach sacrificed some imagination to functionalism and technique but in the American context of the 1920s, it was the only viable philosophy. The metropolis was here to stay; it was absurd to believe that it was about to collapse or that it could be abandoned. While planners should engage in a long-term programme of educating the general public towards a more ideal form of community building, in the short run they had to make existing cities more tolerable and efficient and ensure that future accretions were in the right places and avoided the errors of past additions to the urban mass. Adams believed that there was 'nothing to be gained by conceiving the impossible'. Moreover, visionary nostrums were potentially dangerous for 'A Utopia can be achieved only on the basis of despotism'[31].

The Utopian vision set out in Wright's outline for a state plan and in other R.P.A.A. writings was not feasible in the booming, bourgeois 1920s nor was it within reach even in the more benevolent atmosphere of the New Deal of the 1930s, for the R.P.A.A.'s recommendations were based upon a positive collectivism of proportions quite alien to anything in the American experience. The public acceptance of the R.P.A.A.'s idyllic Fabianism would have required a

political revolution which was never forthcoming, even in the depths of the
Great Depression, while the New Deal itself was meliorism personified.

The immediate situation favoured the meliorists but there is no denying
the truth of the insurgents' prophecy that meliorism would not solve the
fundamental problems of the great city and its vassal neighbours; their radical
prescription might have done so. The makers of the Regional Plan recognized
that America is a business civilization and swam with the current, the insurgents nagging away, more or less impotently, at the mainstream's edge. There
was, therefore, no meeting of minds between the Regional Plan group and the
members of the R.P.A.A.; they 'sailed past each other in the night'. Despite
their mutual interest in Radburn and their common inheritance from Howard
and Geddes, Adams and Mumford, though they remained on good personal
terms and constantly regretted their inability to collaborate on regional planning, represented incompatible traditions which predated them and which
survive them. It was an old dilemma of reformers everywhere which divided
them; Adams contended that the point of difference was 'Whether we stand
still and talk ideals or move forward and get as much realization of our ideals
as possible in a necessarily imperfect society, capable only of imperfect
solutions to its problems'[32].

FROM PLAN TO REALITY

The realization of the Regional Plan was a major problem for its sponsors
since the committee had no official standing and faced a highly fragmented
regional governmental structure, and so in 1929 there was formed a Regional
Plan Association, incorporating the Regional Plan Committee and some of its
staff. It was headed by a well-known New York lawyer, newspaperman and
politician, George McAneny. The other new-comers were also members of
the local elite. Adams wished to enjoy more freedom of employment and ruled
himself out of consideration for the Directorship of the R.P.A., though he
agreed to devote six weeks each year to consultative work. He recommended
his friend John Nolen for the post but the latter was unable to undertake it
on a full-time basis and it went to George B. Ford, equally well-known in
planning circles and another long-standing friend of Adams[33].

The R.P.A. intended 'To foster county, city, town and village planning
within the region centring upon the Port of New York', to liaise with both
public and private institutions in an effort to carry out the plan's proposals
and to raise the public's consciousness of the plan's recommendations. This
last aim was tackled, Chicago style, by the publication of a popular manual
summarizing the plan[34].

The other ambitions were more difficult of attainment. The whole plan was
very nearly wrecked before its voyage had begun. George Ford, who had a
strong social conscience, was disappointed at the plan's lack of positive proposals for social reform, particularly its shyness on the question of low-cost

housing. He wanted an immediate revision of the housing proposals and hinted that the Regional Plan itself should be abandoned in favour of a new one, presumably with a social rather than an economic basis. Fortunately for an embarrassed Adams and other members of the Regional Plan group, Ford was unable to frustrate their intentions, for he died after no more than four months in office. The failure to replace him for several years may account for the R.P.A.'s failure to update the plan substantially, a vital function on which Adams laid great emphasis[35].

Nevertheless, the adroit, persistent and rugged McAneny pushed ahead with the plan's implementation. However, he was not a professional planner nor even as intimately connected with the field as Norton or Delano. His vision was narrower and he thought in terms of projects rather than comprehensive planning. He wrote proudly in 1938 that 'the physical development of the Region is proceeding in accordance with a comprehensive plan which is frankly a composite of proposals by many agencies and individuals'[36]. Viewed in terms of projects completed, the Regional Plan's achievements were high in proportion to its proposals; it outscored easily all of its contemporaries in London, Chicago, Los Angeles and Philadelphia. Despite the freezing climate of the Great Depression, it went ahead at a rapid pace in its early years. Indeed, the anti-depression programmes of Hoover and Roosevelt and their state and local counterparts helped so much to carry out this ready-made agenda of public works that one wonders whether the plan would have enjoyed such a high degree of implementation if times had remained prosperous. The ubiquitous Robert Moses also drew heavily on the shelf of projects for his massive programmes throughout the region. By 1938, McAneny could report that over 40 per cent of the highway and park proposals were completed or in progress, that there was substantial advance in the regional airport system and steady construction on harbour, sewerage, garbage and waterfront improvements. Ultimately, highway construction soared far beyond the apparently adequate proposals of the original Regional Plan and about a half of the recommended open space was acquired for the public. The other major achievement was a notable increase in the number of zoning and planning commissions in the region, so that by 1940, 351 of the region's 495 local authorities had some form of zoning and there were numerous county and city planning commissions[37].

It is doubtful whether Adams was very active as a consultant to the Regional Plan Association but he watched his brainchild's progress with pride. On his last visit to the United States in the summer of 1938, he summed up the plan's achievements in an address to the R.P.A. Acknowledging that New York was a quarter-century ahead of London in planning, he believed that the execution of such a high proportion of the plan's recommendations was 'proof of its soundness and practicability'. He heaped praise, somewhat surprisingly, upon Robert Moses and said of him, 'I know of no-one in our generation who has combined so successfully, as Mr. Moses has, high ideals and a vigorous determination to achieve'; he dismissed Moses's 'occasional skepticism of long-term planning with friendly feelings'. A later generation has been less charitable in its evaluation of Moses's czardom. During the 1930s, Adams seems to have become more reconciled to a higher degree of public activity, since he called finally for the collaboration of public and private enterprise in the clearance and rebuilding of decayed areas and in meeting housing needs[38].

VERDICT ON THE REGIONAL PLAN

The Regional Plan of New York and its Environs certainly fulfilled more of its objectives than any comparable plan but even in areas where its apparent success was greatest – highways, recreation and local planning and zoning – there were reservations to be made. In the first place, general trends in administrative development, transportation and leisure provision would have led to many of the projects recommended being adopted regardless of a regional plan, though almost certainly with less co-ordination and less speedily than was the case. Similarly, public regulation of environmental development was a growing if marginal feature of the American scene though the spread of planning agencies in the region would have been slower without the deliberate encouragement of the Regional Plan's staff. However, the R.P.A. had to admit by 1942 that it was 'becoming increasingly clear that many local planning boards were relatively inactive' while zoning, though covering 96 per cent of the region's population, was largely divorced from planning and served chiefly to ensure the exclusiveness of the wealthier suburbs[39].

The expansion of road building far beyond the Regional Plan's estimates illustrates both the independent dynamic of the motoring phenomenon and the relative failure of the other parts of the plan's transportation proposals. New York City refused to co-operate on rapid transit and the recommendations in that sphere made slow progress. Road-borne public transport suffered from lack of appreciation and investment and the new roads catered largely for private traffic. The railroads, mutually antagonistic dinosaurs from an earlier, cruder age of entrepreneurship, declined to co-operate either with each other or with the planning bodies to any considerable degree, little being achieved on the rails beyond a measure of electrification. Indeed, the railroads were declining and played a far less significant role in regional development than the planners had imagined (though the likelihood of their contraction should have been apparent by the mid-1920s). The region's transport network came to favour the truck and the car, a policy given a substantial boost by the predilection of Robert Moses, the principal highway and park builder in the region, for the private automobile. Similarly, the bulk of the recreation provision was related to the interests of the motoring public, since most of the newly-acquired parks were on distant shores or deep in the countryside, accessible only to car owners. In practice, then, the Regional Plan offered extensive benefits to the suburban, homeowning, commuting, car-driving middle class[40].

If the middle class was the principal beneficiary, the working class gained least – despite Norton's clear identification with their needs. Though the plan called for low-cost housing and satellite towns as an escape from inner-city congestion, it willed the ends without sanctioning the means. Adams was coy on the method of establishment and the location of satellite towns. Wholesale, publicly-regulated decentralization would have undermined land values in both developed and developing districts. The insistence on self-supporting public transport also militated against the relocation of poorer families. In his proposals for low-cost housing, Adams, like his sponsors, remained wedded to futile nineteenth-century policies. By the mid-twentieth century, as more advanced reformers like Catherine Bauer, Edith Elmer Wood and Ernest Bohn recognized, only public authorities could meet low-income housing needs by subsidized construction. The New Deal, though disappointingly slow to recognize the economic opportunities and social needs of this unsatisfied market, did begin to make a contribution, amounting in the New York region to some sixty projects[41].

Assessed in terms of project realization, the Regional Plan was a greater success than any of its contemporaries but its impact on the region was lop-sided in favour of privatism and the mobile middle class. Moreover, it produced what Lewis Mumford had predicted – a slightly more orderly dilution of metropolitan New York over an extensive area, solving neither the problem of dispersal at uneconomically low densities nor the congestion of traffic and commercial functions at the centre. The tentacular spread of New York over its tributary region has continued. Furthermore, the plan's utility was strictly circumscribed in a number of ways. In the first place, cataclysmic events like the Great Depression and World War II altered radically public perceptions of environmental control and government action, in a more positive direction. The first crisis played a major role in the attainment of the plan's projects while the rather different demands of the second effectively finished it off. Secondly, the failure of the R.P.A. to follow Adams's advice constantly to update the plan meant that once the immediately-realizable projects were exhausted, the plan lost its relevance and its momentum was already waning before Pearl Harbor. Thirdly, the planners placed severe limitations upon themselves, for they had no clear conception of what they were aiming at, simply accepting that they could have only a marginal influence on the nature of regional growth. They rejected out of hand any alternative strategies and in almost every aspect of their work shied away from radical proposals that might have displeased the establishment on whose behalf they laboured. The fact that so much of what they proposed was carried into effect is testimony not necessarily to the plan's soundness but to its close correspondence with the requirements and ambitions of its business and professional elite constituency. Its reliance on voluntarism stamped it with the seal of the 1920s yet it depended, ironically, for much of its fulfilment on the collectivism of the 1930s. It is doubtful whether the New York region would have grown up in a substantially different way without it. The Regional Plan gave the region a degree of physical unity through its roads and parks, it educated the public to higher environmental standards, trained future professional leaders, and pushed forward the frontiers of planning law and economic planning and gave New Deal planning much of its rationale. The R.P.A. continued to be a valuable centre of research, information and propaganda. Finally the Regional Plan brought about a fundamental debate on the nature of American planning[42].

Adams as Educator and Publicist

During his period as Director of the Regional Plan, Adams was responsible for a new initiative in planning education. He had been convinced for many years that planning was a distinct profession and that there must be grafted onto a training in one of the environmental professions the elements of others which bore directly upon a planner's work. The New York plan, with its stimulation of local planning activity on a large scale, revealed the need for a greater output of trained planners. Furthermore, the extensive research work the plan entailed demonstrated the need for systematic enquiry into common problems facing planners by members of the profession unhampered by the routine of regular planning though not divorced entirely from professional practice.

Adams's concerns led to a 'Conference on a Project for Research and Instruction in City and Regional Planning' at Columbia University in 1928. Out of this arose a Rockefeller Foundation grant to Harvard University for the establishment of the Charles Dyer Norton chair of Regional Planning and a School of City Planning. Harvard had pioneered in the provision of courses in city planning in 1909 and in 1923 offered a Master's degree programme in the field. Adams himself had given a number of lectures there and by 1930 John Nolen, Arthur C. Comey and Arthur A. Shurtleff were regular lecturers on the programme[43]. When the School was set up in 1930, Henry Vincent Hubbard, an associate of the younger Olmsted and a noted landscape architect, was appointed to the chair. Adams became a part-time associate professor and a director of research in what was then the only independent professional school of city planning. Adams was delighted with the outcome of his initiative. As he told Nolen in 1930, the Harvard work 'is going to be one of my own chief interests in future'. Unfortunately, no new funds were found to continue the work after the Rockefeller money ran out in 1936 but during his spell at Harvard, Adams put in some teaching, contributed a volume to the 'Harvard City Planning Studies' and co-authored a second with another former associate from the New York plan, Robert Whitten. He carried on with his well-established course of lectures at M.I.T. and had the satisfaction of seeing his second son, Frederick, appointed to the faculty there to teach city planning. A second enterprise in which he had collaborated, the Planning Foundation of America, set up in 1928 to provide for the nation a research and advisory service in lieu of the hoped-for Federal bureau, and operating under the umbrella of the National Conference on City Planning and supported largely by Adams's professional friends and New York associates, failed to develop because of the onset of the Great Depression[44].

Despite the termination of his central role in New York planning, the failure to sustain the Planning Foundation and the brief lifespan of the Harvard School, the 1930s were productive years for Adams. The event which gave him most pleasure was the award of an honorary doctorate of engineering from New York University (1932). He spent only a quarter of each year in the United States but in those years he published the two Harvard books, numerous articles and a major textbook which became one of the standard works on planning for a decade[45]. This *Outline of Town and City Planning* (1935) was based on his M.I.T. lectures and was intended to introduce the subject, explain the necessity for planning, survey the history of the movement, discuss the growth of planning in twentieth-century America and suggest what its future might be. He defined planning as 'a science, an art, and a movement of policy concerned with the shaping and guiding of physical growth and the arrangement of towns in harmony with their social and economic needs'. He identified the aim of planning as the creation of 'a stable and well-balanced physical structure so designed as to secure health, safety, amenity, order and convenience, and, generally, to promote human welfare'. His approach, as was general in those days, was heavily historical and essentially physical though he was more cognisant of social and economic factors than most of his contemporaries. As always, he emphasized a careful balance between community action and individual liberty. He saw the planner as a team leader, co-ordinating the efforts of specialists in other fields[46].

Drawing upon his rural and urban background in Edinburgh, he affirmed that 'planning must be based on a blending of artificial structure with the informal, natural features inherent in the land on which the city is built'. He expected planning to advance slowly in democratic states and stressed the need for patient public education by information and examples. Condemning the urban disorder resulting from the Industrial Revolution, he called for severe limitations on land speculation. While welcoming the swing away from aesthetic to economic emphases, he warned that 'one of the chief dangers ahead in modern city planning is that the technique of planning will become completely subservient to legal and administrative control'. Professionalization carried with it the danger of routinization to the exclusion of that insistence upon social reform which still lay at the heart of Adams's planning.

Apart from the maintenance of a social purpose, he saw planning's greatest needs as the retention of the voluntary initiative, a proper balance between architectural and engineering elements and a more comprehensive treatment. It was necessary also to maintain flexibility of approach, to ensure 'the greater spaciousness of cities, the great compactness of rural communities, and the better co-ordination of both'. The wisdom of thirty years of pragmatic practice and shrewd observation was distilled in this volume, which synthesized the views he had retailed in hundreds of addresses and articles[47].

In *Neighborhoods of Small Homes* (1931), Robert Whitten studied the American evidence while Adams outlined the British experience in seeking 'Economic densities of low-cost housing'. In an extensive discussion of costs, Adams endorsed Unwin's standard of twelve houses to the acre and adduced examples from the two garden cities, an industrial village designed by his own firm and London County Council subsidized housing, refraining from commenting on the wisdom or otherwise of public housing[48]. In *The Design of Residential Areas* he exposed rationally the fallacies underlying speculative suburban development and taught patiently the principles of sound site planning on economical, aesthetically-pleasing and socially-desirable lines, tasks he had been engaged in since first settling in North America. Most of his points were simple, common sense ones, such as 'The cost of congestion is greater than the cost of preventing it'. Though much of the book dealt with the technique of neighbourhood design, he emphasized a broader approach. 'Civic design should embody the material objects of communities', he acknowledged, 'but should also express the ideas born of their spiritual and purely social aspirations'. It was characteristic of him to remark that 'wisdom in our aims is more important than skill in our methods'. He conceded that housing provision had long fallen short of need and that 'Public aid of some kind is essential in slum clearance' but, while acknowledging that it appeared impossible for private enterprise to build decent new housing for the poorest third of the American people, he gave scant encouragement to the rising public housing lobby[49].

In his many articles for the lay and professional press, Adams dealt chiefly with themes he had adumbrated at the outset of his North American career – the planner as co-ordinator of the several forms of environmental expertise, planning as a discernible science and the necessity of doing 'What can be practically done and to avoid fads'. He inveighed constantly against the excesses of speculation and the North American tendency to place 'liberty of property' before 'liberty of life'. The promotion of economic efficiency remained the first object of city planning with adequate social conditions a vital complement. His philosophy was still a trend-adjusting meliorism which recognized severe limits to accomplishment, especially in built-up districts. By the early 1920s, he was expounding the need for metropolitan regional rather than city planning and allotted the Federal Government a planning role as a trunk route designer, map-maker, and research and advisory agency, co-operating with the states, which possessed the legislative and judicial powers. During the inter-war period, he advanced some new ideas of his own, appealing, for example, for agricultural wedges, rather than artificial and constricting green belts, since they would fit in with the natural tendency of cities to grow along radial routes. Much of his thought was on planning as a profession and a discipline and he lamented the lack of basic research into fundamental problems as well as the absence of 'a body of doctrine', a corpus of principles on which all planners agreed. By the 1930s, he was well attuned to the demands of the motor age and forecast a system of interstate expressways, motels and a New York–Philadelphia parkway. He welcomed the New Deal's national resources enterprise in its quest for data and for involving the states in the planning process. In a decade when the idea of 'planning' was discussed in all aspects of life, he urged 'technical men to keep planning related to physical features (i.e. planning in its true sense as "design")' and warned against the superficiality and lack of expertise consequent upon planning 'embracing too many phases of human activity'. However, his last writings reveal a depth of thought on social and economic trends unmatched by any contemporary planner writing in English. He remained a firm advocate of co-operation rather than compulsion, of voluntarism rather than collectivism, and of the liberal principle that 'all human interests are harmonious'. In his last statement on planning in America, in 1938, he affirmed that 'My attitude to city planning is also coloured by my belief in a conception of society in which the self-reliance of the individual is regarded as of vital consequence'[50].

After his New York masterpiece was completed he seems to have done little consultancy work. He advised a housing company on the layout of apartment blocks in Queensborough, New York City. His one formal plan was for the Lawrence Farms estate in Westchester County, made in conjunction with the architect Penrose V. Strout. He described it as a small, compact village community and it was laid out in a semi-formal manner reminiscent of the New England townships he admired. It retained the bosky nature of the undulating landscape and had a broad central avenue leading to a public square around which the shops and public buildings were grouped and had a curvilinear road system with individual road widths related to their traffic function. It did not separate traffic and pedestrians to the same degree as Radburn, for Adams thought complete segregation unnecessary and inconvenient, but it represented many of the same design principles and was as near an ideal neighbourhood as he was ever able to create[51].

ADAMS'S CONTRIBUTION TO AMERICAN PLANNING

When Adams paid his first visit to America in 1911, the country was on the threshold of widespread and regular city planning activity and swinging away from the euphoric 'City Beautiful' towards the quintessentially American 'City Scientific'. When he made his last trip in 1938, planning, though still far from being a part of the municipal routine, had advanced far on all fronts. There were potentially powerful new planning bodies – the American Institute of Planners and the American Society of Planning Officials – numerous university courses in the field, professional journals and a prolific technical literature. Legislation had extended planning to the state and rural levels. New Deal policies built upon Hoover's pioneering stimulation and enquiries and the rising tide of professional, business and academic interest in the idea of planning, even national planning, which received an immense boost from the Great Depression experience. The New Deal's planning enterprises ranged from the grand conception (essentially Roosevelt's own) of regional planning in the Tennessee Valley (though it failed ultimately to fulfil its promise) and the Greenbelt new towns programme, through the National Resources Planning Board, which fostered state planning, to the assistance given by various Federal agencies to the carrying out of existing plans. Planning, which before America's entry into the First World War had signified physical resource allocation on the ground, had become before the Second World War a multi-disciplinary process integrating social and economic policies with physical planning[52].

Over a span of nearly thirty years, Adams had visited the United States on an almost annual basis, engaged in one aspect or another of the planning function. His contribution to American planning in its formative generation, if not crucial was at least sizeable. His principal aims were, first, to spread the gospel of planning so that it would be accepted as a vital public policy. He emphasized also not only satisfactory land-use patterns but the necessity of meeting the community's economic interests and providing for its social well-being; thus, while endorsing the 'City Scientific' creed of civic efficiency championed by his friends, he attempted to add a missing dimension to American planning. His insistence on the consideration of economic and social factors was born out of his British planning experience and also his own background as an avid student of economic and social questions. As a publicist for planning, he had no rival, despite frequent absences from America. Finally, he was an enthusiastic advocate of an independent professional fraternity on the lines of those he had established in Britain and Canada, though he met with a resistance that proved, in the end, superior to his entreaties; the profession never gained an institute of true independence and vigour. Validation for professionals was achieved eventually via postgraduate courses in the universities and here Adams made a significant contribution in pioneering instruction and research in two of America's most influential institutions, M.I.T. and Harvard. His teaching was orthodox but rich in experience, wisdom and breadth of vision. His attachment to research was almost unique before 1930, though his work was somewhat dry and rather factual. He has been criticized as incapable of being ahead of his time and certainly in the area of positive government intervention in environmental policy-making, particularly publicly-provided low-cost housing, he was conservative, appearing to fear public interference with personal liberty more than the evils of slumdom and speculative excess. However, he was the first advocate of regional and state planning and a pioneer of the concept of Federal-state-municipal co-operation in planning[53].

Well attuned to the pragmatic business civilization and the conservative shade of progressive thought of his day, he was regarded by 1923 as the outstanding figure on the American planning scene. Given the self-imposed constraints of the Regional Plan Committee, he was the ideal person to head the New York regional plan staff. The end product, a co-ordinated if essentially project-oriented attack on the region's major land use, communications and recreation problems, was very much his own work and exhibited his salient characteristics – pragmatism, an attachment to voluntarism, zeal for efficiency, clarity of thought, polished expression, and shrewd realism. American planning would have ploughed much the same furrow without his contribution but he leant it his international prestige, widened its audience immeasurably, offered it an extraneous perspective, agitated for adequate professional education, organization and standards and carried to completion the largest single planning enterprise of his generation. He was acknowledged by his peers as a giant in his time[54].

Chapter Eight

Elder Statesman,
1921–1940

During his domicile in Canada, Adams was a frequent visitor to his home-land, even in wartime. He returned to see his kinsfolk, to maintain contact with fellow-pioneers of planning, to keep abreast of British planning – which he regarded as the model for other countries – and to cast a paternal eye over his infant foundation, the Town Planning Institute.

The demise of the Commission of Conservation and the frustration of his hopes for social reconstruction in Canada threw his career into a state of flux between 1920 and 1923. Though he had numerous consultancy commitments in North America and, from 1921, a developing teaching role at M.I.T., he had no longer a secure base on the sub-continent. He sought therefore to establish his permanent home in Britain, perhaps for family reasons, and to return to private practice, ideally on a transatlantic basis.

THE BRITISH PLANNING SCENE, 1918–1940

British planning made little progress in any direction during Adams's absence in Canada. The war further handicapped statutory planning and reinforced planners' central concern with the solution of the housing problem. Inter-war legislation lurched haphazardly in the direction of autonomous, comprehen-sive and compulsory planning, though most planners chafed at the grudging and tardy extension of their powers and at 'the almost sacred rights of property'. The new Ministry of Health assumed responsibility for planning, in place of the defunct Local Government Board, in 1919. However, planning remained a cinderella function of the ministry, enjoying a much lower priority than housing which, together with highways (under the new Ministry of Transport), experienced an enormous expansion after the war. Both of these key functions thus remained outside the ambit of planning for the most part and the codification of planning law as a separate entity from 1925 exacerbated this divorce. Furthermore, most planners and politicians shied away from a direct confrontation with the most crucial but terrifying issue of planning in a democratic capitalist society – the taking over by the community of the responsibility for the distribution of scarce resources between competing interests, with its implication of shifts in land values and hence the need for an acceptable system of compensation and betterment. Finally, Francis Longstreth Thompson's comment that 'town planning has not yet succeeded in establishing itself in the minds of the great bulk of the people' was still valid in 1940. As in North America, planners were often still regarded as visionary radicals, impractical academics, extravagant bureaucrats or mere adjuncts to housing departments[1].

In fact, most planners were conservative, not to say complacent, and politically impotent. They became attached more to the technical than the social aspects of their art. Their philosophy was essentially meliorist, they deferred readily to the perceived susceptibilities of their clients and, like their North American counterparts, they were anxious to demonstrate that planning 'is a firm business proposition' and sought only the minimal adjustment of current economic and social trends in the interests of the community. Despite their eagerness to please, they found the period a frustrating one. Few comprehensive plans were made and fewer implemented, the Garden City movement struggled for existence, fruitless calls were made for motorways and national parks, the problems of London remained unsolved, the environmental reform lobby was split between the protagonists of flats and the advocates of cottages, and planners were slow to appreciate the connection between physical and economic and social planning. Planners' horizons did expand quickly to embrace a form of regional planning and, more circumspectly, national planning but the main preoccupation of regional planning was the conservation of amenity in the face of suburban sprawl and motor-borne pleasure seekers. Abercrombie sounded the tocsin: ' . . .this rural England of ours is . . . menaced with a more sudden and thorough change than ever before' but such protection as the shires enjoyed was due as much to voluntary agencies as to official planning. Neville Chamberlain, though he raised many hopes, was ultimately a disappointment as the planning Minister, the prisoner of his own Victorian provincialism, business-progressivism and parsimony. The fact that most of the country was covered by some form of tentative planning control by 1939 was due largely to the gentle incrementalism practised by the arch-persuader, George Pepler, the Ministry of Health's senior planning officer[2].

Mainstream orthodoxy met criticism from within the profession – notably from A. Trystan Edwards, R. H. Mattocks and Thomas Sharp, the *enfant terrible* of the calling. All of them argued for compact development at twenty to forty houses per acre, envisaging Georgian cities differentiated sharply from their rural environs. Sharp, inveighing against the 'symbolic dozen' cottages to the acre, charged that attachment to Garden City nostrums led to neglect of other problems. Conventional regional planning was vague, aroused local jealousies and worked from selective agendas. He accused fellow-practitioners of promoting middle-class amenity at the expense of the working class; garden suburbia practised effective class segregation[3]. Even advocates of the garden city were uncomplimentary about inter-war planning; Frederic Osborn, harbinger of the coming orthodoxy, characterized it as 'the uninspiring task of putting a little local order into the hateful process of suburban sprawl'[4]. The civil servant, I. G. Gibbon, challenged professional assumptions in trenchant fashion. Such leaps of imagination as there were came from outside the profession. At the end of the period, the emigré German geographer M. R. G. Conzen, arguing from the term 'Geoproscopy', called for a systems approach to planning resting on the social and natural sciences (notably geography), firmly based in the universities and supported by systematic research, here, for better or worse, was the true precursor of the modern discipline[5].

ADAMS, THOMPSON AND FRY

On his return to Britain in 1921, Adams associated first with his old friend, the doyen of British landscapists, Thomas Mawson, then nearing the end of his career and about to be succeeded by his sons. The firm was reconstructed, Adams assuming 'active direction' of its work in town planning and park design. Within a year, however, Adams had formed a new partnership with a man almost twenty years his junior, Francis Longstreth Thompson, Pepler's half-brother. A prize-winning engineering graduate of London University and a surveyor, Thompson had worked for the Port of London Authority, Pepler's former partner Ernest Allen and the Ministry of Health. The partnership was to 'act in close collaboration' with the Mawsons and the two firms co-operated for more than a decade. Adams may have found a close relationship with the elder Mawson irksome and was probably disgruntled with a junior partnership. The new arrangements, which dated from August 1922, gave him both independence and access to the full range of skills involved in planning, thus realizing in practice his belief in planning as a team exercise. Shortly after starting with Thompson, Adams was offered a partnership in the Boston firm of Olmsted and Hubbard but declined it with regret owing to his extensive new British commitments. However, in the hope of exploiting Adams's North American connections, his firm opened an office in New York as well as in London[6].

In about 1924, the young architect Maxwell Fry, a graduate of the Liverpool University School of Architecture, arrived in London armed with a letter of introduction from his professor, Charles Reilly, to his former colleague Stanley Adshead, then professor of planning at London University.

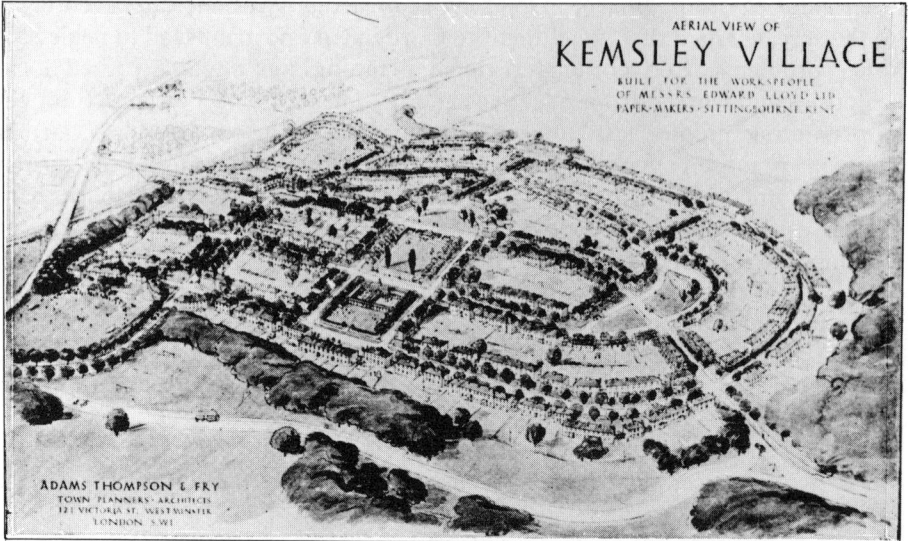

FIGURE 19. Kemsley Village, Sittingbourne, Kent: Aerial View, 1926.

Principally the work of Longstreth Thompson. The village is sited away from the works and is laid out to garden city standards. There is ample open space and the main feature is the community centre at the heart of the village. Attractive features terminate the streets. (Thomas Adams, *Recent Advances in Town Planning*, 1932)

Adshead recommended Fry to 'Try Tommy Adams if all else fails' and the young architect was taken on by Adams to prepare the working drawings for Kemsley Papers' model industrial village near Sittingbourne, Kent, then being laid out by Thompson. Fry recalled Adams as 'a canny Scot . . . with a twinkle in his eye' and struck up a happy relationship with him but 'his shy, stiff partner' he found 'difficult of access'. After eighteen months, Fry left to join the Southern Railway but was tempted back about 1927 with the offer of a partnership. Adams, Thompson and Fry occupied 'a gloomy enough office in gloomy Victoria Street', near Buckingham Palace and then the haunt of engineers, surveyors and other planning consultants like W. R. Davidge. 'The motive for the partnership', Fry recollected, 'was to bolster the low fees paid for town planning with the higher ones paid for architecture'. Adams's almost total commitment to the New York plan left Thompson virtually in sole control of the British work. The office was always busy, chiefly on advisory regional plans, and employed many young men who became leaders of the profession after World War II – Thomas Sharp, Bernard Collins, Colin Buchanan and Adams's son James[7].

The firm's output, though weighted towards regional planning, embraced a wide spectrum of civic design, including the resource towns of Corner Brook in Newfoundland and Kemsley in Kent, an entry for the Birmingham civic centre competition (1923), a handful of architectural designs by Fry (notably the Sassoon flats at Peckham of 1934, an explicit statement of the modern movement) and half-a-dozen conventional town plans. Noteworthy among these was a series of general development reports on the Edinburgh district (1929–31), appropriately recommending, in the heart of Geddes's territory, a detailed civic survey. Scotland being backward in planning, the exercise was primarily educational, demonstrating planning's capacity to promote economy, efficiency, stable values and civic improvement at negligible cost. Recommending the guidance rather than the control of urban growth, flexibility since the future could not be foretold with accuracy, and co-operation with landowners to avoid the problem of compensation, it was a confession of faith in voluntarism and ameliorative planning. It nudged the burghers gently along the path towards planning, recommending the division of the city into five districts for detailed planning schemes, a general development plan and a possible Lothians regional plan[8]. At Rugby and Northampton, the partnership was dealing with medium-sized industrial towns and their environs, recommending principally land-use zoning, adequate reservations

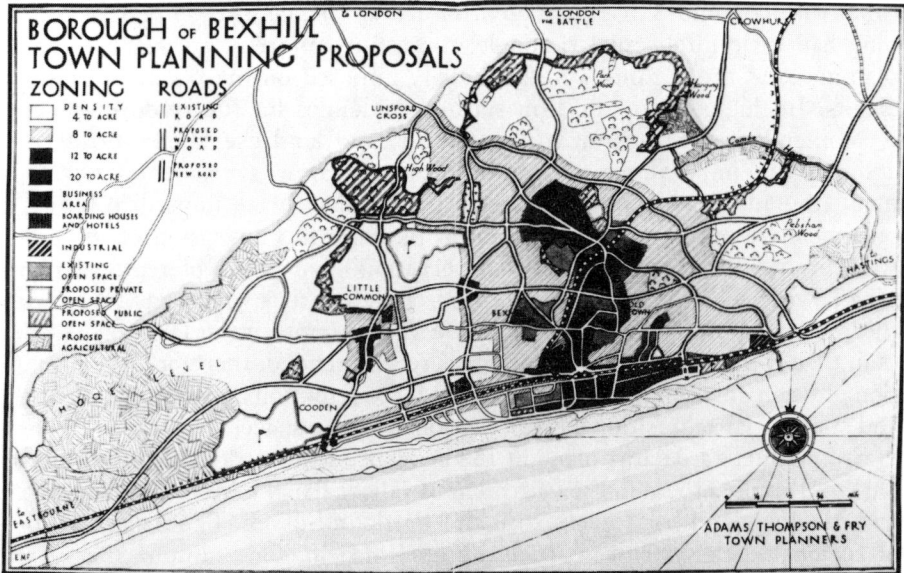

FIGURE 20. Borough of Bexhill, Sussex: Town Planning Proposals, 1931.

There was to be a steady reduction of density of development away from the urban core and a variegated greenbelt to prevent undue sprawl and preserve much fine country. Numerous but relatively minor road improvements were proposed. (Thomas Adams, *Recent Advances in Town Planning*, 1932)

for industrial and residential expansion, additional open spaces, sites for public buildings and road improvements[9].

Adams had a particular attachment to seaside resorts, seeing in them the possibility of blending traditional English landscaping and amenity provision with modern American resort design. The plans for Eastbourne (under the Dukes of Devonshire 'an outstanding example of planning'), Hastings, Bexhill and Felixstowe sought to preserve fine natural features including trees, unspoilt sea fronts, historic open spaces and genteel villas and squares while making discreet provision for the motor- and rail-borne visitors which were their lifeblood. In particular they suggested greenbelts, civic centres, the avoidance of ribbon development, the strict control of advertising and garages and the removal of cheap and nasty holiday cottages – Thompson referring to 'acres of downland spattered over with shanties only worthy of some mad gold rush'[10].

The firm's dozen or so advisory regional plans were drawn up largely by Thompson, though Adams paid occasional 'state visits' to the regions and no doubt cast an eye over the draft plans. They were representative examples of their genre, notable for their lucid if wooden exposition, relatively unsophisticated analyses of physical, economic and social conditions in the sketchy surveys and straightforward recommendations which unashamedly had more to do with common sense than environmental science. British regional planning had little intellectual rationale, it was an empirical extension of town planning and the regions were arbitrarily imposed on the planners by their clients. In this context, the firm set out guidelines for future development, recommended three or four major categories of land use, the co-ordination and marginal improvement of communications, compact residential development (though in attractive country districts houses were limited to between one and four per acre) and economical public utility provision. The accent was emphatically upon amenity conservation. 'No phase of regional planning', wrote Thompson, 'is more important than that which has to do with the preservation of amenity and no amenity is more important to preserve than that of the countryside'. The plans recommended, therefore, the protection of beautiful scenery and historic sites, the retention and planting of trees, and substantial acquisitions or reservations of open space[11].

From America Adams brought the concept of the parkway and the linear park and applied them to the treatment of valleys like the Mole in Mid-Surrey and the downland between Bexhill and Battle in Sussex. The American idea of regional park systems was adumbrated also in, for example, the North Middlesex plan. 'Green girdles' to curb urban sprawl were suggested in most plans, together with agricultural wedges, for example in the West Middlesex plan. The reports on Surrey and Kent stressed the vital necessity of preserving unspoilt the crest of the North Downs and the ancient Pilgrim's Way. The amenity priority was at its height in the two reports on the Thames above London, where bungaloid and other undesirable developments threatened

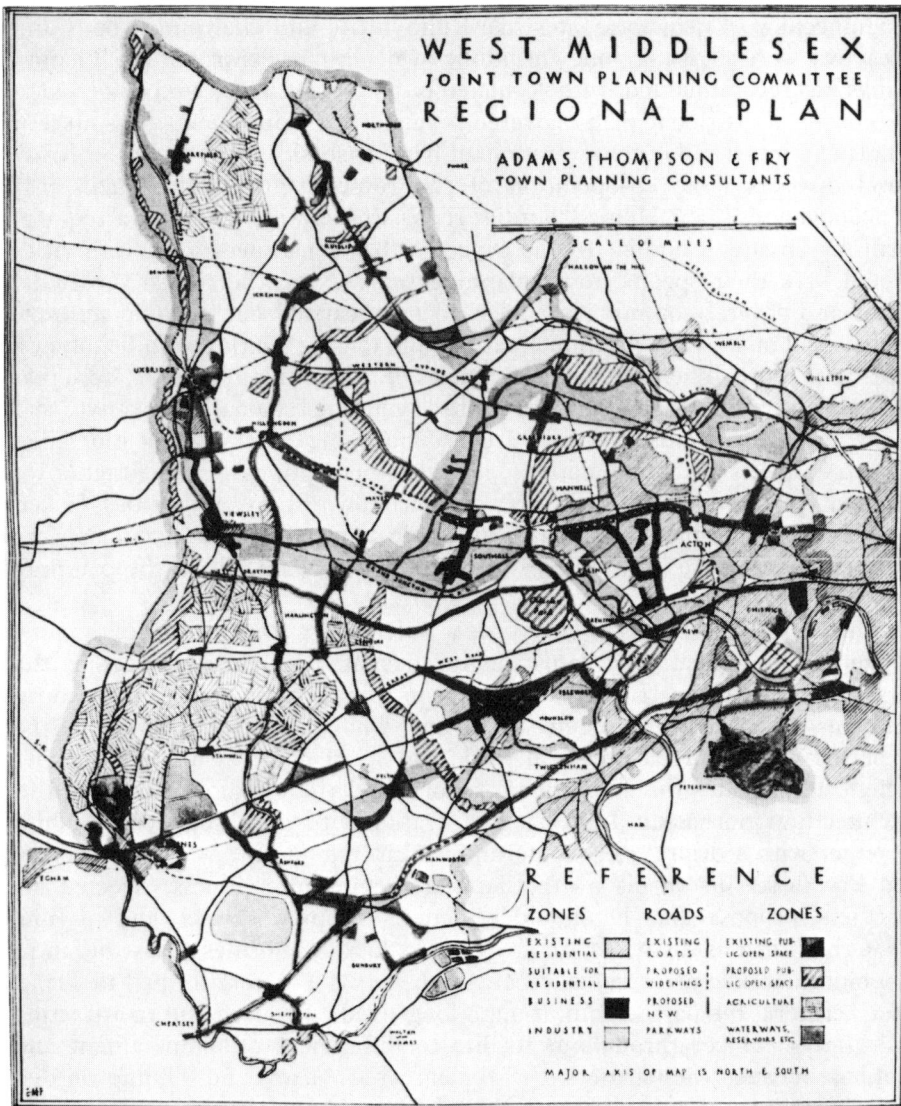

FIGURE 21. West Middlesex Regional Plan, 1924.

Inner suburban London shading westwards into open country but developing
outward at a rapid pace. Adams attempted to prevent suburbs coalescing by establishing a variety of greenbelts-linear parks, agricultural wedges and parkways. Business
and industry were kept close to the main lines of communications. The plan proposed
to strengthen north-south communications. (Thomas Adams, *Recent Advances in
Town Planning*, 1932)

fine reaches in London's 'greatest playground'. Here great houses and their magnificent parks, historic sites like Runnymede and charming woods and meadows were at risk; a policy of public ownership or control of the Thames banks was recommended, with regulated public access in selected places[12].

The firm's regional plans covered a range of environments in southern England – inner and outer metropolitan fringes, seaside areas and thoroughly rural districts. The co-operation of the respective county councils was welcomed and in the Home Counties reports pleas were made for a regional plan for Greater London. It was expected that constituent local authorities would base their specific town planning schemes on the advisory regional plans and several committees appear to have carried out major communications and open space recommendations and to have continued in being for a decade or more. The principal deficiencies of this form of planning were that the areas were too small and arbitrary for a genuine regional perspective, that some authorities refused to join a consortium and others which did failed to carry out its recommendations, and that perceptions of the function of regional planning were both hazy and narrow. Many authorities lacked professional planning staff to carry out their plans and county councils were only tardily admitted to no more than an *amicus curiae* role in the planning process[13].

The year 1934 appears to have been a watershed in the firm's life, the prologue to its termination. Adams was incapacitated for almost a year by the first in a series of heart attacks. Thompson won a contract in Johannesburg and this absorbed much of his time. Fry, who had failed to bring in the expected volume of architectural work, had spent much of his time making delightful sketches for the regional reports and the New York plan and in architectural journalism. Increasing frustration with 'an irksome partnership' together with a desire 'to become unmistakably modern' in his architecture led Fry to set up on his own. Adams, returning after illness, rejected his partners' proposal that he should become a 'sleeping partner' and in June 1936 the firm was dissolved. In any case, as local authorities at last began to appoint their own professional planners, there was less work for private firms. Furthermore, the partnership, though long-lived and successful in attracting work, was subject throughout its life to differences of temperament and outlook between the partners. Fry remembered Adams and Thompson disagreeing heatedly over expenses though their personal relations remained amicable. Adams's generous wooing of prospective clients was opposed by Thompson, who may have resented also Adams's lengthy absences on the lucrative New York contract[14].

For the last four years of his life, Adams practised alone, with the aid of an assistant, the architect T. A. Jeffryes. However, few commissions came his way and he filled his time increasingly with lectures and journalism. He retained one or two municipal consultancies and judged a competition for a housing estate at Kincorth, Aberdeen. One of his few tasks of note was an

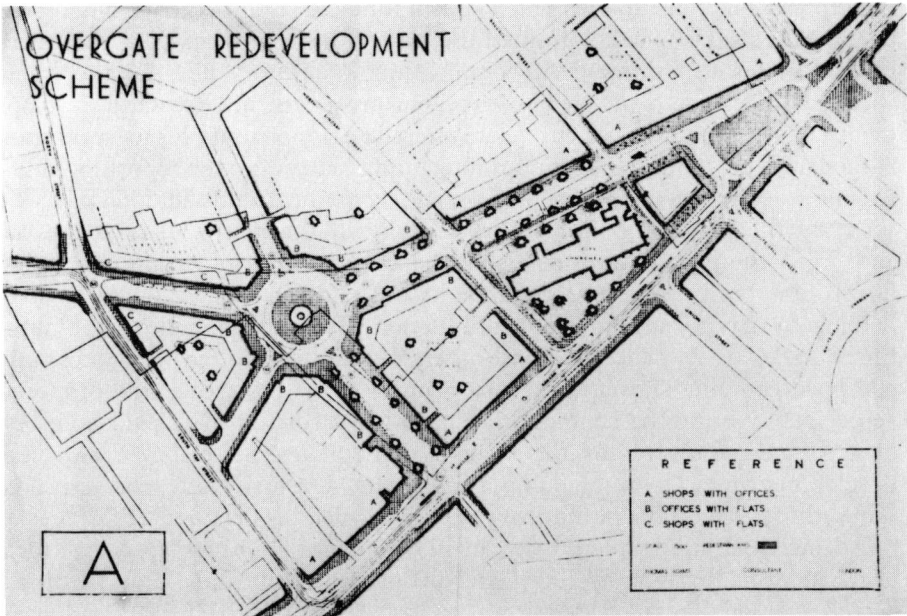

FIGURE 22. Dundee: Overgate Redevelopment Scheme, 1937.
A bold exercise in urban renewal, intended to replace a slum with a fine broad commercial avenue, integrating the best of the old property. It was to be almost exclusively non-residential. (Courtesy of Dundee City Libraries)

exercise in redevelopment for the City of Dundee. It was an aspect of planning to which he had given little attention but he seized on the opportunity boldly, proposing the clearance of a downtown slum and its replacement by a mile-long broad commercial thoroughfare on the scale of London's Kingsway or Birmingham's Corporation Street. The new Overgate was designed to revitalize and double the city's business quarter. Link roads were to connect it with neighbouring business streets and with the University College. At its western end, Adams proposed a large island flanked by offices and at the eastern terminal two small rest parks. From the New York plan he borrowed the idea of arcaded sidewalks. In an early exercise in citizen participation, he called for suggestions from local citizens and proposed that the cost of three million pounds be spread over a generation and borne equally by public and private agencies. The council approved the scheme but the war prevented its implementation[15].

A report made by Adams for the town of Barrow-in-Furness in 1938 illustrates his procedure. Engaged to report on the prospects of the town's western rim, Walney Island, as a seaside resort, he paid two short visits to reconnoitre the ground and consult with officials; two junior assistants then spent a week on a detailed survey, which formed the basis of his report, made within three months of his appointment. Recommending a statutory plan for the whole island, he considered that it has 'excellent prospects, of successful development as a seaside resort'. A virgin site offered an opportunity for its realization at moderate cost. Several small but interesting features of the report highlight Adams's awareness of wider social and economic trends and factors. He sketched the regional holiday market, outlined the merits of rival resorts, and urged the preservation of historic villages and the retention of existing farmland not only on grounds of amenity but also for the strategic purpose of helping to maximize home food production. The Adams hallmark, a West Shore parkway, was included and other transatlantic borrowings were fully equipped camping sites and the provision of a viewing area at the proposed aerodrome. Noting the contemporary trend towards universal paid holidays, he envisaged a future for the resort bright enough to justify a two-year development plan, to be made by a consultant. Unfortunately, the arrival of war within a year of his preliminary report stymied his proposal[16].

Adams's last known plan, made in 1939–40, was for a holiday village for a client identified only as 'Westminster people' at Whitelands, near Hastings. A well-wooded, irregular area, it was to have a long approach road leading to a village green surrounded by two circular roads, holiday homes, shops, a club house, playing fields, allotments and market gardens; the design was reminiscent of American national and state park resorts[17].

ADAMS'S CONTRIBUTION TO PLANNING THOUGHT

Adams was a prolific contributor to the debate on British planning, notably in his *Recent Advances in Town Planning* (1932), the distillation of thirty years of problem-solving and rumination. Like its American companion, *Outline of Town and City Planning* (1935), it became a standard text for a generation, surveying in evolutionary fashion the history of planning prior to the modern era, summarizing twentieth-century progress world-wide, and expounding the essential components and techniques of planning in his accustomed pragmatic vein[18]. His philosophic stance remained unchanged; it was still the cautious, negatively-regulatory adaptation of Classical liberalism characteristic of the mainstream of the Liberal revival of 1905 and of American Progressivism – one foot planted in the time of his youth and the other in the contemporary world. 'Town planning in Britain has always been inspired by a social purpose', he affirmed in the spirit of 1914, 'it must be allied with liberty and pay respect to all that is sound and true in tradition'. He sought 'some practical and common sense solution to problems' while 'avoiding fads'. Like most of his contemporaries, he felt planning stood to gain more by persuasion, foresight, agreement, sympathetic understanding and co-operation than by the force of law. Thus he advocated only the amelioration of current social and economic conditions and the adjustment of trends to the benefit of the community rather than to individuals, assuming, as always, an inherent consensus[19].

Adams's definition of planning – 'The art of shaping and guiding the physical growth of towns and also of rural communities, in harmony with social and economic needs' – accorded with the conventional view. Nothing better described his own experience than the dictum that the planner's 'proper function is that of the co-ordinator of design'. Among the many features of American planning he carried home was the conviction that planners had to undertake vigorous public relations campaigns to instil in the public mind a positive perception and acceptance of planning, beginning in the schools. He was emphatic, however, that planning 'should show by works rather than words' and that its scope was circumscribed by what democratic societies could be persuaded to accept at given times. He cautioned planners not to spread themselves over too wide a field, arguing that they would lack competence in essentials and that planning would be weakened if it strayed beyond the design of physical features. Nevertheless, he was alive to the current interest in political and economic planning and counselled exchanges of professional advice between the two distinct fields[20].

Adams shared much of the contemporary dissatisfaction with British planning. Surveying its history between 1909 and 1931, he wrote that it 'can hardly be claimed to be a record of adequate accomplishment' and 'the expectations of enthusiasts have not been realised'. Legislation had consistently lagged behind thought and practice and even the reasonably satisfactory 1932 Act was retrogressive on procedure and failed to consider economic development or co-ordinate housing and communications with general planning. He had wanted local authorities to have greater scope and had hoped for two schedules, one basic and compulsory, the other advanced and permissive. He called for 'one constructive Ministry dealing, through co-ordinated branches, with the regional, city and rural planning of the country' and suggested that the Ministry should play less of a judicial and more of an advisory role, thus speeding up the planning process. After 1932, planning authorities had all the necessary powers but lacked the will to use them, while central government imposed a depressing uniformity on statutory planning. 'The chief general weakness in English planning', he thought, 'is the almost complete subordination of design to legal requirements. . . Positive or creative planning is not encouraged and most planning takes the form of restrictions'. What he meant by 'positive or creative planning' was unclear but presumably it included privately-initiated satellite towns and bolder programmes of open space provision, parkways, expressways and large-scale landscaping. He lamented the paucity and inadequacy of completed schemes and the fact that 'we are only at the beginning of town planning in this country. All we have done in the past twenty years has been experimental'. However Adams shared the general optimism and faith in the ultimate triumph of the cause. Moreover, he stressed the 'broad, intangible results' of public planning. 'Much of modern development' was 'a great improvement on development before 1909', an advance he attributed to the Burns Act's elevation of public environmental standards[21].

Adams's advice on procedure and technique, though fundamentally conventional, was both more imaginative and more widely informed than that of most of his contemporaries. He absorbed Geddes's message about the prior necessity of a survey but characteristically added his own variation – a preliminary outline survey to determine a plan's objectives and area, followed by a detailed and comprehensive civic survey to supply data for the plan. In preparing plans, the first step should be 'a comprehensive programme for the development of the whole town', uninhibited by current legal and other constraints, an imaginative and long-term outline of ideals and possibilities; this would be followed by specific planning schemes, selective and short-term agendas dealing with immediate needs. The planner must first identify the principal economic activities of the town, find convenient and adequate sites for them and thus improve their efficiency. Associated closely with this priority must be the establishment of 'wholesome living conditions' for the workforce, followed by the provision of adequate open space and satisfactory communications. Zoning, an important tool but no substitute for proper planning, should be kept simple, elastic and negative, establishing dominant, permitted and prohibited uses and, as in Ontario, embracing the entire metropolitan area. It was characteristic of Adams's thoroughness, precision and wisdom that he cautioned against both over-planning, since many of Britain's finest features were 'accidental', and over-hasty redevelopment, which might destroy the individuality which was the heart of the British character in favour of a tasteless uniformity. He was cautious about redevelopment not only on the grounds of cost and the power of vested interests but also because 'We have not yet begun to appreciate the disadvantage of congestion nor the unprofitable character of obsolete buildings sufficiently to know how and when to pursue a bold policy of reconstruction'. He conceded that 'democratic countries are too timid in getting rid of obsolete buildings' but, ignoring contemporary opinion, believed that 'the tendency in town planning will be more in the direction of the regulation of the use of land and the density of buildings by zoning than in promoting elaborate schemes of re-planning'. His caution is explicable also by the fact that redevelopment would have involved a high degree of positive collectivism which was alien to his spirit[22].

Adams's approach to regional planning was as simple and pragmatic as that of his fellows. He differed from most of them, however, in his attachment to advisory rather than executive or statutory regional plans, which he regarded as probably not worth the time and effort. Advisory plans were

a greater factor in promoting town planning on sound lines than is commonly realised. They have a great value in developing good feeling between adjacent.

authorities, in giving them a wider outlook, and in co-ordinating proposals for the improvement of circulation and the control of land uses and densities throughout large regions[23].

This faith he derived from the relative success of the advisory Regional Plan of New York and from his predilection for persuasion rather than compulsion. His prescription for the protection of amenity was similar; planners should recognize the severe practical limitations of the law in this regard and rely primarily upon the steady education of the public in higher standards. From his American and Canadian experience he drew suggestions for publicly-sponsored resorts, camp sites and national parks 'as part of our duty in making provision for the healthy use of increased leisure time and developing a fitter people'. Endorsing the Howardian principle of the interdependence of town and country, he acknowledged realistically that 'the hunger of urban England for rural England is something that cannot be denied', urging the countryside to protect itself from despoliation and city folk to be sensitive to the interests of the countryside. He introduced his own variation on the greenbelt theme, arguing that wedges of open space were more natural features than belts, since they accorded more accurately with normal urban growth patterns[24].

Apart from amenity, the two most vital environmental questions of the day were housing and roads. Adams had much to say on both, regretting as did most planners, their dissociation from the statutory planning structure. Calling for a national road system based on aerial surveys on the Canadian model, he envisaged a hierarchical structure. Drawing on American practice, he suggested 'a national system of new express roads as an addition to the system of existing tributary roads', with easy gradients and curves, steady traffic flows, flyover junctions, three lanes each way, railway interchanges and urban arterial links. British road design was backward and engineers needed the assistance of landscape architects to help integrate roads into their environment. He was a constant advocate of the American parkway as a contribution to traffic relief, the enhancement of the landscape and the increase of rateable values while in towns he appealed for arcading, separate levels for pedestrians and vehicles and the avoidance of ribbon development, castigating the Restriction of Ribbon Development Act (1935) as ineffective. The lack of a relationship between road programmes and general planning was 'the greatest single cause of the considerable degree of failure. . . (of) our efforts in planning during the last thirty years'[25].

Adams was at odds with most of his colleagues on the issue of low-cost housing. Nothing revealed more clearly his orthodox Liberalism than his resolute opposition to subsidized housing. While conceding that public housing projects were 'superior to those carried out by private enterprise, both in regard to spaciousness about buildings and to the design and arrangement of groups of buildings' and that public action may have been necessary in the immediate post-war crisis, he believed that it was no 'more than a palliative' and that the subsidy was 'in effect, a gratuity to those who will live in the houses, and however justified to meet an emergency is, of course, economically unsound'. The 'worst thing' about council housing was that it discouraged owner-occupation, a badge of self-respect, independence and thrift. The enormous cost of the subsidies was unjustified. He did, however, suggest areas of legitimate state intervention – the purchase of the value of potential building land and a joint state and landlord insurance fund for housing maintenance and replacement. Together with almost all planners, he condemned 'the continuing trend' to inner-city flats in the 1930s, a response to high travel costs and the economics of slum clearance. 'American experience', he declared, 'showed us that we were wrong in building tenements with the objects of solving the housing problem'. He shared William Thompson's view that 'the cottage home is the unit of the nation' and believed that Unwin's twelve houses to the acre represented good value in health, convenience, traffic flow and amenity and, sensibly handled, was just as compact a form of development as flats with the requisite amount of open space. Many flats lacked adequate open space and were an insoluble problem when they became obsolete. The solution to inner-city congestion was 'recentralization' of people and workplaces to satellite towns having the requisite degree of concentration necessary to provide economical services[26].

Nowhere was the flats versus cottages and satellites battle fought out more intensively and persistently than in London. Adams, the pre-war architect of the Arterial Roads Conferences and the planner of the great transatlantic comparison, New York, plunged with enthusiasm into the London morass, undertaking regional plans in the Home Counties and speaking and writing on the subject throughout the period. He subscribed to the conventional wisdom on the relief of the capital's problems – decentralization into satellite towns separated from the metropolis by a greenbelt, parkways and river valley country parks and north and south circular roads. Like his contemporaries, he would have welcomed an invitation to plan the metropolitan region and saw London's planning as a touchstone for the nation. It was 'of national importance that London should be well-planned' and Adams's prescription for it was reminiscent of his New York plan. Acknowledging that 'we cannot stop the expansion of London', he declared that 'What is wrong with London is not its size, but the fact that it is a swollen and shapeless mass'. It was possible to correct this 'by constructive methods of town planning, ameliorating the effects of much of the congestion'. Cautioning that planners should not 'destroy the charm of its traditional features', he called for a thorough survey and a three-year planning exercise looking ahead for two generations. He was emphatic that 'the solution of the problems of congestion will be best attained by the creation of new centres surrounded by large areas of open land in the Home Counties, together with the strengthening of sub-centres within the County of London'. The ground for Abercrombie had been well-tilled by Adams, Unwin, Pepler, Davidge and others of their generation[27].

Britain's difficulties in this period and the examples of New Deal America, Nazi Germany and Stalinist Russia led to a vogue for national planning which embraced not only professional planners but also politicians, economists and other savants. Adams had made an early plea for a national survey and outline resource, power, land and communications planning when still in Canada and Stanley Adshead had argued for the same programme in post-war Britain. Adams continued to press for a national survey on his return to Britain, serving on the Town Planning Institute's sub-committee which gave evidence to the Barlow Commission of 1937–40 but he never expanded his 1918 ideas because he held that economic and political planning was essentially distinct from physical planning and that there were severe limits to the practicability of national planning. He regarded a national survey essentially as a basis for sound regional planning. Noting the regional imbalance so marked in the inter-war years, he commented that 'What we have been most neglectful of in England is in the planning of industrial growth'. He concluded guardedly that it might be possible to control the movement of population and industry for greater efficiency through a national Garden City programme but 'It is not possible to prepare a comprehensive national plan to cover the same ground as a regional plan'. Most planners subscribed to this cautious view and enthusiasm for more positive and comprehensive national planning came largely from other disciplines[28].

INSTITUTIONAL ACTIVITIES

Adams re-established himself as a major public figure almost immediately upon his return to Britain in 1921, gathered many honours and served on numerous professional and other bodies. An Honorary Member of the American Institute of Architects and a member of the Architectural League of New York, he received in 1934 the proud distinction of election to a Fellowship of the Royal Institute of British Architects. An Honorary Member of the Institution of Municipal and County Engineers, he held an Honorary Doctorate of Engineering from New York University (1932). He served again as an External Examiner in Civic Design at Liverpool University, lectured at the Architectural Association's School of Planning and Research for National Planning, lamented the backwardness of British universities compared with American institutions in the provision of courses in planning and landscape architecture and floated a grand scheme for an International Institute of Research in City Planning with offices in America and Europe. In 1937, while a member of a distinguished party examining German road design, he had the dubious pleasure of hearing Hitler and Mussolini speak in the Olympic Stadium in Berlin. At the same time, he was chairman of the Technical Advisory Committee of the Coronation Planting Committee and strove hard to establish playparks along American lines in British towns[29].

Described by the distinguished road planner Rees Jeffreys as 'a true missionary who knows how to enthuse and inspire others', Adams was active in attempts to broaden the base of popular support for planning and to improve the education of its lay as well as professional supporters. In 1933 he financed the first of the annual Town and Country Planning Summer Schools. His eldest son James was the Honorary Secretary and Frederic Osborn the Honorary Treasurer. Attracting an attendance of great public figures and most of the nation's leading planners, it helped to fill a major gap in planning education. Adams was its mainspring, guiding its early progress with his well-known wise counsel and genial chairmanship[30].

The Summer School was taken over in due course by the Town Planning Institute. Adams remained a prominent member of his principal institutional creation throughout his life. Based in London throughout the inter-war period, he was a frequent speaker at Institute meetings and from 1920 to 1936 he was a regular attender at Council meetings. On his retirement from the Council he was elected to an Honorary Vice-Presidency. He sat on the Competitions and Professional Practice Committee until his death and served also on the Sub-Committee on a National Survey and National Plan. By the outbreak of war in 1939, membership of the Institute exceeded 900 and many of these were student members, a particular source of satisfaction to one who had pioneered planning education. The Institute, and its *Journal*, changed in character during the inter-war period, one President, Ewart Culpin, remarking that it became more technical and essentially professional in interest and membership; the social reform element faded away and there was a general failure to respond to major social and economic questions. Engagement in public controversy and propaganda was frowned upon. The Institute sought political, public and professional acceptability and pursued a primly respectable course. Apart from a sizeable increment of student members consequent upon the rising opportunities for planners in the later 1930s, there was a more significant shift in the character of the senior membership; local authority planning officers outweighed the assortment of idealists, consultants and emigrés from other professions who had helped Adams to found the Institute twenty years earlier, becoming almost a state within a state[31].

Adams returned from North America in 1921 not only with new ideas on the scope, techniques and preparation for town planning but also with a redoubled 'ambition to make town planning ... a distinct profession'. In a joint paper with the architect and planner T. Alwyn Lloyd (later President) in 1926, he made a vigorous attack upon interlopers who merely adopted the title of 'town planner' without obtaining professional training or qualifications and often undercut members' fees, at best not very profitable and described as 'barely adequate'. The authors recommended a university training on the lines of the Harvard School of Landscape Architecture's postgraduate course and a proper schedule of technical work to aid in the fixing of fees. Their view of the Institute's purpose was noticeably broader and bolder than that of other senior members. 'It is very important', they declared, 'that the Institute should make itself felt as a vigorous, public-spirited, professional body'. However, private practitioners, social reformers and evangelists for a new discipline like Adams and Lloyd were already in a minority and in the inter-war era the Institute progressed largely as a validating body for local authority technical staff. It was not until after the Second World War that Adams's dream of 1909, as expanded in 1926, was realized and then only in part; planning was recognized as a normal public activity, a regular university course and as a distinct profession though its identification with the social sciences was greater and its connection with social reform rather less than Adams had anticipated[32].

Despite being one of the principal architects of the present-day Town and Country Planning Association, Adams seems to have played little part in its inter-war activities but he did become active in the National Housing and Town Planning Council in the late 1930s. He joined the General Committee in 1937 and spoke regularly at its regional conferences, where 'his inspiring addresses were received with enthusiasm by the delegates'. He acted as a consultant for the Council, preparing memoranda, leading discussions and answering technical questions. His most 'valuable memorandum' was on 'Town and Country Planning during the War', written early in 1940. Drawing on his Canadian experience, he argued that 'continuing planning efforts during the war' were 'a national duty'. Existing plans should be carried out, with suitable modifications to meet war needs, civil defence and a long war. The joint advisory regional committees were admirable vehicles for emergency work and it was especially important that the country began to devise plans for post-war reconstruction at once to avoid being caught out by a sudden peace as in 1918. After the war, he foresaw an enormous housing programme, much greater provision for civil aviation, heavier vehicles and the need for planned decentralization. Planners should undertake more fundamental research and seize the opportunity to arouse public interest in post-war planning. Having lectured to the British Association for the Advancement of Science on 'Some Economic Aspects of Urban Concentration', a summary of the Barlow Report and the Regional Survey of New York, he began work on a new book for the American market, *Modern Trends in City, Town and Regional Planning*, a revision and broadening of his synthesis of 1935. A few days before his death, he announced his intention to review the Barlow Commission's findings for the National Housing and Town Planning Council[33].

Adams's principal institutional contribution in the inter-war years was the formation of the Institute of Landscape Architects (now the Landscape Institute). He was not actually present at the creation but his was the formative influence in its first decade. It was founded following the International Exhibition of Garden Design in October 1928, on the initiative of the landscape gardener S. V. Hart who, 'realising the lack of unity shown in the

British section, urged the necessity for forming an association of Garden Architects'. In February 1929 a provisional gathering formed the British Association of Garden Architects. For President, the founders looked naturally to the doyen of British landscapists, Thomas Mawson, who peremptorily dismissed the new body on the grounds that there was not enough work to justify it. However, the accession of Geoffrey Jellicoe and other architects and the promptings of Adams, then still in New York, persuaded Mawson to become the first President. Nevertheless, as Brenda Colvin has recalled, 'we all thought mainly in terms of garden design' and 'the enormous field of wider landscape planning was not foreseen until our attention was drawn to it by Thomas Adams, who was working in the U.S.A. and had seen the role opening there for landscape design'. Indeed, at times Adams thought of himself principally as a landscape architect, having been influenced by his close associates in America. Frederick Law Olmsted, Jr., John Nolen and Henry Vincent Hubbard[34].

Within a year of its foundation the Association had become the Institute of Landscape Architects. 'Thomas Adams influenced the choice of title', said Colvin, 'but was abroad too much to take a more active part' in the Institute's earliest days. The architects' 'influence on its future was to be of critical importance . . . without their support it could well have foundered or become confined to purely horticultural design'. The initial steering was undertaken by people like Jellicoe, E. Prentice Mawson and Barry Parker, imparting a grander perspective than simply garden design. A takeover bid from the R.I.B.A. was resisted and within a year forty-two members had been recruited. However, the Institute's 'sights were still set low' and its membership was little more than a stage army'[35].

Following his return from New York in 1931, Adams almost single-handedly transformed the struggling and uncertain Institute into a credible professional body. By 1934, a constitution had been drafted, by-laws made, a scale of fees fixed, an examination syllabus drawn up, papers read and a quarterly journal, *Landscape and Garden,* launched. Adams gave increasing attention to the fledgling organization, ending the decade as its President (1937–9). Not only did he lend it his enormous prestige, his wealth of experience, his unrivalled range of contacts, his capacity for organization and his flair for publicity, most crucially he gave it an intellectual rationale and professional self-respect. He capped his Presidential term by giving it a revised constitution, setting rigorous standards for admission, with several classes of membership culminating in Fellows who were required to have had seven years of practice and to have satisfied the Council as to their standing. The Institute's objects were defined as the advancement of landscape architecture; the theory and practice of garden, landscape and civic design; the promotion of research; professional education; and the creation and maintenance of a high standard of professional qualification[36].

Adams's greatest contribution to modern landscape architecture in Britain was to define the subject, point out its pedigree, draw attention to progress abroad (notably in America and Germany) and press for the integration of landscape design into current planning and development. As so often with Adams, a literary allusion provided him with a starting point. Noting that Sir Walter Scott had appreciated the distinction between gardening and design, he pointed out that the latter required long training and imagination. The problem for both landscape architects and planners was how to reconcile aesthetic enjoyment and civic pride with efficiency and convenience and Adams believed that the landscapist's training began where the planner's finished – adding the fine clothes of design to the bare flesh of technical expertise. His definition of landscape architecture was entirely derivative and sprang from Charles Eliot: 'Landscape Architecture is a fine art concerned with the improvement of the habitations of men as well as with the preservation and development of scenic beauty'. The landscapist's ambit included the site planning of open spaces, a knowledge of plants and their decorative value, the selection of sites for and the design of parks and other recreation grounds, the landscaping of civic centres and other public places, the planning of subdivisions and their relation to the environment, the design of highways with reference to the surrounding topography and buildings, the preservation and improvement of amenities along roads and detailed zoning. There was, deliberately, a wide overlap between landscape architecture and planning and other environmental professions but Adams regarded it as related most closely to architecture[37].

A countryman by origin and probably by inclination, too, Adams was attached to the countryside of Britain and wished to see it preserved. However, he recognized the impossibility of even the remotest landscape standing still in the hectic twentieth century, hence he counselled that 'If we are to save the beauty of England it must be done by design and planting that is adaptable to new conditions, in addition to such preservation of good landscape as is possible'. Observing that the landscape was largely an artificial arrangement of natural features, he wished to carry on the traditions of the past in designing landscapes that reflected man and Nature in harmony; in place of the great landowners of past ages, public authorities must now assume this responsibility. He condemned their reluctance to do so, complaining that 'Because in this country we have had so much fine landscape handed down to us we are more indifferent to it than people in newer countries, like the United States'[38].

Britain's great inheritance was threatened by careless destruction from both public and private agencies and town planning's greatest weakness lay in its failure to appreciate the need for constructive landscaping. 'In England', he declared, 'we are content with the wholly ineffective method of relying on the existing scenery, which we mutilate in the process of road building and of the super-imposition of some tree planting or what we call "road beautification" on the verges of arterial roads'. The Germans and Americans wisely

used the services of landscape architects in designing their new expressways
so that they blended into the environment. British road design, by contrast,
was dangerous, dull and out of date. Condemning Peacehaven-style bungalow
developments, the speculative destruction of former great estates and the
garish and badly-sited petrol stations which appeared like a blight in these
years, he commended the county councils for their enlightened preservation
work and hoped that, with Government backing, they would be able to retain
many large estates and their buildings in their traditional form. In North
America, he had been closely associated with national and regional wilderness
and scenic parks and believed that the British planning lobby 'should
immediately press for the establishment of at least two great National Parks' –
the forerunners of a national programme to reserve 6400 square miles over a
twenty-year period[39].

Adams's principal cultural acquisition from North America, however, was
the parkway. Devised originally by the father of modern American landscape
architecture, Frederick Law Olmsted, Sr., it came to maturity in the
Westchester County Park system developed in the commuter and recreation
belt outside New York City in the 1920s. Adams was thrilled by it as by no
other aspect of planning save the Garden City. He lost no opportunity of
urging its widespread adoption on both sides of the Atlantic. A landscaped
road, hugging the contours, reserved for private cars and immune from building on its frontages, it was almost self-financing if wealthy people could be
persuaded to build villas in its vicinity. It separated private and commercial
traffic, introduced city folk to fine country without destroying it – indeed, it
could rehabilitate decayed environments – and linked parks into regional
systems. In Britain, its most publicized use was in the satellite town of
Wythenshawe near Manchester, designed by Barry Parker[40].

Adams, who regarded old country roads fringed by trees, hedges and
verges as in effect parkways, was anxious to give Britain an even more complete demonstration of the parkway's potential. When he and his partners
prepared a general development plan for the small Sussex seaside resort of
Bexhill in 1930, he felt he had found the perfect opportunity to plan a
four-mile section between Bexhill and Battle, a part of a proposed London-
South Coast parkway. It was to be an example of swift, safe motorized travel
without the usual accompanying destruction of the environment; indeed,
winding along the contours of the South Downs, it would enhance the traditional scene, opening up vistas of nature, woods and tranquil meadows. The
persuasive and enthusiastic Adams obtained the agreement of Bexhill Council
and local landowners to the preparation of a design but the county highways
authority refused to survey the route on the grounds of cost. 'Had it been
built', lamented a greatly disappointed Adams, 'it would have resulted in a
fine improvement and an enormous saving of public money in comparison
with adequate widening' of existing roads. The parkway never enjoyed in
Britain the vogue it had in North America – probably because there were still

many traditional scenic country roads, which were, as Adams had perceived, taken for granted[41].

ADAMS AT HOME

It was not until his return from New York in 1930 that Adams bought a house in Britain. Until then, his family had accompanied him across the Atlantic on

FIGURE 23. Thomas Adams, c. 1937.

many occasions, in the intervals settling in a succession of homes in the outer London suburbs, such as Thames Ditton in Surrey, where Adams was able to indulge himself in his favourite relaxation of gardening. He acquired in 1930

Yew Tree Cottage at Henleys Down near Battle. It was a 200-year old property, in reality three farm cottages knocked into one. It fulfilled Thomas
Adams's long-held dream of a country cottage and it would have fitted any
Briton's vision of the idyllic home. All the quintessential features of the
Englishman's home were there – low beams, an inglenook, six bedrooms and
a smoker. The grounds comprised two fields, a one-acre garden, a pond and a
paddock. A barn was fitted up with a swing-cum-trapeze hung from the
beams and badminton and table tennis were played there. Adams made himself an office in the cowshed and also built a tennis court. In the summer, he
made hay, stacking it Scots fashion. He employed a gardener and a chauffeur.
For two years, the cottage was a summer retreat and the family moved there
permanently only in 1932, Adams renting flats in London for business use.
His children, now reaching adulthood, were occasional visitors to the cottage,
along with many of his acquaintances – Adams, an amiable but essentially shy
man, made few close friends. In the village, he and his wife attended the
parish church. As Thomas Adams's career ebbed away in the late 1930s, he
retired increasingly to his garden and his study. Over the Easter week-end of
1940, following an over-enthusiastic spell of gardening, he suffered the last in
a series of heart attacks and, after a short illness, he died, aged 68, on 24
March. He had just begun to write his autobiography[42].

During the inter-war years, and especially in the 1930s when he spent most
of his time in Britain, Adams fulfilled the role of an elder statesman of British
planning. He was uniquely fitted for the task. No one, save Unwin, rivalled
his experience of planning at home and abroad. No one held so many high
public and institutional posts and none could match him as the instigator,
galvanizer and publicist for professional bodies of planners and landscape
architects. On public platforms, in popular newspapers like the London *Star*
and *Evening Standard,* in the journals and meetings of other professions and
on the radio, he did more than anyone to educate people on the need for
and nature of planning and landscape architecture. His accumulated wisdom
and experience was projected with lucidity and persuasiveness. While he had
a fundamentally conservative and cautious cast of mind, innovative only in
detail, he was a masterly synthesizer of current thought. Apart from Geddes,
no one gave planning a more intellectual flavour or drew on the output of
other disciplines like economics and philosophy. Above all, his work and
writing was informed by a transatlantic perspective at once singular and
perspicacious.

Chapter Nine

Conclusion

Thomas Adams died in the spring of 1940, followed in the summer by Raymond Unwin. Their passing marked the end of the pioneer phase in modern British planning. From 1940, total war quickened markedly the pace of progress in planning; for the first time, the national government took the lead in shaping planning policy, establishing a comprehensive system, with its own ministry. Within a decade or so of his death, Adams's contribution to planning was little remembered by a new generation whose approach to planning was substantially more sophisticated, fragmented and anonymous than that of the pioneers.

The obscurity into which Adams has slipped is undeserved for he was one of the handful of great builders of the modern planning movement, and, moreover, was recognized as such in his own lifetime. He was, above all, an initiator and creator of major institutions and schemes without parallel in his day. It is doubtful whether any of his contemporaries matched his remarkable record of 'firsts' – the Presidency of the British Amateur Press Association, the first paid planning official in Britain as Secretary of the Garden City Association, the first Manager of First Garden City, the first full-time British planning consultant, the first Town Planning Inspector, the first national Town Planning Advisor, and the first President of both the British and Canadian Town Planning Institutes. He was also a co-founder of the American City Planning Institute, the creative inspiration behind the British landscape architecture profession, the initiator of the Town and Country Planning Summer School, the progenitor of the planning school at M.I.T. and the instigator of planning research at Harvard, as well as the founder of numerous clubs and societies – cultural, sporting, intellectual, political, religious and literary – such as the Young Scots Society and a host of others at Letchworth.

Adams suffered many of the misfortunes which often befall pioneers. Many of his schemes were abortive and others were only partially implemented. He had to compromise his ideals in order to gain lay acceptance of the idea of

191

planning. Some of his initiatives, notably in Canada, petered out because the times were not propitious. Even when he was in high office – at the Local Government Board, the Commission of Conservation and the Regional Plan of New York – he must have felt frustrated at his inability to have his own way as often as he would have liked. However, he was realistic enough to understand that his career, and those of his fellow-pioneers, must be largely chronicles of failure. The price of pioneering often is rebuff and rejection yet Adams had the patience, optimism, faith and the historical determinism to recognize that he and his colleagues were performing a 'John the Baptist' role. They sowed the seed from which a later generation gathered the harvest, chalking up a handful of landmarks – Letchworth, *Rural Planning and Development,* the planning school at M.I.T. and the like. They preached, educated and demonstrated, laying brick upon brick until the nations they served should accept the edifice of planning as a vital structure in the land-scape of twentieth-century man. Adams never lost sight of his ultimate goal, the public recognition of planning as a normal and necessary function of government in modern society, and he remained confident to his end that it would come to pass. That faith sustained him in a forty-year struggle to formulate, explicate, institutionalize, professionalize and implement his gospel.

It would be a hackneyed truism to say that he was 'a planner's planner' yet that was essentially what he became. His great gifts of charm, persuasion, patience, practicality, dynamism, shrewdness and lucidity were allied to substantial talents for organization, administration and publicity and were harnessed most effectively in his work for the emerging profession of plan-ning. Perhaps because he owed everything to planning, he was quicker to perceive the necessity for a coherent disciplinary, professional and edu-cational apparatus for planning than colleagues who had prior professional attachments. Between 1910 and his death, he was the prime mover in the pro-fessionalization and education of planners in all three countries. His textbooks of the 1930s were the standard works of their time in the English-speaking world and his research monographs for the Commission of Conservation and Harvard were about the earliest examples of what has now become a familiar genre.

Adams was the greatest planning 'manager' or administrator of his day. He was a natural co-ordinator, synthesizer and conciliator and was well fitted for the three high posts to which he was called. No one of his generation held so many high commands and he filled all of them with dedication, zest and no small measure of distinction.

He was also the leading publicist for planning in all three countries, as his hundreds of addresses and over 300 publications testify. At once comprehen-sive, learned, lucid, persuasive and good humoured, no one did more to carry the gospel of planning to a wide audience, reaching politicians, fellow professionals, academics and the general public.

As a designer, Adams was derivative rather than original. He learned quickly from others more gifted in this respect and was adept at combining the best features of several modes of planning. He empathized with nature and few could match his ability to integrate artificial features into a natural landscape. He made the leap from city to metropolitan and regional planning earlier and more boldly than anyone else and even flirted, somewhat circumspectly, with the idea of national planning.

Because of the unique shape of his career – he crossed the Atlantic almost annually, often three or four times a year, between 1911 and 1938 – Thomas Adams was a perfect vehicle for the transatlantic traffic in ideas which has become such a significant aspect of the relationship between the Old and New Worlds in this century. In North America, he espoused (though generally with little success) the primarily social objects of British planning – good health and decent housing – and its legislative and institutional framework, agitated constantly for Garden City standards of housing and planning, and pressed on Americans and Canadians the British mode of professional organization. From North America, he derived a more comprehensive and more metropolitan perspective on planning, a belief in the primacy of the economic function of cities, an interest in purpose-built campsites and resorts, an obsession with parkways, an attachment to the art and profession of landscape architecture and a belief in university-based instruction and research in planning. His addresses, writings and reports abound with references to and comparisons with planning in other countries.

Philosophically, Adams remained what he had become in his youth, a late Victorian liberal, a disciple of J. S. Mill's mildly regulatory utilitarianism. He had an essentially simple view of society, perceiving no internal conflicts, only external sores like disease and inefficiency which could be overcome by rational resource allocation. Like many of his contemporaries, he had a somewhat naive faith in the disinterestedness and omnicompetence of the professional planner and in the total applicability of scientific method to planning. He refused to accommodate to the growing polarization of classes which was a major feature of the twentieth century, re-affirming constantly his belief in an essentially harmonious society. An individualist to gladden the heart of Samuel Smiles, he approved of collectivism only in so far as it was generated by self-help on a mutual basis, which he described as 'associated individualism'. Had he survived the Second World War, he would have found himself at odds with the degree of Government intervention and direction inherent in the planning policies of 1940–7. Adams's adherence to a liberal philosophy was his greatest handicap, not because the philosophy itself was intellectually faulty but because he chose to work in a field in which his goals were unattainable by a philosophy which was essentially negative in its attitude to the power of the state.

This study has focused, inevitably, on Adams's professional career. Little has been said about Adams the man. Nevertheless, his personal attributes – a quiet, smiling, good-humoured disposition, patience, tolerance, kindliness, integrity, common sense and, at times, a genuine sense of fun – were crucial to his success in a field in which persuasion rather than compulsion was the organizing principle throughout his life. There is ample testimony in many records to Thomas Adams's rich store of the great human qualities.

Thomas Adams was a great planner whose contribution to the modern planning movement has been unjustly neglected. It may well be that the British, American and Canadian planning movements would have progressed in much the same way and perhaps at the same pace without his presence, for they were subject to complex forces beyond the capacity of one person to change in any drastic fashion. However, there is no gainsaying the facts that Adams was the first to tackle a large number of important issues and tasks, that he was crucial to the establishment and survival of Letchworth, that his was the principal hand shaping the British planning and landscape architecture professions, that he was a prime mover in American planning education, and that he won planning much of its present audience and standing. By 1914 he was regarded as the head of the planning profession in Britain; between 1914 and 1919, very largely he *was* Canadian planning; and in 1923, he was regarded as the best man for the largest task in American planning up to that time, ahead of native rivals. It is at least arguable that between 1914 and 1930, Thomas Adams was the greatest figure in planning, if not in the world as a whole, at least in the English-speaking part of it.

A Note on Sources

PAPERS OF THOMAS ADAMS

There is no central collection of these in a public archive. What little remains of his papers consists chiefly of copies of his books, articles and planning reports, random newspaper cuttings, a handful of letters and some material on housing in Canada at the end of the First World War. During this study, it has been largely in the author's possession, on loans from the family. There are a few letters by Adams in other archives, notably in the *John Nolen papers* at Cornell University. For a comprehensive guide to Adams's voluminous writings, see Hulchanski, J. D. (1978) *Thomas Adams: A Biographical and Bibliographic Guide*. Toronto: Department of Urban and Regional Planning, University of Toronto, *Papers on Planning and Design*, no. 15.

OTHER SOURCES IN BRITAIN

Of first class importance for an understanding of British planning and related subjects between 1900 and 1914 are the numerous books of newspaper cuttings at the Garden City Museum, Letchworth, which has also some papers of the Garden City Association, the Garden City Pioneer Company and First Garden City, Ltd., together with a few other materials. Most other sources are in archives not normally open to non-members of the institutions concerned. A few records of the Garden City Association remain in the care of the Town and Country Planning Association. The National Housing and Town Planning Council has most of its papers and those of its predecessor, the National Housing Reform Council. The few documents of the Institute of Landscape Architects are at the Landscape Institute. The Town Planning Institute's archives are at the Royal Town Planning Institute. All of these bodies are in London. Supplementary material was obtained chiefly from public libraries and archives. The Public Record Office has the Local Government Board papers. The libraries of the greatest value were those of the Royal Town Planning Institute and the Royal Institute of British Architects and the Civic Design Library of the University of Liverpool.

CANADIAN SOURCES

Virtually none of the records of the Commission of Conservation survive other than its *Annual Reports* and other publications, but its progress, and that of Canadian planning in general, can be followed in the admirable and extensive *Noulan Cauchon papers* at the Public Archives of Canada in Ottawa, supplemented by the papers of *Horace Seymour, Sir Clifford Sifton, Sir John Willison* and the various Prime Ministers at the same place. The Public Archives and the adjoining National Library of Canada have between them the Commission's publications, including its magazine, *Town Planning and Conservation of Life*. The Canadian Institute of Planners, also in Ottawa, has the papers and the *Journal* of the Town Planning Institute of Canada, and papers of *A. G. Dalzell, W. F. Burditt* and *J. M. Kitchen*; it is not normally open to non-members. Other Canadian material was found in the Archives of Ontario or was supplied by Professor David Hulchanski.

AMERICAN SOURCES

The *Regional Plan of New York papers*, which are extremely comprehensive, are in the Olin Library, Cornell University, as are the useful *John Nolen papers*. The School of Design Library at Harvard University has most of Adams's published works from 1914; its holdings can be supplemented by those of the Library of the Massachusetts Institute of Technology. All three universities have first-rate libraries on the history of planning.

Notes

CHAPTER ONE

1. Robert Forsyth (1805), quoted in Daiches, D. (1978) *Edinburgh*. London: Hamish Hamilton, p. 220. Stevenson, R. L. (1924) *Edinburgh : Picturesque Notes*. London: Heinemann, pp. 138, 141, 143, 174–5. Adams, I. H. (1977) *The Making of Urban Scotland*. London: Croom Helm, pp. 117–9, 134, 140, 156, 188–9. Keir D. (1966) *The Third Statistical Account of Scotland: The City of Edinburgh*. Glasgow: Collins, pp. 47, 88, 99. See also Smith, P. J. (1980) Planning an environmental improvement: slum clearance in Victorian Edinburgh, in Sutcliffe, A. R. (ed.) *The Rise of Modern Urban Planning*. London: Mansell, pp. 99–133, and Gray, R. Q. (1977) Religion, culture and social class in late nineteenth century Edinburgh, in Crossick, G. (ed.) *The Lower Middle Class in Britain, 1870–1914*. London: Croom Helm, p. 135.

2. Stevenson (1924), p. 143 (see note 1). Keir (1966), pp. 19, 69–72, 730 (see note 1). Nimmo, I. (1969) *Portrait of Edinburgh*. London: Hale, p. 129. Cormack, E. A. *et al.* (1975) *Corstorphine Notes*. Edinburgh; The Corstorphine Trust, p. 55. I am indebted to Dr. Cormack and to the late Mr. David Wilson of Corstorphine for much valuable information on the old village.

3. *Plan of the Estate of Corstorphine* (1845, copy in the possession of the Corstorphine Trust). Ordnance Survey, 25 in. : 1 mile series (1895), sheet 111.9. *Edinburgh and Leith Post Office Directory*. Edinburgh: G.P.O., annually, issues for 1897–8 and 1901–2. All information on the family from General Register Office for Scotland, Edinburgh.

4. Mr. R. H. Morgan, Principal of Daniel Stewart's and Melville College, Edinburgh, to the author, 20 August 1979. Thompson, J. (1971) *A History of Daniel Stewart's College*. Edinburgh: The College, pp. 43–5. Extract from news release from Regional Plan Association, Inc. (New York, 6 February 1932) in *Adams papers* (in author's possession).

5. Ordnance Survey, 25 in. : 1 mile series (1896), sheet 111.6. *Edinburgh and Leith Post Office Directory*, 1887–8, pp. 2, 519, 622, 1069; and *Directory Plans*, vol. 1 (1828–94), in Edinburgh Room, Central Public Library, Edinburgh.

6. Information from General Register Office and Registers of Scotland, Edinburgh. Stevenson (1924), pp. 189–97 (see note 1). Biographies in Brief of Famous Scots: No. 14, Dr. Thomas Adams, London *Sketch*, n.d., 1938, cutting in *Adams papers*.

7. Mrs. Margaret Adkins (Adams's daughter) to the author, 26 May 1979. *Post Office Directory*, 1887–8, p. 622. Cormack *et al.* (1975), p. 49 (see note 2).

8. Mrs. Adkins to author, 26 May 1979. Four scrapbooks of cuttings contain Adams's published and manuscript writings for the years 1888–1914 (in the family's possession). *Interesting Items* (an amateur magazine), August 1941, in *Adams papers*. A name written across the world, *Letchworth Pictorial*, 2 February 1932.

10. Douglas, R. (1974), God gave the land to the people, in Morris, A. J. A. (ed.), *Edwardian Radicalism, 1900–1914*. London: Routledge, p. 152. Adams, T. (1938) *State, Regional and City Planning in America* (ms.), p. 2, in *Adams papers*. His identifiable articles (copies in scrapbooks) were: Science in farming (1894). Rural sketches (1895), Farming: a gambling occupation (1899), all in *Peeblesshire Advertiser*; An ill-lambin': a story of the Pentland Hills (in local dialect), *North British Agriculturalist*, 21 April 1897; The land problem in the rural districts, *Edinburgh Evening News*, 8 and 13 July 1897. On the 1900 Election, see *The Scotsman*, 14 September and 8, 10 and 11 October 1900. Adams had worked for Elibank when he had contested Peebles in 1895. *Scottish Home Rule Association Press Cuttings*, in Scottish Secretariat Papers, Acc. 3721, box 2, f.29, and box 124, f.21, National Library of Scotland, Edinburgh. Cuttings of press reports of inaugural meetings in *Adams papers*. London *Sketch*, c. 1938, in *Adams papers*.

11. It is said by his family that when Adams sought the advice of the popular novelist Mrs. Humphry Ward on how to enter upon a literary career, she replied: 'Don't!' Mrs. Adkins to author, 26 May 1979.

12. Adams, T. (n.d.) *Robert Burns: Humanitarian and Radical* (ms.), in *Adams papers*. See also Adams's articles in *Edinburgh Evening News* and his *Garden City and Agriculture*. London: Simpkin, Marshall, 1905, and *Rural Planning and Development*. Ottawa: Commission of Conservation, 1917. Emy, H. V. (1973) *Liberals, Radicals and Social Politics, 1892–1914*. London: Cambridge University Press, p. 81.

13. Adams, T. (1938), *State, Regional and City Planning in America*, p. 3, and (1940) *My Job of Work* (ms.), pp. 2–3, in *Adams papers;* (1919) Partner-owner building societies. *Town Planning and Conservation of Life* (Ottawa: Commission of Conservation), 5, October, p. 75; (1919) Report on National Conference on City Planning, Niagara Falls, N.Y., in First General Meeting of the Town Planning Institute of Canada. *Canadian Engineer*, 26 June; (1906) The political effects of Garden City. *Garden City*, 1 July, pp. 129–30; (1907) Garden City and small-holdings. *Garden City*, 2 February, pp. 286–90; (1921) Site planning at Lindenlea, Ottawa. *Journal of the Town Planning Institute of Canada*, 1, April pp. 4–5. See also, Ottawa Housing Commission has prepared ideal garden development plan. *Contract Record*, 33, 13 August, 1919, pp. 775, 777–8.

14. On Unwin's association with the working class and socialism, see Miller, M. (1981) Raymond Unwin, in Cherry, G. E. (ed.) *Pioneers in British Planning*. London: Architectural Press, pp. 72–7. Day, M. G. (1981) The contribution of Sir Raymond Unwin and Richard Parry Parker to the development of site planning theory and practice, c. 1890–1918, in Sutcliffe, A. R. (ed.) *British Town Planning: the formative years*. Leicester: Leicester University Press, pp. 156, 158. Day, M. G. and Garstang, K. (1975) Socialist theories and Sir Raymond Unwin. *Town and Country Planning*, 43, July, pp. 346–9. On Adams's views, see

Adams, T. and Cromarty, W. D. (1920) England's housing problem. *Journal of the Town Planning Institute of Canada*, **1** (6). pp. 6–8; Adams, T. (1926) Industrial housing and public health in metropolitan regions, address at Johns Hopkins University, Baltimore, 4 January, box 33, *Regional Plan of New York papers*. Cornell University, Ithaca, New York, (1915). A civic improvement organization for Canada. *Town Planning and Conservation of Life*, **2**, October, p. 4; Planning the Greater Halifax, Commission of Conservation, *Tenth Annual Report*, Ottawa, 1919, p. 107; (1932) *Recent Advances in Town Planning*. London: J. and A. Churchill, pp. 16–17. See also Smith, P. J. (1979) The principle of utility and the origins of planning legislation in Alberta, 1912–75, in Artibise, A. F. J. and Stelter, G. A. (eds.) *The Usable Urban Past: planning and politics in the modern Canadian city*. Toronto : Macmillan, pp. 196–217.

15. Extract from news release from Regional Plan Association, Inc. (see note 4).

16. Adams, T. (1924) Planned cities, II: Edinburgh. *Journal of the American Institute of Architects*, **12**, January, p. 1.

17. Adams, T. (1935) *Outline of Town and City Planning*. New York: Russell Sage Foundation, pp. 112–13; Adams (1932), pp. 15, 23–4 (see note 14).

18. Adams, T. (1910) Town planning and housing. Supplements to *Architectural Review*, May, pp. 311–16; October 1910, pp. 197–201; Adams (1935), pp. 112–13 (see note 17); Adams (1932), p. 30 (see note 14); (1907) A Garden City in the Black Country. *Garden City*, **2**, June, p. 349.

19. Adams, T. (1935), pp. 112–13 (see note 17); Adams (1932), pp. 149–50, 158, 167, 301, 337, 338 (see note 14); Adams, Thompson and Fry (1931), *Final Report on Town Planning* (for City of Edinburgh).

20. Stevenson (1924), pp. 196–7 (see note 1).

CHAPTER TWO

1. Adams, T. (1931) Keeping alive the memory of a great man (the first Ebenezer Howard Memorial lecture), *Letchworth Citizen*, 16 January; (1938) *State, Regional and City Planning in America* (ms.), p. 3; (1940) *My Job of Work* (ms.), pp. 2–3.

2. Howard, E., *Tomorrow: a peaceful path to real reform*. London: Swan, Sonnenschein, 1898; reissued in 1902 as *Garden Cities of Tomorrow*. See the edition edited by F. J. Osborn. London: Faber, 1946, reprinted 1974. Adams, T. (1931), *Letchworth Citizen*, 16 January (see note 1).

3. On the crisis at the turn of the century and attempted solutions prior to 1914, see, for example: Shannon, R. T. (1976) *The Crisis of Imperialism*. London: Paladin; Searle, G. R. (1971) *The Quest for National Efficiency*. Oxford: Blackwell; Thompson, F. M. L. (1962) *English Landed Society in the Nineteenth Century*. London: Routledge, pp. 303, 308–9, 315; Emy, H. V. (1973) *Liberals, Radicals and Social Politics, 1892–1914*. London: Cambridge University Press; Cherry, G. E. (1972) *Urban Change and Planning*. Henley-on-Thames: Foulis, pp. 84–127; Offer, A. (1981) *Property and Politics*. London: Cambridge University Press; Weiler, P. (1982) *Liberal Social Thought in Great Britain, 1889–1914*. New York and London: Garland, Wohl, A. S. (1977) *The Eternal Slum*, London:

Arnold. See especially three contemporary works: Masterman, C. F. G. (1909) *The Condition of England*. London: Methuen; Masterman, C. F. G. (ed.) (1901) *The Heart of Empire*. London: T. F. Unwin, Stead, W. T. (ed.) (1905) *Coming Men on Coming Questions*. London: *Review of Reviews*. On Howard's proposals, see Fishman R. (1977) *Urban Utopias in the Twentieth Century*. New York: Basic Books, pp. 25, 29–58, 87–88; Creese, W. L. (1966) *The Search for Environment*. New Haven: Yale University Press; Osborn, F. J. (1950) Ebenezer Howard: the evolution of his ideas. *Town Planning Review*, **21**, pp. 221–34; Rockey, J. (1983). From vision to reality: Victorian ideal cities and model towns in the genesis of Ebenezer Howard's Garden City. *Town Planning Review*, **54**, pp. 83–105; Sutcliffe, A. R. (1982) *Towards the Planned City*. Oxford: Blackwell, pp. 63–6.

4. On the sceptical reception accorded Howard's book, see *Fabian News*, quoted in Moss-Eccardt, J. (1973) *Ebenezer Howard*. Aylesbury: Shire Publications, p. 16; *Times*, 19 October 1898; Brocklehurst, F., Progressive News and Notes. *The Clarion*, 24 November 1900; Purdom, C. B. (1913) *The Garden City: a study in the development of a modern town*. London: Dent, pp. 22–3.

5. Purdom, C. B. (1913), pp. 22–4 (see note 4). Garden City Association, Third Annual Report (1901), *Minute Book, 1901–1966* (in the possession of the Town and Country Planning Association (henceforth T.C.P.A.). Macfadyen, D. (1933) *Sir Ebenezer Howard and the Town Planning Movement*. Manchester: Manchester University Press, pp. 24–5, 33–8. *Times*, 27 October 1899 and 31 October 1900. *People's Journal*, 12 November 1900. *Daily Mail*, 16 November 1900. Most newspaper and periodical references are taken from the exhaustive books of cuttings at the Garden City Museum, Letchworth.

6. Neville, R. (1901) The extension of co-operation: garden cities. *Labour Co-partnership*, March. Donnelly, D. (1949) The Town and Country Planning Association. *Town and Country Planning*, 17, pp. 13–18. Macfadyen (1933), pp. 40–3. Garden City Assn. (henceforth G.C.A.), Third Annual Report (see note 5).

7. Adams, T. (1928) A greater power outside than within. *Letchworth Citizen*, 7 September.

8. Adams, T. (1931) *Letchworth Citizen*, 16 January (see note 1).

9. Adams, T. (1901) *Morning Leader*, 7 May; (1901) Garden City Notes. *Municipal Reformer*, May (and each month thereafter). Adams's first published utterance on behalf of the G.C.A. was a letter, Back to the land, in *The People*, 28 April 1901.

10. Adams, T. (1901) Garden City Notes. *Municipal Reformer*, June.

11. Adams, T. (1901) Garden City Notes. *Municipal Reformer*, July.

12. Purdom (1913) p. 24 (see note 4).

13. Purdom (1913) p. 24 (see note 4). *Times*, 21 and 23 September 1901.

14. Howard, E. (1901) Garden City Notes. *Municipal Reformer*, November. Neville, R., in Third Annual Report (see note 5). *Brotherhood*, December 1901. G.C.A., A Memorandum by the Secretary, 8 January 1904, in G.C.A. papers at Garden City Museum, Letchworth.

15. G.C.A., Fourth Annual Report (1902). Manchester branch, G.C.A., *Minute Book, 1902–1910* (at T.C.P.A.). Adams, T. (1901) letter in *The Echo*, 8 July. *British Sanitarian*, March 1902. Garden City Notes, *Municipal Reformer*, March 1902. *Times*, 26 July 1902.

16. G.C.A., Report of Public Meeting, Westminster Palace Hotel, 10 October 1902, *Minute Book, 1901–1966*. Howard, E. (1902) *Garden Cities of Tomorrow* (see note 2).

17. *Times*, 28 July 1902. *Land and Labour*, August 1902. Purdom (1913), p. 25 (see note 4).

18. *Times*, 6 and 30 August 1902. Adams, T. (1902) *Circular to Prospective Shareholders* and *Circular to Estate Agents*, both October, in Garden City Pioneer Company papers, Garden City Museum, Letchworth. G.C.A., Fourth Annual Report (see note 5).

19. *Finance*, 13 September 1902. *Daily News*, 18 November 1902. *Times*, 6 and 30 August 1902. Garden City Pioneer Company, *Cash Book*.

20. Purdom, C. B. (1964) A glance back. *Town and Country Planning* 32, p. 401; (1951) *Life Over Again*. London: Dent, pp. 36–9; (1913), pp. 28–9 (see note 4). G.C.A., Sites Committee report, July 1901, and Fourth Annual Report, *Minute Book* (see note 5).

21. Garden City Pioneer Company (henceforth G.C.P.C.), circulars from Howard, Adams and directors, December 1902 to March 1903 (Garden City Museum). List of sites, Adams to Howard, 18 November 1902; Adams to Howard, 11 January 1903; Unwin to Howard, 13 January 1903; Howard to Aneurin Williams (a director), 4 March 1903; correspondence between Howard, Adams and J. German and Sons (agents for Chartley), 22 and 24 April, 29 May and 10 July 1903; also correspondence on other sites, all by courtesy of Dr. Mervyn Miller.

22. Purdom (1913), pp. 29–31 (see note 4); (1951), pp. 39–40 (see note 20). Adams to A. Williams, 22 May 1903; Adams to Parker and Unwin, 17 July 1903 (both Dr. Miller). *Times*, 11 July 1903. *Liverpool Echo*, 18 July 1903.

23. G.C.P.C., *Cash Book; Circular to Shareholders*, 20 May 1904.

24. G.C.P.C., *Circular to Shareholders*, 9 September 1903. *Municipal Journal*, 11 September 1903. *Daily Chronicle*, 17 September 1903. *Church Family Newspaper*, 25 September 1903. Purdom (1913), pp. 31, 230 (see note 4). First Garden City, Ltd. (henceforth F.G.C.), *Annual List and Survey, 1904* (Garden City Museum). On the company's aims, see Osborn, F. J. and Whittick, A. (1969) *New Towns: the answer to megalopolis*. London: Leonard Hill, pp. 57–8.

25. *Pall Mall Gazette*, 30 September 1903. Purdom (1913), p. 33 (see note 4); (1951), p. 40 (see note 20); (1949) *The Building of Satellite Towns*. London: Dent, pp. 148–54.

26. F.G.C., *Minutes of Board Meetings*, 7 September, 29 October 1903, 17 March 1904, Garden City Museum.

27. Cranfield, S. W. and Lucas, G. (1904) Report upon preliminary scheme for a proposed town in North Hertfordshire; Ricardo, H. and Lethaby, W. R. (4 January 1904) Scheme for a garden city, both in F.G.C., *Memorandum and*

Articles of Association, etc., and F.G.C., *Minutes,* 12 October 1903, 7 and 15 January, 11 February 1904 (see note 26). Adams to Parker and Unwin, 17 July and 30 October 1903; Parker and Unwin to Adams, 3 November 1903 (Dr. Miller). Purdom (1913) pp. 41–4 (see note 4); (1963) *The Letchworth Achievement.* London: Dent, pp. 16–18. Cutting from *Letchworth Citizen,* n.d. but pre-1940, on Parker and Unwin plans, Garden City Museum. Miller, M. (1981) Raymond Unwin, in Cherry, G. E. (ed.) *Pioneers in British Planning.* London: Architectural Press, pp. 81–3. Howard to Adams, 31 October and 2 November 1903; Adams to Howard, 3 November 1903; Warren to Adams, 6 November 1903 (all Dr. Miller). Unwin, R. (1913) The planning of Garden City, in Purdom (1913), pp. 222–9 (see note 4).

28. F.G.C., *Minutes,* 7 January, 2 June and 4 August 1904 (see note 26). Parker and Unwin to Adams, 11 July 1904, 1 April 1905 (Dr. Miller). Purdom (1913), pp. 66–8 (see note 4); (1951), p. 46 (see note 20). F.G.C., circulars, 25 January, 12 July 1904, Garden City Museum. Adams, T. (1906) *Letchworth Citizen,* 22 September. Interview with the first tenant-resident (A. W. Brunt), unknown newspaper, n.d., cutting Ha 20, Garden City Museum. Stirring times at Letchworth, *Hertfordshire Express* 20 August 1931.

29. Parker and Unwin to Adams, 11 July 1904 (Dr. Miller).

30. Parker and Unwin to Adams, 1 April 1905; Unwin to Howard, 27 April 1904 (Dr. Miller).

31. *Daily Express,* 16 May 1905. F.G.C., *Minutes, passim* (see note 26). Adams rented a house in Hitchin until January 1905, when he was granted the lease of Punchardon Hall on the company's estate. Purdom (1951), p. 48 (see note 20); (1913), pp. 45–6, 58, 230 (see note 4); (1949), pp. 58–63 (see note 25).

32. Adams, T. (1905; 2nd, ed. 1906) *Guide to Garden City.* London: First Garden City. F.G.C., circulars, 1903–6. See frequent newspaper reports on Letchworth's progress in cuttings books at Garden City Museum. See also *The Garden City,* the movement's journal, from October 1904, especially 1, September 1906, pp. 165–8 on Dent's move to Letchworth. See further Dent, J. M. (1938) *The House of Dent.* London: Dent, p. 129. *North Herts. Mail,* 23 August 1906. Adams, T. (1915) Report on the planning of Greater Vancouver. *Town Planning and the Conservation of Life,* 1, January, p. 59.

33. Newspaper cuttings for 7 October 1903, Garden City Museum. The reporter of the *Pall Mall Gazette,* 8 October 1903, remarked that 'under the influence of the pelting rain one might be forgiven for thinking of Mark Tapley and Eden colony in *Martin Chuzzlewit*'.

34. *Bedfordshire Express,* 16 June 1906. *Daily Telegraph,* 11 June 1906.

35. *The Builder,* 23 January 1904. *Property Market Review,* 18 February 1904. *Electrical Investor,* 14 October, 16 and 30 December 1903. *The Clarion,* 6 November 1903. Interview with Adams in *Bedfordshire Express,* 12 December 1903. John Burns, the Liberal working-class leader and later Adams's chief at the Local Government Board, was a prominent sceptic: see *Morning Leader,* 6 January 1902, and Adams's reply, 25 January. See also Macfadyen (1933), p. 13 (see note 5); Wells, H. G. (1905) Utopianisms. *Daily Mail,* 18 March 1905, and Howard's reply, 22 March; Adams, T. (1906) letter in *Edinburgh Evening News,* 3 October,

Early days, by an Early Resident (W. H. Gaunt) *Letchworth Citizen*, 16 October 1931.

36. Adams, T. (1906) letter in *Edinburgh Evening News*, 3 October. *Labour Leader*, 9 June 1905. Knee, F. (Secretary, Workmen's National Housing Council and a socialist councillor in London), letter in *Justice*, 29 July 1905. See also exchange between Knee and Northcroft in *Pall Mall Gazette*, 16 April 1904. *Daily Chronicle*, 5 October 1906. *Tribune*, 9 October 1906. Adams, T. (1906) Pleasant Sunday Afternoon movement. *North Herts. Mail*, 25 October. *The Clarion*, editorially, was well disposed (see 22 September 1905) and in Letchworth itself it was claimed that socialists were in a majority; see Palmer, S. W., reminiscences in unknown local newspaper, 14 July 1953, cutting Ha 94, Garden City Museum.

37. *Bedfordshire Express*, 16 October 1903. *Sheffield Daily Telegraph* and *Daily News*, 10 October 1903.

38. Visits of various groups, advertised in circulars, were reported in *Garden City*; see also press cuttings, Garden City Museum. On Strong and Rowntree, see *Midland Free Press* and *Garden City Press*, 9 July 1904 and *Times*, 1 August 1904. Adams, T., F.G.C. circular on Constructive temperance reform, 19 July 1904, Garden City Museum.

39. *Bedfordshire Express*, 12 September and 31 October 1903. *Hertfordshire Reporter*, 27 November 1903. Tagg, W. (1956) Garden City was given a year to live. *Letchworth Citizen*, n.d., cutting GR 50, Garden City Museum.

40. *Times*, 7 September 1904.

41. Howard (1902, 1974 edn.) pp. 43–5, 58–65, 126 (see note 2). Adams, T. (1905) *Garden City and Agriculture*. London: Simpkin, Marshall, pp. 38–40, 69–72. Burr, H. (1913) Agriculture and smallholdings, in Purdom (1913), pp. 275–83 (see note 4). See also Purdom (1949), pp. 59, 142–5, 154 (see note 25); (1964), p. 402 (see note 20). Adams, T. (1904), F.G.C. circular on Smallholdings, 26 October, Garden City Museum. Adams, T., interview in *Bedfordshire Express*, 12 December 1903, and letter on allotments, 16 April 1904. *Daily News*, 10 September 1904. Adams to Warren, 11 March 1904, Garden City Museum.

42. Osborn and Whittick (1969), p. 57 (see note 24). Haggard, H. R. (1905) Introduction to Adams, T., *Garden City and Agriculture*, pp. 1–11, and p. 115 (see note 41). Haggard to Adams, 31 July 1905, *Adams papers*.

43. See chapter 1, note 10.

44. Adams (1905), pp. 36–7 (see note 41).

45. Adams (1905), pp. 39, 43–6, 72–8, 98 (see note 41).

46. Adams (1905), p. 102 (see note 41).

47. *Garden City*, 1, February 1905, pp. 6–7; 1, April 1905, p. 32; 1, July 1905, p. 60; Williams, Ben (a leading co-operator) Garden City and agriculture. 1, November 1905, pp. 82–3; 1, March 1906, p. 31; 1, May 1906, p. 98; 1, August 1906, p. 155; 1, October 1906, pp. 184–5, 188; Gaunt, W. H., The future of the Garden City agricultural belt, 1, December 1906, pp. 230–2. *Hertfordshire Reporter*, 7 July 1905.

48. Adams, T. (1907) Garden Cities and smallholdings. *Garden City*, 1, January p.

249 and **2**, February, pp. 286–90. See also Adams, T., letter in *Garden City*, **2**, May 1907, pp. 329–30, and replies by Matthews, A. H. H., and Howard, E., to articles, **2**, February 1907, pp. 270–1 and 290–2. See further Pratt, E. A. (1906) *The Transition in Agriculture*. London: Murray, pp. v, 323–7, 331–2, 335; Orwin, C. S. and Whetham, E. H. (1964) *History of British Agriculture*. London: Longmans, pp. 330–5; Thompson (1962), pp. 321–6 (see note 3); Douglas, R. (1976) *Land, People and Politics: a history of the land question*. London: Allison and Busby, pp. 17–163.

49. Unwin, R. (1906) Cottage building in Garden City. *Garden City*, **1**, June, p. 111. For views on the housing question, see *Garden City* generally.

50. Purdom (1913), pp. 45–6, 51 (see note 4); (1949), p. 60 (see note 25). A real conversion, *Christian World*, 11 August 1904. Bastin, S. L. (1905) The making of a Garden City. *World's Work*, May. *Times*, 10 February and 17 April 1905. Howard, E. (1905) Life at Garden City. *Daily Mail*, 25 July. Howard, E., letter in *Daily News*, 6 September 1905. Interview with Adams in *Bedfordshire Express*, 12 December 1903.

51. Vivian, H. (1905) Co-operation in cottage building, I. *Garden City*, **1**, July, p.65. Advertisement for Co-partnership Tenants, Ltd., *Garden City*, **2**, November 1907.

52. Vivian, H. (1906) Co-operation in cottage building, II. *Garden City*, **1**, February, pp. 11–13, Co-partnership in housing. *Garden City*, **1**, October 1906, p. 196. An Irishman's opinion of Garden City, *Hertfordshire Express*, 18 August 1906. Adams, T., letter in *Manchester Guardian*, 28 September 1906.

53. 'Standish O'Grady' on Garden City. *North Herts. Mail*, 16 August 1906. Adams, T. (1906) The great need for labourers' cottages. *Garden City*, **1**, April pp. 55–6. Our record of progress. *Garden City*, **1**, May 1906, p. 82. Unwin, R. (1906) Cottage building in Garden City. *Garden City*, **1**, June, pp. 107–11. There was extensive correspondence on the housing problems of Letchworth in the local press and in *Garden City* during 1906; charges that rents were too high, the number of houses inadequate, the standard of construction poor, and that the designs were not what working-class people wanted, were made and rebutted. The Co-partnership movement and Parker and Unwin were as much the targets of criticism as the company.

54. The housing problem. *Garden City*, **1**, November 1906, p. 208. *Birmingham Gazette*, 18 September 1905. F.G.C., *Minutes*, 25, October 1906 (see note 24). Howard, E. (1906) Who will help to build homes? *Garden City*, **1**, December, p. 237. A new housing scheme, *Garden City*, **2**, May 1907, p. 337. *North Herts. Mail*, 30 August 1906. Purdom (1949), p. 65 (see note 25).

55. Strachey, J. St.Loe (1904) In search of the £150 cottage. *The County Gentleman*, 1 October, reprinted in *The Book of the Cheap Cottages Exhibition*. London: *The County Gentleman*, 1905, pp. 7–8.

56. Adams to directors, 10 November 1904 (Dr. Miller). F.G.C., *Minutes*, 17 November 1904 (see note 24).

57. *The Book of the Cheap Cottages Exhibition*. pp. 11–17 (see note 55). *Garden City*, **1**, February 1905, p. 13; **1**, April 1905, pp. 42–3; **1**, July 1905, articles by

Strachey, M. H. Baillie Scott, C. R. Ashbee, Parker and Unwin, and Lionel F. Crane. Strachey, J. St.Loe, letter in *Times*, 26 December 1904. Cooper, W.V. (Exhibition Secretary), letter in *Times*, 13 February 1905. *Times*, 25 July 1905. See also Foster, Sir Walter, M.P., at the annual meeting of the G.C.A., *Times*, 18 January 1905.

58. Purdom (1913), pp. 49–51 (see note 4).
59. *Garden City*, 1, November 1905, pp. 73–7. *Daily Express*, 18 September 1905. Newton, E., The Garden City, and Macartney, M., Letchworth, both in Service, A. (1975) *Edwardian Architecture and Its Origins*. London: Architectural Press, pp. 412–8 and 418–22.
60. Adams, T., letter in *Times*, 14 September 1905. Adams, T., F.G.C. circular, 19 October 1905, Garden City Museum. On the Exhibition, see press cuttings for summer and autumn of 1905.
61. Purdom (1913), pp. 49–51 (see note 4).
62. Purdom (1949), p. 64 (see note 25). *Birmingham Gazette*, 18 September 1905. See *Garden City* for details of subsequent exhibitions. F.G.C., circular on Proposed Municipal Cottages Exhibition, 22 December 1905; circular on 1907 exhibition, n.d., 1906, Garden City Museum. Parker and Unwin to Adams, 3 July 1906 (Dr. Miller).
63. A lounger at Letchworth, *Hampstead Record*, 16 September 1905. *Times*, 24 March 1906. *North Herts. Mail*, 9 and 23 August 1906. Early days, by an Early Resident (W. H. Gaunt), *Letchworth Citizen*, 16 October 1931. Rogers, F. W. (1932), First things in Garden City, 29 January, unknown newspaper, n.d., cutting GR 23, Garden City Museum. Tagg, W. (1956) Garden City was given a year to live, *Letchworth Citizen*, n.d., cutting GR 50, Garden City Museum. Palmer, S. W., reminiscences in unknown local newspaper, 14 July 1953, cutting Ha 94, Garden City Museum. Purdom (1949), pp. 58–9 (see note 25); (1951), pp. 49, 52 (see note 20); (1913), pp. 51–2 (see note 4). London *Evening News*, 30 July 1906. *Daily News*, 27 July 1906. Brunt, A. W. (1942) *The Pageant of Letchworth*. Letchworth: Letchworth Printers, pp. 41, 81, 101. Mrs. Adams's brother Louis, a talented artist, was an early resident on Norton Way; see obituary of Louis Weierter, *Hertfordshire Express*, 28 January 1932. Garden City leaders attempted to refute these charges; see Adams's letter in *Edinburgh Evening News*, 3 October 1906; 'Standish O'Grady' in *North Herts. Mail*, 16 August 1906; George Northcroft (G.C.A. Secretary), letter in *Southport Guardian*, 28 January 1905.
64. Interview with the first tenant-resident (A. W. Brunt), unknown newspaper, n.d., cutting, Ha 20, Garden City Museum. F. W. Rogers ruminates, *Letchworth Citizen*, 22 January 1932. *Blackburn Telegraph*, 2 January 1905.
65. Purdom (1963) Unwin and the Garden City movement. *Town and Country Planning*, 31, November, pp. 428–9. On Adams's religious activities, see *Letchworth Citizen*, 22 September, 6, 13, 20 and 27 October, and 17 November 1906; *Hertfordshire Express*, 23 June 1906; *Hertfordshire Reporter*, 21 July 1906; *North Herts. Mail*, 20 October 1906.
66. Adams, T. (1904), circular on proposed golf club, 26 October; (1906) circular on

golf competition, 1 December, Garden City Museum. *Blackburn Telegraph*, 2 January 1905. *Times*, 17 April 1905. *Hertfordshire Express*, 7 and 28 July 1906. *Bedfordshire Express*, 11 August 1906. *North Herts. Mail*, 11 and 25 October 1906. *Letchworth Magazine*, 1, August 1906, p. 16. See also *Garden City*, 1, October 1904 to 1 (n.s.), July 1906. Garden City Evening Education Committee, *Minutes*, 16 May and 20 June 1906; Garden City Association (Residents' Branch), *Minutes*, 11 July and 12 September 1906, all in Garden City Museum.

67. Purdom (1913), pp. 53–4 (see note 4); (1951), p. 51 (see note 20). *North Herts. Mail*, 23 August and ('Open Letter to the Democratic Residents of Garden City') 30 August and (letter from 'Pax') 11 October 1906. Letter from 'Oliver Cromwell' in *Hertfordshire Express*, 1 September 1906. *Daily Chronicle*, 5 October 1906. *Tribune*, 9 October 1906.

68. Adams, T., letter on work at Letchworth for London unemployed, *Times*, 13 January 1905. Adams's general philosophy on labour and capital is set out in The political effects of Garden City. *Garden City*, 1, July 1906, pp. 128–30. See *Garden City, passim*, for details of social provision and activities at Letchworth. Brunt (1942), pp. 52–4, 72–6, 83, 87, 97 (see note 63). *North Herts. Mail*, 25 October 1906.

69. S. W. Palmer, reminiscences, 14 July 1935, unknown newspaper, cutting Ha 94, Garden City Museum.

70. F.G.C., *Minutes*, 28 February, 13 July, 10 August, 28 September 1905, Garden City Museum. Purdom (1951), pp. 53–4 (see note 20); (1913), p. 230 (see note 4); (1949), p. 175 (see note 25). *Garden City*, 1, November 1905, p. 70. *Manchester Courier*, 16 August 1905. *Hertfordshire Reporter*, 25 August 1905.

71. Early days, by an Early Resident (W. H. Gaunt), *Letchworth Citizen*, 16 October 1931. Purdom (1951), pp. 52–6 (see note 20). On local opposition to the 'New Policy', see Garden City Residents' Council, *Minutes*, 15 July 1905, Garden City Museum; *Garden City*, 1, November 1906, p. 219; and especially local press in summer and autumn of 1906.

72. *Garden City*, 1, November 1905, p. 79; 1, February 1906, p. 14. G.C.A., Report of special sub-committee appointed to enquire into the financial position of the Association, 6 November 1903; Adams, T., Memorandum by the Secretary as to the *raison d'être* of the Association, its relationship to the Garden City Company, and other matters which require consideration, 8 January 1904; Memorandum concerning the future relation of the Association to First Garden City: for Council, 12 February 1904; Herbert Warren to Alexander W. Payne (G.C.A. Treasurer), 17 May 1904; Adams, T., Secretary's report on organization, 9 October 1905; F.G.C., *Minutes*, 18 May and 24 August 1905; all in Garden City Museum. Interview with G. J. H. Northcroft in unknown newspaper, 6 August 1903. Purdom (1964), pp. 401–2 (see note 20).

73. Adams, T., Memorandum, 8 January 1904, and Appendix to it by Warren, H. (see note 72). See also Memorandum for Council, 12 February 1904 (see note 72) and Report of Executive to Council, 17 April 1905, in G.C.A. papers, Garden City Museum.

74. Adams, T., Memorandum, 8 January 1904 (see note 72).

75. Adams, T., letter in *Western Mail,* 17 September 1903. Adams, T., Memorandum, 8 January 1904 (see note 72). Adams, T. (1906) Hampstead Garden Suburb. *Garden City,* **1,** February, p. 19.

76. Our record of progress became the regular leading feature of *Garden City* from November 1905. See **1,** November 1905, pp. 70, 79, 90 for particulars of Adams's revival of journal and association. G.C.A., Eighth Annual Report, 31 December 1906, Garden City Museum.

77. Culpin later qualified as an architect and town planner and was President of the Town Planning Institute in 1937–8. He was a Labour alderman and vice-chairman of the London County Council in the late 1930s. *Garden City,* **1,** May 1906, p. 90; **1,** September 1906, pp. 165–8.

78. *Garden City,* **1,** August 1906, p. 154.

79. Adams, T. (1931) Keeping alive the memory of a great man. *Letchworth Citizen,* 16 January. *Garden City,* **1,** July 1906, p. 133. Lord Brassey, a notable statesman, became Chairman of First Garden City, Ltd., on Neville's resignation. Purdom (1964), p. 403 (see note 20); (1951), pp. 53–4 (see note 20). *Glasgow Evening Chronicle,* 13 June 1906.

80. Adams, T. (1931) Keeping alive the memory of a great man. *Letchworth Citizen,* 16 January.

81. Purdom (1951), p. 47. *Hertfordshire Express,* 28 July and 4 August 1906. Adams himself made a very judicious statement to the Residents' Branch of the G.C.A.; see *Letchworth Citizen,* 22 September 1906. Stirring times at Letchworth. *Hertfordshire Express,* 22 August, 1931.

82. *Letchworth Citizen,* 22 September, 27 October, 3 and 17 November 1906. *Hertfordshire Express,* 1 September, 27 October, 3 and 17 November 1906. *North Herts. Mail,* 1 and 15 November 1906. *Garden City,* **1,** October 1906, p. 202; **1,** November 1906, p. 216.

83. *Hertfordshire Express,* 28 July and 4 August 1906.

84. *North Herts. Mail,* 1 November, 1906. Some former citizens, unknown newspaper, n.d., cutting Ha 43, Garden City Museum. Interview with the first tenant-resident (A. W. Brunt), unknown newspaper, n.d., cutting Ha 20, Garden City Museum. Brunt (1942), pp. 25–6 (see note 63).

85. Tagg (1956) Garden City was given a year to live. *Letchworth Citizen,* n.d., cutting GR 50, Garden City Museum. On the early days of Letchworth, see particularly *Town and Country Planning,* **21,** September 1953, including reminiscences by Adams's widow Caroline and his eldest son James.

CHAPTER THREE

1. Sutcliffe, A. R. (1981) *Towards the Planned City.* Oxford: Blackwell, pp. 47–87. Cherry, G. E. (1974) *The Evolution of British Town Planning.* Leighton Buzzard: Leonard Hill, pp. 34–43. Ashworth, W. (1954) *The Genesis of Modern British Town Planning.* London: Routledge, pp. 138–41, 147–64.

2. On the growth of the garden suburb movement, see Culpin, E. G. (1913; 2nd. ed. 1914) *The Garden City Movement Up-to-date*. London: Garden Cities and Town Planning Association, *passim*. *Garden City* (from **3**, March 1908 renamed *Garden Cities and Town Planning*) generally.

3. Paget, Sir Richard (1940) letter in *Journal of the Town Planning Institute*, **26**, March–April, p. 156. *Hertfordshire Express*, 10 November 1906. Adams, T. (1906) Address to Residents' Branch of the Garden City Association, *Letchworth Citizen*, 22 September.

4. Adams, T. (1907) Fallings Park Garden Suburb: a great social opportunity. *Wolverhampton Journal*, **6**, February, p. 41. On Adams's career as a consultant, see his typescript *Adventures in town planning* in newspaper cuttings book, *Adams papers*.

5. Adams, T. (1907) A Garden City in the Black Country. *Garden City*, **2**, June, pp. 348–9; (1908) Fallings Park Garden Suburb. *Garden City*, **2**, January, pp. 496–8; (1909) Some new garden suburb schemes. *Garden Cities and Town Planning*, **4**, May, pp. 206–8; (1907) Land reform and garden cities. *Wolverhampton Express and Star*, 28 June; (1907) (writing as 'Reformer'), letter on The housing question: Wolverhampton's position. *Wolverhampton Chronicle*, 9 October.

6. *Wolverhampton Journal*, **6**, February 1907, pp. 28–9, 41–6.

7. (Adams, T.) (1908) *The Story of a Midland Town*. Wolverhampton: Wolverhampton Industrial Development Committee. *Wolverhampton Chronicle*, Messrs. Chubb's new factory, 8 July 1908; Industrial progress: visit to garden suburb, 15 July 1908. (Adams, T.) (1908) *The Book of the Model Housing Exhibition, Wolverhampton*. Wolverhampton, pp. 5–6. *Primitive Methodist Leader*, 3 January 1907.

8. *Midland Evening Press*, 16 and 18 January, 23 February, 13 July, 23 August, 27 November 1907. *Wolverhampton Chronicle*, New garden suburb, 17 July 1907; Town planning: model housing exhibition opened at Fallings Park: cultivation of joyful life, 23 September 1908. *Wolverhampton Journal*, **6**, April 1907, p. 103. See also, The advance of Wolverhampton in *Municipal Journal*, 17 May 1907, and further extensive coverage of Fallings Park in local press in 1907 and 1908, notably editorial in *Wolverhampton Express and Star*, 15 January 1908; Adams, T. (1908) How to improve the town and trade of Wolverhampton, 13 May, (1909) Ideal conditions of labour. 22 January. Both in *Midland Free Press*. See further Culpin (1913, 1914), pp. 28, 53 (see note 2); Abercrombie, L. P. (1910) Modern town planning in England: a comparative review. *Town Planning Review*, **1**, July, pp. 122–3; Adams to Patrick Geddes, 13 November 1908, *Geddes papers*, Acc. 10541, f.134, National Library of Scotland, Edinburgh.

9. Adams, T. (1907) A Garden City in the Black Country, p. 349 (see note 5). Lodge, Sir Oliver (1907) Trees in the Black Country. *Tribune*, 1 February.

10. *Garden City*, **2**, November 1907, p. 449. *Garden Cities and Town Planning*, **4**, November 1909, pp. 245–6. *Birmingham Post*, 26 May 1908; 27 July 1909. Adams to John Burns, 27 January 1909; Adams to George Haw (a Treasury official), 10 September 1909. Both *Adams papers*.

11. *Garden City*, **2**, August 1907, p. 393.

12. *Tribune*, 11 June 1906. *Garden City*, 1, February 1906, p. 5; March 1906, p. 45. *South Wales Daily News*, 22 October 1908. Mawson, T. H. (1911) *Civic Art: studies in town planning, parks, boulevards and open spaces*. London: Batsford, pp. 287–98; (1927) *The Life and Work of an English Landscape Architect*. London: Richards, pp. 105–6. Mawson, D. (1979) T. H. Mawson. *Landscape Design*, August, pp. 30–3.

13. *Garden City*, 2, January, 1908, p. 498; *Garden Cities and Town Planning*, 3, March 1908, p. 12; 1, May 1911, p. 81. Adams, T. (1909) Some new garden suburb schemes. *Garden Cities and Town Planning*, 4, May, pp. 206–8. Culpin (1913, 1914), p. 30 (see note 2). *South Wales Daily News*, 9 June 1909. *Standard*, 16 September 1909. Abercrombie (1910), pp. 113–14 (see note 8).

14. Garden City Association (G.C.A.), Manchester Branch, *Minutes*, 11 May, 12 and 26 October, 16 and 23 November 1906. Culpin (1913, 1914), p. 23 (see note 2). *Manchester Dispatch*, 6 October 1906. *Manchester Evening News*, 8 and 18 October 1906. *Hertfordshire Express*, 20 October, 17 November 1906. *Garden City*, 1, November 1906, pp. 214–15; 2, April 1907, pp. 319–20. *Manchester Guardian*, 27 January 1909. *Middleton Guardian*, 30 January and 7 August 1909. *Alkrington Garden Village* (undated local brochure). I am indebted to Mr. M. Garrett of Middleton Library and Mr. W. John Smith of Alkrington for further information on the estate.

15. Adams (1909), pp. 206–8 (see note 13). Abercrombie (1910), p. 115 (see note 8).

16. *Garden Cities and Town Planning*, 1, May 1911, pp. 98–9; 1, September 1911, p. 195; 2, May 1912, p. 116; 3, July 1913, p. 170. See also entries from *Middleton Guardian* in *Norcross Scrapbooks*, 1, Middleton Area Central Library.

17. *Bedfordshire Express*, 23 September 1905. *Knebworth Garden Village* (undated prospectus of Garden Villages, Ltd.). *Morning Post*, 20 September 1909. Adams (1909), pp. 206–8 (see note 13).

18. *Knebworth Garden Village* (see note 17). *Morning Post*, 20 September 1909.

19. *Edwin Lutyens and Knebworth* (typescript notes, courtesy of Dr. M. Miller). Culpin (1913, 1914), p. 35 (see note 2). *Garden Cities and Town Planning*, 1, May 1911, pp. 97–8; 2, May 1912, pp. 107–8.

20. *Clifton Chronicle*, 4 August 1909, and 2 December 1908. *Western Daily Press*, 6 and 10 July, 15 August, 26 September 1903; 3 December 1909. *Bristol Mercury*, 28 July, 19 September 1903. *Bristol Times and Mirror*, 19 September 1903; 16 December 1908. *Garden City*, 1, February 1906, p. 5; *Garden Cities and Town Planning*, 4, January–February 1909, p. 168; 4, May 1909, p. 195; 1, August 1911, p. 177. Adams, T. (ed.) (1906) *Housing in Town and Country*. London: G.C.A., p. 11. Abercrombie (1910), p. 114 (see note 8). *The Bristol Garden Suburb* (undated local brochure) and clippings and reports relating to Bristol Garden Suburb, Ltd., Acc. B20757, Avon Central Library, Bristol.

21. Culpin (1913, 1914), p. 25 (see note 2).

22. Adams (1909), pp. 206–8 (see note 13). Abercrombie (1910), p. 115 (see note 8). Culpin (1913, 1914), p. 40.

23. Adams, T. (1909), letter in *Liverpool Daily Courier*, 6 November. Adams (1909), pp. 206–8 (see note 13). *Daily News*, 28 October 1909. Culpin (1913, 1914), p. 55.

Garden Cities and Town Planning, 2, May 1912, pp. 111–12; 2, August 1912, pp. 182–4. *Town Planning Review*, 1, July 1910, p. 174; 1, January 1911, pp. 333–4; 2, April 1911, p. 79; 2, October 1911, p. 243.

24. Culpin (1913, 1914), p. 53 (see note 2). *Garden City*, 2, January 1908, p. 498; *Garden Cities and Town Planning*, 4, November 1909, p. 254. *Manchester Evening Chronicle*, 7 August 1909. *Times*, 18 August 1909. *Yorkshire Evening Post*, 1 March 1910.

25. G.C.A., Minute Book, *1901–1966*, minutes of annual meetings and executive council, 1908–14, Town and Country Planning Association. *Municipal Journal*, April 1909. Biographies in Brief of Famous Scots: No. 14, Dr. Thomas Adams, *The Sketch*, c. 1938, cutting in *Adams papers*.

26. On the origins of the Housing, Town Planning, etc., Act of 1909, see *Minute Book (1906–1913)* of the National Housing Reform Council, now in the possession of its successor, the National Housing and Town Planning Council. Adams to Geddes, 8 February 1910, *Geddes papers*, Acc.10542, f.22, National Library of Scotland, Edinburgh. An invaluable guide to early statutory planning is Aldridge, H. R. (1915) *The Case for Town Planning*. London: National Housing and Town Planning Council. See also works by Ashworth, Cherry and Sutcliffe listed in note 1.

27. Aldridge, H. R. (Secretary, National Housing Reform Council, hereafter N.H.R.C.) to Hay, C. (secretary to Walter Long, President of the Local Government Board), 11 May 1905, HLG 29/96; Kershaw, N. T. (Local Government Board official) and others, *Memoranda on Town Planning Bill*, 16 February 1907, HLG 29/96, Public Record Office. On Nettlefold and the Association of Municipal Corporations, see *Report of A.M.C. Deputation*, 7 August 1907, HLG 29/97, Public Record Office (hereafter P.R.O.).

28. Adams, T. (1908) Some criticisms of the Bill. *Garden Cities and Town Planning*, 3, April, pp. 49–50. See other critics in same issue and see *Garden City* and *Garden Cities and Town Planning* generally from 1907. John Burns, quoted in *Garden Cities and Town Planning*, 3, August 1908, p. 92.

29. Housing, Town Planning, etc., Act, 1909, 9 Edward VI, ch. 44. The principal Parliamentary debates are: *Parliamentary Debates*, Fourth Series, vol. 173 (1907), cols. 978–90; vol. 188 (1908), cols. 947–1063; vol. 3 (1909), cols. 734–98, 851–62; vol. 6 (1909), cols. 833–98; vol. 9 (1909), cols. 1688–89; vol. 13 (1909), cols. 445–8. See also reports of Standing Committee 'B', House of Commons, *Times*, 15 July, 6, 13, 17, and 20 November 1908. Masterman, L. (1939) *C. F. G. Masterman*. London: Nicholson and Watson, pp. 104–5, 107–8, 113–17, 121–2, 134, 150–1. Minett, J. (1974) The Housing, Town Planning, etc., Act, 1909. *The Planner*, 60, May pp. 676–80. On Burns, see Brown, K. D. (1977) *John Burns*. London: Royal Historical Society. Adams (1908), pp. 47–51 (see note 28). *Garden City*, 2, September 1907, pp. 414–15; *Garden Cities and Town Planning*, 3, May–June 1908, pp. 62–76; 3, August 1908, pp. 89–92; 4, November 1909, p. 254. Culpin, E. G. (ed.) (1910) *The Practical Application of Town Planning Powers*. London: P. S. King. See also comments and objections by interested parties in HLG 29/97 and 29/99, P.R.O.

30. House of Commons, *Sessional Papers*, 38 (1910), 39th Annual Report of the Local

Government Board (1909–10), Part II (Cd. 5275), p. 607. *Garden Cities and Town Planning*, **4**, February 1910, p. 289. Adams, T. (1938) *State, regional and city planning in the United States*, p. 3. Cutting from unknown Canadian newspaper, n.d., in *Adams papers*. *Parliamentary Debates*, Fourth Series, vol. 188 (12 May 1908), col. 1037 (Alfred Lyttelton); vol. 3 (5 April 1909), col. 749 (Alfred Lyttelton); vol. 10 (31 August 1909), col. 252 (Rt. Hon. John Burns).

31. Anon. (almost certainly Adams), Reply to article 'Strangling town planning'. *Garden Cities and Town Planning*, **3**, December 1913, pp. 301–2. Procedure Regulations discussed in Dowdall, H. C. (1910), including further comments by Adshead, S. D. and Abercrombie, L. P., The Procedure Regulations of the Town Planning Act. *Town Planning Review*, **1**, July, pp. 129–31, 132–6, 164. House of Commons, *Sessional Papers*, 31 (1911), Annual Report of the Local Government Board, pp. 294–5.

32. Anon. (Adams), Reply to 'Strangling Town Planning', p. 302 (see note 31). Dickenson, J. A. E., in 42nd Annual Report of Local Government Board (1912–13), House of Commons, *Sessional Papers*, 31 (1913), p. 338. See also Dickenson in 43rd Annual Report (1913–14), Part II, *Sessional Papers*, 38 (1914), p. 322. See further 40th Annual Report, *Sessional Papers*, 31 (1911), pp. 294–5. *Town Planning Review*, **2**, April 1911, pp. 76–7, 132–6 (Adshead), 164 (Abercrombie). Culpin, E. G. (1911) Progress under the Act. *Garden Cities and Town Planning*, **1**, November–December, pp. 241–3. Adams, T. (1912) The sociological aspect of town planning. *Garden Cities and Town Planning*, **2**, July, p. 150. See also contributions to Culpin, (ed.) (1910) (see note 29).

33. 40th Annual Report of Local Government Board (1911), pp. 294–5 (see note 31). Adams, T. (1912) *Town planning in Great Britain*. Reprint of paper given at International Town Planning Congress, Berlin; (1915) The meaning and practical application of town planning. *Town Planning and Conservation of Life*, **1**, July, p. 75; (1911) Garden cities and town planning in America. *Garden Cities and Town Planning*, **1**, September, p. 197; (1911) Some American impressions. *Town Planning Review*, **1**, July, p. 139; 'A member of the conference' (almost certainly Adams) Town planning and town training. *Transactions of the Town Planning Conference (10–15 October 1910)*. London: Royal Institute of British Architects, pp. 524–33.

34. On Adams's initial impressions of America, see chapter 6, below. See also Adams, T. (1911) American city planning, and Unwin, R. (1911) American town planning. *Garden Cities and Town Planning*, **1**, August, pp. 165–73 and 162–5. On the transatlantic traffic in ideas, see Morgan, K. O. (1976) The future at work: Anglo-American progressivism, 1890–1917, in Allen, H. C. and Thompson, R. (eds.) *Contrast and Connection: Bicentennial essays in Anglo-American history*. London: Bell, pp. 245–71.

35. See reports of inquiries, HLG series, P.R.O.

36. Abercrombie, L. P. (1914) Mr. Adams for Canada. *Town Planning Review*, **5**, October, p. 249.

37. See, for example, Barnet Urban District Council (hereafter U.D.C.), HLG 4/171; Finchley Borough Council (hereafter B.C.), HLG 4/981; Hazelgrove and Bramhall U.D.C., HLG 4/1159. All P.R.O.

38. Middleton Borough Council, HLG 4/1579. Ruislip-Northwood U.D.C., HLG 4/1871, HLG 4/1874, HLG 4/1872 and HLG 4/1873. On opposition to planning, see Gresuolde Williams (a landowner), reported in *Birmingham Daily Post*, 21 June 1912, referring to Birmingham (Stechford and North Yardley) scheme, HLG 4/273; Ratepayers of East Birmingham to Local Government Board, 6 October 1911, Birmingham (East) scheme, HLG 4/283; Association of Finchley Property Owners and Occupiers to Local Government Board, n.d. (c. 1914), Finchley B.C. scheme, HLG 4/981. On support for planning, see Halifax County Borough Council, HLG 4/1093 and HLG 4/1098; Hendon U.D.C., HLG 4/11666; Rev. T. G. Gardiner to Mr. Downes (Local Government Board), 7 March 1913, in Leeds County Borough Council (hereafter C.B.C.), HLG 4/1343; Lincoln C.B.C., HLG 4/1427. All P.R.O.

39. Bournemouth C.B.C., HLG 4/330; Honiton Rural District Council (hereafter R.D.C.), HLG 4/2821; Sutton Coldfield B.C., H.L.G 4/2221; Beckenham U.D.C., HLG 4/189; Surbiton U.D.C., HLG 4/2197. All P.R.O.

40. Wirral R.D.C., HLG 4/3088, HLG 4/3987, HLG 4/3988, HLG 4/3989; Wrexham R.D.C., HLG 4/3095, HLG 4/3096, HLG 4/3098; Sutton Coldfield B.C., HLG 4/2221; Luton B.C., HLG 4/1468. All P.R.O.

41. Birmingham C.B.C., HLG 4/251–4, 257, 259, 269, 273–4, 277, 283–7. Leeds C.B.C., HLG 4/1339, 1341–3, 1397–8. Manchester C.B.C., HLG 4/1525, 1534–5 (and schemes of adjoining councils, HLG 4/560–1, 1159, 1785, 1923, 2135, 2136). Liverpool C.B.C., HLG 4/1438–9, 1441, 1452. All P.R.O. On Sheffield, see *Town Planning Review*, 2, April 1911, pp. 71–4; 2, January 1912, p. 334.

42. See, for example, Barrow U.D.C., HLG 4/177; Beckenham U.D.C., HLG 4/189; Warrington R.D.C., HLG 4/3035; Wrexham B.C., HLG 4/2604; Merton and Morden U.D.C., HLG 4/1573. All P.R.O.

43. See Annual Reports of Local Government Board, House of Commons, *Sessional Papers* (summarized in Cherry (1974), p. 67 (see note 1)). See also Cherry, G. E. (1975) *Factors in the Origins of Town Planning in Britain: the example of Birmingham*. Centre for Urban and Regional Studies: *Working Paper 36*. Birmingham: University of Birmingham, pp. 18–30. Ratepayers of East Birmingham to Local Government Board, 6 October 1911, Birmingham C.B.C., HLG 4/283; Town Clerk, Birmingham C.B.C., to Local Government Board, 25 January 1913, HLG 4/286; Hayes and Harlington U.D.C., HLG 4/1152. All P.R.O.

44. Thompson, Ald. W., quoted in *Garden Cities and Town Planning*, 2, June 1912, pp. 133–5. Aldridge, H. R. (1911) The Advisory Town Planning Committee. *Garden Cities and Town Planning*, 1, May, pp. 102–3. Pepler, G. L. (1911) Town planning for rural districts. *Garden Cities and Town Planning*, 1, October, pp. 204–9. *Daily Chronicle*, quoted in *Garden Cities and Town Planning*, 2, October 1912, p. 214. Anon., Strangling town planning, and comments by Pepler, G. L. and Horsfall, T. C., all in *Garden Cities and Town Planning*, 3, November 1913, pp. 303–6. Wilkes, J. E. (1914) Comment on 'Strangling town planning'. *Garden Cities and Town Planning*, 4, January, p. 27. Abercrombie, L. P. (1913) A study of town planning: the English contribution. *Town Planning Review*, 4, April, p. 108.

Adshead, S. D. (1914) A democratic view of town planning. *Town Planning Review*, **5**, October, p. 186.

45. Abercrombie (1913), p. 109 (see note 44). Culpin (1911), p. 241 (see note 32).

46. Adams (1912), p. 150 (see note 32).

47. *Ibid.*

48. Adams, (1913), p. 302 (see note 31).

49. Burns, Rt. Hon. John, speech at inaugural dinner of Town Planning Institute, reported in *Garden Cities and Town Planning*, **4**, February 1914, p. 50. See also *Town Planning Review*, **5**, April 1914, pp. 9–10. Annual Reports of Local Government Board, House of Commons, *Sessional Papers*, 1910–16, *passim*.

50. *Town Planning Review*, **5**, April 1914, pp. 1–2. *Garden Cities and Town Planning*, **3**, June 1913, p. 145. Annual Reports of the Local Government Board for 1914 and 1916, House of Commons, *Sessional Papers*. The Town Planning Act: revised regulations. *Garden Cities and Town Planning*, **4**, February 1914, pp. 51–2. On Samuel, see *Garden Cities and Town Planning*, **4**, April 1914, pp. 75–6.

51. 42nd Annual Report, Local Government Board (1913), p. 341 (Doncaster), p. 342 (London); 43rd Annual Report, Local Government Board (1914), p. 332 (Doncaster), pp. 333–9 (London), House of Commons, *Sessional Papers*. Ruislip U.D.C., HLG 4/1871 and 1873. Hayes and Harlington U.D.C., HLG 4/1152.

52. *Report of the Royal Commission on London Traffic*. London: H.M. Stationery Office, 1905. Cherry (1974), pp. 69–70 (see note 1).

53. Twickenham U.D.C., HLG 4/2322. Ham U.D.C., HLG 4/3958.

54. Culpin, E. G. (1914) Progress. *Garden Cities and Town Planning*, **4**, June, pp. 144–5.

55. See 42nd and 43rd Annual Reports of Local Government Board (1913 and 1914) and planning press for frequent discussions of planning for London, especially Meath, Lord (1906) A green girdle round London. *Garden City*, **1**, April, pp. 59–60 (reprint of a 1901 article).

56. 43rd Annual Report of Local Government Board (1914), p. 336). *Town Planning Review*, **5**, October 1914, p. 339. Adams, T. (1914–15) Town planning in Greater London. *Papers of the Town Planning Institute*, **1**, pp. i–xi. See also Pepler, G. L. (1910) Greater London. *Transactions of the Town Planning Conference*. London: Royal Institute of British Architects, pp. 611–24.

57. Adams (1938), p. 4 (see note 30); (1914–15) Some recent developments in town planning. *Papers of the Town Planning Institute*, **1**, p. 144.

58. Adams (1910) The practical administration of town planning powers, in Culpin (ed.), pp. 11, 61 (see note 29). Adams (1914–15), pp. 141–3 (see note 57). Potter, A. R. (1963) The history of the Institute. *Journal of the Town Planning Institute*, **49**, December, p. 368.

59. Adams (1914–15), p. 144 (see note 57).

60. Abercrombie, L. P. Landscape architect or city planner?, pp. 172–3; Adshead, S. D., The town planning conference at West Bromwich, pp. 175–7; Mawson, T. H., The position and prospects of landscape architecture in Britain, pp.

225–8, all in *Town Planning Review*, **2**, October 1911. Reilly, C. H., quoted in Cherry (1974), p. 54 (see note 1).

61. Lloyd, T. A. (1940) The late Thomas Adams. *Journal of the Town Planning Institute*, **26**, March–April, p. 115. Town Planning Institute (hereafter T.P.I.), *Minute Book of Council, 1913–32*, Provisional Committee, 17 October 1913. On the foundation of the Institute, see Cherry (1974), pp. 33–62 (see note 1) and Hawtree, M. G. (1975) *The Origins of the Modern Town Planner: a study in professional ideology*. Unpublished Ph.D. thesis, Liverpool University. This section leans fairly substantially on Dr. Hawtree's work.

62. Unwin, R. (1909) *Town Planning in Practice*. London: T. F. Unwin; (1910) 'Wholesale' planning, in Culpin (ed.), p. 39 (see note 29); (1910) The city development plan. *Transactions of the Town Planning Conference*, pp. 247–82. See also J. W. Simpson in *ibid.*, pp. iii–iv. Triggs, H. I. (1909) *Town Planning: past, present and possible*. London: Methuen. Hawtree (1975), pp. 77, 90, 95 (see note 61).

63. A Member of the Conference (almost certainly Adams) (1910) Town planning and town training. *Transactions of the Town Planning Conference*, p. 530.

64. Royal Institute of British Architects, *Memorandum*, 3 December 1907, HLG 29/96; letter to Rt. Hon. John Burns, 17 January 1908, HLG 29/97, Public Record Office. A Member (almost certainly Adams) (1911) The conference and after. *Garden Cities and Town Planning*, **1**, February, pp. 16–17. See also Adshead (1909) The study of town planning. *Garden Cities and Town Planning*, **4**, May, p. 194, and Lanchester, H. V., Town and country; some aspects of town planning, in *ibid.*, pp. 209–11. Adams (1911) in Culpin (ed.), p. 11 (see note 29). Royal Institute of British Architects (1911) Suggestions to promoters of town planning schemes. *Town Planning Review*, **2**, October 1911, pp. 239–40.

65. Hawtree (1975), pp. 120, 122, 126–31 (see note 61). Davidge, W. R. (1910) The surveyor's point of view, in Culpin (ed.), pp. 47–50 (see note 29). Surveyors' Institution, *Memorandum to Rt. Hon. John Burns*, May 1908, HLG 29/97, P.R.O. Thompson, F. M. L. (1968) *Chartered Surveyors: the growth of a profession*. London: Routledge, pp. 299–301.

66. Hawtree (1975), pp. 101–2, 105, 110, 117 (see note 61). N.H.R.C., *Minute Book 1*, Committee, 1 September 1906. Institution of Municipal and County Engineers, *Housing and Town Planning Conference, 1911* and *ibid., 1913*. Adshead (1911), pp. 175–8 (see note 60); (1914) The annual meeting of the Institution of Municipal and County Engineers. *Town Planning Review*, **5**, April, pp. 150–4. *Garden Cities and Town Planning*, **4**, January 1914, p. 3. Institution of Municipal and County Engineers, *Memorandum to Rt. Hon. John Burns*, 21 February 1908, HLG 29/97, P.R.O.

67. T.P.I., *Minute Book of Council*, 11 July, 17 October, 21 November, 12 December 1913.

68. T.P.I., *Minute Book of Council*, 9 January, 6 February, 13 March, 3 April, 12 June, 4 September 1914; *Minutes of General Meetings* (1914–67), 13 March, 24 April, 15 May 1914.

69. T.P.I., *Minute Book of Council*, 4 September 1914. See Unwin, R. and Abercrombie, L. P. in *Town Planning Review*, 5, October 1914, pp. 243–4, 248–9.

70. Adams (1914–15), p. 144 (see note 57). Hawtree (1975), pp. 195–6. 201–16 (see note 61).

71. Hawtree (1975), p. 137 (see note 61) and information from Adams family.

72. On the state of British planning in 1914, see Abercrombie (1910) Modern town planning in England. *Town Planning Review*, 1, April, pp. 18–38 and July, pp. 111–23. Culpin (1913, 1914), *passim*. (see note 2). Abercrombie (1913) Town planning in the rut of routine, and The study of town planning: the English contribution. *Town Planning Review*, 4, April, pp. 1–2 and 105–14. Adshead (1914) A democratic view of planning. *Town Planning Review*, 5, October, pp. 183–94. Edwards, A. T. (1913) A criticism of the garden city movement, and (1914) A further criticism of the garden city movement. *Town Planning Review*, 4, April, pp. 150–7 and 4, January, pp. 312–18. Reade, C. C. (1913) A defence of the garden city movement. *Town Planning Review*, 4, October, pp. 245–51. See also *Garden Cities and Town Planning*, *passim*. See further the works by Cherry, Ashworth and Sutcliffe listed in note 1.

73. Adams (1938), pp. 4–5 (see note 30).

74. Abercrombie (1914) in *Town Planning Review*, 5, October, p. 248.

CHAPTER FOUR

1. Brown, R. C. and Cook, R. (1976) *Canada, 1896–1921: a nation transformed.* Toronto: McClelland and Stewart, p. 49. Neatby, H. B. (1967) The new century, in Careless, J. M. S. and Brown, R. C., *The Canadians*. Toronto: Macmillan, pp. 137–71.

2. Brown and Cook (1976), pp. 49, 61–3, 82 (see note 1). See also Preston, W. T. R. (1927) *My Generation of Politics and Politicians*. Toronto: Rose, pp. 214, 262–5; and McGregor, F. A. (1962) *The Fall and Rise of Mackenzie King*. Toronto: Macmillan, pp. 35–6, 54; and Dafoe, J. W. (1931, repr. 1971) *Clifford Sifton in Relation to His Times*. New York: Books for Libraries Press.

3. Dalzell, A. G. (1927) Town planning problems in Canada. *City Planning*, 3, January, pp. 26–31. Adams, T. (1921) *In the Matter of the Public Utilities Act, etc.*, 11 May, p. 2, in vol. 9, *Noulan Cauchon papers* (hereafter *Cauchon papers*), Public Archives of Canada. Bryce, P. H. (1918) *Conservation of Manpower in Canada*, vol. 6, *Cauchon papers*. Rickett, J. E., Jr. (c. 1912) How one railroad is putting new towns on the map. *Canada Monthly*, August (cutting in Design Library, Harvard University). McGahan, E. (1976) The Port of Saint John, New Brunswick, 1867–1911. *Urban History Review*, 3, February, pp. 3–13. Careless, J. M. S., Aspects of Urban Life in the West, 1870–1914; MacDonald, N., A Critical Growth Cycle for Vancouver, 1900–14; Artibise, A. F. J., Divided City: the immigrant in Winnipeg society, 1874–1921, all in Stelter, G. A. and Artibise, A. F. J. (eds.) (1979) *The Canadian City: essays in urban history*. Toronto: Macmillan, pp. 139, 142–5, 303–4.

4. Burditt, W. F. (1917) Civic efficiency and social welfare in the planning of land, in Commission of Conservation, *Urban and Rural Development in Canada*. Ottawa: Commission of Conservation, p. 78.

5. Berlin (now Kitchener) *News Record*, c. 1915, cutting in *Adams papers*. Adams (1921), p. 2 (see note 3). Dalzell (1927) The relation of housing and town planning in cities such as Vancouver. *Municipal Review of Canada*, 23 May, p. 199; (1927) How stop the deadly toll of the streets? *Toronto Star Weekly*, 26 November. Hobbs, W. E. (1922) The suburban problem of Greater Winnipeg. *Journal of the Town Planning Institute of Canada*, 1, June, pp. 22–31. Detweiler, D. B. (Algoma Power Company, Berlin, Ontario) to Sifton, Sir C., 8 November 1915, *Adams papers*.

6. Adams (1921), pp. 2–3 (see note 3).

7. *Apartment houses*, typescript note, n.d., *Adams papers*. Memorandum: *A case for treatment*, typescript, n.d., *Adams papers*. Unwin, R. (1914) Canada and town planning. *The Record* (Hampstead Garden Suburb), 2, February (courtesy of Dr. M. Miller). Hastings, Dr. C. J. C. O. (1912) The significance of sanitary housing, and Suggestions for the housing problem. *Industrial Canada*, June, pp. 1284–6, and August, pp. 66–69. Housing Committee of the Board of Trade, Saint John, N. B. (1914) *Investigation by the Board of Health*, April, *Adams papers*. See also contemporary essays on slum problems reprinted in Rutherford, P. (ed.) (1974) *Saving the Canadian City: the first phase, 1880–1920*. Toronto: University of Toronto Press; Brown and Cook (1976), pp. 62–3, 99–100, 128–9 (see note 1); Artibise, A. F. J. and Stelter, G. A. (1980) Conservation planning and urban planning: the Canadian Commission of Conservation in perspective, in Kain, R. J. P. (ed.) *Planning for Conservation*. London: Mansell, p. 19; Hulchanski, J. D. (1981) *The Origins of Urban Land Use Planning in Alberta, 1900–1945*. Toronto: Centre for Urban and Community Studies, University of Toronto, p. 9; MacDonald (1979), in Stelter and Artibise, pp. 142–5 (see note 3); and Artibise, *ibid.*, pp. 300–36, and (1975) *Winnipeg: a social history of urban growth, 1874–1914*. Montreal: McGill-Queen's University Press.

8. Dalzell (1927) pp. 26–31 (see note 3). Miller, Rev. J. O. (1917) The better government of our cities, in Miller (ed.) *The New Era in Canada*. London and Toronto: Dent, p. 351.

9. Road policy in Northern Ontario. *Toronto Globe*, 12 March 1919, and *ibid.* on rural depopulation, 15 August 1917. Murphy, E. F. (1920) The dual problem of modern social organization. *Social Welfare*, 3, 1 November, pp. 38–9. On the rural problem in general, see Adams, T. (1917) *Rural Planning and Development*. Ottawa: Commission of Conservation.

10. Miller (ed.) (1917), *passim.* (see note 8). Allen, R. (1968) The Social Gospel and the reform tradition in Canada. *Canadian Historical Review*, 49, pp. 381–99. See also Rutherford, P. (1979) Tomorrow's metropolis: the urban reform movement in Canada, 1880–1920, and Weaver, J. C. (1979) Tomorrow's metropolis revisited: a critical assessment of urban reform in Canada, 1890–1920, both in Stelter and Artibise (eds.), pp. 368–92, 393–413 (see note 3). Weaver (1976) Approaches to the history of urban reform; Kitchener, S. (1976) J. W. Bengough and the millenium in Hogtown; Nelles, H. V. and Armstrong, C. (1976) The great fight for clean government, all in *Urban History Review*, 2, pp. 3–11, 30–49, 50–66. Wickett, S. M. (1915) *On Toronto's Need of Reform*. Toronto: the author. Pamphlet 1915, no. 77, Ontario Archives, Toronto. Weaver (1979) The modern

city realized: Toronto civic affairs, 1880–1915; Anderson, J. D. (1979) The municipal government reform movement in Western Canada, 1880–1920, both in Artibise, A. F. J. and Stelter, G. A. (eds.) *The Usable Urban Past.* Toronto: Macmillan, pp. 39–72, 73–111.

11. Walker, B. E., A comprehensive plan for Toronto, in Rutherford (ed.) (1974), p. 225 (see note 7). Buckley, A. (1920) The model city plan. *Ottawa Citizen,* 30 December. Mitchell, C. H. (1912) Town planning and civic improvement. *Canadian Engineer,* 26 December. Toronto Guild of Civic Art (1909) *Report on a Comprehensive Plan for Systematic Civic Improvements in Toronto.* Pamphlet 1909, no. 55, Ontario Archives. Mawson, T. H. (1912) The city of the plain and how to make it beautiful, in *Two Notable Addresses on Town Planning and Housing.* Calgary: City Planning Commission. Pearse, W. to Cauchon, N., 15 June 1912. vol. **1,** *Cauchon papers.* Winnipeg City Planning Commission, *Report, 1911–13.* vol. **10,** *Cauchon papers.* See also Van Nus, W. (1975) *The Plan-Makers and the City: architects, engineers, surveyors and urban planning in Canada, 1890–1939.* Unpublished Ph.D. thesis, Toronto University, esp. chapter 4; (1979) The fate of City Beautiful thought in Canada, 1893–1930, in Stelter and Artibise (eds.), pp. 162–85 (see note 3). Artibise (1975), pp. 267–79 (see note 7).

12. Adams, quoted by Mawson, T. H., in City building. Undated lecture given in Toronto. File 15, Canadian Institute of Planners, Ottawa.

13. Cauchon to Pearse, W., 20 June 1912, vol. **1,** *Cauchon papers.* Adams, T. (1916) The Governors-General of Canada and town planning. *Town Planning and Conservation of Life,* **3,** December, pp. 1–4. Vivian, H. (1912) How to apply town planning in Calgary, and Mawson, T. H. (1912) The city of the plain and how to make it beautiful, both in *Two Notable Addresses on Town Planning and Housing* (see note 11). Unwin, R., Some architectural aspects of town planning, and Adams, T., Some observations on the British Town Planning Act, both in *The First Canadian Housing and Planning Congress, Winnipeg, 15–17 July, 1912,* vol. **10,** *Cauchon papers.*

14. Hastings (1912), p. 1286 (see note 7). Miller (1917), p. 354 (see note 8). Letterhead of Calgary City Planning Commission, example in vol. **1,** *Cauchon papers.* Hayler, G. W. (1912) The essential elements of city planning, in *The First Canadian Housing and Planning Congress,* p. 64 (see note 13).

15. An Act respecting Town Planning. Province of Nova Scotia, ch. 6, 2 George V, 3 May 1912, and An Act relating to Town Planning. Province of New Brunswick, ch. 19, 2 George V, 20 April 1912, both in Commission of Conservation, *Report of Fourth Annual Meeting, 1913,* Ottawa: Commission of Conservation, pp. 206–10, 211–22. An Act relating to Town Planning. Province of Alberta, ch. 25, 3 George V, 25 March 1913. Commission of Conservation: *Report of Fifth Annual Meeting, 1914.* Ottawa: Commission of Conservation, pp. 249–58. Adams, T. (1924) Review of town planning in Canada. *Canadian Engineer,* **46,** 24 June, pp. 651–3. See also Hulchanski (1981), pp. 20–4 (see note 7), and Smith, P. J. (1979) The principle of utility and the origins of planning legislation in Alberta, 1912–75, in Artibise and Stelter (eds.), pp. 204–13 (see note 10).

16. Unwin (1914) (see note 7). City of Halifax, N.S., *City Charter,* sections 591–600 (1914), vol. **9,** *Cauchon papers. Civic Improvement Bulletin,* 2 May 1916, in Nova

Scotia file, *Horace Seymour papers* (hereafter *Seymour papers*), Public Archives of Canada. Burditt, W. F., to Bradford, Marjorie (Assistant Secretary, Social Service Council of Canada, Toronto), 19 March 1928, in *Burditt papers*, Canadian Institute of Planners. Hastings (1912), p. 69 (see note 7). *A Few Facts About the Toronto Housing Company Limited*, undated brochure in vol. 7, *Cauchon papers*. Commission of Conservation, *Annual Reports*, 1912–14, reports of Dr. C. A. Hodgetts and of Public Health Committee.

17. See correspondence for 1909 in vol. 187, *Sifton papers*, Public Archives of Canada. Sifton, C., Inaugural Address in Commission of Conservation, *First Report, 1910*, pp. 1–27, and Chairman's Address in *Fifth Report, 1914*, p. 17. Armstrong, A. (1968) Thomas Adams and the Commission of Conservation, in Gertler, L. O. (ed.) *Planning the Canadian Environment*. Montreal: Harvest House, pp. 19–35. Smith, C. R. and Witty, D. R., Conservation, resources and environment: an exposition and critical assessment of the Commission of Conservation, Canada. *Plan Canada*, 11, 1970, pp. 55–70 and 11, 1972, pp. 199–216. Artibise and Stelter (1980), in Kain (ed.), pp. 17–36 (see note 7).

18. Hodgetts, Dr. C. A., Report of Committee on Public Health, and Housing and town planning, Commission of Conservation, *Third Report, 1912*, pp. 5–9, 130–48. See also Hodgetts, Unsanitary housing, Commission of Conservation, *Second Report, 1911*, pp 50–81; (1914) Town planning in Canada. *Canadian Municipal Journal*, 10, August, pp. 312, 321; The housing problem, *First Canadian Housing and Planning Congress*, pp. 35–43 (see note 13). *Conservation of Life*, from August 1914. Discussion on 'A Town Planning Act for Canada', Commission of Conservation, *Sixth Report, 1915*, pp. 245–82. See further Armstrong (1968), p. 21 (see note 17).

19. Hodgetts, and Osler, Sir E., in Commission of Conservation, *Fourth Report, 1913*, pp. 5, 8–12. Hodgetts (1914), p. 321 (see note 18).

20. Sifton, Sir C., in Commission of Conservation, *Fifth Report, 1914*, pp. 10, 21. Adams, T. in Commission of Conservation, *Sixth Report, 1915*, p. 269; (1914) Remarks at the closing dinner, in *National Conference on City Planning, Toronto*. Boston, Mass.: N.C.C.P., 1915, pp. 311, 313. See also *Canadian Municipal Journal*, 10, June 1914, p. 228, quoted in Van Nus (1975), p. 53 (see note 11).

21. White, J. to Sifton, C., 23 July 1914, cablegram in vol. 202, *Sifton papers*.

22. Hodgetts (1914) Town Planning Adviser to Commission of Conservation. *Conservation of Life*, 1, October, p. 27.

23. White, J. to Tory, Prof. H. M., 12 November 1914, University of Alberta Archives, Edmonton.

24. 'Ajax' (1915) Some big municipal men: Thomas Adams. *Canadian Municipal Journal*, 11, December, p. 438. Atherton, W. H. (1915) Review of civic improvement. *Canadian Municipal Journal*, 11, February, pp. 64–5. See Sifton's correspondence on planning advice, 1913–14, in vols. 201 and 202, *Sifton papers*.

25. Hodgetts (1914), p. 321 (see note 18).

26. Adams, T. (1915) Report on housing and town planning in Canada, Commission of Conservation, *Sixth Report*, p. 162. Adams to Patrick Geddes, 20 October

1914, f. 139, Acc. 10544, *Geddes papers*, National Library of Scotland, Edinburgh.

27. Adams, T., in Commission of Conservation, *Sixth Report, 1915*, pp. 158–77.

28. Adams, T. (1919) Town and rural planning in British Columbia. *Canadian Municipal Journal*, **15**, January, p. 26; (1918) Town planning in British Columbia: the example of Victoria. *Town Planning and Conservation of Life*, **4**, July, p. 65; (1916) The garden as a factor in social well-being. *Town Planning and Conservation of Life*, **2**, January–March, p. 37; (1917) Planning and development in New Brunswick. *The Busy East*, October, p. 35.

29. Adams, T. (1916) Housing conditions in Canada. *Town Planning and Conservation of Life*, **3**, December, p. 10.

30. Adams, T. (1918) The planning of new towns in Canada – Ojibway. *Town Planning and Conservation of Life*, **4**, October, p. 73; (1915) Town planning and housing reform in Canada. *Town Planning and Conservation of Life*, **1**, January, p. 53; (1915) The meaning and practical application of town planning. *Town Planning and Conservation of Life*, **1**, July, p. 75.

31. Adams, T. (1920) The Federal housing project. *Town Planning and Conservation of Life*, **6**, April–June, p. 35; (1918) *Housing and town development in wartime: an opportunity for government enterprise*. New York: National Housing Association, p. 4; (1914) The back-to-the-land movement. *Conservation of Life*, **1**, October, p. 31; Planning the Greater Halifax, Commission of Conservation, *Tenth Report, 1919*, p. 107.

32. Adams, T. (1917) Town planning, housing and local government, and Report of Planning and Development Branch, in Commission of Conservation, *Eighth Report*, pp. 11, 95; (1915) Report on the planning of Greater Vancouver. *Town Planning and Conservation of Life*, **1**, January, p. 59; (1916) Can money be saved by town planning? *Town Planning and Conservation of Life*, **2**, July–September, pp. 84–5.

33. Adams, T. (1914, repr. 1976) What town planning really means. *Plan Canada*, June, pp. 113–14; (1914), p. 31 (see note 31); (1916) Town planning, housing and public health, in Commission of Conservation, *Seventh Report*, p. 121; (1916) Town planning and good roads. *Canadian Municipal Journal*, **12**, May, p. 177; (1918), p. 79 (see note 30); (1918), pp. 6–15 (see note 31); (1915) Garden Cities. *Town Planning and Conservation of Life*, **1**, January, pp. 60–5.

34. Adams, T. (1914, repr. 1976), p. 114 (see note 33); (1915) A civic improvement organisation for Canada. *Town Planning and Conservation of Life*, **2**, October, p. 4; (1915), p. 76 (see note 30); (1918) Town planning in relation to public safety. *Town Planning and Conservation of Life*, **4**, October, p. 90.

35. Adams, T. (1915) Report on housing and town planning in Canada. Commission of Conservation, *Sixth Report*, p. 162; (1916) Civic and social questions in Canada. *Town Planning and Conservation of Life*, **2**, April–June, p.53; (1916) *Town Planning Legislation*, p. 17, typescript for article in *Municipal World*, RG 8, box 101A, Ontario Archives; (1917) The planning and development of land in the Maritime Provinces. *The Busy East*, September, p. 5; (1917) The planning and

development of land, in Commission of Conservation, *Urban and Rural Development in Canada*. Ottawa: Commission of Conservation, p. 82.

36. A comprehensive bibliography of Adams's writings has been compiled by Professor J. D. Hulchanski: *Thomas Adams: a biographical and bibliographic guide*. Papers on Planning and Design, no. 15. Toronto: Department of Urban and Regional Planning, University of Toronto, April 1978.

37. Adams (1915), pp. 1–2 (see note 34).

38. Commission of Conservation, *A Civic Improvement League for Canada: report of a preliminary conference, 19 November 1915*. Ottawa: Commission of Conservation, p. 26, and *passim*.

39. Adams (1915) Statement of objectives. *ibid.*, pp. 9–14, and pp. 44–8.

40. *Ibid.*, pp. 18, 67–70. Adams, T. (1917) Report on Civic Improvement League progress. Commission of Conservation, *Urban and Rural Development in Canada*. Ottawa: Commission of Conservation, p. 55; (1917) Address to Ottawa Civic Improvement League, 17 January. Commission of Conservation, *Eighth Report*, pp. 315–22; (1919) Report on housing, town planning and municipal government. Commission of Conservation, *Tenth Report*, p. 102, and pp. 116–22. Reports on civic improvement in *Town Planning and Conservation of Life*, 1916–19. Adams to Civic Improvement League members, 14 January 1916, 26 September 1917, 12 June 1918, vol. **6**, *Cauchon papers*. Correspondence on civic improvement between Adams, Sifton and White in vols. **205** and **206**, *Sifton papers*. Adams to Willison, Sir John, numerous dates, 1915, 1917 and 1918, *Willison papers*, Public Archives of Canada. Van Nus (1975) p. 68 (see note 11).

41. *Town Planning – a draft Act*. Ottawa: Commission of Conservation, 1915, p. 3. vol. **6**, *Cauchon papers*. Adams, T. (1915) Road improvement in Great Britain, the United States and Canada. *Town Planning and Conservation of Life*, **2**, October, p. 14; (1919) Report on housing, etc., p. 101 (see note 40).

42. *Town Planning – a draft Act* (see note 41). Draft Town Planning Act. Commission of Conservation, *Seventh Report, 1917*, pp. 229–47.

43. Adams, T. (1935) *Outline of Town and City Planning*. New York: Russell Sage Foundation, pp. 247–9.

44. Adams (1917), pp. 217–18 (see note 9).

45. Adams, T. (1916) Town planning, housing and public health. Commission of Conservation, *Seventh Report*, p. 125.

46. Adams (1916), *ibid.*; (1914–15) Some recent developments in town planning. *Papers of the Town Planning Institute*, **1**, p. 149; (1915) Recent town planning progress in the Maritime Provinces. Commission of Conservation, *Sixth Report*, pp. 284–302; (1917), *The Busy East*, pp. 5–7 (see note 35); (1919) Housing, town planning and civic improvement in Canada. *Town Planning and Conservation of Life*, **5**, July, pp. 68–9.

47. Adams (1917) *The Busy East*, p. 7 (see note 35); (1916) p. 126 (see note 45). See also *Town Planning and Conservation of Life, passim*.

48. Adams, T. (1917) Report of the Planning and Development Branch. Commission of Conservation, *Eighth Report*, p. 96; (1919) p. 97 (see note 40). See also *Town Planning and Conservation of Life, passim*.

49. Hulchanski (1981), p. 25 (see note 7). Adams, T. (1916) Housing, town planning and civic improvement in Canada. *Town planning and Conservation of Life*, **3**, December, pp. 19–21; (1918) Town planning and land development. Commission of Conservation, *Ninth Report*, p. 201; (1919), p. 101 (see note 40).

50. Adams, T. (1915) p. 166 (see note 26); (1916) pp. 125, 127 (see note 33); (1917) p. 98 (see note 32); (1918) p. 201 (see note 49); (1919) p. 101 (see note 40); (1917) The progress of civic improvement and town planning in Canada. *Town Planning and Conservation of Life*, **3**, October, p. 96; (1918) Housing, town planning and civic improvement in Canada. *Town Planning and Conservation of Life*, **4**, July, pp. 71–2; (1919) pp. 68–9 (see note 46).

51. Adams (1915), p. 166 (see note 26); (1916) pp. 125, 127 (see note 33); (1917) p. 97 (see note 32); (1919) pp. 100–1 (see note 40).

52. Adams, T. (1919) p. 25 (see note 28); (1916) Report of Planning and Development Branch. Commission of Conservation, *Seventh Report*, p. 99; (1919) p. 102 (see note 40); (1918) pp. 65–70 (see note 28); (1918) Civic improvement, town planning and housing in Canada. *Town Planning and Conservation of Life*, **4**, October, pp. 95–6; (1919) Civic improvement, town planning and housing in Canada. *Town Planning and Conservation of Life*, **5**, January, pp. 23–4; (1919) Housing, town planning and civic improvement in Canada. *Town Planning and Conservation of Life*, **5**, July, pp. 68–9.

53. A Town Planning Act under consideration for Quebec Province. *Canadian Municipal Journal*, **12**, December 1916. Adams (1916) p. 125 (see note 33); (1917) p. 96 (see note 32); (1918) p. 199 (see note 49); (1919) pp. 98–9 (see note 40); (1916) Housing, town planning and civic improvement in Canada. *Town Planning and Conservation of Life*, **3**, December, pp. 19–21; (1918) p. 94 (see note 52); (1919) Federal and Provincial housing schemes. *Town Planning and Conservation of Life*, **5**, January, pp. 4–9, and pp. 23–4; (1919) pp. 68–9 (see note 46). On provincial legislation generally, see Van Nus (1975), chapter 2 (see note 11).

54. Adams (1915) p. 165 (see note 26). South West Ontario Town Planning Conference, *Memorandum to W. H. Hearst, Prime Minister, on the need for a Planning and Development Act and a Department of Municipal Affairs*, 9 February 1917, RG 8, box 93, Ontario Archives. Province of Ontario. An Act respecting surveys and plans of land in certain cities and their suburbs. 2 George V, ch. 43, in Commission of Conservation, *Fourth Report, 1913*, pp. 220–2.

55. See correspondence between Adams and Ontario Government in RG 8, box 93, Ontario Archives. Adams (1916) typescript, p. 11 (see note 35). Province of Ontario, Planning and Development Act, and Bureau of Municipal Affairs Act, in Commission of Conservation, *Ninth Report, 1918*, pp. 226–30, 231–3.

56. Adams (1919) p. 99 (see note 40); (1921) The housing and town planning work of the Commission of Conservation. *Journal of the Town Planning Institute of Canada*, **1**, February, p. 3. Adams to Cauchon, 5 March 1920, vol. 1, *Cauchon papers*.

57. A Town Planning Act under consideration for Quebec Province. *Canadian Municipal Journal*, **12**, December 1916.

58. Adams (1924) pp. 651–3 (see note 15); (1921) No criticism of Toronto harbour

work. *Canadian Engineer*, 24 February, cutting in vol. **9**, *Cauchon papers;* (1920) The future of Ottawa. *Town Planning and Conservation of Life*, **6**, April–June, pp. 32–35; (1916) Housing, town planning and civic improvement in Canada. *Town Planning and Conservation of Life*, **2**, July–September, pp. 85–92; (1921) Town planning powers refused. *Ottawa Journal*, 6 April, vol. **3**, *Cauchon papers*. Town planning report provides for creation of Federal District. *Ottawa Citizen*, 11 March 1916, vol. **3**, *Cauchon papers*.

59. Adams (1916) p. 126 (see note 33); (1917) pp. 96, 319 (see note 32); (1918) pp. 195–7 (see note 49); (1919) pp. 95–7, 106–9 (see note 40); regular reports on Saint John and Halifax schemes in *Town Planning and Conservation of Life*, especially **4**, October 1918, pp. 82–8; (1917) *The Busy East*, pp. 33–5, 52 (see note 28). See also extensive correspondence between Adams and W. F. Burditt of Saint John, *Burditt papers*, Canadian Institute of Planners, Ottawa; and further letters of 5 and 24 August 1918 and 16 September 1921 in File 2731, *Adams papers*, Cornell University Archives, Ithaca, New York. Adams, T., letter on Halifax plan, 4 March 1915, in R6, 35–102 (1B), 1915, *City of Halifax papers*, Nova Scotia Archives, Halifax.

60. Adams to Bell, W. J., Sudbury, Ontario, Park Commission, reprinted in *Sudbury Journal*, 26 July 1917. Adams, T. (1915) Report on planning Greater Vancouver. *Town Planning and Conservation of Life*, **1**, January, pp. 57–60.

61. Adams, T. (1916) Housing, town planning and civic improvement in Canada. *Town Planning and Conservation of Life*, **2**, July–September, p. 85; (1916) Housing, town planning and civic improvement in Canada. *Town Planning and Conservation of Life*, **3**, December, p. 22; (1917) p. 321 (see note 40).

62. Adams, T. (1921), *passim.* (see note 3); (1919) Town planning in relation to land taxation. Commission of Conservation, *Tenth Report*, pp. 113–15.

63. Adams to G. S. Campbell, 4 January, and Campbell to R. L. Borden (Prime Minister), 6 January 1918, vol. **141**, *Borden papers*, Public Archives of Canada. Adams, T. (1918) Reconstruction and redevelopment at Halifax. *Town Planning and Conservation of Life*, **4**, January, pp. 22–3; (1918) Housing, town planning and civic improvement in Canada. *Town Planning and Conservation of Life*, **4**, July, p. 71; (1918) p. 82 (see note 59); (1919) Civic improvement, town planning and housing in Canada. *Town Planning and Conservation of Life*, **5**, January, p. 23.

64. Adams (1919) pp. 95–6 (see note 40). See particularly Weaver, J. C. (1976) Reconstruction of the Richmond district in Halifax: a Canadian episode in public housing and town planning, 1918–1921. *Plan Canada*, **16**, March, pp. 36–47.

65. Adams (1917), pp. 167–72 (see note 9); (1916) pp. 121–2 (see note 33); (1917) p. 93 (see note 32); (1919) p. 100 (see note 40). *Conservation of Life*, **1**, October 1914, p. 33. *Town Planning and Conservation of Life*, **1**, January 1915, pp. 60–5.

66. Adams (1916) pp. 127, 129 (see note 33); (1917) p. 321 (see note 32); (1918) pp. 71–2 (see note 63); (1918) pp. 73–80 (see note 30).

67. Adams (1917) p. 104 (see note 32); (1918) p. 198 (see note 49); (1919) pp. 98–9, 110–12 (see note 40); (1919) The planning and building of new towns in Canada: Kipawa. *Town Planning and Conservation of Life*, **5**, January, pp. 10–16; (1919) The town of Kipawa. *Canadian Engineer*, 27 February, pp. 260–2. See also

Saarinen, O. (1979) The influence of Thomas Adams and the British new towns movement in the planning of Canadian resource communities, in Artibise and Stelter (eds.), pp. 268–92 (see note 10).

68. Adams (1917) *passim.* (see note 9); (1916) p. 128 (see note 33); (1917) p. 94 (see note 32).

69. Adams (1917) pp. 7, 143, 241 (see note 9).

70. *Ibid.*, pp. 143, 228; (1916) p. 122 (see note 33); (1916) p. 4 (see note 13).

71. Adams (1917) pp. 61, 177–8 (see note 9).

72. Reviews of Adams, T. (1917) *Rural Planning and Development.* Ottawa: Commission of Conservation, in vol. 7, *Cauchon papers.*

73. Sifton, Sir C. (1917) Review of the work of the Commission. Commission of Conservation, *Eighth Report,* p. 24, and see also Robertson, Dr. J. W., p. 287 in same. Adams to Geddes, 5 December 1917, f. 164, Acc. 10545, *Geddes papers,* National Library of Scotland, Edinburgh.

74. Adams (1915) p. 17 (see note 38); (1917) pp. 100–1 (see note 32); (1917) pp. 207–16 (see note 9); (1918) p. 203 (see note 49). Buckley, A. (1921) The new town of Lens, Saskatchewan. *Journal of the Town Planning Institute of Canada,* 1, October, pp. 1–2; (1922) Memorial Industrial Village. *Journal of the Town Planning Institute of Canada,* 1, February, pp. 3–6. See also Deville, E.G. (1921) The Lens town site. *Journal of the Town Planning Institute of Canada,* 1, October, p. 8. Bryce, P. H. (1916) Some after-war problems. *Town Planning and Conservation of Life,* 2, April–June, pp. 49–53. Burditt, W. F. (1917) Immigration after the war. *Town Planning and the Conservation of Life,* 3, October, pp. 91–3. Phelps, G. (1918) The need for Government organisation of land settlement. *Town Planning and the Conservation of Life,* 4, January, pp. 3–8. Kon, L. (1917) The problem of returned soldiers. Commission of Conservation, *Urban and Rural Development.* Ottawa: Commission of Conservation, pp. 83–8. See further Sifton to Borden, 27 September 1917, vol. **179,** *Borden papers;* this informs the Prime Minister that Adams is to visit Europe to study the settlement of veterans and other post-war problems.

75. Moon, C. G. (1919) *House Rentals and Costs of Construction in Canada,* in *Adams papers* (author's possession), which include numerous press, social work and official reports on the housing situation all over Canada in the period 1915–20. Adams, T. (1918) *Report on Housing,* 16 November, typescript in same.

76. See *ibid.* for a discussion of proposals by Sir John Willison and G. F. Beer of Toronto, and Sam Carter, M.P., of Guelph, Ontario, among others. City of Winnipeg, Housing Committee, *Report to Council on Housing in the City,* undated typescript (c. 1919), *Adams papers.* Ellis, J. A. (Housing Commissioner, Province of Ontario) (1918) *Memorandum re: Housing Proposition,* RG 8, box 101A, Ontario Archives. See also Hearst, W. H. (Prime Minister of Ontario) (1918) The housing question. *Municipal World,* 28, November, pp. 171–3. Adams, T. (1918) War housing most urgent. *Toronto Globe,* 12 July. See further Holdsworth, D. W. (1979) House and home in Vancouver: images of West Coast urbanism, 1886–1929, in Stelter and Artibise (eds.) pp. 186–211 (see note 3); Spragge, S. (1979) A confluence of interests: housing reform in Toronto, 1900–20, in Artibise and Stelter (eds.) pp. 247–67 (see note 10).

77. Adams (1918) (see note 75).

78. *Ibid.*

79. *Ibid.*

80. *Ibid.* Adams to Willison, 14 August 1918, *Willison papers.* Adams, T. (1919)
    Canada's post war housing progress. *Town Planning and Conservation of Life,* 5,
    July, p. 52; (1920) The improvement of slum areas. *Town Planning and Conser-
    vation of Life,* 6, April–June, p. 39. For Adams's earlier remarks on housing, see
    (1915) pp. 168, 170 (see note 26); (1917) p. 93 (see note 32); Town planning and
    housing reform in Canada. *Town Planning and Conservation of Life,* 1, January,
    pp. 52–6; (1916) The Governors-General of Canada and town planning, and
    Housing conditions in Canada. *Town Planning and Conservation of Life,* 3,
    December, pp. 3, 10–11; (1918) The housing problem and production. *Town
    Planning and Conservation of Life,* 4, July, pp. 49–57.

81. Adams, T. (1918) (see note 75); (1919) Partner-owner building societies. *Town
    Planning and Conservation of Life,* 5, October, p. 75; (1920) England's housing
    problem. *Journal of the Town Planning Institute of Canada,* 1, October, p. 8;
    (1919) Prospects for a town planning profession in Canada, in report on first
    general meeting of Town Planning Institute of Canada, in *Canadian Engineer,* 26
    June, vol. 3, *Cauchon papers.* Quebec declared backward in housing. *Contract
    Record,* 15 September 1920, vol. 3, *Cauchon papers.*

82. *Housing in Canada: general project of Federal Government.* Ottawa: King's
    Printer, 1919, p. 10.

83. *Ibid.* Adams, T. (1919) The Federal housing loan. Commission of Conservation,
    Tenth Report, pp. 103–4, 117; (1919) p. 55 (see note 80). Orders-in-Council on
    Housing. Commission of Conservation, *Tenth Report, 1919,* pp. 123–31.

84. Parry, B. E. (1920) Ottawa Garden Suburb. *Town Planning and Conservation of
    Life,* 6, July–September, p. 68. Site Planning at Lindenlea, Ottawa. *Journal of
    Town Planning Institute of Canada,* 1, April 1921, pp. 4–5. Ottawa Housing Com-
    mission has prepared ideal garden development plan. *Contract Record,* 13 August
    1919, p. 775. Pickett, S. H. (1961) Lindenlea, Ottawa. *Habitat,* 4, March–April,
    p. 18.

85. Buckley, A. (1920) Government housing in Canada. *Canadian Municipal Journal,*
    August, p. 244. Parry (1920) p. 68 (see note 84). Ottawa Housing Commission has
    reply to critics. *Ottawa Citizen,* 30 March 1922.

86. Association of Dominion Land Surveyors, minutes of Topographical Committee,
    11 March 1918, vol. 9, *Cauchon papers.* Henderson, F. D. (Secretary-Treasurer,
    A.D.L.S.) to Challies, J. B. (Secretary, Engineering Institute of Canada), 6
    November 1918, vol. 9, *Cauchon papers.* Adams (1919) (see note 81). Van Nus
    (1975) pp. 81–99 (see note 11).

87. Minutes of meetings and correspondence relating to formation of Town Planning
    Institute of Canada, 1918–19, in vol. 9, and subsequent correspondence in vol. 1,
    Cauchon papers. For Adams's domination of the Town Planning Institute of
    Canada, see *Minute Book 1,* now in possession of successor body, Canadian
    Institute of Planners, Ottawa. See also Adams, T. (n.d.) *Note as to best method of
    promoting education and town planning and desirability of having a separate group of*

professional men for the purpose, and (1922) *Notes on Town Planning Institute of Canada Constitution,* both in vol. **9,** *Cauchon papers.*

88. Agenda for meeting of Architects, Engineers and Surveyors to consider Town Planning Education, 15 November 1918, vol. **9,** *Cauchon papers.*

89. Town Planning Institute of Canada (hereafter T.P.I.C.), *Constitution and By-laws (adopted 5 July 1920); Articles of Incorporation* (1922); *General Report,* 31 May 1920; Adams, T. (1918) *Proposed matters for consideration at meeting of Special Committee appointed re: Town Planning Institute,* 27 November; *Report of Secretary-Treasurer, 1921–22,* all in vol. **9,** *Cauchon papers.* Gerecke, K. (1976) The history of Canadian city planning. *City Magazine,* **2,** Summer, p. 13.

90. Definition on title page, *Journal of T.P.I.C.,* from **2,** May, 1923.

91. T.P.I.C., *Charter of Incorporation,* n.d., vol. **1,** *Cauchon papers.* Adams (1919) (see note 81). Editorial, *Journal of T.P.I.C.,* **1,** October 1920, p.2. *Agenda, etc.,* 15 November 1918, and Adams to a Mr. Vaughan, 6 November 1918, vol. **9,** *Cauchon papers.* Editorial, *Journal of T.P.I.C.,* **1,** April 1921, pp. 1–2. For the development of the university connection, see *Journal of T.P.I.C.,* 1921–3, and *Minute Book 1* of T.P.I.C., Canadian Institute of Planners. Adams, T., reported in Dr. Deville heads town planners. *Ottawa Citizen,* 28 May 1921. Town planning, and Short course in civics and town planning. *Canadian Municipal Journal,* January 1922, vol. **4,** *Cauchon papers.* Ewing, J. (1921) Report of Ways and Means Committee. *Journal of T.P.I.C.,* **1,** June–August, pp. 6–8.

92. Adams (1924) pp. 651–3 (see note 15). Report of Council, *Journal of T.P.I.C.,* **1,** June-August 1921, p. 2. Bliss, J. M. (1968) The Methodist Church and World War One. *Canadian Historical Review,* **49,** p. 229. On the 'New Era', see King, W. L. M. (1917) *Industry and Humanity;* Miller (1917) (see note 8); Allen, R. (1968) (see note 10).

93. Adams (1917) pp. 2–3 (see note 9); (1919) Reconstruction and labour. *Social Welfare,* **1,** July.

CHAPTER FIVE

1. Adams, T. (1924) Review of town planning in Canada. *Canadian Engineer,* **46,** 24 June 1924, p. 652, vol. **9,** *Cauchon papers.* Brown, R. C. and Cook, R. (1976) *Canada, 1896–1921: a nation transformed.* Toronto: McClelland and Stewart, pp. 309–38.

2. Adams, T. (1919) Town planning in Canada. *Canadian Engineer,* **36,** 6 February, pp. 199–200. Sifton, Sir C. (1917) The work of the Commission. Commission of Conservation, *Eighth Report,* p. 25. Armstrong, A. (1968) Thomas Adams and the Commission of Conservation, in Gertler, L. O. (ed.) *Planning the Canadian Environment.* Montreal: Harvest House, p. 31.

3. Adams, T. (1924) pp. 199–200 (see note 2); (1919) Report on housing, town planning and municipal government. Commission of Conservation, *Tenth Report,* p. 102. Adams to Burditt, W. F., 7 May 1919 and 18 July 1921, *Burditt papers,* Canadian Institute of Planners, Ottawa.

4. Armstrong (1968) in Gertler (ed.) p. 32 (see note 2). Artibise, A. F. J. and Stelter,

G. A. (1980) Conservation planning and urban planning: the Canadian Commission of Conservation in historical pespective, in Kain, R. J. P. (ed.) *Planning for Conservation*. London: Mansell, p. 28. Thomas Adams does work for United States. *Ottawa Journal*, 4 and 26 February 1920, vol. 3, *Cauchon papers*. See also Dominion of Canada, *Debates of the House of Commons*, Session 1920, vol. 1, 7 April 1920, col. 1002 (Mr. Demers and Sir George Foster). Thomas Adams. *Toronto Saturday Night*, 26 February 1921, vol. 3, *Cauchon papers*. Thomas Adams's contract now expired. *Ottawa Journal*, 18 September 1923, vol. 4, *Cauchon papers*. Mr. Thomas Adams resigns position under Canadian Government. *Journal of the Town Planning Institute of Canada* (hereafter *Journal of T.P.I.C.*) 2, November 1923, p. 12.

5. Dafoe, J. W. (1931, reprinted 1971) *Clifford Sifton in Relation to His Times*. New York: Books for Libraries Press, pp. 452, 455. Dominion of Canada, *Debates of the House of Commons*, Session 1921, vol. 4, 26 May 1921, col. 3962 (H. S. Béland); see also Session 1921, vol. 1, 14 March 1921, col. 875 (Hon. R. Lemieux); vol. 4, cols. 3967–8 (J. Bureau), 3970–1 (W. S. Fielding); *Senate Debates*, 13 and 19 May 1921, cols. 461–70, 510–20.

6. Adams, T. (1926) Regional planning and urban growth. *Canadian Engineer*, 50, 18 May 1926, pp. 575–6; (1924) pp. 651–3 (see note 1). See also articles by Armstrong and by Artibise and Stelter listed in note 2, and Smith, C. R. and Witty, D. R., Conservation, resources and environment: an exposition and critical assessment of the Commision of Conservation, Canada. *Plan Canada*, 11, 1970, pp. 55–70 and 11, 1972, pp. 199–216.

7. Adams to Burditt, 18 July 1921, *Burditt papers*. Re-arrangement of Town Planning Division. *Journal of T.P.I.C.*, 1, October 1921, p. 10. For Jasper, see: Plan of town of Jasper, Alberta. *Journal of T.P.I.C.*, 1, October 1921, p. 11; Plan of Jasper (with map). *Journal of T.P.I.C.*, 3, January 1924, p. 9; Cory, W. W. (1925) Town planning in Canada. *Journal of T.P.I.C.*, 4, June, p. 35.

8. Meighen, Rt. Hon. A. to Fenwick, G. W. (Secretary, Board of Trade, Prince George, B.C.), 5 May 1921, vol. 30, *Meighen papers*, Public Archives of Canada. See same file for other items of correspondence on housing, 1920–1. Adams, T. (1921) The housing situation in Canada. *Housing Betterment*, 10, April, pp. 40–7; (1922) Town planning in other countries. *Journal of the Institution of Municipal and County Engineers*, 49, 18 July, p. 55. Dalzell, A. G. (1927–8) *Housing in Canada. I. Housing in Relation to Land Development; II. Housing of the Working Classes*. Toronto: Social Service Council of Canada. *Dalzell papers*, Canadian Institute of Planners.

9. Board of Health, City of Winnipeg, *Bulletin*, June–July 1919, pp. 6–7, *Adams papers*. Memorial Industrial Village. *Journal of T.P.I.C.*, 1, February 1922, p. 4.

10. Adams, T., reported in Quebec declared backward in housing. *Contract Record*, 15 September 1920, vol. 3, *Cauchon papers*. Dalzell (1927–8) (see note 8). Ontario housing programme is dealt with in RG 8, boxes 55 and 101A, Ontario Archives. For progress reports on Federal and provincial housing programmes, see *Town Planning and Conservation of Life*, 1919–21. Adams, T. (1921) Suggestions for Montreal housing. *Contract Record*, 9 February, p. 147. See also Civic problems under discussion by Union of Quebec Municipalities. *Contract Record*, 15

September 1920, vol. **3**, *Cauchon papers*. Housing progress, St. Lambert, P.Q. *Town Planning and Conservation of Life*, 5, January-March 1921, pp. 19–20. Adams, T. (1919) Housing and town planning. *Canadian Engineer*, 6 November, pp. 435–7.

11. See comments by Buckley, Dalzell and Seymour in *Journal of T.P.I.C.*, **5**, October 1926, p. 6. Housing for workers still a grave problem in Canada. *Journal of T.P.I.C.*, **2**, November 1923, pp. 11–12.

12. Burditt to Adams, 26 February 1919, *Burditt papers*.

13. Adams, T. (1921) pp. 40–7 (see note 8); (1919) pp. 435–7 (see note 10); and statements in *Town Planning and Conservation of Life*, 1919–21; (n.d.) Notes for *Evening Journal*. Typescript, *Adams papers*. Hearst, W. H. (1918) The housing question. *Municipal World*, **28**, November, RG 8, box 101A; Hearst to Willison, Sir J., 17 July 1918, RG3, box 12; and other correspondence on housing in these boxes and box 55, Ontario Archives. Adams to Willison, 31 July and 14 August 1918, *Willison papers*, Public Archives of Canada. Why houses are dear. *Toronto Globe*, 23 May 1919; Medical Officer of Health, Toronto, *Report on Housing Problem*, 8 July 1918; *Report of Toronto Housing Commission*, 2 December 1918; and other reports, cuttings and memoranda in *Adams papers* (author's possession). See also articles in *Social Welfare*, **3**, November 1920.

14. Buckley, A. (n.d.) *The Provision of Houses for Wage Earners who cannot pay an Economic Rent*, typescript, *Adams papers;* (1920) Government housing in Canada. *Canadian Municipal Journal*, August, pp. 240, 247; (1920) The housing of unskilled wage-earners. *Town Planning and Conservation of Life*, **6**, January–March, pp. 11–14.

15. Would abolish Commission. *Ottawa Citizen*, 3 May 1921. Mr. Thomas Adams under fire. *Ottawa Citizen*, 7 June 1921. Cauchon, N., reported in Speakers address West End Citizens on many problems. *Ottawa Citizen*, 2 May 1924. Adams, T. (1922) Lindenlea, *Ottawa Journal*, 3 March. Ottawa town planning. *Canadian Engineer*, **47**, 30 September 1924. p. 387. All the foregoing in vol. **4**, *Cauchon papers*. Adams, T. (1921) Site planning at Lindenlea, Ottawa. *Journal of T.P.I.C.*, **1**, April, p. 4. Ottawa Housing Commission has reply to critics. *Ottawa Citizen*, 30 March 1922, *Adams papers*. See also Pickett, S. H. (1961) Lindenlea, Ottawa. *Habitat*, **4**, March-April, pp. 17–19.

16. For Adams's criticism of planning legislation in Ontario, see correspondence in RG 8, box 93, and Adams, T. (1916) Town planning legislation. Typescript article for *Municipal World*, box 101A, Ontario Archives. Anon. (probably Adams) (1920) Defects in Ontario's Planning and Development Act. *Social Welfare*, **3**, November, p. 57. Adams, T. (1921) Town Planning powers refused. *Ottawa Journal*, 6 April; (1919) Thomas Adams on Ontario Town Planning Act. *Hamilton Herald*, 28 November, vol. **3**, *Cauchon papers*. *Proposed Act to Amend Ontario Planning and Development Act, 1924*, vol. **9**, *Cauchon papers*.

17. Adams, T., reported in Dr. Deville heads town planners. *Ottawa Citizen*, 28 May 1921; Town planners conclude sessions. *Ottawa Citizen*, 30 May 1921, vol. **4**, *Cauchon papers*. See extensive coverage of planning legislation in *Journal of T.P.I.C.*, notably Town planning news. **1**, October 1920, p. 5; Saskatchewan town planning. **1**, February 1921, p. 5; Canadian Town Planning Acts. **1**, April

1922, pp. 2–3; Saskatchewan Town Planning and Rural Development Act. 1, June–August 1921, pp. 17–20; Editorial, 1, April 1922, pp. 1–3; Saskatchewan Town Planning Branch. 2, November 1923, p. 11; Reports from Provinces – Saskatchewan. 3, June 1924, pp. 15–16; Young, S. (1931) Planning progress in Saskatchewan. 10, February, pp. 5–8. Young, S. to Adams, T., 7 September 1926; Young to Phillips, R. D., Saskatoon, 17 February 1932; *Memorandum regarding Saskatchewan Town Planning Bill*, all in Saskatchewan Archives, Regina, Saskatchewan. Van Nus, W. (1975) *The Plan-Makers and the City: architects, engineers, surveyors and urban planning in Canada*. Unpublished Ph.D. thesis. Toronto: University of Toronto, pp. 114–15.

18. On Manitoba, see *Journal of T.P.I.C.* as follows: Manitoba appoints Town Planning Comptroller: 1, October 1921, pp. 8–10; Manitoba gets under way, 1, February 1922, p. 11; General progress. 1, June 1922, p. 13; Town planning schemes in Manitoba. 2, March 1923, p. 4; Reports from Provinces – Manitoba. 3, June 1924, pp. 13–15. Van Nus (1975) p. 111 (see note 17).

19. Reports from Provinces—Alberta. *Journal of T.P.I.C.*, 3, June 1924, p. 19. Way through for Canadian planning. *Journal of T.P.I.C.*, 10, February 1931, pp. 1–2. Seymour, H. L. (1929) *Annual Report of the Director of Town Planning*. Edmonton: Province of Alberta, Canadian Institute of Planners, Ottawa. Hulchanski, J. D. (1981) *The Origins of Urban Land Use Planning in Alberta, 1900–1975*. Toronto: Centre for Urban and Community Studies, University of Toronto, pp. 31–44. Van Nus (1975) p. 115 (see note 17).

20. Cauchon, N. (1926) Retiring President's address. *Journal of T.P.I.C.*, 5, April, pp. 2, 4. Ewing, J. (1921) Report of Ways and Means Committee. *Journal of T.P.I.C.*, 1, June–August, p. 6. Reports from Provinces. *Journal of T.P.I.C.*, 3, June 1924, pp. 13–19. Young (1931) pp. 5–6 (see note 17). Burditt to Adams, 30 December 1918; Adams to Burditt, 7 May 1919; Dalzell, A. G. to Burditt, 16 April 1928 and 6 March 1929; Burditt to Bradford, Miss M., 19 March 1928, *Burditt papers*. Cauchon's criticisms of Adams appear in occasional marginal comments in his papers and especially in a letter (apparently never sent) to James White (Secretary, Commission of Conservation), 23 October 1919, vol. 1, *Cauchon papers*.

21. On British Columbia planning, see *Journal of T.P.I.C.* as follows: Town planning in British Columbia. 1, June 1922, p. 5; New town planning powers. 1, August 1922, p. 3; Point Grey town planning by-law. 1, November 1922, p. 23; Town planning legislation for British Columbia. 2, November 1923, p. 9; Reports from Provinces – British Columbia. 3, June 1924, p. 19; Good work of Vancouver Branch toward town planning legislation in British Columbia. 3, October 1924, pp. 8–9; British Columbia Town Planning Act. 5, January 1926, pp. 3–6; British Columbia Town Planning Act. 5, April 1926, p. 2; Niagara Regional Plan. 5, June 1926, p. 4. Young to Phillips, 17 February 1932 (see note 17). Province of British Columbia, An Act related to Urban and Rural Planning, etc., undated draft in vol. 9, *Cauchon papers*. Van Nus (1975) pp. 119–20 (see note 17).

22. Dalzell, A. G., quoted in Young (1931), p. 6 (see note 17). See also Faludi, E. G. (1947–8) Planning progress in Canada. *Journal of the American Institute of Planners*, 13, p. 5.

23. Kitchen, J. M. (Secretary-Treasurer, T.P.I.C.) to Sclanders, F. M. (Commissioner, Board of Trade, Saint John, N.B.) 20 February 1928, *Burditt papers*. The extensive *Cauchon papers* in the Public Archives of Canada and his frequent contributions to the *Journal of T.P.I.C.* give an excellent picture of Cauchon's career, interests and imagination. See also Van Nus (1975), *passim*. (see note 17). Gunton, T. I. (1979) The ideas and policies of the Canadian planning profession, 1909–1931, in Artibise, A. F. J. and Stelter, G. A. (eds.) *The Usable Urban Past*. Toronto: Macmillan, pp. 177–95.

24. T.P.I.C., *Memorandum on the Need of a Federal Town Planning Bureau to serve as an Educational Organization for the Dominion*, 7 November 1927, vol. 8, *Cauchon papers*. See also King, W. L. M. (1917) *Industry and Humanity*.

25. The professional aspect. *Journal of T.P.I.C.*, **10**, February 1931, p. 4. Correspondence between Adams and Dean W. Emerson, Department of Architecture, Massachusetts Institute of Technology, June 1921, *Adams papers*.

26. Adams, T. (1922) Modern city planning. *Canadian Engineer*, 3 October, vol. **9**, *Cauchon papers;* (1927) Town planning notes. *Municipal Review of Canada*, 23, December, p. 502. Gerecke, K. (1976) The history of Canadian city planning. *City Magazine*, **2**, Summer, p. 20. Van Nus (1975) *passim*. (see note 17). Gunton (1979) pp. 177–95 (see note 23). Buckley (1920) pp. 11–14 (see note 14); (n.d.) (see note 14); editorials in *Journal of T.P.I.C.*, especially **1**, April 1921, p. 1. Dalzell (1927–8) *passim*. (see note 8); (1929) Social aspects of housing. *Social Welfare*, May, *Dalzell papers*, Canadian Institute of Planners; (1929) *The Need of a New Spirit*. Toronto: Social Service Council of Canada, *Burditt papers*.

27. Editorial, *Journal of T.P.I.C.*, **3**, June 1924, p. 2. Dalzell to Burditt, 20 December 1928, *Burditt papers*.

28. Adams, T. (1926) Regional planning and urban growth. *Canadian Engineer*, **50**, p. 576; (1924) pp. 651–3 (see note 1); (1921) *Municipal and Real Estate Finance in Canada*. Typescript, vol. 9, *Cauchon papers*.

29. Editorial, *Journal of T.P.I.C.*, **3**, June, 1924, pp. 1–3. Ewing, J. (1924) The status of town planning in Canada. *Journal of T.P.I.C.*, **3**, June, pp. 9–10. Philip, G. (Managing Secretary, Chamber of Commerce, London, Ont.) to Cauchon, 3 January 1920, vol. **1**, *Cauchon papers*.

30. Ewing, J. (1921) p. 6 (see note 20). Seymour, H. L. (1922) Credit where credit is due. *Journal of T.P.I.C.*, **1**, November, p. 4. Regina Town Planning Association. *Journal of T.P.I.C.*, **2**, November, p. 10. Buck, F. E. (1924) Advantages of town planning. *Journal of T.P.I.C.*, **3**, March, p. 8. Editorial. *Journal of T.P.I.C.*, **3**, June 1924, p. 1. Keith, J. C. (1928) Regional planning. *Journal of T.P.I.C.*, **7**, December, p. 137.

31. Seymour, H. L. to Cauchon, 13 February 1923, vol. **1**, *Cauchon papers*. Van Nus (1975) p. 213 (see note 17); (1979) Towards the City Efficient: the theory and practice of zoning, in Artibise and Stelter (eds.) pp. 226–46 (see note 23). Adams (1927) p. 502 (see note 26).

32. Burditt, W. F. (1924) Reports from Provinces—New Brunswick. *Journal of T.P.I.C.*, **3**, June, pp. 17–18. See *Burditt papers*, Canadian Institute of Planners, for extensive correspondence with Adams and Dalzell. Saint John Town Plan-

ning Scheme. *Journal of T.P.I.C.*, **1**, April 1921, p. 9. Editorial. *Journal of T.P.I.C.*, **3**, June 1924, p. 2. Town planning movement at Saint John, N.B. *Journal of T.P.I.C.*, **10**, February 1931, p. 8. Adams (1919) pp. 199–200 (see note 2). Town planning news. *Journal of T.P.I.C.*, **1**, October 1920, p. 3. Progress at Halifax. *Journal of T.P.I.C.*, **1**, April 1921, p. 9. Reports from Provinces—Nova Scotia. *Journal of T.P.I.C.*, **3**, June 1924, pp. 18–19. Adams (1921) (see note 17). Van Nus (1975) p. 99 (see note 17).

33. Cauchon, N., President's addresses, T.P.I.C., 14 May 1925 and 22 April 1926, vol. **2**, *Cauchon papers*. New Federal District Commission for Ottawa. Undated cutting, vol. **2**, *Cauchon papers*. Hamilton approves Cauchon highways. *Ottawa Citizen*, 8 January 1920. Mr. Adams to advise on zoning proposal. *Ottawa Journal*, 27 November 1920. Town planning act goes to legislature. *Ottawa Citizen*, 10 December 1920. Adams (1921) (see note 16). All in vol. **3**, *Cauchon papers*. Mr. Cauchon heads Plans Commission. *Ottawa Citizen*, 14 May 1921. Careful plan of Ottawa as capital. *Ottawa Citizen*, 12 May 1922. Town plan for Haileybury. *Hamilton Spectator*, 14 October 1922. All in vol. **4**, *Cauchon papers*. See also correspondence on Ottawa, Hamilton and London in vol. **1**, *Cauchon papers*. Seymour, H. L. (1922) *Preliminary Report on Town Planning, Haileybury, Ontario*, in *Seymour papers*, Public Archives of Canada. Dalzell (1929) p. 19 (see note 26). Van Nus (1975) pp. 99, 108, 109–10 (see note 17). Pearson, N. (1967) From villages to cities, in Careless, J. M. S. and Brown, R. C. (eds.) *The Canadians, 1867–1967*. Toronto: Macmillan, pp. 621–38.

34. Ewing, J. (1922) The Montreal situation with reference to town planning. *Canadian Engineer*, 21 March; (1920) Unplanned cities. *Ottawa Journal*, 16 July 1920, both vol. **3**, *Cauchon papers*. Cauchon, N. (1926) (see note 33). Adams (1926) pp. 575–6 (see note 28); (1921) Suggestions for Montreal housing. *Contract Record*, 9 February. Montreal issue. *Journal of T.P.I.C.*, **1**, December 1921.

35. Regina Town Planning Association, leaflet c. 1924, School of Design Library, Harvard University. Cutting from *Winnipeg Tribune*, 29 April 1919, *Adams papers*. Vancouver City to have a comprehensive plan. *Journal of T.P.I.C.*, **5**, October 1926, p. 1. Vancouver. *Journal of T.P.I.C.*, **7**, December 1928, p. 154. Walker, J. A. (1931) A plan for the City of Vancouver, B. C. *Journal of T.P.I.C.*, **11**, April, pp. 35–43. See also Adams (1919) pp. 199–200 (see note 2). See further essays by Foran, M., Artibise, A. F. J. and Moore, P. W., in Artibise and Stelter (eds.) (1979) (see note 23). On Bartholomew, see Johnston, N. J. (1973) Harland Bartholomew: precedent for the profession. *Journal of the American Institute of Planners*, **39**, March, pp. 115–24. Van Nus (1975) pp. 119–20 (see note 17). Holdsworth, D. W. (1979) House and home in Vancouver: images of West Coast urbanism, 1886–1929, in Stelter, G. A. and Artibise, A. F. J. (eds.) *The Canadian City*. Toronto: Macmillan, p. 205. Seymour, H. L. (1929) (see note 19).

36. Adams, T. (1922) *Report on Welland Parks* and *Report on Plan of the City of Welland*, vol. **9**, *Cauchon papers*. Seymour, H. L. (1925) *A Plan for the City of London*, vol. **10**, *Cauchon papers*. Adams, T. and Seymour, H. L. (1924) *Report on Plan of the Town of Waterloo, Seymour papers*. Why hire experts? *London Free Press*, 25 October 1923; Halifax planner to serve London. *London Free Press*, 24

July 1924, both in vol. **4**, *Cauchon papers*. Seymour, H. L. (1924) Report of town planning survey of Waterloo, Ontario. *Journal of T.P.I.C.*, **3**, January, pp. 3–9. Kitchener plan becomes law. *Journal of T.P.I.C.*, **4**, January, pp. 1–8. Kaufman, A. (1928) Town planning in Kitchener after three years' trial. *Journal of T.P.I.C.*, **7**, December, pp. 134–7. Leonard, I. (1928) Brief history of town planning in London, Ontario. *Journal of T.P.I.C.*, **7**, December, pp. 146–54. Van Nus (1975) pp. 106, 110 (see note 17). Adams, T. (1922) pp. 63–5 (see note 8).

37. See note 36.

38. A Colonial timber village. *Garden Cities and Town Planning*, **13**, 1923, pp. 303–5. Adams, T. (1932) *Recent Advances in Town Planning*. London: Churchill, pp. 162–3; (1924) p. 653 (see note 1).

39. For the earlier view on the impact of the Great Depression, see Carver, H. (1957) Town planning in Canada. *Journal of the Town Planning Institute*, **44**, December, pp. 13–14, and Gerecke, K. (1976) p. 13 (see note 26). See also Moore, P. W. (1979) Zoning and planning: the Toronto experience, 1904–70, in Artibise and Stelter (eds.) p. 326 (see note 23). Van Nus (1975) pp. 120–5 (see note 17). Kitchen, J. M. (Secretary, T.P.I.C.) to Dalzell, A. G. (President) 21 June 1931; Dalzell to members, 19 April 1932, both in *Kitchen papers*, Canadian Institute of Planners, Ottawa. *In the Matter of the Revival of the Charter of the Town Planning Institute of Canada*, 7 February 1952, Canadian Institute of Planners. Faludi (1947–8) p. 5 (see note 22).

40. Allen, R. A. (1968) The Social Gospel and the reform tradition in Canada, 1890–1928. *Canadian Historical Review*, **49**, pp. 381–99. Ewing, J. (1924) The status of town planning in Canada. *Journal of T.P.I.C.*, **3**, June, p. 9. Dalzell, A. G. (1924) A contrast in city planning. *Journal of T.P.I.C.*, **3**, March, p. 20. Cauchon, N. (1926) (see note 33). LeMay, T. D. (1921) Town planning possibilities in Ontario under present legislation. *Canadian Engineer*, 24 February, vol. **9**, *Cauchon papers*. Adams (1921) (see note 28). Van Nus (1979) in Stelter and Artibise (eds.), pp. 162–85 (see note 31).

41. Adams, T. (1938) *State, regional and city planning in America*. Typescript, p. 7, Adams papers.

42. Gunton (1979) p. 187 (see note 23). See also Smith, P. J. (1979) the principle of utility and the origins of planning legislation in Alberta, 1912–1975, *ibid.*, pp. 196–225.

CHAPTER SIX

1. Adams, T. (1911) Some American impressions. I, The 'Art Atmosphere' of New York and the relation of the skyscraper to town planning. *Town Planning Review*, **2**, July, p. 139.

2. Penn, W., quoted in Reps, J. W. (1965) *The Making of Urban America*. Princeton: Princeton University Press, p. 160. Bridenbaugh, C., quoted in Tunnard, C. and Reed, H. H. (1955) *American Skyline*. Boston: Houghton Mifflin, p. 49.

3. Reps (1965) p. 299 (see note 2). Tunnard, C. (n.d.) A city called beautiful. Reprinted from *Journal of Society of Architectural Historians*, p. 31, in box 93, *Regional Plan of New York Papers*, Cornell University, Ithaca, New York (hereafter *R.P.N.Y. papers*). See also Goldfield, D. R. and Brownell, B. A. (1979) *Urban America: from downtown to no town*. Boston: Houghton Mifflin, pp. 198–295.

4. Adams, T. (1911) The British point of view. *National Conference on City Planning, Philadelphia*. Boston: National Conference on City Planning, p. 37 (hereafter *N.C.C.P.*). Morgenthau, H., Sr. (1909) A national constructive program for city planning. *N.C.C.P., New York*, p. 59. Howe, F. C. (1905) *The City: the Hope of Democracy*. New York: Scribners. Strong, J. (1891) *Our Country*. New York: Baker and Taylor, pp. 179–94. Scott, M. C. (1969) *American City Planning Since 1890*. Los Angeles and Berkeley: University of California Press, pp. 1–31. On landscape architecture, see especially Roper, L. W. (1973) *F.L.O.: A Biography of Frederick Law Olmsted*. Baltimore and London: Johns Hopkins University Press. See also Simpson, M. A. (1976) Two traditions of American planning: Olmsted and Burnham. *Town Planning Review*, **47**, April, pp. 174–9. Ford, G. B. and Warner, R. F. (1917) *City Planning Progress in the United States*. Washington: American Institute of Architects, pp. 175–6. Nichols, J. C. (1912) *Real Estate Subdivisions*. Washington: American Civic Association, p. 11. Civic League of St. Louis (1907) *A City Plan for St. Louis*. Boyer, M. C. (1983) *Dreaming the Rational City: the myth of American city planning*. Cambridge, Mass.: M.I.T. Press. This reached me too late to be used.

5. Peterson, J. A. (1976) The City Beautiful movement: forgotten origins and lost meanings. *Journal of Urban History*, **2**, August, pp. 415–34. Reps (1965) pp. 497–525 (see note 2). Croly, H. (1904) What is civic art? *Architectural Record*, 16 July (reprinted in Tager, J. and Goist, P. D. (1970) *The Urban Vision*. Homewood, Illinois: Dorsey, p. 80). Ford, G. B. (1913) The City Scientific. *N.C.C.P., Chicago*, p. 33. See also Scott (1969) pp. 31–84 (see note 4). Hubbard, T. K. and H. V. (1929) *Our Cities Today and Tomorrow*. Cambridge, Mass.: Harvard University Press, pp. 6–8. Wilson, W. H. (1980) The ideology, aesthetics and politics of the City Beautiful movement, in Sutcliffe, A. R. (ed.) *The Rise of Modern Urban Planning*. London: Mansell, pp. 166–98. Hines, T. S. (1974) *Burnham of Chicago*. New York: Oxford University Press, pp. 73–216. Burg, D. F. (1976) *Chicago's White City of 1893*. Lexington, Kentucky: University of Kentucky Press.

6. Ford and Warner (1917) p. iii (see note 4). Knowles, M. (1919) Engineering problems of regional planning. *N.C.C.P., Buffalo*, p. 115. Kantor, H. A. (1974) Benjamin C. Marsh and the fight over population congestion. *Journal of the American Institute of Planners* (hereafter *Journal of A.I.P.*) **40**, November, pp. 422–9.

7. Burnham, D. H. and Bennett, E. H. (1909, reprinted 1970) *.The Plan of Chicago*. New York: DaCapo Press, p. 4. Hines (1974) *passim*. (see note 5).

8. Roper (1973) *passim*. (see note 4). Fein, A. (1967) *Landscape into Cityscape*. Ithaca, N.Y.: Cornell University Press, p. 25. See also Fein, A. (1972) *Frederick Law Olmsted and the American Environmental Tradition*. New York: Braziller.

Simutis, L. J. (1972) Frederick Law Olmsted: a reassessment. *Journal of A.I.P.*, **38**, September, pp. 276–84. Fabos, J. G., Milde, G. T. and Weinmayer, V. M. (1968) *Frederick Law Olmsted, Sr.: founder of landscape architecture*. Amherst, Mass.: University of Massachusetts Press. Simpson (1976) pp. 174–9 (see note 4).

9. Ford, G. B. (1911) Third American city planning conference. *Town Planning Review*, **2**, October, p. 213. Adams (1911) pp. 27–37 (see note 4).

10. Adams, T. (1911) Some American impressions: I. The 'Art Atmosphere' of New York and the relation of the skyscraper to town planning. II. The peculiar social and economic conditions of New York and the need for a city plan. *Town Planning Review*, **2**, July, pp. 139–46 and October, pp. 183–96; (1926) The social objective in regional planning. *National Municipal Review*, **15**, February, p. 82.

11. Adams, T. (1915) Some town planning principles re-stated. *American City*, **12**, March, pp. 213–16; (1915) Speech at closing dinner. *N.C.C.P., Detroit*, p. 220; (1916) *City Planning*. Cleveland: Cleveland Chamber of Commerce, p. 14, in School of Design Library, Harvard University; (1916) Planning for civic betterment in town and country. *American City*, **15**, July, p. 51. See also Adams, T. (1915) The need for a constructive policy in regard to town planning. *City Plan*, **1**, March, pp. 2–6; (1916) An industrial tendency which provides an opportunity for the city planner. *National Municipal Review*, **5**, January, pp. 89–92. Adams to Nolen, J., 16 October 1914, 3 February 1915, 24 April 1918 and 8 October 1919, in box 8, *Nolen papers*, Cornell University.

12. Adams, T. (1916) State, city and town planning. *N.C.C.P., Cleveland*, pp. 119–38; (1916) *City Planning* (see note 11).

13. Nolen, J. (1916) *More Houses for Bridgeport*. Bridgeport, Conn.: Bridgeport Chamber of Commerce, p. 12. Alanen, A. R. and Peltin, T. J. (1978) Kohler, Wisconsin: planning and paternalism in a model industrial village. *Journal of A.I.P.*, **44**, April, pp. 145–59. Scott (1969) pp. 170–4 (see note 4).

14. Adams, T. (1918) *Housing and Town Development in War-Time: an opportunity for Government enterprise*. New York: National Housing Association, p. 14; (1918) To what extent shall war workers be housed in temporary barracks or in permanent homes? in *A Symposium on War Housing*. Philadelphia: National Housing Association, p. 47; (1919) Industry, homes and architecture, I. *Journal of the American Institute of Architects* (hereafter *Journal of A.I.A.*), **7**, December, p. 517. See also Adams, T. (1920) Industry, homes and architecture, II. *Journal of A.I.A.*, **8**, May, pp. 173–7; (1921) An American garden city. *National Municipal Review*, **24**, January, pp. 31–38; (1918) Housing and social reconstruction, in *Housing Problems in America*. New York: National Housing Association, pp. 3–35 and pp. 312–19; (1918) discussion on Olmsted, F. L., Jr., Community planning for war-time industries. *City Plan*, **3**, April, pp. 9–10. Nolen, J. (1919) *New Ideals in the Planning of Cities, Towns and Villages*. New York: American City Bureau, p. 123. Kimball, T. (1918) A review of city planning in the United States, 1917–18. *National Municipal Review*, November, pp. 605–13; (1920) A review of city planning in the United States, 1918–19. *National Municipal Review*, January, pp. 21–31. Lubove, R. (1967) *The Urban Community: housing and planning in the Progressive Era*. Englewood Cliffs, N.J.: Prentice-Hall, pp. 99–114. Kennedy, D. M. (1980) *Over Here*. New York: Oxford University Press, pp. 231–95. Hawley,

E. W. (1979) *The Great War and the Search for a Modern Order, 1917–1933.* New York: St. Martin's Press, pp. 45–57.

15. Kimball, T. (1922) A review of city planning in the United States, 1920–21. *National Municipal Review,* January, p. 32. Nolen, J. (1927) Twenty years of city planning progress in the United States. *N.C.C.P., Washington, D.C.,* pp. 1–20. Johnston, N. J. (1973) Harland Bartholomew: precedent for the profession. *Journal of A.I.P.,* **39,** March, pp. 115–24. See Kimball's (from 1924, Mrs. T. K. Hubbard) annual reports in *National Municipal Review* and (from 1927) *City Planning.* I am indebted to Professor B. A. Brownell for his sage and perceptive comments on American zoning.

16. Scott (1969) pp. 163–70 (see note 4). Krueckeberg, D. A. (1980) The story of the planners' journal. *Journal of the American Planning Association* (hereafter *Journal of A.P.A.*) **46,** January, pp. 5–21. Hancock, J. L. (1972) History and the American planning profession. *Journal of A.I.P.,* **38,** September, pp. 274–5; (1967) Planners in the changing American city. *Journal of A.I.P.,* **33,** September, pp. 290–304. Birch, E. L. (1980) Advancing the art and science of planning: planners and their organizations, 1909–1980. *Journal of A.P.A.,* **46,** January, pp. 23–32. Adams to Nolen, 8 October 1919, 7 July 1920, box 8, and 13 March 1926, box 31, *Nolen papers.*

17. Lohmann, K. B. (1931) *Principles of City Planning.* New York and London: McGraw-Hill, pp. 56, 62, 366–9. See Kimball/Hubbard annual reports, notably in *City Planning,* **5,** January 1929, pp. 43–5. Correspondence between Adams and Dean W. Emerson, Department of Architecture, Massachusetts Institute of Technology, June 1921, *Adams papers.*

18. Thomas Adams to spend several months in America. *American City,* **27,** November 1922, p. 489. *An Opportunity to Secure a Visit during February or March, 1922, from Mr. Thomas Adams.* New York: American City Bureau, 1922, in School of Design Library, Harvard University. Adams, T. (1938) *State, regional and city planning in the United States.* Typescript, p. 8, *Adams papers.* Thomas Adams does work for United States. *Ottawa Journal,* 4 February 1920, and Thomas Adams. *Toronto Saturday Night,* 26 February 1921, both in vol. 3, *Noulan Cauchon papers,* Public Archives of Canada. *Journal of the Town Planning Institute of Canada,* **1,** February 1921, p. 11.

19. Adams and Thompson's New York office was at 16 E 41 Street. *Municipal Journal,* 8 September 1922. Miscellany. *National Municipal Review,* **10,** September 1921, p. 488.

20. Johnson, D. A. (1974) *The Emergence of Metropolitan Regionalism: an analysis of the 1929 Regional Plan of New York and its Environs.* Unpublished Ph.D. thesis, Cornell University, pp. 26–52. Scholars of the Regional Plan of New York are greatly indebted to Professor Johnson's comprehensive and perceptive analysis.

21. Adams, T. *et al.* (1929 and 1931) *Regional Plan of New York and its Environs.* **1.** *The Graphic Regional Plan,* pp. 126–8, 163. **2.** *The Building of the City,* pp. 50, 75, 108–16. New York: Regional Plan of New York (hereafter *R.P.N.Y.,* **1** and **2**); (1927) *Highway Traffic. Regional Survey of New York and its Environs,* **3.** New York: Regional Plan of New York, p. 61 (hereafter *R.S.N.Y.*). See also the

comment of Henry James, Sr. in 1907: 'The City is, of all great cities, the least endowed with any blest item of stately square or goodly garden.' *The American Dream*. New York: Scribners, 1946, p. 101.

22. *R.P.N.Y.*, **1**, p. 388. Adams, T. *et al.* (1929) *Population, Land Values and Government*, *R.S.N.Y.*, **2**, pp. 26, 64. Olmsted, F. L., Jr. to James, H., Jr., *The Definition of the Region*, 27 May 1924, box 11, *R.P.N.Y.* papers. *R.S.N.Y.*, **3**, *passim*.

23. *R.P.N.Y.*, **2**, pp. 38–42. Fein (1967) *passim*. (see note 8). Roper (1973) pp. 353–6 (see note 4). Johnson (1974) pp. 53–61 (see note 20). Tunnard and Reed (1955) pp. 59–64 (see note 2). James, H., Jr. (1929) Review of earlier planning efforts in New York and its environs, in Lewis, H. M. *et al.*, *Physical Conditions and Public Services*, *R.S.N.Y.*, **8**, pp. 156–75.

24. Johnson (1974) pp. 61–95, 114–21 (see note 20). *R.S.N.Y.*, **2**, p. 160. Newark City Planning Commission (1913) *City Planning for Newark*. Newark, N. J. Mumford, L. (n.d.) Botched cities. *American Mercury*, pp. 147–8, box 93, *R.P.N.Y.* papers. Adams, T. (1935) *Outline of Town and City Planning*. New York: Russell Sage Foundation, pp. 242–4, 300–4. Logan, T. H. (1976) The Americanization of German zoning. *Journal of A.I.P.*, **42**, October, pp. 377–85.

25. Obituary notice of C. D. Norton, *New York Herald*, 7 March 1923, and other obituaries, box 43, *R.P.N.Y. papers*. Johnson (1974) pp. 96–113 (see note 20).

26. Statement concerning publications of the Russell Sage Foundation, in front endpapers of Adams (1935) (see note 24). Biographical notes on Trustees, as well as members of the Regional Plan Committee and its staff, box 30, *R.P.N.Y. papers*. Norton, C. D. (1921) *Proposal for the Creation of a Plan of New York*, 31 January; (1921) *The Plan of New York, with References to the Chicago Plan*, 24 November (printed by R.P.N.Y., May 1923), box 43, *R.P.N.Y. papers*.

27. Norton, *ibid*. Russell Sage Foundation (1920) *Conference Concerning City Plan*, 10 December; Delano, F. A. to Norton, 22 February 1921; Norton to Glenn, J. M. (Secretary, Russell Sage Foundation), 31 January 1921, box 43, *R.P.N.Y. papers*.

28. Norton (1921) *Proposal* (see note 26). See also Kantor, H. A. (1973) Charles Dyer Norton and the origins of the Regional Plan of New York. *Journal of A.I.P.*, **39**, January, pp. 35–42.

29. Norton (1921) *Plan of New York* (see note 26); (1921) *Memorandum to Committee*, 5 December. *Minutes of Committee Meetings*, 30 December 1921, 13 January, 24 February, 17 April, 3 May 1922, all in box 43, *R.P.N.Y. papers*.

30. Lewis, N. P. to Norton, 24 March and 25 May 1921. Norton (1922) *The Plan of Chicago*; (1921) *Plan of New York* (see note 26). *Minutes of Committee Meetings*, 3 March 1922. DeForest, R. W. to Norton, 27 October 1921. Norton to Wacker, C. H. (Chicago) April 1921. Moore, C. (Burnham's first biographer) to Norton, 8 February, and Norton to Moore, 9 February 1921. All in box 43, *R.P.N.Y. papers*. See also Schlereth, T. J. (1981) Burnham's *Plan* and Moody's *Manual*: city planning as Progressive reform. *Journal of A.P.A.*, **47**, January, pp. 70–82.

31. Norton to Polk, F. C. (a Sage Trustee) 4 August 1922; Norton to Delano, 21 August 1922; Norton to Keppel, F. P., 11 January 1923; Shurtleff, F. (Liaison

Officer, R.P.N.Y.) to Norton, January 1923; Norton to Shurtleff, 16 January 1923; Delano to Senator E. Root (a Carnegie Trustee) 21 December 1922; Unwin, R., reported at Committee, 30 October 1922; Lewis to Norton, 24 March 1921; Adams, T., *Committee Staff Minutes*, 9 April 1922; all in box 43. Olmsted, F. L., Jr. to Glenn, 21 February 1921, box 46. Adams to Norton, 14 April 1922, box 15, *R.P.N.Y. papers.*

32. Unwin, R. (1922) *Lectures at the Russell Sage Foundation; Preliminary Report on the General Situation; Report 2: Economic Survey; Report 3: Procedure and Organization*; all in box 43. *Composite of Unwin Conferences, 2–7 October 1922*, box 30, *R.P.N.Y. papers.*

33. Adams, T., *Committee Staff Minutes*, 9 April 1922, box 43; *Staff Meeting*, 1 February 1923, box 30, *R.P.N.Y. papers.*

34. Advisory Planning Group, meetings and memoranda, 31 December 1922–21 November 1923, box 28, *R.P.N.Y. papers.*

35. *Reports on Sectors by City Planners, 1923* (especially Sector II by Adams), box 18, *R.P.N.Y. papers.* Johnson (1974) p. 203 (see note 20).

36. Adams, T. (1923) The nature of the region, in Reports on Sectors (see note 35). Johnson (1974) p. 216 (see note 20).

37. Norton to Carnegie Corporation, 5 January 1923; Norton to Delano, 21 August 1922, box 43, *R.P.N.Y. papers.*

38. Obituaries of Norton, especially appreciation by Chief Justice Taft, *New York Times*, 10 March 1923; *Minutes of Committee Meetings*, 13 March and 29 May 1923; Keppel, F. P. (1923) *Memorandum*, 23 May; Glenn to Keppel, 23 May 1923; James, H., Jr. to Delano, 4 October 1923; *Committee Staff Minutes*, 7 June 1923; all in box 43, *R.P.N.Y. papers.*

39. Keppel (1923) *Memorandum*, 20 March, box 29. *Minutes of Committee*, 27 February, 13 March, 2 May, 29 May 1923; Glenn to Delano, 15 June 1923, and other correspondence between Glenn, Delano and Adams of that period; conference between Adams, Glenn and Keppel, 15 June 1923; Delano (1923) *Memorandum in Connection with Organizing the Work of the Plan of New York and its Environs after 1 October 1923*, 6 June, and subsequent comments by others; Adams, T. (1923) *Memorandum to Chairman on Organization*, 14 June; Keppel (1923) *Notes for Mr. Adams*, 17 September; Keppel (1923) *Memorandum*, 17 September; see also Keppel (1923) *Memorandum to Committee*, 9 March; all in box 43, *R.P.N.Y. papers.*

40. Adams, T., memorandum on organization, *Minutes of Committee*, 20 November 1923; *Committee Staff Minutes* from 7 November 1923; Adams, T. (1923) *Memorandum of General Director*, 18 December; all in box 43, *R.P.N.Y. papers.*

41. *Minutes of Committee*, 20 November and 18 December 1923; James to Delano, 4 October 1923; Adams to Delano, 24 October 1923; Adams to Glenn, 9 November 1923; Glenn to Delano, 12 December 1923; Delano to Adams, 14 November 1923; Adams to Keppel, 22 November 1923, 19 February 1924; Adams (1923) *Memorandum of General Director*, 18 December; all in box 43. *Ins and Outs of*

Regional Plan Staff, 10 March 1926, box 17, and annual staff dinners notes, box 30. See Adams's articles in boxes 11, 15, 30, 33, etc., all in *R.P.N.Y. papers.*

42. *Minutes of Committee,* 20 November 1923–19 February 1929; *Committee Staff Minutes,* 25 October 1926; Adams to Delano, 17 November 1924, box 43. *Regional Council Meeting,* 27 May 1929, box 16. *Regional Plan Current Notes and Comments,* 1 May, 15 July, 15 October 1927, March 1928, box 29, *R.P.N.Y. papers.* Caro, R. A. (1975) *The Power Broker: Robert Moses and the fall of New York.* New York: Vintage Books, pp. 9–21. Johnson (1974) pp. 390–1 (see note 20). Lewis, H. M. (1929) p. 172 (see note 23).

43. Johnson, *ibid.,* pp. 408–16, 442–3, 449. The remainder of this section relies chiefly on Dr. Johnson's work.

44. Johnson, *ibid.,* pp. 450–78. Caro (1975) pp. 143, 148, 166–7, 171–220, 240, 256–7, 262, 273–4, 278–80 (see note 42).

45. Johnson (1974) pp. 478–86.

46. *Regional Survey of New York and its Environs,* 8 vols. New York: Regional Plan of New York, 1927–31 (cited as *R.S.N.Y.*).

47. Adams, T. (1928) Preface to the Regional Survey, in Haig, R. M. and McCrea, R. C., *Major Economic Factors in Metropolitan Growth and Arrangement. R.S.N.Y.,* 1, p. xiii.

48. Adams to Keppel, 11 March 1923, box 28. Adams to Keppel, *Memorandum on Organization,* summer 1923; *Committee Staff Minutes,* 14 October 1924; Adams, T. (1924) *Memorandum of General Director,* 21 October; Adams, T. (1924) *Draft Regional Plan,* 10 November; Adams to Delano, 7 April 1925; all in box 43, *R.P.N.Y. papers.* On Bassett, see Krueckeberg, D. A. (1983) From the autobiography of Edward M. Bassett, in Krueckeberg (ed.) *The American Planner.* New York and London: Methuen, pp. 100–19.

49. Adams (1928) p. xi (see note 47); (1929) The Regional Survey: a final chapter. *R.S.N.Y.,* 8, pp. 182–4.

50. Haig and McCrea (1928) pp. 10, 12, 15, 18, 44, 103, 106–7 (see note 47).

51. Lewis, H. M. (1929) pp. 18–153 (see note 23).

52. Adams (1929) p. 109 (see note 22).

53. *Ibid.,* pp. 49–50, 127.

54. Wilgus, W. J. (1929) Transportation in the New York region, in Lewis, H. M. *et al., Transit and Transportation. R.S.N.Y.,* 4, p. 161.

55. Adams, T. *et al.* (1931) *Buildings: their uses and the spaces about them. R.S.N.Y.,* 6, pp. 22, 31, 65, 123, 216, 221–2, 224–5, 260–2, 272, 274, 333.

56. Adams, T. *et al.* (1929) The problems of planning unbuilt areas. *Neighborhood and Community Planning. R.S.N.Y.,* 7, pp. 214, 220–1, 223, 231, 245.

57. Perry, C. A. (1929) The neighborhood unit. *ibid.,* pp. 30–1, 34–46, 88–100, 113–14, 123.

58. Hanmer, L. F. *et al.* (1928) *Public Recreation. R.S.N.Y.,* 5, pp. 20, 28, 31, 35–6, 139–41.

Chapter Seven

1. Adams, T. (1929) The planning of the New York region. *Journal of the Royal Institute of British Architects*, **36**, 10 August, p. 706; (1924) *Draft Regional Plan: A Brief Outline of the Scope of the Plan, etc.*, in *Committee Staff Minutes*, 14 November, box 43; (1927) *Planning the New York Region: The Basic Principles and Assumptions Underlying the Regional Plan*, box 29, *Regional Plan of New York papers* (hereafter *R.P.N.Y. papers*), Cornell University, Ithaca, New York.

2. Adams, T. *et al.* (1929 and 1931) *Regional Plan of New York and its Environs*. 1. *The Graphic Regional Plan*. 2. *The Building of the City*. New York: Regional Plan of New York (hereafter *R.P.N.Y.*, **1** and **2**).

3. Adams, T. (1929) *R.P.N.Y.*, **1**, p. 132; (1931) *R.P.N.Y.*, **2**, p. 214 (see note 2); (1932) A communication in defense of the Regional Plan. *New Republic*, **71**, 6 July, p. 208.

4. Adams, T. (1929) Twenty-one million New Yorkers. *Survey*, **62**, 15 July, p. 437; *R.P.N.Y.*, **1**, pp. 208, 342, 405; (1929) Some concluding observations on the Regional Survey, in Lewis, H. M. *et al.*, *Physical Conditions and Public Services. Regional Survey of New York and its Environs*, **8**, p. 184. New York: Regional Plan of New York. (Hereafter *R.S.N.Y.*). See also Johnson, D. A. (1974) *The Emergence of Metropolitan Regionalism: an analysis of the 1929 Regional Plan of New York and its Environs*. Unpublished Ph.D. thesis, Cornell University, pp. 85–95, 415–16, 482.

5. Adams, T. (1929) *R.P.N.Y.*, **1**, pp. 208, 407; (1931) *R.P.N.Y.*, **2**, pp. 35, 44, 79, 311, 587; (1926) Regional planning and garden cities. *Conference on the Third Garden City, Glasgow*, 3 June, box 33, *R.P.N.Y. papers*; Adams to Mumford, L., 9 January 1930, box 44, *R.P.N.Y. papers*; (1929) *Population, Land Values and Government. R.S.N.Y.*, **2**, p. 35.

6. *R.P.N.Y.*, **1**, pp. 134, 309. *R.P.N.Y.*, **2**, pp. 90, 142.

7. *R.P.N.Y.*, **1**, p. 310.

8. *R.P.N.Y.*, **1**, pp. 311, 322–9. *R.P.N.Y.*, **2**, pp. 108–12, 153–93, 223–32, 345–473, 527–47, 568–9.

9. *R.P.N.Y.*, **1**, pp. 140, 309, 312, 322, 327, 329–30, 382, 390, 408, 549–73. *R.P.N.Y.*, **2**, pp. 141–8, 153, 158–9, 166–77.

10. *R.P.N.Y.*, **1**, pp. 149–52, 310, 312, 333. *R.P.N.Y.*, **2**, pp. 42, 142, 219, 341, 568–73.

11. *R.P.N.Y.*, **1**, p. 312. *R.P.N.Y.*, **2**, pp. 341–2, 568–70, 587. Johnson (1974) pp. 286–8 (see note 4).

12. *R.P.N.Y.*, **1**, pp. 135–6, 162, 175–81.

13. *R.P.N.Y.*, **1**, pp. 135–9, 182–307, 331, 366–75. *R.P.N.Y.*, **2**, pp. 221–73.

14. *R.P.N.Y.*, **1**, pp. 171–3, 311, 352, 384, 387–8. *R.P.N.Y.*, **2**, pp. 208, 212, 345–54, 375, 404, 419–22, 433, 436, 442–3, 557.

15. *R.P.N.Y.*, **1**, pp. 269–71, 299–305, 336–44, 355–66, 377–95. *R.P.N.Y.*, **2**, pp. 339, 549, 557–63.

16. *R.P.N.Y.*, **2**, pp. 195–219. See also Marcuse, P. (1980) Housing policy and city planning: the puzzling split in the United States, 1893–1931, in Cherry, G. E. (ed.) *Shaping an Urban World.* London: Mansell, pp. 23–58.

17. *R.P.N.Y.*, **2**, pp. 202–3. Johnson (1974) pp. 280–2 (see note 4).

18. Reviews of *R.P.N.Y.*, **1** and **2**, and congratulations from President Hoover, etc., box 15; press reactions, box 43; Franklin D. Roosevelt to Delano, 14 May 1929, and Veiller, L. to Adams, 28 May 1929, box 44, *R.P.N.Y. papers.* Nolen, J. to Adams, 27 May 1929, box 31, *Nolen papers,* Cornell University. Johnson (1974) p. 75 (see note 4).

19. Lubove, R. (1963) *Community Planning in the Nineteen-Twenties: the contribution of the Regional Planning Association of America.* Pittsburgh: University of Pittsburgh Press; (1967) American Institute of Architects (1925) Report of the Committee on Community Planning, in Lubove (ed.) *The Urban Community: housing and planning in the Progressive Era.* Englewood Cliffs, N.J.: Prentice-Hall, pp. 116–44. Sussman, C. (ed.) (1976) *Planning the Fourth Migration: the neglected vision of the Regional Planning Association of America.* Cambridge, Mass.: M.I.T. Press, pp. x, 1–23, 43. Schaffer, D. (1982) *Garden Cities for America.* Philadelphia: Temple University Press, pp. 29–72. Mumford, L. (1926) The intolerable city. *Harpers,* February, p. 293.

20. State of New York (1926) *Report of the Commission of Housing and Regional Planning,* 7 May. Caro, R. A. (1975) *The Power Broker: Robert Moses and the fall of New York.* New York: Vintage, pp. 135, 166–7, 240, 256–7, 262, 273–4, 666–77. The plan is reproduced in Sussman (1976) (see note 19). See also Schaffer (1982) pp. 87–94, 98–9 (see note 19). On Wright, see Churchill, H. (1983) Henry Wright: 1878–1936, in Krueckeberg, D. A. (ed.) *The American Planner.* New York and London: Methuen, pp. 208–24.

21. (Mumford, L.) (1923) Wilt thou play with Leviathan? *New Republic,* 24 January; Wright, H. to Adams, 18 January 1926, box 30; Adams to Hubbard, T. K., 23 February 1926; Adams–Mumford correspondence, January 1930; Adams to Glenn, J. M. and Harrison, S. M. (of Sage staff), 20 January 1930, and their comments, box 44, *R.P.N.Y. papers.* See also Nolen to Unwin, R., 23 November 1927, box 8, *Nolen papers.*

22. *Survey Graphic,* **54**, 1 May 1925, especially pp. 129, 134. Howard, E., reported in *News Bulletin,* no. 8, April–May 1925, of New York State Bureau of Housing and Regional Planning.

23. Mumford, L. (1925) Realities versus dreams. *Journal of the American Institute of Architects,* **13**, June, p. 198.

24. Geddes Smith (pseudonym of Mumford) (1927) 'Friction of space' among twenty millions. *Survey,* 15 March, pp. 797–9; (1926) p. 288 (see note 19).

25. Mumford, L. (n.d.) Botched cities. *American Mercury,* p. 144, cutting in box 93, *R.P.N.Y. papers.*

26. Adams–Mumford correspondence, January 1930, and Adams to Glenn, J. M. and Harrison, S. M., 20 January 1930, box 44, *R.P.N.Y. papers.*

27. *R.P.N.Y.*, **1**, pp. 327, 331. *R.P.N.Y.*, **2**, pp. 78, 93, 134, 568. Adams, T. (1935) *Outline of Town and City Planning*. New York: Russell Sage Foundation, pp. 232–3; (1934) *The Design of Residential Areas: basic considerations, principles and methods*. Cambridge, Mass.: Harvard University Press, pp. 244–9. Stein, C. S. (1966) *Toward New Towns for America*. Cambridge, Mass.: M.I.T. Press, pp. 37–73. Birch, E. L. (1980) Radburn and the American planning movement: the persistence of an idea. *Journal of American Planning Association* (hereafter *Journal of A.P.A.*) **46**, October, pp. 424–39. Johnson (1974) pp. 72–3 (see note 4). City Housing Corporation (1930) *A Town for the Motor Age*. Schaffer (1982) pp. 134–65 (see note 19). Lubove (1963) pp. 62–8 (see note 19).

28. Mumford, L. (1932) The plan of New York. *New Republic*, **71**, 15 June, pp. 122–6 and 22 June, pp. 146–54.

29. *Ibid.*

30. Adams, T. (1932) A communication in defense of the Regional Plan. *New Republic*, **71**, 6 July, pp. 207–10.

31. *R.P.N.Y.*, **2**, pp. 104–8, 577–8.

32. Johnson (1974) p. 383 (see note 4). Professor Mumford to author, 23 June 1977. Adams–Mumford correspondence, January 1930, box 44, *R.P.N.Y. papers*. For Mumford's general views, see his *The City in History*. Harmondsworth, Middx: Penguin Books, 1961, pp. 586–646. Adams, T. (1929) p. 706 (see note 1); (1932) pp. 207–10 (see note 30). Is there hope for the city? and Editorial. *New Republic*, 5 June 1929 and 29 January 1930 (both probably by Mumford). Aronovici, C. (1932) review of *R.P.N.Y.* in *American Journal of Sociology*, **38**, July; (1932) Let the cities perish, and The planners' five-foot shelf. *Survey Graphic*, **68**, 1 October, pp. 437–40 and 479. Wright, H. (1932) To plan or not to plan. *Survey Graphic*, **68**, 1 October, pp. 468–9. Goist, P. D. (1972) Seeing things whole: a consideration of Lewis Mumford. *Journal of American Institute of Planners* (hereafter *Journal of A.I.P.*) **38**, November, pp. 379–91. On New Deal Greenbelt programme, see Myhra, D. (1974) Rexford Guy Tugwell: the initiator of America's Greenbelt new towns, 1935–36. *Journal of A.I.P.*, **40**, May, pp. 176–88. Conkin, P. (1959) *Tomorrow A New World*. Ithaca, N.Y.: Cornell University Press. Arnold J. L. (1971) *The New Deal in the Suburbs*. Columbus: Ohio State University Press. Stein (1966) pp. 119–87 (see note 27).

33. Adams to Nolen, 6 January 1930; Nolen to Adams, 22 November 1928; Nolen to McAneny, G., 30 December 1929, box 31, *Nolen papers*. McAneny to Adams, 2 September 1931; Adams to McAneny, 24 February 1932, box 17; Minutes of Committee Meetings, 14 November, 13 December 1927, 23 October 1928, 19 February 1929, 14 January, 18 February 1930; *Agreement* between Planning Foundation of America and Regional Plan Association, 18 June 1929; *Proposal for a C. D. Norton Memorial Fund*, June 1930, box 43; *Sub-committee on Continuing Organization*, 8 December 1927, 4 April 1928, box 26, *R.P.N.Y. papers*.

34. *Proposal for a C. D. Norton Memorial Fund*, July 1930, box 43, *R.P.N.Y. papers*. Duffus, R. L. (1930) *Mastering a Metropolis: planning the future of the New York region*. New York: Harper and Row.

35. Adams to Ford, G. B., 10 and 20 May, 20 June 1930, box 17, *R.P.N.Y. papers.* Johnson (1974) pp. 342–57.

36. McAneny, G. (1938) Foreword. *From Plan to Reality,* 2. New York: Regional Plan Association.

37. *From Plan to Reality: four years of progress on the regional development of New York and its environs; From Plan to Reality,* 2; *From Plan to Reality,* 3. New York; Regional Plan Association, 1933, 1938, 1942. Caro (1975) pp. 339–46, 362, 465 (see note 20).

38. Adams, T. (1938) Address at Regional Plan Association luncheon, 2 June, box 45, *R.P.N.Y. papers.*

39. *From Plan to Reality,* 3, p. 4 (see note 37). Johnson (1974) p. 503 (see note 4).

40. *From Plan to Reality,* 1, pp. 14–17; *From Plan to Reality,* 2, section 1, p. 2, section 6, pp. 1–16, section 8, p. 4; *From Plan to Reality,* 3, section 1, p. 1, section 6, p. 1. (see note 37). Johnson (1974) pp. 487–520 (see note 4). Caro (1975) p. 563 (see note 20). For a general discussion of the contest between public and private transportation, see Foster, M. S. (1981) *From Streetcar to Superhighway: American city planners and urban transportation, 1900–1940.* Philadelphia: Temple University Press. I am indebted to Professor Blaine Brownell for stressing the connection between Moses and private motoring.

41. Caro (1975) p. 465 (see note 20). Johnson (1974) pp. 493, 497, 500, 502 (see note 4). *From Plan to Reality,* 2, sec. 8, p. 1. *From Plan to Reality,* 3, sec. 1, p. 4 (see note 37). Sussman (1976) pp. 2, 8–9, 42 (see note 19). Simpson, M. A. (1969) *People and Planning: a history of the Ohio Planning Conference, 1919–1969.* Bay Village, Ohio: Ohio Planning Conference, pp. 44, 58. Scott, M. C. (1969) *American City Planning since 1890.* Los Angeles and Berkeley: University of California Press, pp. 257, 284, 290–2, 316–35.

42. Johnson (1974) pp. 505–73 (see note 4). Scott (1969) p. 293 (see note 41).

43. Thomas Adams to speak to School of Landscape Architecture. *Harvard Crimson,* 7 May 1920, cutting in School of Design Library, Harvard University. *Report of a Conference on a Project for Research and Instruction in City and Regional Planning,* 3 May 1928, box 16, *R.P.N.Y. papers.* Instruction on city planning in the United States. *City Planning,* 5, January 1929, pp. 43–5. *New York World,* 3 September 1929, V.736.2; *Harvard University Catalog, 1929–1930,* pp. 550–4, Harvard University Archives. Johnson (1974) pp. 385–9 (see note 4). Scott (1969) pp. 265–7 (see note 41).

44. School of City Planning entries in *Harvard University Catalogs,* 1930–7, Harvard University Archives. Adams to Nolen, 6 January 1930, box 44, *R.P.N.Y. papers.* Adams to Nolen, 20 May, 7 July 1930, box 31, *Nolen papers.* Whitten, R. H. and Adams, T. (1931) *The Neighborhoods of Small Homes: economic densities of low-cost housing in America and England.* Cambridge, Mass.: Harvard University Press. Adams, T. (1934) *The Design of Residential Areas: basic considerations, principles and methods.* Cambridge, Mass.: Harvard University Press. *The Planning Foundation of America, Inc.,* box 43, *R.P.N.Y. papers.* Scott (1969) pp. 267–9 (see note 41).

45. *Letchworth Citizen,* 17 June 1932, cutting in Garden City Museum, Letchworth.

46. Adams (1935) pp. 21–2, 28, 143, 147, 152, 317 (see note 27).

47. *Ibid.*, pp. 25–6, 151–3, 162, 180–2, 197–8, 204, 208, 214, 287, 316, 318, 325, 328.

48. Whitten and Adams (1931) pp. 90–137 (see note 44).

49. Adams (1934) pp. 81–5, 103, 105, 114, 265 (see note 44).

50. Adams, T. (1925) City planning problems, in Wright, J. (ed.) *Selected Readings in Municipal Problems.* Boston: Ginn, p. 501; (1919) Reconstruction in Great Britain. *National Municipal Review,* **8**, March, pp. 118–25; (1919) The planning of land in relation to social problems. *Proceedings of the American Society for Municipal Improvements,* pp. 355–6; (1921) Reserving productive areas within and around cities. *Journal of American Institute of Architects,* **9**, October, pp. 316–19; (1927) The technical approach to the study and planning of regions. *City Planning,* **3**, April, pp. 87–95; (1928) Forecast: The regional community of the future. *Transactions of the American Society of Civil Engineers,* **92**, pp. 1153–6, 1180; (1928) A statement of city planning principles. *Community Builder,* **2**, August, pp. 23–4; (1932) The American community in fifty years. *National Conference on City Planning, Pittsburgh,* pp. 1–6; (1938) Town and country planning in Old and New England. *The Planners' Journal,* **3**, July–August, p. 91; (1938) *Synopsis of Lectures at Massachusetts Institute of Technology,* May, mimeographed copy, School of Design Library, Harvard University; (1938) *State, regional and city planning in America.* Typescript, p. 3, *Adams papers;* (1935) pp. 227–9, 287–9 (see note 27).

51. Adams (1934) pp. 259–60, 231–6 (see note 41).

52. Adams, T. (1929) *Regional Planning in the United States.* Washington: American Civic Association; (1935) pp. 208–51, 287–314 (see note 27); (1938) Town and country planning in Old and New England (see note 50); (1938) *State, regional and city planning in America* (see note 50). See also Scott (1969) pp. 270–361 (see note 41). Conkin (1959) (see note 32). Arnold (1971) (see note 32). Foster (1981) pp. 132–50 (see note 40). Karl, B. D. (1974) *Charles E. Merriam and the Study of Politics.* Chicago: University of Chicago Press, pp. 226–59. Clawson, M. (1981) *New Deal Planning: the National Resources Planning Board.* Baltimore: Johns Hopkins University Press. Warken, P. (1979) *A History of the National Resources Planning Board, 1933–1943.* New York: Garland. Myhra (1974) (see note 32). Hancock, J. L. (1967) Planners in the changing American city, 1900–40. *Journal of A.I.P.,* **33**, September, pp. 274–301. Birch, E. L. (1980) Advancing the art and science of planning: planners and their organizations, 1909–80. *Journal of A.P.A.,* **46**, January, pp. 22–32. Krueckeberg, D. A. (1980) The story of the Planners' Journal. *Journal of A.P.A.,* **46**, January, pp. 5–11; (1980) From backyard garden to the whole U.S.A.: a conversation with Charles W. Eliot, II. *Journal of A.P.A.,* **46**, October, pp. 441–6. Sussman (1976) p. 43 (see note 19). Schaffer (1982) pp. 224–6 (see note 19).

53. Adams, T. (1918) The need of town planning legislation and procedure for the control of land as a factor in house building development, in Whitaker, C. H. (ed.) *The Housing Problem in War and Peace.* Washington: Journal of American Institute of Architects, pp. 109–15; (1921) Efficient industry and wholesome housing the true aims of zoning. *American City,* **24**, March, pp. 287–9; (1921) City planning and city building. *Journal of American Institute of Architects*

(hereafter *Journal of A.I.A.*) **9**, June, pp. 195–7; (1922) Architects and city planning, II. *Journal of A.I.A.*, **10**, August, pp. 245–6; (1926) *Industrial Housing and Public Health in Metropolitan Regions*, address at Johns Hopkins University, 4 January, box 33, *R.P.N.Y. papers*; (1926) The social objective in regional planning. *National Municipal Review*, **15**, February, pp. 83–4, 87; (1931) Proper directions for public effort in housing. *American City*, **44**, May, p. 118; (1938) Problems in the rebuilding of cities. *Planners' Journal*, **4**, May–June, pp. 69–71. Scott (1969) p. 293 (see note 41). Birch (1980) pp. 26–32, and notes 31–5 (see note 52).

54. *An Opportunity to Secure a Visit during February or March, 1922, from Mr. Thomas Adams*. New York: American City Bureau, School of Design Library, Harvard University. Dedicatory note, *From Plan to Reality*, 1 (see note 37). Delano, F. A., at Regional Plan Association meeting, 11 December 1931, box 16; McAneny, G., Regional Plan Association circular, 25 May 1938, box 45, *R.P.N.Y. papers*. See obituaries of Adams: *New York Times*, 25 March 1940; *American City*, **55**, April 1940, p. 135; *Planning and Civic Comment*, **6**, April–June 1940, pp. 24–5; *Planners' Journal*, **6**, April–June 1940, pp. 56–7; *National Conference on City Planning, San Francisco, 1940*, p. 189.

CHAPTER EIGHT

1. Culpin, E. G. (1934–5) Still it moves. *Journal of the Town Planning Institute* (hereafter *Journal of T.P.I.*) **21**, p. 119. Thompson, F. L. (1932–3) Presidential Address: the new act. *Journal of T.P.I.*, **19**, p. 2. Nicholson, M. (1935–6) A factual basis for territorial planning. *Journal of T.P.I.*, **22**, p. 287. See *Journal of T.P.I.* between the wars generally for assessments of the state of British planning. See also Lloyd, T. A. (1931) The evolution of the post-war subsidised house. *Annual Report* of National Housing and Town Planning Council (hereafter N.H.T.P.C.), pp. 16–21; N.H.T.P.C., *Annual Report, 1932*, pp. 12–13.

2. Hilton-Young, Sir E. (1931–2) Remodelling town and country. *Journal of T.P.I.*, **18**, pp. 120–2. Abercrombie, L. P. (1926) The preservation of rural England. *Town Planning Review*, **12**, May, p. 56. Cherry, G. E. (1980) The place of Neville Chamberlain in British town planning, in Cherry (ed.) *Shaping an Urban World*. London: Mansell, pp. 161–78; (1974) The development of planning thought, in Bruton, M. (ed.) *The Spirit and Purpose of Planning*. London: Heinemann, pp. 66–84; (1981) George Pepler, in Cherry (ed.) *Pioneers in British Planning*. London: Architectural Press, pp. 133–7; (1974) The Housing, Town Planning, etc., Act, 1919. *The Planner*, **60**, May, pp. 681–4. Ward, S. V. (1974) The Town and Country Planning Act. *The Planner*, **60**, May, pp. 685–9. Sheail, J. (1981) *Rural Conservation in Inter-war Britain*. London: Oxford University Press. Swenarton, M. (1981) *Homes Fit for Heroes*. London: Heinemann.

3. Mattocks, R. H. (1919–20) Town planning in relation to housing and the provision of open spaces. *Town Planning Review*, **8**, pp. 169–78. Sharp, T. (1933) Urbanism and rusticism. *Report of the Town and Country Planning Summer School, 1933*, p. 39; (1936–7) Segregation in town development. *Journal of T.P.I.*,

22, pp. 166–71, and A. T. Edwards, p. 173. Stansfield, K. (1981) Thomas Sharp, in Cherry (ed.) pp. 150–76 (see note 2).

4. Osborn, F. J. (1947) Planning comes of age. *Town and Country Planning*, **15**, Spring, pp. 6–9, 22.

5. Gibbon, I. G. (1924) Town planning and regional development, *Garden Cities and Town Planning*, **14**, December, pp. 253–6; (1937–8) Problems of town and country planning. *Journal of T.P.I.*, **24**, pp. 301–8; see review of his book of same title, same vol., pp. 31–4. Conzen, M. R. G. (1938) Towards a systematic approach in planning science: Geoproscopy. *Town Planning Review*, **18**, July, pp. 1–25. See also De Caseres, J. M. (1936) Principles of Planology. *Town Planning Review*, **17**, June, pp. 103–14. For an academic critique of contemporary planning, see Holford, W. G. and Eden, W. A. (1937) *The Future of Merseyside*. Liverpool: University Press of Liverpool. See further Adams, T. (1933) The Garden City under fire. *Town and Country Planning*, **1**, August, pp. 124–7.

6. Miscellany. *National Municipal Review*, **10**, September 1921, p. 488. *Municipal Engineering and the Sanitary Record*, 17 August 1922, *Adams papers*. Adams, T. (1938) *State, regional and city planning in America*. Typescript, pp. 7–8, *Adams papers. Municipal Journal*, 8 September 1922.

7. Fry, E. M. (1975) *Autobiographical Sketches*. London: Elek, pp. 120–7. I am indebted to Sir Colin Buchanan and Mr. Bernard Collins for their recollections of Adams and the partnership's work.

8. McRae, J. F. (1926) A new garden village in Kent. *Architects' Journal*, 10 November, pp. 567–70. Club house in a Kentish village. *Architects' Journal*, 1 January 1930, pp. 6–12. Housing Supplement 2. *Architects' Journal*, 26 April 1934. R. E. Sassoon House: working class flats. *Architects' Journal*, 29 November 1934. Dougill, W. (1928) Birmingham Civic Centre Competition. *Town Planning Review*, **13**, May, pp. 19–29. Adams, T. (1932) *Recent Advances in Town Planning*. London: Churchill, pp. 97, 149–50. Whitten, R. H. and Adams, T. (1931) *The Neighborhoods of Small Homes: economic densities of low-cost housing in England and America*. Cambridge, Mass.: Harvard University Press, p. 135. Adams, Thompson and Fry (1930) *Intermediate Report on Plan of Development of Granton-Cramond Area;* (1931) *Final Report on Town Planning*, both in Edinburgh Room, Central Library, Edinburgh.

9. Adams (1932) pp. 129, 144 (see note 8). Adams, Thompson and Fry (1931) *Rugby and District*. Thomas H. Mawson and Son in collaboration with Adams and Thompson (1925) *County Borough of Northampton: Proposals for Development and Reconstruction*.

10. Thomas H. Mawson and Son and Adams, Thompson and Fry (1930) *Report on a General Development Plan: Borough of Hastings*. Adams, Thompson and Fry (1930) *Borough of Bexhill: General Development Plan*. Adams, Thompson and Fry (n.d.) *Felixstowe Town Planning Scheme*, summarized in Abercrombie, L. P. and Kelly, S. A. (1935) *East Suffolk Regional Planning Scheme*. Liverpool: University Press of Liverpool and Hodder and Stoughton, pp. 76–8. Adams (1932) p. 144 (see note 8); (1934–5) in report of Eastbourne meeting of Town Planning Institute. *Journal of T.P.I.*, **21**, pp. 327–8. Inter-war regional and local plans were often reviewed in *Town Planning Review*.

11. Sir Colin Buchanan to author, 18 July 1983. Mr. Bernard Collins to author, 9 August 1983. Adams, Thompson and Fry (1930) *North East Kent Regional Planning Scheme*, p. 61.

12. The firm's regional plans were as follows: *West Middlesex: Preliminary Report* (1922) and *Final Report* (1924); *Thames Valley: Preliminary Report* (1923) and *Final Report* (1925); *Mid-Surrey* (1928); *North West Surrey* (1928); *North Middlesex* (1928); *The Thames from Putney to Staines* (1930); *North East Kent* (1930); *West Surrey* (1931); *Mid-Northamptonshire* (1931); *South East Sussex* (1931); *Mid-Essex* (c. 1935–6); *North East Essex* (c. 1935–6); *North West Essex* (c. 1935–6). Reviews appeared in *Town Planning Review* between 1928 and 1935. For an early perspective on regional planning, see Abercrombie, L. P. (1923) Regional planning. *Town Planning Review*, **10**, January, pp. 109–18.

13. For assessments of inter-war regional planning, see essays in Cherry (ed.) (1981) (see note 2); (1974) *The Evolution of British Town Planning*. Leighton Buzzard: Leonard Hill, pp. 87–91. See also Adams, T. (1924) Regional planning: the location of commercial, industrial and housing areas. *Proceedings of International Garden Cities and Town Planning Congress, Amsterdam;* (1932) pp. 113–39 (see note 8); (1936) *Regional Planning in England and Wales*. London: National Housing and Town Planning Council. See further Pepler, G. L. (1926–7) Recent developments in regional planning. *Journal of T.P.I.*, **13**, pp. 179–80; (1949) Presidential address. *Journal of T.P.I.*, **36**, November–December, pp. 1–5. Reiss, R. L. (1927) Regional planning in relation to garden cities and satellite towns. *Garden Cities and Town Planning*, **17**, July, pp. 169–71.

14. Mr. E. M. Fry to author, 2 September 1975, and conversation with Mr. Fry, 30 July 1975. Fry, E. M. (1975) *Autobiographical Sketches*. London: Elek, pp. 134–6, 147. Conversations with Mrs. M. Adkins, Mr. J. R. K. Adams and Professor F. M. L. Thompson.

15. Information from Mr. J. R. K. Adams. Kincorth Competition. *Journal of T.P.I.*, **23**, 1936–7, p. 389. Dundee newspaper cuttings, May and October, 1937, *Adams papers*. Extract from Special Meeting, Dundee Town Council, 22 October 1937, by courtesy of Dundee City Library. Overgate redevelopment scheme, Dundee. *Journal of T.P.I.*, **24**, 1937–8, pp. 225–6.

16. For the Barrow plan, I am greatly indebted to Mr. B. D. Beckett, Chief Planning Officer, Borough of Barrow-in-Furness, for a communication of 5 October 1983 and copies of minutes of the County Borough Council in 1937–8, detailing meetings of the Walney Island Development Sub-committee, and of correspondence between Town Clerk and E. G. Culpin, President of T.P.I., and Town Clerk and Adams, 1938, and Adams, T. (1938) *Report on Survey and Preliminary Proposals for Development*, June, and *Schedule of Work*, 24 March.

17. Photostat of plan for a holiday village, dated 25 November 1942, School of Design Library, Harvard University.

18. Adams, T. (1932) (see note 8); (1935) *Outline of Town and City Planning*. New York: Russell Sage Foundation.

19. Adams, T. (1931) What London might be: looking forward forty years. *Listener*, 29 July, p.xii; (1937–8) Road planning. *Journal of T.P.I.*, **24**, p. 154; (1932) p. 17 (see note 8).

20. Adams, T. (1932) p. 1 (see note 8); (1932) Regional planning and economy. *Surveyor and Municipal and County Engineer,* 12 February, pp. 219–20; (1929–30) comments on Townroe, B.S., Town planning and the man in the street. *Journal of T.P.I.,* **16,** p. 149; (1938) Town and country planning in Old and New England. *Planners' Journal,* 3, July–August, p. 91.

21. Adams, T. (1920) Some phases of England's housing and town planning problem. *Landscape Architecture,* **11,** October, p. 4; (1931) The meaning and scope of landscape architecture and its relation to town planning. *Quarterly Notes,* **2,** April, p. 5 (of Institute of Landscape Architects); (1938) p. 93 (see note 20); (1932) pp. 64, 69, 164–5 (see note 8). Adams to Neville Adams, 13 October 1927, *Adams papers.*

22. Adams (1932) pp. 15, 94–5, 140–1, 174–5, 184–7, 301–2, 369 (see note 8). See discussion of Pepler, G. L. (1921–2) Zoning. *Papers of T.P.I.,* **8,** pp. 44–6.

23. Adams (1932) p. 64 (see note 8).

24. Adams, T. (1914–15) Some recent developments in town planning. *Papers of T.P.I.,* **1,** p. 142; (1921) Reserving productive areas in and around cities. *Journal of American Institute of Architects,* **9,** October, pp. 316–19; (1935–6) remarks at T.P.I. annual dinner. *Journal of T.P.I.,* **22,** p. 334; (1937–8) Planning seaside towns. *Journal of T.P.I.,* **24,** pp. 344–52; (1932) p. 370 (see note 8). See also Adams, T. (1933) What others think: shacks at seaside resorts. 26 August, cutting from unknown newspaper; and Looking around. *The Star* (London), 21 August 1937, both in *Adams papers.*

25. Adams, T. (1927) Regional planning around London. Typescript of address in New York, 16 November, School of Design Library, Harvard University; (1929) New methods in arterial road planning. *Modern Transport,* 26 January; (1930) The improvement of British roads. *Modern Transport,* 28 June; (1930) Landscape road design. *Journal of London Society,* no. 150, August, pp. 117–28; (1932) pp. 59, 208–12, 217, 229, 231, 237–8, 252–4; (1935) *Town and Country Planning in Relation to Transport.* Paper to Public Works Congress, London, p. 2, in Massachusetts Institute of Technology Library; (1937–8) Road planning. *Journal of T.P.I.,* **24,** pp. 149–57; (1937–8) p. 349 (see note 24); (1938) Essential road conditions governing the safety of modern traffic, I; road planning. *Journal of the Institution of Municipal and County Engineers,* March, pp. 1635–50.

26. Adams, T. (1920) pp. 5–6 (see note 21); (1922) Town planning in other countries. *Journal of the Institution of Municipal and County Engineers,* **49,** 18 July, pp. 55, 57, 59; (1931) Proper directions for public effort in housng. *American City,* **44,** May, p. 118; (1935) pp. 271–2 (see note 18); (1936) Problems arising out of the administration of the Town and Country Planning Act, 1932. *36th Annual Report.* London: National Housing and Town Planning Council, p. 4; (1938) p. 3 (see note 6); (1939) *Some Economic Aspects of Urban Concentration.* Typescript paper to Economic Section, British Association for the Advancement of Science. August, p. 16; see various newspaper cuttings for 1937, *Adams papers,* for Adams's condemnation of flats.

27. Adams, T. (1926) The planning of London. *Town Planning Review,* **11,** February, pp. 285–90; (1930–1) London as it ought to be (with several other contributors). *Journal of T.P.I.,* **17,** pp. 187–205; (1931) p. vi (see note 19) (see also

Part I: Planning the future of London, by R. Unwin in same issue); (1932) p. 9 (see note 8); (1933) The replanning of built areas in London. *Journal of London Society*, no. 184, June, pp. 84–9; (1938) Regional planning in England and Wales. *38th Annual Report*. London: National Housing and Town Planning Council, pp. 2–3. Scot who planned New York looks at London. *The Star*, 25 June 1937, *Adams papers*. There was extensive discussion in the planning press of the planning of Greater London. Buchanan, C. (1971) *London Road Plans, 1900–1970*. London: Greater London Council. Young, K. and Garside, P. L. (1982) *Metropolitan London: politics and urban change, 1837–1981*. London: Arnold.

28. Adams, T. (1932) pp. 137–9; (1932) pp. 219–20 (see note 20); (1933) letter to *Times*, 26 January; (1938) pp. 1–3 (see note 27); (1940) *Modern Trends in City, Town and Regional Planning*. Typescript of proposed book, pp. 23, 23a, 24, 41, *Adams papers*. T.P.I., *Council Minutes*, 2, 22 May 1936. Adshead, S.D. (1918–19) Presidential address. *Papers of T.P.I.*, 5, p. 3. Nicholson, M. (1935–6) A factual basis for territorial planning. *Journal of T.P.I.*, 22, pp. 287–90. Report of T.P.I. National Survey and National Plan Committee, *Journal of T.P.I.*, 24, 1937–8, pp. 237–55. *Statement* by School of Planning and Research for National Development, 1939, in School of Design Library, Harvard University. See also Pinder, J. (ed.) (1981) *Fifty Years of Political and Economic Planning: looking forward, 1931–1981*. London: Heinemann. Sheail (1981) pp. 123–38 (see note 2). Robson, W. A. (ed.) (1971) *The Political Quarterly in the Thirties*. London: Allen Lane. Marwick, A. (1964) Middle opinion in the thirties; planning, progress and political 'agreement'. *English Historical Review*, 79, pp. 285–98.

29. T.P.I., *Council Minutes*, 2, 10 March 1939. *Journal of T.P.I.*, 13, 1926–7, p. 290. Information on Adams's election to F.R.I.B.A. from Royal Institute of British Architects. Adams, T. (1929) Town planning: teaching at the universities. Letter in *Times*, 13 July. Adams, T. (1931) application form for election to Institute of Landscape Architects, 10 January, in *Early Important Papers*, Landscape Institute, London. Biographical and Civic Portrait, no. 19, Dr. Thomas Adams. *The Scots Town and County Councillor*, November 1936, pp. 14–15. *News Release from Regional Plan Association, Inc.*, 2 June 1932, *Adams papers*.

30. Rees Jeffreys, *Papers of T.P.I.*, 4, 1917–18, p. 26. Summer school. *Journal of T.P.I.*, 20, 1933–4, pp. 324–8. *Report of the First Town and Country Planning Summer School* (1933). London: Garden Cities and Town Planning Association.

31. T.P.I., *Council Minutes*, 1, 23 July 1920, etc.; 2, 10 July 1936, etc. Culpin, E. G. (1929–30) A town planning majority. *Journal of T.P.I.*, 16, pp. 275–6. Cherry (1974) pp. 94–7, 107–17 (see note 13).

32. Adams, T. and Lloyd, T. A. (1925–6) Professional practice. *Journal of T.P.I.*, 12, pp. 204–9.

33. Adams, T. (1939) (see note 26); (1939–40) Town and country planning during the war. *Journal of T.P.I.*, 26, pp. 28–31; (1940) (see note 28). National Roll of Associates. *36th. Annual Report;* Council Report. *37th. Annual Report*. London: National Housing and Town Planning Council. See also N.H.T.P.C., *Minute Book, 1936–9*, Annual General Meeting, 22 April 1937, etc.; *Minute Book, 1940–46*, 26 January to 15 March 1940.

34. Institute of Landscape Architects, Formation and progress. *Quarterly Notes*, 1,

January 1931, p. 3. Adams, T. (1931) pp. 2–6 (see note 21). Fricker, L. J. (1969) Forty years a-growing. *Journal of the Institute of Landscape Architects,* **86,** May, p. 8. Colvin, B. (1979) Beginnings. *Landscape Design,* February, p. 6. Mawson, D. J. (1979) T. H. Mawson. *Landscape Design,* August, pp. 30–3.

35. Colvin (1979) (see note 34). Jellicoe, G. A. (1979) War and peace. *Landscape Design,* February, p. 10.

36. Institute of Landscape Architects, *Quarterly Notes,* **3,** July 1931, p. 2; **5,** January 1932, pp. 3–5; **7,** July 1932, pp. 3, 9; **8,** October 1932, pp. 3–4; **11,** July 1933, pp. 3–6. *Landscape and Garden,* **1,** Spring 1934, p. 15. Institute of Landscape Architects, *Minute Book: Council Meetings,* 22 August 1938 to 10 January 1939; Adams, T., *Memorandum,* November 1938; Constitution Committee, 17 January 1939; Constitution, 24 April 1939; Constitution Committee, 8 May 1939, *Early Important Papers,* in possession of Landscape Institute, London.

37. Adams, T. (1932) Sir Walter Scott and landscape architecture. *Journal of Royal Institute of British Architects,* **39,** 15 October, p. 856; (1938) *Memorandum,* November (see note 36).

38. Adams, T. (1931) p. 3 (see note 21); (1936) Preserving and developing the beauties of the English landscape. *Landscape and Garden,* **3,** Autumn, p. 148; (1936) letter to *Times,* 21 September.

39. Adams, T. (1934) Landscape design in relation to buildings and site-planning. *Landscape and Garden,* **1,** Autumn, p. 45; (1936) Gardening and landscape architecture. *Landscape and Garden,* **3,** Summer, pp. 83–4; (1937) Planting and design for the Coronation. *Landscape and Garden,* **4,** Spring, p. 15; (1937) Landscape design and preservation in East Sussex. *Landscape and Garden,* **4,** Winter, pp. 232–4; (1937) A talk to the people on town planning (script of radio talk, North Region, B.B.C.). *Landscape and Garden,* **4,** Winter, pp. 248–9; (1937) The preservation of open spaces. *Bexhill-on-Sea Observer,* 3 October 1937; (1938) Presidential address: Urban and rural landscape design. *Landscape and Garden,* **5,** Winter, p. 201.

40. Adams, T. (1927) p. 6 (see note 25); (1929) The planning of the New York region. *Journal of Royal Institute of British Architects,* **36,** 10 August, p. 708; (1930) pp. 117–28 (see note 25); (1932) pp. 121–4, 227–38 (see note 8); (1935) (see note 25). See also Parker, R. B. (1935) Parkways. *Town Planning Review,* **16,** June, pp. 182–5. Dougill, W. (1935) Wythenshawe. *Town Planning Review,* **16,** June, pp. 209–15.

41. Adams, Thompson and Fry (1930) *Bexhill,* p. 15 (see note 10). Adams (1935) p. 8 (see note 25); (1937) *Bexhill-on-Sea Observer;* (1937–8) p. 350 (see note 24). 'Astragal' (1940) Notes and Topics. *Architects' Journal,* **91,** 11 April, p. 379.

42. Information from Dr. Adams's children. The autobiography, a brief fragment of which is in typescript in *Adams papers,* was entitled provisionally *My Job of Work.* Adams to Nolen, J., 20 May 1930, box 31, *Nolen Papers,* Cornell University, Ithaca, New York.

Index

Mawson, Thomas H. 45–6, 56, 64,
  74, 88, 119, 171, 186
Meadow House Farm
  (Edinburgh) 1–2
Meath, Lord 62
megalopolis 155
Meighen, Arthur 103, 104, 105
Merchants' Club (Chicago) 132
Middleton (Lancashire) 47–8, 57
Midland Re-afforestation
  Association 44
Miles, Philip Napier 50
Mill, John Stuart 5, 79, 193
Miller, Rev. J. O. 73
Ministry of Health 169, 170, 171, 179
Ministry of Transport 169
Mole Valley (Surrey) 174
Montreal 87, 100, 113, 123
Moody, Walter D. 132
Morgenthau, Henry, Sr. 120
Morning Leader 11
Moses, Robert 138, 154, 159–60
Mumford, Lewis 153–8, 161
Municipal Reformer 11, 12
Mussolini, Benito 183

National Conference on City
  Planning 56, 76, 119, 120, 121,
  124, 126, 130, 163
National Housing and Town Planning
  Council 185
National Housing Association
  (U.S.A.) 130–1
National Housing Reform
  Council 13, 53, 54, 65
national parks 105, 170, 181, 188
National Resources Planning
  Board 166
neighbourhoods 10, 48, 141, 164, 165
Netherlands 93
Nettlefold, J. S. 13, 41, 43, 44, 54,
  59, 60, 64, 75
Neville, Ralph 10–13, 14, 16, 19, 20,
  30, 35, 36, 38, 39
New Brunswick 75, 85
New Deal 125, 157, 158, 161, 162,
  165, 166, 183
New England 165

New Jersey 130, 132, 150, 153
New Republic 156–7
new towns 80, 84, 90–2, 93, 125, 135,
  148, 166
New York: city 56, 72, 121, 122, 127,
  128–30, 138, 140, 145, 157, 160, 165,
  171, 186, 188, 189
  region 129, 130–42, 143–53, 159,
    160, 161, 162, 163, 165
  state 130, 132, 134, 138, 154
New York Advisory Committee on the
  City Plan 129, 130
New York City Improvement
  Commission 129
New York State Commission of
  Housing and Regional
  Planning 154
New York University 163, 183
Newark (New Jersey) 130, 147, 150
Newcastle-upon-Tyne 32
Newfoundland 114–15, 128, 172–3
Newfoundland Power and Paper
  Company 114
Newton Moor Garden Suburb (near
  Manchester) 51
Niagara Frontier Region 114, 127
Nolen, John 56, 67, 92, 123, 125,
  126, 133, *134*, 153, 158, 162, 186
normalcy 103, 125
North Adams (Massachusetts) 127
North America 69, 71, 77, 82, 127,
  164, 169, 170, 171, 184, 188, 193
North British Railway 1
North Downs (Surrey/Kent) 174
North Middlesex 174
Northampton (England) 173
Northcroft, George J. H. 36, 37
Norton, Charles Dyer 130–3, 136,
  137, 139, 143, 144, 159, 161, 162
Nova Scotia 75, 85, 108

Ohio 125
Ojibway (Ontario) 90
Olmsted and Hubbard 171
Olmsted Brothers 127
Olmsted, Frederick Law Jr., 67, 92,
  123, 133, *134*, 162, 186